Kaplan Publishing are constantly finding new ways to make a difference to your studies and our excit' offer something different to students lo

This book comes with free MyKaplan on study anytime, anywhere. **This free onli separately and is included in the pric**

Having purchased this book, you have access to the following online study materials:

CONTENT	ACCA (including FBT, FMA, FFA)		FIA (excluding FBT, FMA, FFA)	
	Text	Kit	Text	Kit
Electronic version of the book	✓	✓	✓	✓
Check Your Understanding Test with instant answers	✓			
Material updates	✓	✓	✓	✓
Latest official ACCA exam questions*		✓		
Extra question assistance using the signpost icon**		✓		
Timed questions with an online tutor debrief using clock icon***		✓		
Interim assessment including questions and answers	✓		✓	
Technical answers	✓	✓	✓	✓

* Excludes BT, MA, FA, FBT, FMA, FFA; for all other papers includes a selection of questions, as released by ACCA
** For ACCA SBL, SBR, AFM, APM, ATX, AAA only
*** Excludes BT, MA, FA, LW, FBT, FMA and FFA

How to access your online resources

Kaplan Financial students will already have a MyKaplan account and these extra resources will be available to you online. You do not need to register again, as this process was completed when you enrolled. If you are having problems accessing online materials, please ask your course administrator.

If you are not studying with Kaplan and did not purchase your book via a Kaplan website, to unlock your extra online resources please go to www.mykaplan.co.uk/addabook (even if you have set up an account and registered books previously). You will then need to enter the ISBN number (on the title page and back cover) and the unique pass key number contained in the scratch panel below to gain access. You will also be required to enter additional information during this process to set up or confirm your account details.

If you purchased through the Kaplan Publishing website you will automatically receive an e-mail invitation to MyKaplan. Please register your details using this email to gain access to your content. If you do not receive the e-mail or book content, please contact Kaplan Publishing.

Your Code and Information

This code can only be used once for the registration of one book online. This registration and your online content will expire when the final sittings for the examinations covered by this book have taken place. Please allow one hour from the time you submit your book details for us to process your request.

Please scratch the film to access your unique code.

Please be aware that this code is case-sensitive and you will need to include the dashes within the passcode, but not when entering the ISBN.

ACCA

Strategic
Professional – Options

Advanced Financial Management
(AFM)

Study Text

British library cataloguing-in-publication data

A catalogue record for this book is available from the British Library.

Published by:

Kaplan Publishing UK
Unit 2 The Business Centre
Molly Millars Lane
Wokingham
Berkshire
RG41 2QZ

ISBN 978-1-78740-870-8

© Kaplan Financial Limited, 2021

Acknowledgements

These materials are reviewed by the ACCA examining team. The objective of the review is to ensure that the material properly covers the syllabus and study guide outcomes, used by the examining team in setting the exams, in the appropriate breadth and depth. The review does not ensure that every eventuality, combination or application of examinable topics is addressed by the ACCA Approved Content. Nor does the review comprise a detailed technical check of the content as the Approved Content Provider has its own quality assurance processes in place in this respect.

We are grateful to the Association of Chartered Certified Accountants and the Chartered Institute of Management Accountants for permission to reproduce past examination questions. The answers have been prepared by Kaplan Publishing.

Contents

Introduction

How to use the Materials

These Kaplan Publishing learning materials have been carefully designed to make your learning experience as easy as possible and to give you the best chances of success in your examinations.

The product range contains a number of features to help you in the study process. They include:

1   Detailed study guide and syllabus objectives

2   Description of the examination

3   Study skills and revision guidance

4   Study text

5   Question practice

The sections on the study guide, the syllabus objectives, the examination and study skills should all be read before you commence your studies. They are designed to familiarise you with the nature and content of the examination and give you tips on how to best to approach your learning.

The **study text** comprises the main learning materials and gives guidance as to the importance of topics and where other related resources can be found. Each chapter includes:

- The **learning objectives** contained in each chapter, which have been carefully mapped to the examining body's own syllabus learning objectives or outcomes. You should use these to check you have a clear understanding of all the topics on which you might be assessed in the examination.

- The **chapter diagram** provides a visual reference for the content in the chapter, giving an overview of the topics and how they link together.

- The **content** for each topic area commences with a brief explanation or definition to put the topic into context before covering the topic in detail. You should follow your studying of the content with a review of the illustration/s. These are worked examples which will help you to understand better how to apply the content for the topic.

- **Test your understanding** sections provide an opportunity to assess your understanding of the key topics by applying what you have learned to short questions. Answers can be found at the back of each chapter.

- **Summary diagrams** complete each chapter to show the important links between topics and the overall content of the syllabus. These diagrams should be used to check that you have covered and understood the core topics before moving on.

- **Question practice** is provided at the back of each text.

Quality and accuracy are of the utmost importance to us so if you spot an error in any of our products, please send an email to mykaplanreporting@kaplan.com with full details, or follow the link to the feedback form in MyKaplan.

Our Quality Coordinator will work with our technical team to verify the error and take action to ensure it is corrected in future editions.

Icon Explanations

 Definition – Key definitions that you will need to learn from the core content.

 Key point – Identifies topics that are key to success and are often examined.

 New – Identifies topics that are brand new.

 Test your understanding – Exercises for you to complete to ensure that you have understood the topics just learned.

 Illustration – Worked examples help you understand the core content better.

 Tricky topic – When reviewing these areas care should be taken and all illustrations and Test your understanding exercises should be completed to ensure that the topic is understood.

 Supplementary reading – These sections will help to provide a deeper understanding of core areas. The supplementary reading is **NOT** optional reading. It is vital to provide you with the breadth of knowledge you will need to address the wide range of topics within your syllabus that could feature in an exam question. **Reference to this text is vital when self studying.**

On-line subscribers

Our on-line resources are designed to increase the flexibility of your learning materials and provide you with immediate feedback on how your studies are progressing. Ask your local customer services staff if you are not already a subscriber and wish to join.

If you are subscribed to our on-line resources you will find:

1   On-line reference ware: reproduces your Study Text on-line, giving you anytime, anywhere access.

2   On-line testing: provides you with additional on-line objective testing so you can practice what you have learned further.

3   On-line performance management: immediate access to your on-line testing results. Review your performance by key topics and chart your achievement through the course relative to your peer group.

Syllabus

Examination background

The aim of Advanced Financial Management (AFM) is to apply relevant knowledge, skills and exercise professional judgement as expected of a senior financial executive or advisor, in taking or recommending decisions relating to the financial management of an organisation in private and public sectors.

Objectives of the syllabus

Main capabilities

On successful completion of this exam, candidates should be able to:

A   Explain and evaluate the role and responsibility of the senior financial executive or advisor in meeting conflicting needs of stakeholders and recognise the role of international financial institutions in the financial management of multinationals

B   Evaluate potential investment decisions and assessing their financial and strategic consequences, both domestically and internationally

C   Assess and plan acquisitions and mergers as an alternative growth strategy

D   Evaluate and advise on alternative corporate re-organisation strategies

E   Apply and evaluate alternative advanced treasury and risk management techniques

F   Apply employability and technology skills

ACCA Performance Objectives

In order to become a member of the ACCA, as a trainee accountant you will need to demonstrate that you have achieved nine performance objectives. Performance objectives are indicators of effective performance and set the minimum standard of work that trainees are expected to achieve and demonstrate in the workplace. They are divided into key areas of knowledge which are closely linked to the exam syllabus.

There are five Essential performance objectives and a choice of fifteen Technical performance objectives which are divided into five areas.

The performance objectives which link to this exam are:

PO2   Stakeholder relationship management (Essential)

PO3   Strategy and innovation (Essential)

PO5 Leadership and management (Essential)

PO9 Evaluate investment and financing decisions (Technical)

PO10 Manage and control working capital (Technical)

PO11 Identify and manage financial risk (Technical)

The following link provides an in depth insight into all of the performance objectives:

https://www.accaglobal.com/content/dam/ACCA_Global/Students/per/PER-Performance-objectives-achieve.pdf

Progression

There are two elements of progression that we can measure: first how quickly students move through individual topics within a subject; and second how quickly they move from one course to the next. We know that there is an optimum for both, but it can vary from subject to subject and from student to student. However, using data and our experience of student performance over many years, we can make some generalisations.

A fixed period of study set out at the start of a course with key milestones is important. This can be within a subject, for example 'I will finish this topic by 30 June', or for overall achievement, such as 'I want to be qualified by the end of next year'.

Your qualification is cumulative, as earlier papers provide a foundation for your subsequent studies, so do not allow there to be too big a gap between one subject and another. We know that exams encourage techniques that lead to some degree of short term retention, the result being that you will simply forget much of what you have already learned unless it is refreshed (look up Ebbinghaus Forgetting Curve for more details on this). This makes it more difficult as you move from one subject to another: not only will you have to learn the new subject, you will also have to relearn all the underpinning knowledge as well. This is very inefficient and slows down your overall progression which makes it more likely you may not succeed at all.

In addition, delaying your studies slows your path to qualification which can have negative impacts on your career, postponing the opportunity to apply for higher level positions and therefore higher pay.

You can use the following diagram showing the whole structure of your qualification to help you keep track of your progress.

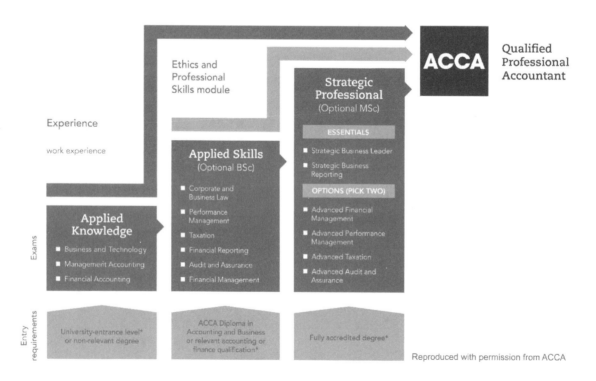

Reproduced with permission from ACCA

Syllabus objectives

We have reproduced the ACCA's syllabus below, showing where the objectives are explored within this book. Within the chapters, we have broken down the extensive information found in the syllabus into easily digestible and relevant sections, called Content Objectives. These correspond to the objectives at the beginning of each chapter.

Syllabus learning objective	Chapter reference

A   ROLE OF SENIOR FINANCIAL ADVISER IN THE MULTINATIONAL ORGANISATION

1   The role and responsibility of senior financial executive/ advisor

(a)	Develop strategies for the achievement of the organisational goals in line with its agreed policy framework.[3]	1
(b)	Recommend strategies for the management of the financial resources of the organisation such that they are utilised in an efficient, effective and transparent way.[3]	1
(c)	Advise the board of directors or management of the organisation in setting the financial goals of the business and in its financial policy development[2] with particular reference to:[2]	1

    (i)   investment selection and capital resource allocation

    (ii)   minimising the cost of capital

    (iii) distribution and retention policy

    (iv) communicating financial policy and corporate goals to internal and external stakeholders

    (v)   financial planning and control

    (vi) the management of risk.

2   Financial strategy formulation

(a)	Assess organisational performance using methods such as ratios and trends.[3]	14
(b)	Recommend the optimum capital mix and structure within a specified business context and capital asset structure.[3]	4
(c)	Recommend appropriate distribution and retention policy.[3]	5

Syllabus learning objective	Chapter reference

(d) Explain the theoretical and practical rationale for the management of risk.[3] — 9

(e) Assess the organisation's exposure to business and financial risk including operational, reputational, political, economic, regulatory and fiscal risk.[3] — 9

(f) Develop a framework for risk management comparing and contrasting risk mitigation, hedging and diversification strategies.[3] — 9

(g) Establish capital investment monitoring and risk management systems.[3] — 9

(h) Advise on the impact of behavioural finance on financial strategies/securities prices and why they may not follow the conventional financial theories.[3] — 1

3 Ethical and governance issues

(a) Assess the ethical dimension within business issues and decisions and advise on best practice in the financial management of the organisation.[3] — 1

(b) Demonstrate an understanding of the interconnectedness of the ethics of good business practice between all of the functional areas of the organisation.[2] — 1

(c) Recommend, within specified problem domains, appropriate strategies for the resolution of stakeholder conflict and advise on alternative approaches that may be adopted.[3] — 1

(d) Recommend an ethical framework for the development of an organisation's financial policies and a system for the assessment of its ethical impact upon the financial management of the organisation.[3] — 1

(e) Explore the areas within the ethical framework of the organisation which may be undermined by agency effects and/or stakeholder conflicts and establish strategies for dealing with them.[3] — 1

(f) Establish an ethical financial policy for the financial management of the organisation which is grounded in good governance, the highest standards of probity and is fully aligned with the ethical principles of the Association.[3] — 1

(g) Assess the impact on sustainability and environmental issues arising from alternative organisational business and financial decisions.[3] — 1

KAPLAN PUBLISHING

Syllabus learning objective		Chapter reference

(h) Assess and advise on the impact of investment and financing strategies and decisions on the organisation's stakeholders, from an integrated reporting and governance perspective.[2] — Chapter reference: 1

4 Management of international trade and finance

(a) Advise on the theory and practice of free trade and the management of barriers to trade.[3] — Chapter reference: 3

(b) Demonstrate an up-to-date understanding of the major trade agreements and common markets and, on the basis of contemporary circumstances, advise on their policy and strategic implications for a given business.[3] — Chapter reference: 3

(c) Discuss how the actions of the World Trade Organisation, the International Monetary Fund, The World Bank and Central Banks can affect a multinational organisation.[2] — Chapter reference: 3

(d) Discuss the role of international financial institutions within the context of a globalised economy, with particular attention to the principal Central Banks (the Fed, Bank of England, European Central Bank and the Bank of Japan).[2] — Chapter reference: 3

(e) Discuss the role of the international financial markets with respect to the management of global debt, the financial development of the emerging economies and the maintenance of global financial stability.[2] — Chapter reference: 3

(f) Discuss the significance to the organisation of the latest developments in the world financial markets such as the causes and impact of the recent financial crisis, growth and impact of dark pool trading systems, the removal of barriers to the free movement of capital and the international regulations on money laundering.[2] — Chapter reference: 3

(g) Demonstrate an awareness of new developments in the macroeconomic environment, assessing their impact upon the organisation, and advising on the appropriate response to those developments both internally and externally.[2] — Chapter reference: 3

Syllabus learning objective	Chapter reference

5 Strategic business and financial planning for multinationals

(a) Advise on the development of a financial planning framework for a multinational organisation taking into account:[3]

    (i) compliance with national regulatory requirements (for example, the London Stock Exchange admission requirements)

    (ii) the mobility of capital across borders and national limitations on remittances and transfer pricing

    (iii) the pattern of economic and other risk exposures in the different national markets

    (iv) agency issues in the central coordination of overseas operations and the balancing of local financial autonomy with effective central control.

Chapter reference: 3

6 Dividend policy in multinationals and transfer pricing

(a) Determine a corporation's dividend capacity and its policy given:[3]

    (i) the corporation's short- and long-term reinvestment strategy

    (ii) the impact of capital reconstruction programmes such as share repurchase agreements and new capital issues on free cash flow to equity

    (iii) the availability and timing of central remittances

    (iv) the corporate tax regime within the host jurisdiction.

Chapter reference: 5

(b) Advise, in the context of a specified capital investment programme, on an organisation's current and projected dividend capacity.[3]

Chapter reference: 5

(c) Develop organisational policy on the transfer pricing of goods and services across international borders and be able to determine the most appropriate transfer pricing strategy in a given situation reflecting local regulations and tax regimes.[3]

Chapter reference: 5

KAPLAN PUBLISHING

Syllabus learning objective	Chapter reference

B   ADVANCED INVESTMENT APPRAISAL

1   Discounted cash flow techniques

(a)   Evaluate the potential value added to an organisation arising from a specified capital investment project or portfolio using the net present value model.[3] Project modelling should include explicit treatment and discussion of: **2**

    (i)   inflation and specific price variation

    (ii)   taxation including tax allowable depreciation and tax exhaustion

    (iii) single period and multi-period capital rationing. Multi-period capital rationing to include the formulation of programming methods and the interpretation of their output

    (iv)   probability analysis and sensitivity analysis when adjusting for risk and uncertainty in investment appraisal

    (v)   risk adjusted discount rates

    (vi)   project duration as a measure of risk.

(b)   Outline the application of Monte Carlo simulation to investment appraisal.[2] Candidates will not be expected to undertake simulations in an exam context but will be expected to demonstrate an understanding of: **9**

    (i)   the significance of the simulation output and the assessment of the likelihood of project success

    (ii)   the measurement and interpretation of project value at risk.

(c)   Establish the potential economic return (using internal rate of return and modified internal rate of return) and advise on a project's return margin. Discuss the relative merits of NPV and IRR.[3]   **2**

Syllabus learning objective	Chapter reference

2 Application of option pricing theory in investment decisions

(a) Apply the Black-Scholes Option Pricing (BSOP) model to financial product valuation and to asset valuation:[3] — 8

   (i) determine and discuss, using published data, the five principal drivers of option value (value of the underlying, exercise price, time to expiry, volatility and the risk-free rate)

   (ii) discuss the underlying assumptions, structure, application and limitations of the BSOP model.

(b) Evaluate embedded real options within a project, classifying them into one of the real option archetypes.[3] — 8

(c) Assess, calculate and advise on the value of options to delay, expand, redeploy and withdraw using the Black Scholes model.[3] — 8

3 Impact of financing on investment decisions and adjusted present values

(a) Identify and assess the appropriateness of the range of sources of finance available to an organisation including equity, debt, hybrids, lease finance, venture capital, business angel finance, private equity, asset securitisation and sale, Islamic finance and initial coin offerings. Including assessment on the financial position, financial risk and the value of an organisation.[3] — 4

(b) Discuss the role of, and developments in, Islamic financing as a growing source of finance for organisations; explaining the rationale for its use, and identifying its benefits and deficiencies.[2] — 4

(c) Calculate the cost of capital of an organisation, including the cost of equity and the cost of debt, based on the range of equity and debt sources of finance. Discuss the appropriateness of using the cost of capital to establish project and organisational value, and discuss its relationship to such value.[3] — 6

(d) Calculate and evaluate project specific cost of equity and cost of capital, including their impact on the overall cost of capital of an organisation. Demonstrate a detailed knowledge of business and financial risk, the capital asset pricing model and the relationship between equity and asset betas.[3] — 7

Syllabus learning objective		Chapter reference
(e)	Assess an organisation's debt exposure to interest rate changes using the simple Macaulay duration and modified duration methods.[3]	6
(f)	Discuss the benefits and limitations of duration, including the impact of convexity.	6
(g)	Assess the organisation's exposure to credit risk, including:[2]	6
	(i) explain the role of, and the risk assessment models used by, the principal rating agencies	
	(ii) estimate the likely credit spread over risk free	
	(iii) estimate the organisation's current cost of debt capital using the appropriate term structure of interest rates and the credit spread.	
(h)	Assess the impact of financing and capital structure upon the organisation with respect to:[3]	4
	(i) Modigliani and Miller propositions, before and after tax	
	(ii) pecking order propositions	
	(iii) static trade-off theory	
	(iv) agency effects.	
(i)	Apply the adjusted present value technique to the appraisal of investment decisions that entail significant alterations in the financial structure of the organisation, including their fiscal and transactions cost implications.[3]	7
(j)	Assess the impact of a significant capital investment project upon the reported financial position and performance of the organisation taking into account alternative financing strategies.[3]	7

4 Valuation and the use of free cash flows

(a)	Apply asset based, income based and cash flow based models to value equity. Apply appropriate models, including term structure of interest rates, the yield curve and credit spreads, to value corporate debt.[3]	13
(b)	Forecast an organisation's free cash flow and its free cash flow to equity (pre- and post-capital reinvestment).[3]	13

Syllabus learning objective	Chapter reference

	(c)	Advise on the value of an organisation using its free cash flow and free cash flow to equity under alternative horizon and growth assumptions.[3]	13
	(d)	Explain the use of the BSOP model to estimate the value of equity of an organisation and discuss the implications of the model for a change in the value of equity.[2]	8
	(e)	Explain the role of BSOP model in the assessment of default risk, the value of debt and its potential recoverability.[2]	8
5	**International investment and financing decisions**		
	(a)	Assess the impact upon the value of a project of alternative exchange rate assumptions.[3]	3
	(b)	Forecast project or organisation free cash flows in any specified currency and determine the project's net present value or organisation value under differing exchange rate, fiscal and transaction cost assumptions.[2]	3
	(c)	Evaluate the significance of exchange controls for a given investment decision and strategies for dealing with restricted remittance.[3]	3
	(d)	Assess the impact of a project upon an organisation's exposure to translation, transaction and economic risk.[3]	3
	(e)	Assess and advise upon the costs and benefits of alternative sources of finance available within the international equity and bond financial markets.[3]	4
C	**ACQUISITIONS AND MERGERS**		
1	**Acquisitions and mergers versus other growth strategies**		
	(a)	Discuss the arguments for and against the use of acquisitions and mergers as a method of corporate expansion.[2]	12
	(b)	Evaluate the corporate and competitive nature of a given acquisition proposal.[3]	12
	(c)	Advise upon the criteria for choosing an appropriate target for acquisition.[3]	12

KAPLAN PUBLISHING

Syllabus learning objective	Chapter reference

(d) Compare the various explanations for the high failure rate of acquisitions in enhancing shareholder value.[3] 12

(e) Evaluate, from a given context, the potential for synergy separately classified as: 12

    (i)   revenue synergy

    (ii)   cost synergy

    (iii) financial synergy.

(f) Evaluate the use of the reverse takeover as a method of acquisition and as a way of obtaining a stock market listing.[3] 12

2   Valuation for acquisitions and mergers

(a) Discuss the problem of overvaluation.[1] 13

(b) Estimate the potential near-term and continuing growth levels of a corporation's earnings using both internal and external measures.[3] 13

(c) Discuss, assess and advise on the value created from an acquisition or merger of both quoted and unquoted entities using models such as:[3] 13

    (i)   'Book value-plus' models

    (ii)   Market based models

    (ii)   Cash flow models, including free cash flows.

Taking into account the changes in the risk profile and risk exposure of the acquirer and the target entities.

(d) Apply appropriate methods, such as: risk-adjusted cost of capital, adjusted net present values and changing price-earnings multipliers resulting from the acquisition or merger, to the valuation process where appropriate.[3] 13

(e) Demonstrate an understanding of the procedure for valuing high growth start-ups.[2] 13

Syllabus learning objective	Chapter reference

3 Regulatory framework and processes

(a) Demonstrate an understanding of the principal factors influencing the development of the regulatory framework for mergers and acquisitions globally and, in particular, be able to compare and contrast the shareholder versus the stakeholder models of regulation.[2]   12

(b) Identify the main regulatory issues which are likely to arise in the context of a given offer, and: 12

   (i) assess whether the offer is likely to be in the shareholders' best interests

   (ii) advise the directors of a target entity on the most appropriate defence if a specific offer is to be treated as hostile.[3]

4 Financing acquisitions and mergers

(a) Compare the various sources of financing available for a proposed cash-based acquisition.[3]   12

(b) Evaluate the advantages and disadvantages of a financial offer for a given acquisition proposal using pure or mixed mode financing and recommend the most appropriate offer to be made.[3]   12

(c) Assess the impact of a given financial offer on the reported financial position and performance of the acquirer.[3]   12

D CORPORATE RECONSTRUCTION AND REORGANISATION

1 Financial reconstruction

(a) Assess an organisational situation and determine whether a financial reconstruction is the appropriate strategy for a given business situation.[3]   14

(b) Assess the likely response of the capital market and/or individual suppliers of capital to any reconstruction scheme and the impact their response is likely to have upon the value of the organisation.[3]   14

KAPLAN PUBLISHING

Syllabus learning objective	Chapter reference

2 Business reorganisation

(a) Recommend, with reasons, strategies for unbundling parts of a quoted company.[3] — 14

(b) Evaluate the likely financial and other benefits of unbundling.[3] — 14

(c) Advise on the financial issues relating to a management buy-out and buy-in.[3] — 14

E TREASURY AND ADVANCED RISK MANAGEMENT TECHNIQUES

1 The role of the treasury function in multinationals

(a) Discuss the role of the treasury management function within:[2] — 1

    (i) the short term management of the organisation's financial resources

    (ii) the longer term maximisation of corporate value

    (iii) the management of risk exposure.

(b) Discuss the operations of the derivatives market including:[3] — 8, 9, 10, 11

    (i) The relative advantages and disadvantages of exchange traded versus OTC agreements.

    (ii) Key features such as standard contracts, tick sizes, margin requirements and margin trading.

    (iii) The source of basis risk and how it can be minimised.

    (iv) Risks such as delta, gamma, vega, rho and theta, and how these can be managed.

2 The use of financial derivatives to hedge against forex risk

(a) Assess the impact on an organisation to exposure in translation, transaction and economic risks and how these can be managed.[2] — 10

(b) Evaluate, for a given hedging requirement, which of the following is the most appropriate strategy, given the nature of the underlying position and the risk exposure:[3] — 10

    (i) the use of the forward exchange market and the creation of a money market hedge

    (ii) synthetic foreign exchange agreements (SAFEs)

Syllabus learning objective	Chapter reference

    (iii)   exchange-traded currency futures contracts

    (iv)   currency swaps

    (v)   FOREX swaps

    (vi)   currency options.

(c)   Advise on the use of bilateral and multilateral netting and matching as tools for minimising FOREX transactions costs and the management of market barriers to the free movement of capital and other remittances.[3]   **10**

3   The use of financial derivatives to hedge against interest rate risk

(a)   Evaluate, for a given hedging requirement, which of the following is the most appropriate given the nature of the underlying position and the risk exposure:[3]   **11**

    (i)   forward rate agreements

    (ii)   interest rate futures

    (iii)   interest rate swaps

    (iv)   interest rate options (including collars).

F   EMPLOYABILITY AND TECHNOLOGY SKILLS

1   Use computer technology to efficiently access and manipulate relevant information   **15**

2   Work on relevant response options, using available functions and technology, as would be required in the workplace   **15**

3   Navigate windows and computer screens to create and amend responses to exam requirements, using the appropriate tools   **15**

4   Present data and information effectively, using the appropriate tools   **15**

The superscript numbers in square brackets indicate the intellectual depth at which the subject area could be assessed within the examination. Level 1 (knowledge and comprehension) broadly equates with the Knowledge module, Level 2 (application and analysis) with the Skills module and Level 3 (synthesis and evaluation) to the Professional level. However, lower level skills can continue to be assessed as you progress through each module and level.

The examination

Approach to examining the syllabus

The **Advanced Financial Management (AFM)** exam builds upon the skills and knowledge examined in the Financial Management (FM) exam. At this stage candidates will be expected to demonstrate an integrated knowledge of the subject and an ability to relate their technical understanding of the subject to issues of strategic importance to the organisation. The study guide specifies the wide range of contextual understanding that is required to achieve a satisfactory standard at this level.

Examination structure

The syllabus is assessed by a three-hour 15 minutes examination.

Section A

Section A will always be a single 50 mark case study, which will contain four professional marks in which candidates are required produce a business document such as a report or a briefing paper for the board of directors.

Candidates should understand that they will be expected to undertake calculations, draw comparison against relevant information where appropriate, analyse the results and offer recommendations or conclusions as required.

Financial managers are required to look across a range of issues which affect an organisation and its finances, so candidates should expect to see the case study focus on a range of issues from at least two syllabus sections from A – E. These will vary depending on the business context of the case study.

Section B

Section B will consist of two compulsory 25 mark questions.

All section B questions will be scenario based and contain a combination of calculation and narrative marks. There will not be any wholly narrative questions.

All topics and syllabus sections will be examinable in either section A or section B of the exam, but every exam will have questions which have a focus on syllabus sections B and E.

Total 100 marks

Strategic Professional Computer Based Examination (CBE)

In March 2020, ACCA introduced Strategic Professional computer based examinations (CBE) in selected locations. Strategic Professional CBE has been extended to other locations over time, across subsequent examination sessions. Once CBE are offered in a location, the paper-based exam will no longer be available. From September 2021 onwards, all AFM exams in all locations will be CBE.

It is essential that students who will be sitting the CBE become familiar with the CBE environment as part of their exam preparation. For additional support please refer to Chapter 15 in this Text and to the ACCA Global website.

Examination tips – Computer Based Exam (CBE)

In addition to reading the tips contained here, we recommend that you review the resources available on the ACCA Global Website before sitting the CBE. Here you will find guidance documents, videos and a link to the CBE question practice platform.

Before the exam starts – You will be given 10 minutes to read the introductory page and the four pages of instructions. These will be the same for each AFM exam and therefore it is important that you familiarise yourself with these (using the ACCA practice exams) during your revision. The exam time (3 hours and 15 minutes) will start automatically at the end of the 10 minutes or earlier if requested by you.

Plan your strategy before you go in; allocating 90 minutes to Section A, 45 minutes to each question in Section B (1.8 minutes per mark) and 15 minutes to skim through the questions at the start and as a buffer to review your answers at the end.

Planning your answers – When the exam starts spend a few minutes skimming through the whole exam to get a feel for what is included. Once you have done this carry out an initial review of Section A. This will include a number of **exhibits** breaking down the scenario into relevant sections and including the detailed requirement. It will also include a list of the summarised **requirements** and an option to complete your answer in a **word processing** document and/or a **spreadsheet** document.

You can move around and resize the windows that you open to lay the screen out in a format that suits you.

Now copy and paste the specifics of the requirement into your answer document, perhaps highlighting in bold the different parts of the requirement and the verb used. Once complete review the exhibits in detail, highlighting and making notes as you do so and copy and pasting any relevant information to your answer document. These steps will help with your planning and structure but will also enable you to minimise the number of windows you have open.

The procedure will be similar for Section B.

Completing your answers – Start by revisiting the relevant exhibits for each requirement. Decide on the use of a word processing format, a spreadsheet format or both. For calculations, use a logical and well laid out structure. Calculations should be labelled and referenced in to any relevant discussion. For discursive answers use bold headings and sub-headings and professional language. Ensure all aspects of the requirement are covered in a sensible and balanced way. It is vital that you relate your answer to the specific circumstances given. In Section A you will usually be required to produce a report. Head up your answer as a report and use the requirements as a basis for your introduction.

If you get completely stuck with a question return to it later.

If you do not understand what a question is asking, state your assumptions. Even if you do not answer in precisely the way the examiner hoped, you should be given some credit, if your assumptions are reasonable.

Finally, use your buffer time to read through the answers, ensuring they are clear and organised, and to make any necessary changes.

Study skills and revision guidance

This section aims to give guidance on how to study for your ACCA exams and to give ideas on how to improve your existing study techniques.

Preparing to study

Set your objectives

Before starting to study decide what you want to achieve – the type of pass you wish to obtain. This will decide the level of commitment and time you need to dedicate to your studies.

Devise a study plan

Determine which times of the week you will study.

Split these times into sessions of at least one hour for study of new material. Any shorter periods could be used for revision or practice.

Put the times you plan to study onto a study plan for the weeks from now until the exam and set yourself targets for each period of study – in your sessions make sure you cover the course, course assignments and revision.

If you are studying for more than one exam at a time, try to vary your subjects as this can help you to keep interested and see subjects as part of wider knowledge.

When working through your course, compare your progress with your plan and, if necessary, re-plan your work (perhaps including extra sessions) or, if you are ahead, do some extra revision/practice questions.

Effective studying

Active reading

You are not expected to learn the text by rote, rather, you must understand what you are reading and be able to use it to pass the exam and develop good practice. A good technique to use is SQ3Rs – Survey, Question, Read, Recall, Review:

1   **Survey the chapter** – look at the headings and read the introduction, summary and objectives, so as to get an overview of what the chapter deals with.

2   **Question** – whilst undertaking the survey, ask yourself the questions that you hope the chapter will answer for you.

3   **Read** through the chapter thoroughly, answering the questions and making sure you can meet the objectives. Attempt the exercises and activities in the text, and work through all the examples.

4   **Recall** – at the end of each section and at the end of the chapter, try to recall the main ideas of the section/chapter without referring to the text. This is best done after a short break of a couple of minutes after the reading stage.

5   **Review** – check that your recall notes are correct.

You may also find it helpful to re-read the chapter to try to see the topic(s) it deals with as a whole.

Note-taking

Taking notes is a useful way of learning, but do not simply copy out the text. The notes must:

*   be in your own words

*   be concise

*   cover the key points

*   be well-organised

*   be modified as you study further chapters in this text or in related ones.

Trying to summarise a chapter without referring to the text can be a useful way of determining which areas you know and which you don't.

Three ways of taking notes:

Summarise the key points of a chapter.

Make linear notes – a list of headings, divided up with subheadings listing the key points. If you use linear notes, you can use different colours to highlight key points and keep topic areas together. Use plenty of space to make your notes easy to use.

Try a diagrammatic form – the most common of which is a mind-map. To make a mind-map, put the main heading in the centre of the paper and put a circle around it. Then draw short lines radiating from this to the main sub-headings, which again have circles around them. Then continue the process from the sub-headings to sub-sub-headings, advantages, disadvantages, etc.

Highlighting and underlining

You may find it useful to underline or highlight key points in your study text – but do be selective. You may also wish to make notes in the margins.

Revision

The best approach to revision is to revise the course as you work through it. Also try to leave four to six weeks before the exam for final revision. Make sure you cover the whole syllabus and pay special attention to those areas where your knowledge is weak. Here are some recommendations:

Read through the text and your notes again and condense your notes into key phrases. It may help to put key revision points onto index cards to look at when you have a few minutes to spare.

Review any assignments you have completed and look at where you lost marks – put more work into those areas where you were weak.

Practise exam standard questions under timed conditions. If you are short of time, list the points that you would cover in your answer and then read the model answer, but do try to complete at least a few questions under exam conditions.

Also practise producing answer plans and comparing them to the model answer.

If you are stuck on a topic find somebody (a tutor) to explain it to you.

Read good newspapers, websites and professional journals, especially ACCA's **Student Accountant** – this can give you an advantage in the exam.

Ensure you **know the structure of the exam** – how many questions and of what type you will be expected to answer. During your revision attempt all the different styles of questions you may be asked.

Further reading

- A Student's Guide to Corporate Finance and Financial Management by David Evans – Kaplan Publishing

- A Student's Guide to Writing Business Reports by Zoe Robinson and Stuart Pedley-Smith

You can find further reading and technical articles under the student section of ACCA's website.

FORMULAE AND TABLES

Modigliani and Miller Proposition 2 (with tax)

$$k_e = k^i_e + (1 - T)(k^i_e - k_d)\frac{V_d}{V_e}$$

The Capital Asset Pricing Model

$$E(r_i) = R_f + \beta_i(E(r_m) - R_f)$$

The asset beta formula

$$\beta_a = \left[\frac{V_e}{(V_e + V_d(1-T))}\beta_e\right] + \left[\frac{V_d(1-T)}{(V_e + V_d(1-T))}\beta_d\right]$$

The Growth Model

$$P_0 = \frac{D_0(1+g)}{(r_e - g)}$$

Gordon's growth approximation

$$g = br_e$$

The weighted average cost of capital

$$WACC = \left[\frac{V_e}{V_e + V_d}\right]k_e + \left[\frac{V_d}{V_e + V_d}\right]k_d(1-T)$$

The Fisher formula

$$(1 + i) = (1 + r)(1 + h)$$

Purchasing power parity and interest rate parity

$$S_1 = S_o \times \frac{(1+h_c)}{(1+h_b)} \qquad F_0 = S_o \times \frac{(1+i_c)}{(1+i_b)}$$

Modified Internal Rate of Return

$$MIRR = \left[\frac{PV_R}{PV_I}\right]^{\frac{1}{n}}(1+re) - 1$$

The Black-Scholes option pricing model

$$c = P_a N(d_1) - P_e N(d_2)e^{-rt}$$

Where:

$$d_1 = \frac{\ln(P_a/P_e) + (r + 0.5s^2)t}{s\sqrt{t}}$$

$$d_2 = d_1 - s\sqrt{t}$$

The Put Call Parity relationship

$$p = c - P_a + P_e e^{-rt}$$

KAPLAN PUBLISHING

Present value table

Present value of 1, i.e. $(1 + r)^{-n}$

Where   r = discount rate

             n = number of periods until payment

Periods	Discount rate (r)									
(n)	1%	2%	3%	4%	5%	6%	7%	8%	9%	10%
1	0.990	0.980	0.971	0.962	0.952	0.943	0.935	0.926	0.917	0.909
2	0.980	0.961	0.943	0.925	0.907	0.890	0.873	0.857	0.842	0.826
3	0.971	0.942	0.915	0.889	0.864	0.840	0.816	0.794	0.772	0.751
4	0.961	0.924	0.888	0.855	0.823	0.792	0.763	0.735	0.708	0.683
5	0.951	0.906	0.863	0.822	0.784	0.747	0.713	0.681	0.650	0.621
6	0.942	0.888	0.837	0.790	0.746	0.705	0.666	0.630	0.596	0.564
7	0.933	0.871	0.813	0.760	0.711	0.665	0.623	0.583	0.547	0.513
8	0.923	0.853	0.789	0.731	0.677	0.627	0.582	0.540	0.502	0.467
9	0.914	0.837	0.766	0.703	0.645	0.592	0.544	0.500	0.460	0.424
10	0.905	0.820	0.744	0.676	0.614	0.558	0.508	0.463	0.422	0.386
11	0.896	0.804	0.722	0.650	0.585	0.527	0.475	0.429	0.388	0.350
12	0.887	0.788	0.701	0.625	0.557	0.497	0.444	0.397	0.356	0.319
13	0.879	0.773	0.681	0.601	0.530	0.469	0.415	0.368	0.326	0.290
14	0.870	0.758	0.661	0.577	0.505	0.442	0.388	0.340	0.299	0.263
15	0.861	0.743	0.642	0.555	0.481	0.417	0.362	0.315	0.275	0.239

Periods	Discount rate (r)									
(n)	11%	12%	13%	14%	15%	16%	17%	18%	19%	20%
1	0.901	0.893	0.885	0.877	0.870	0.862	0.855	0.847	0.840	0.833
2	0.812	0.797	0.783	0.769	0.756	0.743	0.731	0.718	0.706	0.694
3	0.731	0.712	0.693	0.675	0.658	0.641	0.624	0.609	0.593	0.579
4	0.659	0.636	0.613	0.592	0.572	0.552	0.534	0.516	0.499	0.482
5	0.593	0.567	0.543	0.519	0.497	0.476	0.456	0.437	0.419	0.402
6	0.535	0.507	0.480	0.456	0.432	0.410	0.390	0.370	0.352	0.335
7	0.482	0.452	0.425	0.400	0.376	0.354	0.333	0.314	0.296	0.279
8	0.434	0.404	0.376	0.351	0.327	0.305	0.285	0.266	0.249	0.233
9	0.391	0.361	0.333	0.308	0.284	0.263	0.243	0.225	0.209	0.194
10	0.352	0.322	0.295	0.270	0.247	0.227	0.208	0.191	0.176	0.162
11	0.317	0.287	0.261	0.237	0.215	0.195	0.178	0.162	0.148	0.135
12	0.286	0.257	0.231	0.208	0.187	0.168	0.152	0.137	0.124	0.112
13	0.258	0.229	0.204	0.182	0.163	0.145	0.130	0.116	0.104	0.093
14	0.232	0.205	0.181	0.160	0.141	0.125	0.111	0.099	0.088	0.078
15	0.209	0.183	0.160	0.140	0.123	0.108	0.095	0.084	0.074	0.065

Annuity table

Present value of an annuity of 1, i.e. $\dfrac{1-(1+r)^{-n}}{r}$

Where   r = discount rate

            n = number of periods

Periods (n)	Discount rate (r)									
	1%	2%	3%	4%	5%	6%	7%	8%	9%	10%
1	0.990	0.980	0.971	0.962	0.952	0.943	0.935	0.926	0.917	0.909
2	1.970	1.942	1.913	1.886	1.859	1.833	1.808	1.783	1.759	1.736
3	2.941	2.884	2.829	2.775	2.723	2.673	2.624	2.577	2.531	2.487
4	3.902	3.808	3.717	3.630	3.546	3.465	3.387	3.312	3.240	3.170
5	4.853	4.713	4.580	4.452	4.329	4.212	4.100	3.993	3.890	3.791
6	5.795	5.601	5.417	5.242	5.076	4.917	4.767	4.623	4.486	4.355
7	6.728	6.472	6.230	6.002	5.786	5.582	5.389	5.206	5.033	4.868
8	7.652	7.325	7.020	6.733	6.463	6.210	5.971	5.747	5.535	5.335
9	8.566	8.162	7.786	7.435	7.108	6.802	6.515	6.247	5.995	5.759
10	9.471	8.983	8.530	8.111	7.722	7.360	7.024	6.710	6.418	6.145
11	10.368	9.787	9.253	8.760	8.306	7.887	7.499	7.139	6.805	8.495
12	11.255	10.575	9.954	9.385	8.863	8.384	7.943	7.536	7.161	6.814
13	12.134	11.348	10.635	9.986	9.394	8.853	8.358	7.904	7.487	7.103
14	13.004	12.106	11.296	10.563	9.899	9.295	8.745	8.244	7.786	7.367
15	13.865	12.849	11.938	11.118	10.380	9.712	9.108	8.559	8.061	7.606

Periods (n)	Discount rate (r)									
	11%	12%	13%	14%	15%	16%	17%	18%	19%	20%
1	0.901	0.893	0.885	0.877	0.870	0.862	0.855	0.847	0.840	0.833
2	1.713	1.690	1.668	1.647	1.626	1.605	1.585	1.566	1.547	1.528
3	2.444	2.402	2.361	2.322	2.283	2.246	2.210	2.174	2.140	2.106
4	3.102	3.037	2.974	2.914	2.855	2.798	2.743	2.690	2.639	2.589
5	3.696	3.605	3.517	3.433	3.352	3.274	3.199	3.127	3.058	2.991
6	4.231	4.111	3.998	3.889	3.784	3.685	3.589	3.498	3.410	3.326
7	4.712	4.564	4.423	4.288	4.160	4.039	3.922	3.812	3.706	3.605
8	5.146	4.968	4.799	4.639	4.487	4.344	4.207	4.078	3.954	3.837
9	5.537	5.328	5.132	4.946	4.772	4.607	4.451	4.303	4.163	4.031
10	5.889	5.650	5.426	5.216	5.019	4.833	4.659	4.494	4.339	4.192
11	6.207	5.938	5.687	5.453	5.234	5.029	4.836	4.656	4.486	4.327
12	6.492	6.194	5.918	5.660	5.421	5.197	4.968	4.793	4.611	4.439
13	6.750	6.424	6.122	5.842	5.583	5.342	5.118	4.910	4.715	4.533
14	6.982	6.628	6.302	6.002	5.724	5.468	5.229	5.008	4.802	4.611
15	7.191	6.811	6.462	6.142	5.847	5.575	5.324	5.092	4.876	4.675

KAPLAN PUBLISHING

Standard normal distribution table

	0.00	0.01	0.02	0.03	0.04	0.05	0.06	0.07	0.08	0.09
0.0	.0000	.0040	.0080	.0120	.0160	.0199	.0239	.0279	.0319	.0359
0.1	.0398	.0438	.0478	.0517	.0557	.0596	.0636	.0675	.0714	.0753
0.2	.0793	.0832	.0871	.0910	.0948	.0987	.1026	.1064	.1103	.1141
0.3	.1179	.1217	.1255	.1293	.1331	.1368	.1406	.1443	.1480	.1517
0.4	.1554	.1591	.1628	.1664	.1700	.1736	.1772	.1808	.1844	.1879
0.5	.1915	.1950	.1985	.2019	.2054	.2088	.2123	.2157	.2190	.2224
0.6	.2257	.2291	.2324	.2357	.2389	.2422	.2454	.2486	.2517	.2549
0.7	.2580	.2611	.2642	.2673	.2703	.2734	.2764	.2794	.2823	.2852
0.8	.2881	.2910	.2939	.2967	.2995	.3023	.3051	.3078	.3106	.3133
0.9	.3159	.3186	.3212	.3238	.3264	.3289	.3315	.3340	.3365	.3389
1.0	.3413	.3438	.3461	.3485	.3508	.3531	.3554	.3577	.3599	.3621
1.1	.3643	.3665	.3686	.3708	.3729	.3749	.3770	.3790	.3810	.3830
1.2	.3849	.3869	.3888	.3907	.3925	.3944	.3962	.3980	.3997	.4015
1.3	.4032	.4049	.4066	.4082	4099	.4115	.4131	.4147	.4162	.4177
1.4	.4192	.4207	.4222	.4236	.4251	.4265	.4279	.4292	.4306	.4319
1.5	.4332	.4345	.4357	.4370	.4382	.4394	.4406	.4418	.4430	.4441
1.6	.4452	.4463	.4474	.4484	.4495	.4505	.4515	.4525	.4535	.4545
1.7	.4554	.4564	.4573	.4582	.4591	.4599	.4608	.4616	.4625	.4633
1.8	.4641	.4649	.4656	.4664	.4671	.4678	.4686	.4693	.4699	.4706
1.9	.4713	.4719	.4726	.4732	.4738	.4744	.4750	.4756	.4761	.4767
2.0	.4772	.4778	.4783	.4788	.4793	.4798	.4803	.4808	.4812	.4817
2.1	.4821	.4826	.4830	.4834	.4838	.4842	.4846	.4850	.4854	.4857
2.2	.4861	.4864	.4868	.4871	.4875	.4878	.4881	.4884	.4887	.4890
2.3	.4893	.4896	.4898	.4901	.4904	.4906	.4909	.4911	.4913	.4916
2.4	.4918	.4920	.4922	.4925	.4927	.4929	.4931	.4932	.4934	.4936
2.5	.4938	.4940	.4941	.4943	.4945	.4946	.4948	.4949	.4951	.4952
2.6	.4953	.4955	.4956	.4957	.4959	.4960	.4961	.4962	4963	.4964
2.7	.4965	.4966	.4967	.4968	.4969	.4970	.4971	.4972	.4973	.4974
2.8	.4974	.4975	.4976	.4977	.4977	.4978	.4979	.4980	.4980	.4981
2.9	.4981	.4982	.4982	.4983	.4984	.4984	.4985	.4985	.4986	.4986
3.0	.4987	.4987	.4987	.4988	.4988	.4989	.4989	.4989	.4990	.4990

This table can be used to calculate $N(d_i)$, the cumulative normal distribution functions needed for the Black-Scholes model of option pricing. If $d_i > 0$, add 0.5 to the relevant number above. If $d_i < 0$, subtract the relevant number above from 0.5.

KAPLAN PUBLISHING

The role and responsibility of the financial manager

Chapter learning objectives

Study guide section	Study guide outcome
A1: The role and responsibility of senior financial executive/ advisor	(a) Develop strategies for the achievement of the organisational goals in line with its agreed policy framework.
	(b) Recommend strategies for the management of the financial resources of the organisation such that they are utilised in an efficient, effective and transparent way.
	(c) Advise the board of directors or management of the organisation in setting the financial goals of the business and in its financial policy development with particular reference to: (i) Investment selection and capital resource allocation (ii) Minimising the cost of capital (iii) Distribution and retention policy (iv) Communicating financial policy and corporate goals to internal and external stakeholders (v) Financial planning and control (vi) The management of risk.

A2: Financial strategy formulation

(h) Advise on the impact of behavioural finance on financial strategies/securities prices and why they may not follow the conventional financial theories.

A3: Ethical issues in financial management

(a) Assess the ethical dimension within business issues and decisions and advise on best practice in the financial management of the organisation.

(b) Demonstrate an understanding of the interconnectedness of the ethics of good business practice between all of the functional areas of the organisation.

(c) Recommend, within specified problem domains, appropriate strategies for the resolution of stakeholder conflict and advise on alternative approaches that may be adopted.

(d) Recommend an ethical framework for the development of an organisation's financial policies and a system for the assessment of its ethical impact upon the financial management of the organisation.

(e) Explore the areas within the ethical framework of the organisation which may be undermined by agency effects and/or stakeholder conflicts and establish strategies for dealing with them.

(f) Establish an ethical financial policy for the financial management of the organisation which is grounded in good governance, the highest standards of probity and is fully aligned with the ethical principles of the Association.

(g)   Assess the impact on sustainability and environmental issues arising from alternative organisational business and financial decisions.

(h)   Assess and advise on the impact of investment and financing strategies and decisions on the organisation's stakeholders, from an integrated reporting and governance perspective.

E1: The role of the treasury function in multinationals

(a)   Discuss the role of the treasury management function within: (i) The short term management of the organisations financial resources (ii) The longer term maximisation of corporate value (iii) The management of risk exposure.

Four of the five ACCA PER Essentials performance objectives apply to the AFM paper (PO1, PO2, PO3 and PO5).Working through this chapter will give you an introduction to these objectives.

PER

1   Key roles and responsibilities of the financial manager

The financial manager is responsible for making decisions which will increase the wealth of the company's shareholders.

The specific areas of responsibility are listed below.

However, it is also important that the financial manager considers the impact of his or her role on the other stakeholders of the firm.

You may be asked in the exam to assess the

- strategic impact

- financial impact

- regulatory impact

- ethical impact

- environmental impact.

of a financial manager's decisions.

Link between strategy and financial manager's role

You will remember from your earlier studies that the process of strategy selection starts with the development of a mission statement. A mission statement:

- is the overriding purpose of the firm

- guides and directs all decisions taken.

The mission is then broken down into broad-based goals, and then further, into detailed objectives. Strategies can then be developed to bridge the gap between current forecast performance and the targets set.

Policy framework

The mission will also provide the basis for the development of a **policy framework**.

The purpose of this framework is:

- to govern the way in which decisions are taken, and

- specify the criteria to be considered in the evaluation of any potential strategy.

At a broad level, this framework will incorporate guidance on issues such as:

Ethics and social responsibility

A consideration of the role of business in society. It covers responsibilities towards society as a whole, the extent to which the company should fulfil or exceed its legal obligations towards stakeholders and the behaviour expected of individuals within the firm itself.

Stakeholder protection

The extent to which the needs and wishes of individual stakeholders are incorporated into decisions and the development of a framework to ensure their needs are met and their rights upheld.

Corporate governance

The system by which companies are directed and controlled, including issues of risk management.

Sustainable development

Ensuring that projects and developments that meet the needs of the present, do not compromise the ability of future generations to meet their own needs.

This guidance is often formulated as a general principle:

e.g. all suppliers used must demonstrate commitment to employee welfare,

but may also form the basis for the generation of specific targets:

e.g. increase by 10% the amount of raw materials sourced locally in the next 12 months.

Financial policy

Policies will also be developed to govern decisions within each operational area of the business. These policies specify generally applicable processes or procedures to be followed when decisions are being made, or state one overarching principle which the sets the boundaries for all decisions taken.

For example, within the finance function, policies will be developed over areas such as:

- investment selection

- overall cost of finance

- distribution and retentions

- communication with stakeholders

- financial planning and control

- risk management

- efficient and effective use of resources.

Key areas of responsibility for the financial manager

The main roles and responsibilities of the financial manager can be summarised by the following headings:

- investment selection and capital resource allocation

- raising finance and minimising the cost of capital

- distribution and retentions (dividend policy)

- communication with stakeholders

- financial planning and control

- risk management

- efficient and effective use of resources.

The Advanced Financial Management syllabus (and the rest of this Text) covers these areas in detail. This chapter gives a brief introduction to each of them.

Investment selection and capital resource allocation

The primary goal of a company should be the maximisation of shareholder wealth, but any number of stakeholders may have views on the objectives a company should pursue.

Therefore, key policy decisions need to be made:

- How to incorporate ethical issues, such as minimising potential pollution or refusal to trade with unacceptable regimes, into the investment appraisal process?

- What method of investment appraisal should be used?

    – NPV?

    – IRR?

- In times of capital rationing, how are competing projects to be evaluated?
  - use of theoretical methods
  - incorporation of non-financial factors such as:
    1. closeness of match to objectives
    2. degree to which all goals will be achieved.

- As markets are not truly efficient, and investors treat earnings and dividend announcements as new information, to what extent should the impact on, for example:
  - ROCE
  - EPS
  - DPS

  be considered when evaluating a project?

More on investment selection

Incorporation of corporate policy issues

If for example, a decision has been taken to pay a 'fair' wage to all employees regardless of the legal minimum requirement in the country where the business is operating, this rule must be applied to the wages figure used in any project evaluation.

The financial executive must be aware of the policy requirement and ensure that sufficient research is carried out in advance that the correct figure is used.

Methods of investment appraisal

Assuming that the discounted cash flow techniques are preferred over Payback and ARR (which do not assure the maximisation of shareholder wealth), it is still necessary to designate which of the DCF methods is to be applied. Although NPV is theoretically superior, it is not as well liked by non-financial managers. IRR as a percentage is deemed clearer and simpler (although the point could be argued!). It is for the senior financial executive to decide on a method and ensure it is applied correctly.

Capital rationing

The rule for an NPV evaluation states that all projects with a positive NPV should be accepted. However, this presupposes no limits on the available funds. Where restrictions exist, theoretical models can be applied:

- Shortages in one period only – use limiting factor analysis (covered in the Financial Management exam).

- Shortages in multiple periods – see Chapter 2: Investment appraisal.

However, these methods do not build in evaluation of non-financial factors such as how well each strategy will meet the objectives set and practical difficulties that might be encountered along the way.

Forms of evaluation such as Cost Benefit Analysis and Weighted Benefit Scoring can be used where these factors are significant. These methods, pioneered by the public sector where such problems are commonplace, include techniques to assign money values to non-financial factors and to weight subjective factors against each other. Detailed knowledge of such methods is outside the syllabus.

Earnings and dividend measures

Even where improving shareholder wealth is the primary concern of the financial executive, the impact of the investment decisions on the reported position and perceived performance of the firm cannot be ignored. In an imperfect market, the earnings of a company and the dividends paid, are treated as relevant information for evaluating a company's worth and may impact the share price. Yet it is the share price that the executive is trying to improve.

Behavioural finance

Introduction

Conventional financial management is based on the assumption that markets are efficient, and that investors behave in ways that are logical and rational.

The efficient market hypothesis (EMH)

The EMH states that security prices fully and fairly reflect all relevant information. This means that it is not possible to consistently outperform the market by using any information that the market already knows, except through luck.

The idea is that new information is quickly and efficiently incorporated into asset prices at any point in time, so that old information cannot be used to predict future price movements.

Behavioural finance

Despite the evidence in support of the efficient markets theory, some events seem to contradict it, such as significant share price volatility and boom/crash patterns e.g. the stock market crash of October 1987 where most stock exchanges crashed at the same time. It is virtually impossible to explain the scale of those market falls by reference to any news event at the time.

An explanation has been offered by the science of behavioural finance. Behavioural finance is a relatively new field that seeks to combine behavioural and cognitive psychological theory with conventional economics and finance to provide explanations for why people make irrational financial decisions.

Key concepts of behavioural finance

Pioneers in the field of behavioural finance have identified the following factors as some of the key factors that contribute to irrational and potentially detrimental financial decision making:

Anchoring – investors have a tendency to attach or 'anchor' their thoughts to a reference point – even though it may have no logical relevance to the decision at hand e.g. investors are often attracted to buy shares whose price has fallen considerably because they compare the current price to the previous high (but now irrelevant) price.

Gambler's fallacy – investors have a tendency to believe that the probability of a future outcome changes because of the occurrence of various past outcomes e.g. if the value of a share has risen for seven consecutive days, some investors might sell the shares, believing that the share price is more likely to fall on the next day. This is not necessarily the case.

Herd behaviour – this is the tendency for individuals to mimic the actions (rational or irrational) of a larger group. There are a couple of reasons why herd behaviour happens. The first is the social pressure of conformity – most people are very sociable and have a natural desire to be accepted by a group. The second is the common rationale that it's unlikely that such a large group could be wrong. This is especially prevalent in situations in which an individual has very little experience.

Over-reaction and availability bias – according to the EMH, new information should more or less be reflected instantly in a security's price. For example, good news should raise a business' share price accordingly. Reality, however, tends to contradict this theory. Often, participants in the stock market predictably over-react to new information, creating a larger-than-appropriate effect on a security's price.

Confirmation bias – it can be difficult to encounter something or someone without having a preconceived opinion. This first impression can be hard to shake because people also tend to selectively filter and pay more attention to information that supports their opinions, while ignoring or rationalising the rest. This type of selective thinking is often referred to as the confirmation bias.

In investing, the confirmation bias suggests that an investor would be more likely to look for information that supports his or her original idea about an investment rather than seek out information that contradicts it. As a result, this bias can often result in faulty decision making because one-sided information tends to skew an investor's frame of reference, leaving them with an incomplete picture of the situation.

Hindsight bias and overconfidence – hindsight bias occurs in situations where a person believes (after the fact) that the onset of some past event was predictable and completely obvious, whereas in fact, the event could not have been reasonably predicted.

Many events seem obvious in hindsight. For example, many people now claim that signs of the technology bubble of the late 1990s and early 2000s were very obvious. This is a clear example of hindsight bias: If the formation of a bubble had been obvious at the time, it probably wouldn't have escalated and eventually burst.

For investors and other participants in the financial world, the hindsight bias is a cause for one of the most potentially dangerous mind-sets that an investor or trader can have: overconfidence. In this case, overconfidence refers to investors' or traders' unfounded belief that they possess superior stock-picking abilities.

Student Accountant article

The article 'Patterns of behaviour' in the Technical Articles section of the ACCA website provides further details on behavioural finance.

Raising finance and minimising the cost of capital

A key aspect of financial management is the raising of funds to finance existing and new investments. As with investment decisions, the main objective with raising finance is assumed to be the maximisation of shareholder wealth.

The following issues thus need to be considered when setting criteria for future finance and deciding policies:

- Is the firm at its optimal gearing level with associated minimum cost of capital?
- What gearing level is required?
- What sources of finance are available?
- Tax implications.
- The risk profile of investors and management.
- Restrictions such as debt covenants.
- Implications for key ratios.

Distribution and retention (dividend) policy

When deciding how much cash to distribute to shareholders, the company directors must keep in mind that the firm's objective is to maximise shareholder value:

- Shareholder value arises from the current value of the shares which in turn is derived from the cash flows from investment decisions taken by the company's management.

- Retained earnings are a significant source of finance for companies and therefore directors need to ensure that a balance is struck:

  - Paying out too much may require alternative finance to be found to finance any capital expenditure or working capital requirements.

  - Paying out too little may fail to give shareholders their required income levels.

- The dividend payout policy, therefore, should be based on investor preferences for cash dividends now or capital gains in future from enhanced share value resultant from re-investment into projects with a positive NPV.

It is the task of the financial manager to decide on the appropriate policy for determining distributions and retentions.

Communication with stakeholders

A vital role for those running a company is to keep both external and internal stakeholders informed of all significant matters.

External stakeholders

External stakeholders to be kept informed would include:

- shareholders
- government
- suppliers
- customers
- community at large.

Internal stakeholders

Corporate goals and financial policies must be communicated to all those involved within the organisation, whether at a senior level or in operational positions

- managers/directors
- employees.

Test your understanding 1

Suggest reasons why it would be important to keep each of the above stakeholders informed of general corporate goals and intentions.

In addition to information about corporate goals, key matters of financial policy will also need to be communicated to stakeholders:

- Shareholders will need information about:
    - dividend policy
    - expected returns on new investment projects
    - gearing levels
    - risk profile.
- Suppliers and customers will need information about:
    - payment policies
    - pricing policies.

Financial planning and control

Financial planning and control is the main role of the management accountant within a company.

The senior financial executive will need to oversee the development of policies to govern the way in which the process is carried out.

Policies will be needed over areas such as:

- the planning process
- business plans
- budget setting
- monitoring and correcting activities
- evaluating performance.

The management of risk

One of the key matters to consider when developing a financial policy framework is the way risk and risk management is to be incorporated into the decision making process.

A number of policy decisions must be made:

- What is the firm's appetite for risk?
- How should risk be monitored?
- How should risk be dealt with?

A major part of the AFM syllabus involves the choice and use of many alternative methods and products to manage risk exposure.

More detail on risk management

Appetite for risk

Shareholders will invest in companies with a risk profile that matches that required for their portfolio. Management should be wary of altering the risk profile of the business without shareholder support. An increase in risk will bring about an increase in the required return and may lead to current shareholders selling their shares and so depressing the share price.

Inevitably management will have their own attitude to risk. Unlike the well-diversified shareholders, the directors are likely to be heavily dependent on the success of the company for their own financial stability and be more risk averse as a consequence.

Monitoring risk

The essence of risk is that the returns are uncertain. As time passes, so the various uncertain events on which the forecasts are based will occur. Management must monitor the events as they unfold, reforecast predicted results and take action as necessary. The degree and frequency of the monitoring process will depend on the significance of the risk to the project's outcome.

Dealing with risk

Risk can be either accepted or dealt with. Possible solutions for dealing with risk include:

- mitigating the risk – reducing it by setting in place control procedures

- hedging the risk – taking action to ensure a certain outcome

- diversification – reducing the impact of one outcome by having a portfolio of different ongoing projects.

Policy decisions about which methods are to be preferred should be made in advance of specific actions being required.

Use of resources

It will be important to develop a framework to ensure all resources (inventory, labour and non-current assets as well as cash) are used to provide value for money. Spending must be:

- economic
- efficient
- effective
- transparent.

Performance measures can be developed in each area to set targets and allow for regular monitoring.

Definitions of the 3 Es

Economy:	Minimising the costs of inputs required to achieve a defined level of output.
Efficiency:	Ratio of outputs to inputs – achieving a high level of output in relation to the resources put in.
Effectiveness:	Whether outputs are achieved that match the predetermined objectives.
Transparency:	Ensuring all spending is recorded and reported correctly.

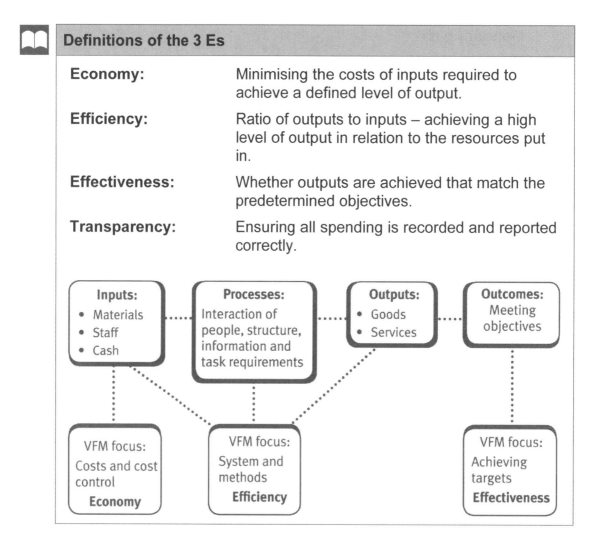

2 Treasury

The role of the treasury function

Most large companies have a separate treasury function to undertake some of the above listed roles.

Developments in technology, the breakdown of exchange controls, increasing volatility in interest rates and exchange rates, combined with the increasing globalisation of business have all contributed to greater opportunities and risks for entities. To survive in today's complex financial environment, entities need to be able to actively manage both their ability to undertake these opportunities, and their exposure to risks.

A separate treasury function is more likely to develop the appropriate skills, and it should also be easier to achieve economies of scale; for instance in achieving lower borrowing rates, or netting-off balances.

Treasury and financial control

In a large entity the finance function may be split between treasury and financial control, with both functions reporting to the chief financial officer.

The financial control function will be concerned primarily with the allocation and effective use of resources, and will have responsibility for investment decisions.

The treasury function is usually responsible for obtaining finance and managing relations with the financial stakeholders of the entity who will include shareholders and lenders.

Close liaison is often required between financial control and treasury, for example:

- In investment appraisal decisions, the treasurer is best able to assess the cost of capital and quantify the entity's aversion to risk, while the financial controller relates these factors to group strategy.

- When managing currency risks, the financial controller will play an important role in identifying the entity's currency risks, while the treasurer advises on the best means to hedge the risk.

In larger entities, treasury will usually be centralised at head office, providing a service to all the various units of the entity and thereby achieving more effective control over financial risks and also achieving economies of scale (for example, by obtaining better borrowing rates).

Financial control is frequently delegated to individual units, where it can more closely impact on customers and suppliers and relate more specifically to the competition that those units have to face.

As a result, treasury and financial control may often tend to be separated by location as well as by responsibilities.

Test your understanding 2

Compare and contrast the roles of the treasury and financial control departments with respect to a proposed investment.

Treasury: Cost centre or profit centre?

As a cost centre the aggregate treasury function costs would simply be charged throughout the group on a fair basis. If no such fair basis can be agreed, the costs can remain as central head office unallocated costs in any group segmental analysis.

However it is also possible to identify revenues arising from treasury departments and thus to establish the treasury as a profit centre. Revenues could be realised as follows:

- Each division can be charged the market value for the services provided by the treasury. The total value charged throughout the group should exceed the treasury's costs enabling it to report a profit.

- By deciding not to hedge all currency and interest rate risks. Experts in the treasury could decide which risks not to hedge, hoping to profit from unhedged favourable exchange rate and interest rate movements.

- Hedging using currency and interest rate options leaves an upside potential which could be realised if the rate moves in the company's favour.

- Taking on additional exchange rate or other risks purely as a speculative activity, e.g. writing options on currencies or on shares held.

The trend in recent years has been for large companies to turn their treasuries from cost centres into profit centres and to expect the treasury to pay its way and generate regular profits each year.

However the following points should be noted:

- A treasury engaged in speculation must be properly controlled by the company's board of directors. Millions of dollars can be committed in one telephone call by a treasurer, so it is crucial that limits are set on traders' risk exposures and that these limits are monitored scrupulously. The temptation has been for directors to let treasurers 'get on with whatever they do' as long as regular profits are being earned. Such a policy is no longer acceptable; the finance director in particular must control the treasury on a day-to-day basis.

- For example, the German oils and metals company Metallgesellschaft managed to lose $1 billion after becoming over-exposed to oil derivative contracts.

- Treasury staff must be well trained and probably well paid, so that staff of the right calibre can be secured.

- The low volume of foreign currency transactions undertaken by a small company would probably make a profit centre approach unviable. A regular flow of large foreign transactions is needed before the cost centre approach is abandoned.

International aspects

The international treasury function

The corporate treasurer in an international group of companies will be faced with problems relating specifically to the international spread of investments.

- Setting transfer prices to reduce the overall tax bill.

- Deciding currency exposure policies and procedures.

- Transferring of cash across international borders.

- Devising investment strategies for short-term funds from the range of international money markets and international marketable securities.

- Netting and matching currency obligations.

The centralisation of treasury activities

The question arises in a large international group of whether treasury activities should be centralised or decentralised.

- If centralised, then each operating company holds only the minimum cash balance required for day to day operations, remitting the surplus to the centre for overall management. This process is sometimes known as cash pooling, the pool usually being held in a major financial centre or a tax haven country.

- If decentralised, each operating company must appoint an officer responsible for that company's own treasury operations.

Advantages of centralisation

- No need for treasury skills to be duplicated throughout the group. One highly trained central department can assemble a highly skilled team, offering skills that could not be available if every company had their own treasury.

- Necessary borrowings can be arranged in bulk, at keener interest rates than for smaller amounts. Similarly bulk deposits of surplus funds will attract higher rates of interest than smaller amounts.

- The group's foreign currency risk can be managed much more effectively from a centralised treasury since only they can appreciate the total exposure situation. A total hedging policy is more efficiently carried out by head office rather than each company doing their own hedging.

- One company does not borrow at high rates while another has idle cash.

- Bank charges should be lower since a situation of carrying both balances and overdraft in the same currency should be eliminated.

- A centralised treasury can be run as a profit centre to raise additional profits for the group.

- Transfer prices can be established to minimise the overall group tax bill.

- Funds can be quickly returned to companies requiring cash via direct transfers.

Advantages of decentralisation

- Greater autonomy leads to greater motivation. Individual companies will manage their cash balances more attentively if they are responsible for them rather than simply remitting them up to head office.

- Local operating units should have a better feel for local conditions than head office and can respond more quickly to local developments.

3 Incorporating the interests of other stakeholders

We usually assume that the primary objective of a business is to maximise shareholder wealth.

However, a company is unlikely to be successful unless it also aims to satisfy the needs of its other stakeholders. The financial manager will have to identify potential conflicts between stakeholders' objectives and aim to resolve these conflicts.

A further, but associated, problem is the potential agency problem i.e. if the management of a firm act in their own best interests, rather than in the best interests of the shareholders.

Agency theory

Agency theory identifies that, although individual members of a business team act in their own self-interests much of the time, the well-being of each individual and of the business overall depends on the well-being of the other team members too. The separation of owners and management in many businesses leads to the classic 'agency problem'.

Definition of 'Agency Problem'

A conflict of interest inherent in any relationship where one party is expected to act in another's best interests.

The problem is that the agent who is supposed to make the decisions that would best serve the principal is naturally motivated by self-interest, and the agent's own best interests may differ from the principal's best interests.

Application to shareholders/managers

In corporate finance, the agency problem usually refers to a conflict of interest between a company's management and the company's owners or shareholders.

The manager, acting as the agent for the shareholders, or principals, is supposed to make decisions that will maximise shareholder wealth. However, it is in the manager's own best interest to maximise his or her own wealth.

While it is not possible to eliminate the agency problem completely, the manager can be motivated to act in the shareholders' best interests through incentives such as performance-based compensation, direct influence by shareholders, the threat of firing and the threat of takeovers.

Application to not-for-profit organisations

In not-for-profit and public sector organisations, the agency problem changes, because of the ambiguity in identifying the principals, or owners, of the organisation.

It could be argued that the owner of a public sector organisation such as a hospital is society as a whole, so there is more a moral rather than a legal ownership in place.

As with a profit-focussed organisation, the managers have to make decisions in the best interests of the 'owners' rather than in their own interests, so the agency problem doesn't disappear in a not-for-profit organisation.

Examples of stakeholder conflict

Stakeholders	Potential conflict	Costs resulting from the conflict
Employees v Shareholders	Employees may resist the introduction of automated processes which would improve efficiency but cost jobs. Shareholders may resist wage rises demanded by employees as uneconomical.	Costs of strike or work to rule from employees. Costs of additional compensation to redundant staff. Costs of strikes etc. as above. Costs of reassuring shareholders – additional meetings for example.
Customers v Community at large	Customers may demand lower prices and greater choice, but in order to provide them a company may need to squeeze vulnerable suppliers or import products at great environmental cost.	Costs of overcoming negative publicity. Time spent renegotiating supplier contracts/ sourcing new suppliers.
Shareholders v Finance providers	Shareholders may encourage management to pursue risky strategies in order to maximise potential returns, whereas finance providers prefer stable lower risk policies that ensure liquidity for the payment of debt interest.	Agency costs: loan covenants restricting further borrowing, dividend payouts, investment policy etc.
Government v Shareholders	Government will often insist upon levels of welfare (such as the minimum wage and Health and Safety practices) which would otherwise be avoided as an unnecessary expense.	Costs of complying with legislation.

NB: You may have come up with different suggestions in an exam scenario. The point is to recognise that there are a huge range of potential conflicts of interest and each one results in additional costs for the business and therefore a reduction in returns to shareholders.

Strategies for the resolution of stakeholder conflict

Hierarchies of decision making (corporate governance codes)

In order to prevent abuse of decision-making power by the executive, control over decisions tends to be distributed between:

- the full board
- individual executive directors making operational decisions
- non-executive directors
  - audit committee
  - remuneration committee
- shareholders in general meeting
- specific classes of shareholders where particular rights are concerned.

In addition, a company may elect to take some key decisions in consultation with the employees.

 More on Corporate Governance

The full board

Whilst for most operational matters, decisions may be taken by the appropriate functional director, matters of corporate policy, investment decisions over a certain limit, sensitive decisions etc. are likely to require the consent of the full board. This ensures that all salient factors are considered when the decision is taken.

Non-executive directors

Whilst executive directors are employees involved in the day-to-day running of the business, non-executives are independent of the company, and appointed to monitor and challenge the executives as well as to advise and support them.

Removing decisions such as director remuneration and appointment from the remit of the executive, mitigates the likelihood of directors making self-serving decisions contrary to the interests of other stakeholders.

In addition, creating an audit committee to provide an independent reporting line for internal auditors and external auditors alike, provides a safeguard for shareholders against potential cover-ups of poor management practices.

Shareholders in general meeting

Legislation reserves for the shareholders certain key corporate decisions such as the appointment and removal of auditors and directors. When taking decisions, the directors will be aware that ignoring the wishes of the shareholders would put them at risk of removal. Shareholders may also use the company general meetings as an opportunity to express their concerns and remind the directors of their voting control.

Specific classes of share

In order to protect the rights of non-voting shareholders such as those holding preference shares, it is common to allow them voting rights in particular circumstances such as where their dividend goes into arrears.

The principles of corporate governance

Corporate governance is usually defined as 'the system by which companies are directed and controlled'. The concept encompasses issues of ethics, risk management and stakeholder protection.

The Organisation for Economic Cooperation and Development (OECD) issues specific guidelines for national legislation and regulation in the form of the Principles of Corporate Governance. These were explored in the Strategic Business Leader syllabus.

Practical implications

The implications of the guidelines for companies in all countries are a need for the:

- Separation of the supervisory function and the management function.

- Transparency in the recruitment and remuneration of the board.

- Appointment of non-executive directors.

- Establishment of an audit committee.

- Establishment of risk control procedures to monitor strategic, business and operational activities.

Performance monitoring and evaluation systems

Managers are more likely to act in accordance with shareholders' wishes when their performance is regularly monitored and appraised against prescribed targets. To be of real value, the targets must be congruent with the maximisation of shareholder value.

Performance appraisal methods – Link to s/h wealth maximisation

Listed below are some of the ways in which management performance may be appraised. For each method we have considered the extent to which it is congruent with the maximisation of shareholder wealth objective.

Financial measures

Accounting ratios:

- EPS/ROCE/RI – both suffer from the same criticism – that earnings are not directly related to shareholder wealth and therefore may encourage non-goal congruent behaviour.

- DPS – is a measure of immediate improvement in wealth but must be looked at in conjunction with the company share price. Dividends may be reduced in order to invest in positive NPV projects, but in that case, the gain should be reflected in the share price.

- Economic value added – EVA is a more sophisticated method of residual income (registered as a trademark by Stern, Stewart & Co.), which more accurately measures improvements in shareholder wealth by adjusting the accounting data to eliminate much of the subjectivity and incorporating the company's WACC into the calculation.

Stock market figures:

- Share price – reflects the expectations of the investors. Is a direct measure of company success but is hard to link directly to directors' performance as it is affected by so many outside factors.

- PE ratio – as a multiple of share price over earnings it does reflect investors' view of the investment potential of the company but suffers from the same weakness as all other earnings related measures and is not easy to relate to directors activities.

Shareholder value added

A calculation of the present value free cash flows, this method is a more accurate measure of improvements in shareholder wealth, but its complexity makes it of little use as a regular performance measure.

Specific cost/revenue targets

A vast array of financial targets may be set around the levels of spending and investment, or around revenues earned. Care must be taken to ensure that the targets are achievable and within the control of the person being assessed. Particular attention must be paid to the interdependence of the various aspects of performance. If managers are incentivised to achieve a reduction in purchase spending for example, alternative measures must also confirm that quality is maintained.

Non-financial measures

Balanced scorecard

Many businesses operate a balanced scorecard approach to management appraisal. This involves setting targets in all of those aspects of the business where success is necessary if positive NPVs are to be earned. In addition to financial targets, managers are measured on the satisfaction of customers, improvement of business practices and levels of innovation. Since achieving these targets should lead to improved project returns and greater cost efficiency, a balanced scorecard approach should lead to improved shareholder wealth.

Employee/satisfaction

In addition, some businesses specifically set management targets related to employee satisfaction ratings, or related targets such as absenteeism or staff turnover.

Non-financial information

According to the International Accounting Standards Board's (IASB's) conceptual framework, the objective of financial reporting is to 'provide information about the reporting entity that is useful to existing and potential investors, lenders and other creditors in making decisions about providing resources to the entity'.

Financial statements provide historic financial information. To help users make decisions, it may be helpful to provide information relating to other aspects of an entity's performance.

For example:

* how the business is managed

* its future prospects

* the entity's policy on the environment

* its attitude towards social responsibility etc.

There has been increasing pressure for entities to provide more information in their annual reports beyond just the financial statements since non-financial information can also be important to users' decisions.

Non-financial reporting

The important additional non-financial information can be reported in a number of ways, for example:

A management commentary (sometimes called an operating and financial review) will assess the results of the period and discuss future prospects of the business.

An environmental report will discuss responsibilities towards the environment and a social report will discuss responsibilities towards society. Both these issues could be combined in a report on sustainability which will also encompass economic issues.

Integrated Reporting

The International Integrated Reporting Council (IIRC)

The IIRC was formed in 2010 and aims to create a globally accepted framework for a process that results in communications by an organisation about value creation over time. The IIRC brings together a cross section of representatives from corporate, investment, accounting, securities, regulatory, academic and standard-setting sectors as well as civil society.

Objective of the IIRC

At the time of its formation, the IIRC's stated objective was to develop an internationally accepted integrated reporting framework to create the foundations for a new reporting model to enable organisations to provide concise communications of how they create value over time. After a consultation process, the IIRC published the first version of its 'International Integrated Reporting Framework' in 2013. This framework is intended as a guide for all businesses producing integrated reports.

The concept of Integrated Reporting (<IR>)

Integrated Reporting (<IR>) is seen by the IIRC as the basis for a fundamental change in the way in which entities are managed and report to stakeholders.

A stated aim of <IR> is to support integrated thinking and decision-making. Integrated thinking is described in the <IR> Framework as "the active consideration by an organization of the relationships between its various operating and functional units and the capitals that the organization uses or affects".

The objectives for integrated reporting include:

- To improve the quality of information available to providers of financial capital to enable a more efficient and productive allocation of capital.

- Provide a more cohesive and efficient approach to corporate reporting that draws on different reporting strands and communicates the full range of factors that materially affect the ability of an organisation to create value over time.

- Enhance accountability and stewardship for the broad base of capitals (financial, manufactured, intellectual, human, social and relationship, and natural) and promote understanding of their interdependencies.

- Support integrated thinking, decision-making and actions that focus on the creation of value over the short, medium and long term.

Purpose and content of an integrated report

The <IR> Framework sets out the purpose of an integrated report as follows:

> The primary purpose of an integrated report is to explain to providers of financial capital how an entity creates value over time. An integrated report benefits all stakeholders interested in an entity's ability to create value over time, including employees, customers, suppliers, business partners, local communities, legislators, regulators, and policy-makers.

The 'building blocks' of an integrated report are:

Guiding principles – these underpin the preparation of an integrated report, informing the content of the report and how information is presented.

Content elements – the key categories of information required to be included in an integrated report under the Framework, presented as a series of questions rather than a prescriptive list of disclosures.

<IR> illustration

Key requirements of an integrated report

An integrated report should be a designated, identifiable communication.

A communication claiming to be an integrated report and referencing the <IR> Framework should apply all the key requirements (identified using bold type below), unless the unavailability of reliable data, specific legal prohibitions or competitive harm results in an inability to disclose information that is material (in the case of unavailability of reliable data or specific legal prohibitions, other information is provided).

The integrated report should include a statement from those charged with governance that meets particular requirements (e.g. acknowledgement of responsibility, opinion on whether the integrated report is presented in accordance with the <IR> Framework) – and if one is not included, disclosures about their role and steps taken to include a statement in future reports (a statement should be included no later than an entity's third integrated report referencing the <IR> Framework).

Guiding principles

Strategic focus and future orientation – insight into the organisation's strategy.

Connectivity of information – showing a holistic picture of the combination, inter-relatedness and dependencies between the factors that affect the organisation's ability to create value over time.

Stakeholder relationships – insight into the nature and quality of the organisation's relationships with its key stakeholders.

Materiality – disclosing information about matters that substantively affect the organisation's ability to create value over the short, medium and long term.

Conciseness – sufficient context to understand the organisation's strategy, governance and prospects without being burdened by less relevant information.

Reliability and completeness – including all material matters, both positive and negative, in a balanced way and without material error.

Consistency and comparability – ensuring consistency over time and enabling comparisons with other organisations to the extent material to the organisations own ability to create value.

Content elements

Organisational overview and external environment – What does the organisation do and what are the circumstances under which it operates?

Governance – How does an organisation's governance structure support its ability to create value in the short, medium and long term?

Business model – What is the organisation's business model?

Risks and opportunities – What are the specific risk and opportunities that affect the organisation's ability to create value over the short, medium and long term, and how is the organisation dealing with them?

Strategy and resource allocation – Where does the organisation want to go and how does it intend to get there?

> **Performance** – To what extent has the organisation achieved its strategic objectives for the period and what are its outcomes in terms of effects on the capitals?
>
> **Outlook** – What challenges and uncertainties is the organisation likely to encounter in pursuing its strategy, and what are the potential implications for its business model and future performance?
>
> **Basis of preparation and presentation** – How does the organisation determine what matters to include in the integrated report and how are such matters quantified or evaluated?

Integrated reporting (<IR>) and performance appraisal

<IR> enables an organisation to prepare a much wider range of information that can be used by stakeholders to appraise the performance of the management. The <IR> information covers both financial and non-financial performance.

Therefore, when making decisions, the financial manager must consider the impact of the decisions on all aspects of the organisation's performance, not just its financial performance.

4 The strategic impact of the financial manager's decisions

Strategic issues are those which impact the whole business in the long term.

Key strategic issues which may arise from decisions made by the financial manager are:

Does the new investment project help to enhance the firm's competitive advantage?

For example, if the firm has traditionally competed on the basis of cost leadership, the financial manager needs to ensure that new projects maintain this position, and that any new finance is raised at the lowest possible cost.

Fit with environment

A knowledge of the main Political, Economic, Social and Technological factors which impact the business will help the financial manager to identify likely opportunities.

Use of resources

The financial manager should identify new investment opportunities which make the best use of the firm's key resources. Knowledge of the firm's current strengths (core competencies) and weaknesses is critical in assessing which new projects are most likely to be successful.

Stakeholder reactions

As discussed above, it is critical that the views of all stakeholders are considered when financial management decisions are made. Theoretically, the directors have a primary objective to maximise shareholder wealth. However, decisions which appear to satisfy this requirement by ignoring other stakeholders' views in the short term can damage the firm's prospects for longer term shareholder wealth maximisation.

Impact on risk

Investors will have been attracted to the firm because they deem its risk profile to be acceptable. Making decisions which change the overall risk of the firm may alienate shareholders and damage the firm's long term prospects.

5 The financial impact of the financial manager's decisions

It is common to assess the financial impact of a financial manager's decision by focussing on the likely Net Present Value (NPV) of investment projects undertaken. After all, the primary aim of a company is to maximise the wealth of its shareholders, and NPV represents the increase in shareholder wealth if a project is undertaken.

However, it is also important to consider the following issues:

Likely impact on share price

In a perfect capital market, the NPV of the project would immediately be reflected in the company's share price. In the real world, unless the details of the project are communicated effectively to the market, the share price will not be impacted.

Likely impact on financial statements

In theory, a positive NPV project should increase shareholder wealth. However, if the project has low (or negative) cash flows in the early years, the negative impact on the financial statements in the short term may give a negative signal to the market, thus causing the share price to fall.

Impact on cost of capital

As discussed in detail elsewhere, raising new finance causes the firm's cost of capital to change. However, undertaking projects of different business risk from the firm's existing activities can also impact cost of capital. Projects will be more valuable when discounted at a low cost of capital, so the financial manager should avoid high risk projects unless it is felt that they are likely to deliver a high level of return.

> ### Test your understanding 3
>
> The directors of Ribs Co, a listed company, are reviewing the company's current strategic position. The firm makes high quality garden tools which it sells in its domestic market but not abroad.
>
> Over the last few years, the share price has risen significantly as the firm has expanded organically within its domestic market. Unfortunately, in the last 12 months, the influx of cheaper, foreign tools has adversely impacted the firm's profitability. Consequently, the share price has dropped sharply in recent weeks and the shareholders expressed their displeasure at the recent AGM.
>
> The directors are evaluating two alternative investment projects which they hope will arrest the decline in profitability.
>
> **Project 1:** This would involve closing the firm's domestic factory and switching production to a foreign country where labour rates are a quarter of those in the domestic market. Sales would continue to be targeted exclusively at the domestic market.
>
> **Project 2:** This would involve a new investment in machinery at the domestic factory to allow production to be increased by 50%. The extra tools would be exported and sold as high quality tools in foreign market places.
>
> Both projects have a positive Net Present Value (NPV) when discounted at the firm's current cost of capital.
>
> **Required:**
>
> **Discuss the strategic and financial issues that this case presents.**

6 The regulatory impact of the financial manager's decisions

The extent to which the financial manager's actions are scrutinised by regulators is determined by:

- the type of industry – some industries (for example the privatised utility industries in the UK) are subject to high levels of regulation

- whether the company is listed – listed companies are subject to high levels of scrutiny.

The UK City Code

The City Code applies to takeovers in the UK. It stresses the vital importance of absolute secrecy before any takeover announcement is made. Once an announcement is made, the Code stipulates that the announcement should be as clear as possible, so that all shareholders (and potential shareholders) have equal access to information.

7 The ethical impact of the financial manager's decisions

Ethics, and the company's ethical framework, should provide a basis for all policy and decision making. The financial manager must consider whether an action is ethical at a:

- society level
- corporate level
- individual level.

Explanation of levels of ethics

Society level

The extent to which the wishes of all stakeholders both internal and external should be taken into account, even where there is no legal obligation to do so.

Corporate level

The extent to which companies should exceed legal obligations to stakeholders, and the approach they take to corporate governance and stakeholder conflict.

Individual level

The principles that the individuals running the company apply to their own actions and behaviours.

As key members of the decision-making executive, financial managers are responsible for ensuring that all the actions of the company for which they work:

- are ethical
- are grounded in good governance
- achieve the highest standards of probity.

In addition to general rules of ethics and governance, members of the ACCA have additional guidance to support their decision making.

ACCA Code of Ethics

At an individual level, members of the ACCA are governed by a set of fundamental ethical principles. These principles are binding on all members and members review and agree to them each year when they renew their ACCA membership and submit their CPD return.

The fundamental principles are:

- integrity
- objectivity
- professional competence and due care
- confidentiality
- professional behaviour.

Integrity

Members should be straightforward and honest in all professional and business relationships.

Objectivity

Members should not allow bias, conflicts of interest or undue influence of others to override professional or business judgements.

Professional competence and due care

Members have a continuing duty to maintain professional knowledge and skill at a level required to ensure that a client or employer receives competent professional service based on current developments in practice, legislation and techniques. Members should act diligently and in accordance with applicable technical and professional standards when providing professional services.

Confidentiality

Members should respect the confidentiality of information acquired as a result of professional and business relationships and should not disclose any such information to third parties without proper and specific authority or unless there is a legal or professional right or duty to disclose. Confidential information acquired as a result of professional and business relationships should not be used for the personal advantage of members or third parties.

Professional behaviour

Members should comply with relevant laws and regulations and should avoid any action that discredits the profession.

In working life, a financial manager may:

- have to deal with a conflict between stakeholders

- face a conflict between their position as agent and the needs of the shareholders for whom they act.

An ethical framework should provide a strategy for dealing with the situation.

More on ethics

Ethical financial policy

All senior financial staff would be expected to sign up and adhere to an ethical financial policy framework. A typical code would cover matters such:

- acting in accordance with the ACCA principles

- disclosure of any possible conflicts of interest at the first possible opportunity to the appropriate company member

- ensuring full, fair, accurate, complete, objective, timely and understandable disclosure in all reports and documents that the company files

- ensuring all company financial practices concerning accounting, internal accounting controls and auditing matters meet the highest standards of professionalism, transparency and honesty

- complying with all internal policy all external rules and regulations

- responsible use and control of assets and other resources employed

- promotion of ethical behaviour among subordinates and peers and ensuring an atmosphere of continuing education and exchange of best practices.

Assessing the ethical impact of decisions

Once a framework has been developed it is essential that all decisions are made in accordance with it.

This will involve:

- all employees explicitly signing up to the framework

- providing employees with guidelines to apply to ethical decisions

- offering resources for consultation in ethical dilemma

- ensuring unethical conduct can be reported without reprisal

- taking disciplinary action where violations have occurred.

Guidelines for making ethical decisions often take the form of a series of questions which employees are encouraged to ask themselves before implementing a decision.

For example:

- Have colleagues been properly consulted?
- Are actions legal and in compliance with professional standards?
- Is individual or company integrity being compromised?
- Are company values being upheld?
- Is the choice of action the most ethical one?
- If the decision were documented would a reviewer agree with the decision taken?

In addition to written ethical guidelines firms often provide employees with a list of people who can be consulted in the case of an ethical dilemma. For example:

- Line manager.
- Appointed quality and risk leaders.
- Firm legal team.
- Ethics hotline within the firm (obviously only in larger companies is this likely to be affordable).
- Professional hotline – the ACCA for example, provides its members with ethical advice and support, as do many other professional organisations.

Interconnectedness of the ethics of good business practice

The ethical financial manager understands the importance of the interconnectedness of the ethics of good business practice.

It is vitally important that decision makers throughout an organisation appreciate the impact of their decisions on the likely success of all the other, interconnected parts of the organisation. Unethical business practices undertaken in one part of the business can have disastrous consequences elsewhere. For example, an unethical marketing campaign could have a knock-on impact on the sales of a business, leading to a reduction in production and a subsequent cut in purchasing and staffing.

Test your understanding 4

Suggest ways in which ethical issues would influence the firm's financial policies in relation to the following:

- shareholders
- suppliers
- customers
- investment appraisal
- charity.

8 The environmental impact of the financial manager's decisions

In the last few years, the issue of sustainable development has taken on greater urgency as concerns about the long-term impact of business on the planet have grown.

The United Nations defines sustainable development as:

Development that meets the needs of the present without compromising the ability of future generations to meet their own needs.

The underlying principle for firms is that environmental, social and economic systems are interdependent and decisions must address all three concerns coherently.

In developing corporate policies and objectives, specific attention should be given to matters of sustainability and environmental risk.

Specific examples of environmental issues

Carbon-trading and emissions

Firms with high energy use may need to set objectives for their emissions of greenhouse gases in order to achieve targets set by governments under the Kyoto Protocol.

This may include:

- reducing emissions to reduce liability for energy taxes
- entering a carbon emissions trading scheme.

The Kyoto Protocol

The Kyoto Protocol was negotiated by 160 nations in 1997. It is an attempt to limit national emissions of greenhouse gases in order to slow or halt an associated change of climate. The agreement sets emission targets for the individual nations. Australia, for instance, agreed to limit its annual emission by the year 2012 to no more than 108% of its emission in 1990.

The Protocol was negotiated based on an economic mechanism of 'carbon trading' evolving; i.e. nations issuing permits for carbon emission, set to match the targets set by the Kyoto Protocol or its follow-on agreements. The permits, tradeable, both nationally and internationally, are intended to operate such that market forces ultimately replace government direction in the process of encouraging more efficient use of fossil fuel.

Individual companies will be able to decide whether to spend money on new 'carbon efficient' technology or on the acquisition of carbon credits from those industries or countries which have a surplus.

In the UK for example, there is a carbon emissions trading scheme, which is run by the Department of Energy and Climate Change. Details are provided here only to provide a clear picture of how such a scheme works.

The UK scheme

Organisations in the scheme volunteer to reduce emissions in return for a financial incentive provided by the government. They are set emissions targets based on a formula. If they overachieve they can sell or bank the excess allowances. If they underachieve they must buy the allowances they need.

Some firms already have targets as a result of Climate Change Levy Agreements (CCLs – see below) set up to help businesses with intensive energy use mitigate the effects of the UK energy tax. These firms can sell their surpluses or buy needed credits.

Other firms, even if they do not emit greenhouse gases, may set up an account to trade in the allowances.

The climate change levy is a tax on the use of energy in industry, commerce and the public sector, with offsetting cuts in employers' National Insurance Contributions – NICs – and additional support for energy efficiency schemes and renewable sources of energy. The levy forms a key part of the Government's overall Climate Change Programme.

The role of an environment agency

Government environment agencies (in the UK – Defra – the Department for the environment, food and rural affairs) work to ensure that business meets the environmental targets set internationally. They set local business targets in key areas such as:

- energy conservation
- recycling
- protection of the countryside
- sustainable development.

which will need to be taken into account when setting objectives for the business as a whole.

Triple Bottom Line (TBL) reporting

Environmental audits and the triple bottom line approach

First coined in the mid-1990s, the phrase triple bottom line, refers to the need for companies to focus on the:

- economic value and
- environmental value and
- social value.

both added and destroyed by the firm.

Providing stakeholders with corporate performance data in each of these areas is known as **triple bottom line reporting**.

In order to provide credible data, companies will need to:

- set up a suitable management system to capture the information
- ensure the reports are subject to an appropriate audit scrutiny.

Triple bottom line reporting

A triple bottom line approach requires a shift in culture and focus, and the development of appropriate policies and objectives. It can also be used as a framework for measuring and reporting corporate performance.

Many leading companies are now publishing environmental and sustainability reports – demonstrating to stakeholders that they are addressing these issues.

In order to provide meaningful data, a business must be able to assess the environmental and social impact of their operations. One way to do this is to adopt the framework provided by ISO 14000. ISO 14000 is a series of international standards on environmental management. It provides a framework for the development of an environmental management system and a supporting audit programme.

Environmental auditing is a systematic, documented, periodic and objective process in assessing an organisation's activities and services in relation to:

- Assessing compliance with relevant statutory and internal requirements.

- Facilitating management control of environmental practices.

- Promoting good environmental management.

- Maintaining credibility with the public.

- Raising staff awareness and enforcing commitment to departmental environmental policy.

- Exploring improvement opportunities.

- Establishing the performance baseline for developing an Environmental Management System (EMS).

9 Chapter summary

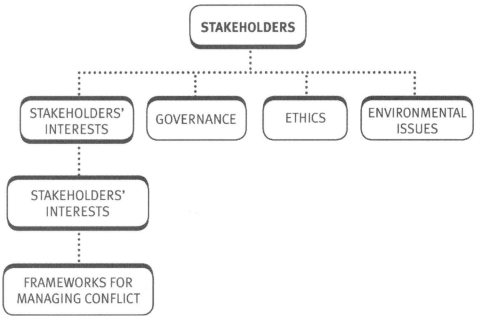

Test your understanding answers

Test your understanding 1

Shareholders – The support of shareholders is necessary for the smooth running of the business. Actions from awkward questions at AGMs through to (in the worst case) a vote to remove the directors, are available to aggrieved shareholders. The goals set by a company should reflect their concerns as key stakeholders, and communication of them should reassure shareholders that the firm is acting as they would wish.

Government – Government targets and policies often include specific expectations of the business community. Keeping government departments informed of activities and consulting in key areas can help prevent later government intervention, or punitive action from regulators.

Customers – A business will struggle to continue without the support of its customers. Today, consumers are increasingly concerned about how the goods and services they buy are provided. Companies are therefore keen to demonstrate their commitment to ethical, environmental policies. They can do so by communicating clearly the specific goals and policies they have developed to ensure they meet customer expectations.

Suppliers – If shareholder and customer concern over the provenance of the supply chain is to be addressed, it is essential that suppliers are clear about the expectations of the company. This may include requirements for their own suppliers, the treatment of their own staff, the way in which their products are produced etc. The company must ensure such policies are clear and enforced.

Community at large – The larger community may not have any direct involvement with the company but can be quick to take action such as arranging boycotts or lobbying if it disapproves of the way the company conducts business. Reassurance about corporate goals can reduce the likelihood of disruptive action.

Managers/directors/employees – Senior staff will need to be kept fully up-to-date about all goals and policies set by the firm, so they can apply them when taking decisions. Explaining to employees why decisions are being taken can help to ensure co-operation in their implementation.

Test your understanding 2

Treasury is the function concerned with the provision and use of finance and thus handles the acquisition and custody of funds whereas the Financial Control Department has responsibility for accounting, reporting and control. The roles of the two departments in the proposed investment are as follows:

Evaluation

- Treasury will quantify the cost of capital to be used in assessing the investment.

- The financial control department will estimate the project cash flows.

Implementation

- Treasury will establish corporate financial objectives, such as wanting to restrict gearing to 40%, and will identify sources and types of finance.

- Treasury will also deal with currency management – dealing in foreign currencies and hedging currency risks – and taxation.

- The financial control department will be involved with the preparation of budgets and budgetary control, the preparation of periodic financial statements and the management and administration of activities such as payroll and internal audit.

Interaction

- The Treasury Department has main responsibility for setting corporate objectives and policy and Financial Control has the responsibility for implementing policy and ensuring the achievement of corporate objectives. This distinction is probably far too simplistic and, in reality, both departments will make contributions to both determination and achievement of objectives.

- There is a circular relationship in that Treasurers quantify the cost of capital, which the Financial Controllers use as the criterion for the deployment of funds; Financial Controllers quantify projected cash flows which in turn trigger Treasurers' decisions to employ capital.

Test your understanding 3

Strategic issues

Competitive advantage – currently the firm is a differentiator (it competes on quality rather than cost). The new entrants into the market seem to be cost leaders. Undertaking Project 1 might reduce the quality of the Ribs Co tools and undermine the firm's long standing competitive advantage.

Fit with environment – clearly the environment has changed in the last 12 months. The new imports indicate that perhaps the economic environment has changed (movement in exchange rates? removal of import tariffs?), and also that customers are seemingly looking for cheaper tools (social factor). Ribs Co is right to try to find new projects which enable it to compete in this new environment.

Stakeholder reactions – the shareholders are not happy, so they will welcome the new projects (providing the directors communicate the positive NPV information effectively). However, other stakeholders are likely to be less impressed. For example, under Project 1 there are likely to be job cuts in the domestic market, so the employees, local community and domestic government are likely to be unhappy about this option. The directors must consider the long term consequences of upsetting these key stakeholders in the short term.

Risk – Project 2 appears to be the more risky option – it involves exporting goods into a foreign market where Ribs Co currently has no operations. There is no guarantee that the Ribs tools will be a success in the new market. However, there is huge potential under this option. Clearly the domestic market is becoming saturated, so perhaps now is the time for Ribs to seek out new opportunities abroad.

Financial issues

Positive NPVs – both prospective projects have positive NPVs, so theoretically shareholder wealth should increase whichever is undertaken. However, the cash flow estimates need to be analysed and sensitivity analysis should be performed to see what changes in estimates can be tolerated.

Impact on cost of capital – Ribs Co's current cost of capital has been used for discounting the projects. However the change in risk (caused by the exposure to foreign factors in both projects) is likely to change the cost of capital.

Financing – both projects are likely to require significant short term capital expenditure. The directors will have to consider the size of investment required, and the firm's target gearing ratio, as they assess whether debt or equity funding should be sought.

Test your understanding 4

Shareholders:

- Providing timely and accurate information to shareholders on the company's historical achievements and future prospects.

Suppliers:

- paying fair prices

- attempting to settle invoices promptly

- co-operating with suppliers to maintain and improve the quality of inputs

- not using or accepting bribery or excess hospitality as a means of securing contracts with suppliers.

Customers:

- charging fair prices

- offering fair payment terms

- honouring quantity and settlement discounts

- ensuring sufficient quality control processes are built in that goods are fit for purpose.

Investment appraisal:

- payment of fair wages

- upholding obligations to protect, preserve and improve the environment

- only trading (both purchases and sales) with countries and companies that themselves have appropriate ethical frameworks.

Charity:

- Developing a policy on donations to educational and charitable institutions.

Investment appraisal

Chapter learning objectives

Study guide section	Study guide outcome	
B1: Discounted cash flow techniques	(a)	Evaluate the potential value added to an organisation arising from a specified capital investment project or portfolio using the net present value (NPV) model. Project modelling should include explicit treatment and discussion of: (i) Inflation and specific price variation (ii) Taxation including tax allowable depreciation and tax exhaustion (iii) Single period and multi-period capital rationing. Multi-period capital rationing to include the formulation of programming methods and the interpretation of their output. (vi) Project duration as a measure of risk.
	(c)	Establish the potential economic return (using internal rate of return (IRR) and modified internal rate of return) and advise on a project's return margin. Discuss the relative merits of NPV and IRR.

PER

One of the PER performance objectives (PO09 – Evaluate Investment and Financing Decisions) is to be able to review the financial and strategic consequences of undertaking a particular investment decision.

Working through this chapter should help you understand how to demonstrate that objective.

1 Introduction – Investment, financing and dividend decisions

Three of the key decisions facing the financial manager (identified in Chapter 1 above) are:

Investment – what projects should be undertaken by the organisation?

Finance – how should the necessary funds be raised?

Dividends – how much cash should be allocated each year to be paid as a return to shareholders, and how much should be retained to meet the cash needs of the business?

This chapter and the next three chapters of this Text cover these three key decisions in detail.

However, as well as considering these three areas separately, it is vital that we understand that the three decisions are very closely interlinked.

Examples of links between these three key decisions

Investment decisions cannot be taken without consideration of where and how the funds are to be raised to finance them. The type of finance available will, in turn, depend to some extent on the nature of the project – its size, duration, risk, capital asset backing, etc.

Dividends represent the payment of returns on the investment back to the shareholders, the level and risk of which will depend upon the project itself, and how it was financed.

Debt finance, for example, can be cheap (particularly where interest is tax deductible) but requires an interest payment to be made out of project earnings, which can increase the risk of the shareholders' dividends.

Throughout this chapter and the next three, it is critical that we continue to consider these inter-relationships. Exam questions rarely focus on just a single area of the syllabus, so we must consider such links throughout in order to prepare fully for the exam.

2 Investment appraisal

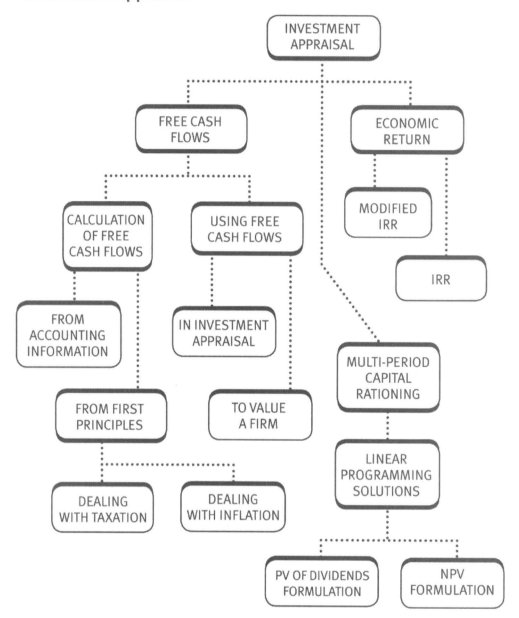

3 A key concept in investment appraisal – Free cash flow

 Cash that is not retained and reinvested in the business is called free cash flow.

It represents cash flow available:

- to all the providers of capital of a company
- to pay dividends or finance additional capital projects.

Uses of free cash flows

Free cash flows are used frequently in financial management:

- as a basis for evaluating potential investment projects – see below

- as an indicator of company performance – see Chapter 14: Corporate failure and reconstruction

- to calculate the value of a firm and thus a potential share price – see Chapter 13: Business valuation.

Calculating free cash flows for investment appraisal

Free cash flows can be calculated simply as:

Free cash flow = Revenue – Costs – Investments

The free cash flows used to evaluate investment projects are therefore essentially the net **relevant cash flows** you will recall from your earlier studies.

Use of free cash flows in investment appraisal

This chapter covers the following investment appraisal methods, all of which incorporate the use of free cash flows:

- Net Present Value (NPV)

- Internal Rate Of Return (IRR)

- Modified Internal Rate Of Return (MIRR)

- Discounted Payback Period

- Duration (Macaulay Duration and Modified Duration).

4   Net Present Value

Capital investment projects are best evaluated using the net present value (NPV) technique. You should recall from earlier studies that this involved discounting the relevant cash flows for each year of the project at an appropriate cost of capital.

As mentioned above the net relevant cash flows associated with the project are the free cash flows it generates. The discounted free cash flows are totalled to provide the NPV of the project.

Some basic NPV concepts (relevant cash flows, discounting, the impact of inflation, the impact of taxation) are covered below.

Relevant cash flows

Relevant costs and revenues

Relevant cash flows are those costs and revenues that are:

- future
- incremental.

Some basic NPV concepts are revised as follows:

You should therefore ignore:

- sunk costs
- committed costs
- non-cash items
- apportioned overheads.

Discounting

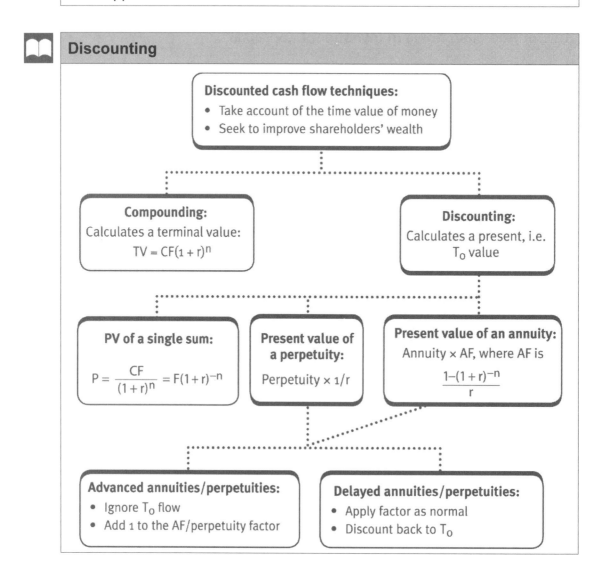

Discounted cash flow techniques:
- Take account of the time value of money
- Seek to improve shareholders' wealth

Compounding:
Calculates a terminal value:
$$TV = CF(1 + r)^n$$

Discounting:
Calculates a present, i.e. T_0 value

PV of a single sum:
$$P = \frac{CF}{(1 + r)^n} = F(1+r)^{-n}$$

Present value of a perpetuity:
Perpetuity $\times$ 1/r

Present value of an annuity:
Annuity $\times$ AF, where AF is
$$\frac{1-(1 + r)^{-n}}{r}$$

Advanced annuities/perpetuities:
- Ignore T_0 flow
- Add 1 to the AF/perpetuity factor

Delayed annuities/perpetuities:
- Apply factor as normal
- Discount back to T_0

The impact of inflation

The treatment of inflation was introduced in the Financial Management syllabus. A brief recap follows:

Inflation is a general increase in prices leading to a general decline in the real value of money.

In times of inflation, the fund providers will require a return made up of two elements:

- Real return for the use of their funds.

- Additional return to compensate for inflation.

The overall required return is called the **money or nominal rate of return**.

Real and nominal rates are linked by the Fisher formula:

$$(1 + i) = (1 + r)(1 + h)$$

Or

$$(1 + r) = (1 + i)/(1 + h)$$

in which:

r = real rate

i = money/nominal interest rate

h = general inflation rate.

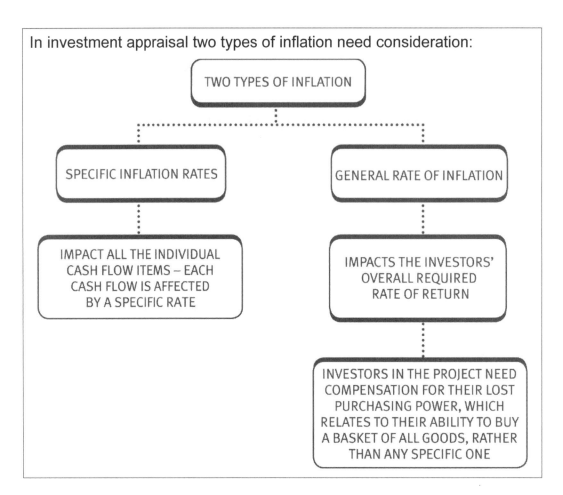

In investment appraisal two types of inflation need consideration:

TWO TYPES OF INFLATION

SPECIFIC INFLATION RATES

GENERAL RATE OF INFLATION

IMPACT ALL THE INDIVIDUAL CASH FLOW ITEMS – EACH CASH FLOW IS AFFECTED BY A SPECIFIC RATE

IMPACTS THE INVESTORS' OVERALL REQUIRED RATE OF RETURN

INVESTORS IN THE PROJECT NEED COMPENSATION FOR THEIR LOST PURCHASING POWER, WHICH RELATES TO THEIR ABILITY TO BUY A BASKET OF ALL GOODS, RATHER THAN ANY SPECIFIC ONE

Calculating the free cash flows of a project under inflation

In project appraisal the impact of inflation must be taken into account when calculating the free cash flows to be discounted.

The impact of inflation can be dealt with in two different ways – both methods give the same NPV.

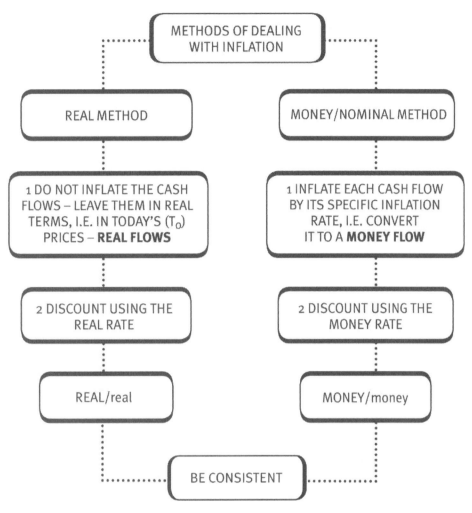

Note:

- The real method can only be used if all cash flows are inflating at the general rate of inflation.

- In questions involving specific inflation rates, taxation or working capital, the money/nominal method is usually more reliable.

Illustration of inflation in investment appraisal

A company is considering investing $4.5m in a project to achieve an annual increase in revenues over the next five years of $2m.

The project will lead to an increase in wage costs of $0.4m per year and will also require expenditure of $0.3m per year to maintain the level of existing assets to be used on the project.

Additional investment in working capital equivalent to 10% of the increase in revenue will need to be in place at the start of each year.

The following forecasts are made of the rates of inflation each year for the next five years:

Revenues	10%
Wages	5%
Assets	7%
General prices	6.5%

The real cost of capital of the company is 8%.

All cash flows are in real terms. Ignore tax.

Find the free cash flows of the project and determine whether it is worthwhile.

Solution

$000

	T_0	T_1	T_2	T_3	T_4	T_5
Increased revenues (infl. @ 10%)		2,200	2,420	2,662	2,928	3,221
Increased wage costs (infl. @ 5%)		(420)	(441)	(463)	(486)	510)
Operating cash flows		1,780	1,979	2,199	2,442	2,711
New investment	(4,500)					
Asset replacement spending (infl. @ 7%)		(321)	(343)	(367)	(393)	(421)
Working capital injection (W1)	(220)	(22)	(24)	(27)	(29)	322
Free cash flows	(4,720)	1,437	1,612	1,805	2,020	2,612
PV factor @ 15% (W2)	1.000	0.870	0.756	0.658	0.572	0.497
PV of free cash flows	(4,720)	1,250	1,219	1,187	1,155	1,298

The NPV = $1,389,000 which suggests that the project is worthwhile.

(W1) Working capital injection

	T_0	T_1	T_2	T_3	T_4	T_5
Increased revenues		2,200	2,420	2,662	2,928	3,221
Working capital required 10% in advance	220	242	266	293	322	
Working capital injection	(220)	(22)	(24)	(27)	(29)	322

(W2) Cost of capital

$(1 + i) = (1 + r)(1 + h) = (1.08)(1.065) = 1.15$, giving $i = 15\%$

Test your understanding 1 – NPV with inflation revision

A company plans to invest $7m in a new product. Net contribution over the next five years is expected to be $4.2m per year in real terms.

Marketing expenditure of $1.4m per year will also be needed.

Expenditure of $1.3m per year will be required to replace existing assets which will now be used on the project but are getting to the end of their useful lives. This expenditure will be incurred at the start of each year.

Additional investment in working capital equivalent to 10% of contribution will need to be in place at the start of each year. Working capital will be released at the end of the project.

The following forecasts are made of the rates of inflation each year for the next five years:

Contribution	8%
Marketing	3%
Assets	4%
General prices	4.7%

The real cost of capital of the company is 6%.

All cash flows are in real terms. Ignore tax.

Required:

Forecast the free cash flows of the project and determine whether it is worthwhile using the NPV method.

Note that in the CBE you can use the NPV spreadsheet function to save time here.

The impact of taxation

There are two main impacts of taxation in an investment appraisal:

- tax is charged on operating cash flows, and

- tax allowable depreciation (sometimes referred to as capital allowances or writing down allowances) can be claimed, thus generating tax relief.

Revision of taxation on operating cash flows

Tax on operating flows

Corporation tax charged on a company's profits is a relevant cash flow for NPV purposes. It is assumed that:

- operating cash inflows will be taxed at the corporation tax rate

- operating cash outflows will be tax deductible and attract tax relief at the corporation tax rate

- tax is paid in the same year the related operating cash flow is earned unless otherwise stated

- investment spending attracts tax allowable depreciation which gets tax relief (see the section below)

- the company is earning net taxable profits overall.

Revision of Tax Allowable Depreciation

For tax purposes, a business may not deduct the cost of an asset from its profits as depreciation (in the way it does for financial accounting purposes). Instead the cost must be deducted in the form of tax allowable depreciation (TAD).

The basic rules that follow are based on the current UK tax legislation:

- TAD is calculated on a reducing balance basis.

- The total TAD given over the life of an asset equates to the fall in value over the period (i.e. the cost less any scrap proceeds).

- TAD is claimed as early as possible.

- TAD is given for every year of ownership except the year of disposal.

- In the year of sale or scrap a balancing allowance or charge arises.

	$
Original cost of asset	X
Cumulative TAD claimed	(X)
Written down value of the asset	X
Disposal value of the asset	(X)
Balancing allowance or charge	X

You should carefully check the information given in the question however, since the examiner could ask you to examine the impact on the project of potential changes in the rules, for example:

- giving 50% TAD in the first year of ownership and 25% thereafter
- giving 100% first year TAD allowances (these are sometimes available to encourage investment in certain areas or types of assets)
- changing the calculation method from reducing balance to straight line.

Calculating the free cash flows of a project taking account of taxation

In project appraisal the effects of taxation must be taken into account when calculating the free cash flows to be discounted.

 Illustration of taxation in investment appraisal

A company buys an asset for $26,000. It will be used on a project for three years after which it will be disposed of on the final day of year 3 for $12,500.

Tax is payable at 30%. Tax allowable depreciation is available at 25% reducing balance, and a balancing allowance or charge should be calculated when the asset is sold.

Net trading income from the project is $16,000 per year and the cost of capital is 8%.

Required:

Forecast the free cash flows of the project and determine whether it is worthwhile using the NPV method.

Solution

Time		$
T$_0$	Initial investment	26,000
T$_1$	TAD @ 25%	(6,500)
	Written down value	19,500
T$_2$	TAD @ 25%	(4,875)
	Written down value	14,625
	Sale proceeds	(12,500)
T$_3$	Balancing allowance	2,125

NPV calculation

Time	T₀	T₁	T₂	T₃
Net trading inflows		16,000	16,000	16,000
TAD (from working)		6,500	4,875	2,125
		–––––––	–––––––	–––––––
Taxable profit		9,500	11,125	13,875
Tax payable (30%)		(2,850)	(3,338)	(4,163)
Add back TAD		6,500	4,875	2,125
Initial investment	(26,000)			
Scrap proceeds				12,500
	–––––––	–––––––	–––––––	–––––––
Free cash flows	(26,000)	13,150	12,662	24,337
Discount factor @ 8%	1.000	0.926	0.857	0.794
	–––––––	–––––––	–––––––	–––––––
Present value	(26,000)	12,177	10,852	19,324
	–––––––	–––––––	–––––––	–––––––
NPV	16,353			
	–––––––			

Test your understanding 2 – NPV with taxation revision

A project will require an investment in a new asset of $10,000. It will be used on a project for four years after which it will be disposed of on the final day of year 4 for $2,500.

Tax is payable at 30% one year in arrears. Tax allowable depreciation is available at 25% (reducing balance), and a balancing allowance or charge should be calculated when the asset is sold.

Net operating flows from the project are expected to be $4,000 per year.

The company's cost of capital is 10%. Ignore inflation.

Required:

Forecast the free cash flows of the project and determine whether it is worthwhile using the NPV method.

Note that in the CBE you can use the NPV spreadsheet function to save time here.

5   The Internal Rate of Return (IRR)

As well as NPV, the other discounting technique used to appraise investment projects, which you should recall from earlier studies, is the calculation of the internal rate of return or the IRR.

A brief recap follows:

IRR – The basics

The IRR of a project has the following features:

*   It represents the discount rate at which the NPV of an investment is zero.

*   It can be found by linear interpolation.

*   Standard projects (outflow followed by inflows) should be accepted if the IRR is greater than the firm's cost of capital.

The steps in linear interpolation are:

1   Calculate two NPVs for the project at two different costs of capital.

2   Use the following formula to find the IRR:

$$IRR = L + \frac{N_L}{(N_L - N_H)} \times (H - L)$$

where:

L = Lower rate of interest.

H = Higher rate of interest.

N_L = NPV at lower rate of interest.

N_H = NPV at higher rate of interest.

3   Compare the IRR with the company's cost of borrowing.

If the IRR is higher than the cost of capital, the project should be accepted.

Test your understanding 3

An initial investment of $2,000 in a project yields cash inflows of $500, $500, $600, $600 and $440 at 12 months intervals. There is no scrap value. Funds are available to finance the project at 12%.

Required:

Decide whether the project is worthwhile, using:

(a)   **net present value approach**

(b)   **internal rate of return approach.**

Note that in the CBE you can use the IRR spreadsheet function to save time here.

Interpreting the IRR

The IRR provides a decision rule for investment appraisal, but also provides information about the riskiness of a project – i.e. the sensitivity of its returns. The project will only continue to have a positive NPV whilst the firm's cost of capital is lower than the IRR.

A project with a positive NPV at 14% but an IRR of 15% for example, is clearly sensitive to:

- an increase in the cost of finance
- an increase in investors' perception of the potential risks
- any alteration to the estimates used in the NPV appraisal.

Interpretation of IRR

Increases in interest rates will clearly increase the company's costs of finance as will concerns affecting the stock market as a whole and hence the returns demanded by investors.

However, other, company specific factors – such as the actions of competitors may affect the firm's position in the market place and the viability of its business model. This could impact the level of systematic risk it faces and result in an increase in the required return of shareholders.

Where the IRR is close to the company cost of capital, any changes to estimates in the NPV calculation will have a significant impact on the viability of the project. Any unexpected changes such as an increase in the costs of raw materials, or an aggressive advertising campaign run by a competitor will erode the return margin and may make the project unacceptable to investors.

6 The modified IRR (MIRR)

Problems with using IRR

There are a number of problems with the standard IRR calculation:

- The assumptions. IRR is often mistakenly assumed to be a measure of the return from a project, which it is not. The IRR only represents the return from the project if funds can be reinvested at the IRR for the duration of the project.

- The decision rule is not always clear cut. For example, if a project has 2 IRRs (or more), it is difficult to interpret the rule which says "accept the project if the IRR is higher than the cost of capital".

- Choosing between projects. Since projects can have multiple IRRs (or none at all) it is difficult to usefully compare projects using IRR.

It is therefore usually considered more reliable to calculate the NPV of projects for investment appraisal purposes.

More on the problems with IRR

For conventional projects (those with a cash outflow at time 0 followed by inflows over the life of the project), the decision rule states that projects should be accepted if the IRR exceeds the cost of capital.

However unconventional projects with different cash flow patterns may have no IRR, more than one IRR, or a single IRR but the project should only be accepted if the cost of capital is greater.

The IRR calculates the discount rate that would cause the project to break-even assuming it:

- is the cost of financing the project

- is the return that can be earned on all the returns earned by the project.

Since, in practice, these rates are likely to be different, the IRR is unreliable.

A project with a high IRR is not necessarily the one offering the highest return in NPV terms and IRR is therefore an unreliable tool for choosing between mutually exclusive projects.

A more useful measure is the modified internal rate of return or MIRR.

This measure has been developed to counter the above problems since it:

- is unique

- gives a measure of the return from a project

- is a simple percentage.

It is therefore more popular with non-financially minded managers, as a simple rule can be applied:

MIRR = Project's return

If Project return > company cost of finance $\Rightarrow$ Accept project

The interpretation of MIRR

MIRR measures the economic yield of the investment under the assumption that any cash surpluses are reinvested at the firm's current cost of capital.

Although MIRR, like IRR, cannot replace net present value as the principle evaluation technique it does give a measure of the maximum cost of finance that the firm could sustain and allow the project to remain worthwhile. For this reason it gives a useful insight into the margin of error, or room for negotiation, when considering the financing of particular investment projects.

Calculation of MIRR

There are several ways of calculating the MIRR, but the simplest is to use the following formula which is provided on the formula sheet in the exam:

$MIRR = [PVR/PVI]^{1/n}(1 + r_e) - 1$

where

PVR = the present value of the 'return phase' of the project

PVI = the present value of the 'investment phase' of the project

r_e = the firm's cost of capital.

Test your understanding 4

A project with the following cash flows is under consideration:

$000	T_0	T_1	T_2	T_3	T_4
	(20,000)	8,000	12,000	4,000	2,000

Cost of capital 8%

Required:

Calculate the MIRR.

Note that in the CBE you can use the MIRR spreadsheet function to save time here.

Alternative calculation of MIRR

One other feature of the MIRR is that it can be calculated even if the firm's depositing and borrowing rates of interest are different. In this case, the calculation has to be adapted as follows:

Method

1   Find the terminal value of the cash inflows from the project if invested at the company's reinvestment rate.

2   Find the present value of the cash outflows, discounted at the company's cost of finance.

3   The MIRR is then found by taking the n th root of (TV inflows/PV outflows) and subtracting 1. (Note that n is the length of the project in years.)

Example

A project requires an initial investment of $20,000 and will generate annual cash flows as follows:

Year	Cash flow $
1	4,000
2	(2,000)
3	6,000
4	7,600
5	10,000

The firm's financing rate (for negative cash flows) is 9%, and its reinvestment rate for positive cash flows is 6%.

What is the MIRR?

Year	Equivalent cash flow at time 0 $		Equivalent cash flow at time 5 $	
0		(20,000)		
1			$4,000 \times 1.06^4 =$	5,050
2	$(2,000) \times 1/1.09^2 =$	(1,683)		
3			$6,000 \times 1.06^2 =$	6,742
4			$7,600 \times 1.06 =$	8,056
5			$10,000 \times 1 =$	10,000
		(21,683)		29,848

$$\sqrt[5]{\frac{29,848}{21,683}} - 1 = 6.6\%$$

Since the MIRR, the return on the project, is less than the cost of finance, the project should be rejected.

7 Discounted Payback Period (DPP)

Traditional payback period

The payback period was introduced in Financial Management (FM).

Payback period measures the length of time it takes for the cash returns from a project to cover the initial investment.

The main problem with payback period is that it does not take account of the time value of money.

Discounted payback period

Hence, the discounted payback period can be computed instead.

Discounted payback period measures the length of time before the discounted cash returns from a project cover the initial investment.

The shorter the discounted payback period, the more attractive the project is. A long discounted payback period indicates that the project is a high risk project.

Illustration 1 – Discounted Payback Period

A project with the following cash flows is under consideration:

$000	T_0	T_1	T_2	T_3	T_4
	(20,000)	8,000	12,000	4,000	2,000

Cost of capital 8%

Required:

Calculate the Discounted Payback Period.

Solution

Year	Discounted cash flow	Cumulative discounted cash flow
0	(20,000)	(20,000)
1	$8,000/(1.08) = 7,407$	(12,593)
2	$12,000/(1.08)^2 = 10,288$	(2,305)
3	$4,000/(1.08)^3 = 3,175$	870

Hence discounted payback period =

2 years + (2,305/3,175) = 2.73 years

8 Duration (Macaulay duration)

Introduction to the concept of duration

Duration measures the average time to recover the present value of the project (if cash flows are discounted at the cost of capital).

Duration captures both the time value of money and the whole of the cash flows of a project. It is also a measure which can be used across projects to indicate when the bulk of the project value will be captured.

Projects with higher durations carry more risk than projects with lower durations.

Calculation of duration

There are several different ways of calculating duration, the most common of which is Macaulay duration, illustrated below.

More details on duration

As mentioned above, duration measures the average time to recover the present value of the project if discounted at the cost of capital.

However, if cash flows are discounted at the project's IRR, it can be used to measure the time to recover the initial investment.

As well as being used in project appraisal, duration is commonly used to assess the likely volatility (risk) associated with corporate bonds. An example of duration in the context of bonds is shown in Chapter 8.

Payback, discounted payback and duration

Payback, discounted payback and duration are three techniques that measure the return to liquidity offered by a capital project.

In theory, a firm that has ready access to the capital markets should not be concerned about the time taken to recapture the investment in a project. However, in practice managers prefer projects to appear to be successful as quickly as possible.

Payback period

Payback as a technique fails to take into account the time value of money and any cash flows beyond the project date. It is used by many firms as a coarse filter of projects and it has been suggested to be a proxy for the redeployment real option.

Discounted payback period

Discounted payback does surmount the first difficulty but not the second in that it is still possible for projects with highly negative terminal cash flows to appear attractive because of their initial favourable cash flows. Conversely, discounted payback may lead a project to be discarded that has highly favourable cash flows after the payback date.

Duration

Duration measures either the average time to recover the initial investment (if discounted at the project's internal rate of return) of a project, or to recover the present value of the project if discounted at the cost of capital. Duration captures both the time value of money and the whole of the cash flows of a project. It is also a measure which can be used across projects to indicate when most of the project value will be captured.

Its disadvantage is that it is more difficult to conceptualise than payback and may not be employed for that reason.

Illustration 2 – Macaulay duration

A project with the following cash flows is under consideration:

$000	T0	T1	T2	T3	T4
	(20,000)	8,000	12,000	4,000	2,000

Cost of capital 8%

Required:

Calculate the project's Macaulay duration.

Solution

The Macaulay duration is calculated by first calculating the discounted cash flow for each future year, and then weighting each discounted cash flow according to its time of receipt, as follows:

$000	T0	T1	T2	T3	T4
Cash flow		8,000	12,000	4,000	2,000
D F @ 8%		0.926	0.857	0.794	0.735
PV @ 8%		7,408	10,284	3,176	1,470
PV × Year		7,408	20,568	9,528	5,880

Next, the sum of the (PV × Year) figures is found, and divided by the present value of these 'return phase' cash flows.

Sum of (PV × Year) figures = 7,408 + 20,568 + 9,528 + 5,880 = 43,384

Present value of return phase cash flows
= 7,408 + 10,284 + 3,176 + 1,470 = 22,338

Hence, the Macaulay duration is 43,384/22,338 = 1.94 years

Test your understanding 5

A project with the following cash flows is under consideration:

$m	T0	T1	T2	T3	T4	T5	T6
Net cash flow	(127)	37	52	76	69	44	29

Cost of capital 10%

Calculate the project's discounted payback period and Macaulay duration.

Modified Duration

As well as the Macaulay Duration, there is another commonly used measure of duration, known as Modified Duration.

Comparison of Macaulay Duration and Modified Duration

Macaulay Duration is the name given to the weighted average time until cash flows are received, and is measured in years.

Modified Duration is the name given to the price sensitivity and is the percentage change in price for a unit change in yield.

Macaulay Duration and Modified Duration differ slightly, and there is a simple relationship between the two (assuming that cash flows are discounted annually), namely:

Modified Duration = Macaulay Duration/(1+ cost of capital)

Therefore, in the above illustration, where the project cash flows were discounted at 8% and the Macaulay Duration was 1.94 years, the Modified Duration is (1.94/1.08 =) 1.80.

9   Investment appraisal and capital rationing

Capital rationing was first introduced in Financial Management (FM). A brief recap follows:

Capital rationing – The basics

Shareholder wealth is maximised if a company undertakes all possible positive NPV projects.

Capital rationing is where there are insufficient funds to do so.

This shortage of funds may be for:

- a single period only – dealt with as in limiting factor analysis by calculating profitability indexes (PIs)

  PI = NPV/PV of capital invested

- more than one period – extending over a number of years or even indefinitely.

Test your understanding 6 – Single period capital rationing

Peel Co has identified 4 positive NPV projects, as follows:

Project	NPV ($m)	Investment at t_0 ($m)
A	60	9
B	40	12
C	35	6
D	20	4

Peel Co can only raise $12m of finance to invest at t_0.

Required:

Advise the company which project(s) to accept if the projects are:

(i)   **independent and divisible**

(ii)   **independent and indivisible**

(iii) **mutually exclusive.**

Multi-period capital rationing

A solution to a multi-period capital rationing problem cannot be found using PIs. This method can only deal with one limiting factor (i.e. one period of shortage). Here there are a number of limiting factors (i.e. a number of periods of shortage) and linear programming techniques must therefore be applied.

In the exam you will not be expected to produce a solution to a linear programming problem, but you may be asked to formulate the linear programme.

In practice, long term capital rationing is a signal that the firm should be looking to expand its capital base through a new issue of finance to the markets.

Revision of linear programming (LP)

In your previous studies, you were introduced to the details of linear programming. In AFM, we are interested only in formulating the linear programming problem and this revision example therefore only reviews those first key stages.

Linear programming is a technique for dealing with scarce or rationed resources. The solution calculated identifies the optimum allocation of the scarce resources between the products/projects being considered.

A brief recap follows:

The linear programme is formulated in three stages:

1   Define the unknowns.

2   Formulate the objective function.

3   Express the constraints in terms of inequalities including the non-negativities.

Simple LP example

A company makes two products, brooms and mops. Each product passes through two departments, manufacture and packaging. The time spent in each department is as follows:

	Departmental time (hours)	
	Manufacture	**Packaging**
Brooms	3	2
Mops	4	6

There are 4,800 hours available in the manufacturing department and 3,600 available in the packaging department. Production of brooms must not exceed 1,100 units.

The contribution earned from one broom is $15 and from a mop is $10.

Formulate the linear programme needed to identify the optimum use of the scarce labour resource.

Solution

1 **Define the unknowns**

Let m = number of mops to be produced.

Let b = number of brooms to be produced.

Let z = contribution earned from the products made.

2 **Formulate the objective function**

The aim is to maximise contribution:

$z = 15b + 10m$.

3 **Express the constraints in terms of inequalities including the non-negativities**

Manufacturing	$3b + 4m \leq 4{,}800$
Packaging	$2b + 6m \leq 3{,}600$
Production	$b \leq 1{,}100$

$b, m \geq 0$

The main constraints simply say that you cannot use any more of the resource than you have available.

Since only 4,800 hours of manufacturing time is available, the constraint shows that the number of hours taken to make a broom times the number of brooms made (3b) plus the number of hours needed to make a mop times the number of mops made (4m) must not exceed 4,800.

The same principle is applied to packaging time.

The third constraint restricts the production of brooms to 1,100.

The non-negative constraints at the end, prevent negative quantities from being produced. (If this seems unnecessary, remember that a computer solving the problem does not have a sense of this being ridiculous and producing negative quantities would, on paper, actually contribute scarce resource!)

Example of LP in capital rationing

A company has identified the following independent investment projects, all of which are divisible and exhibit constant returns to scale. No project can be delayed or done more than once.

Project Cash flows at time:	0	1	2	3	4
	$000	$000	$000	$000	$000
A	−10	−20	+10	+20	+20
B	−10	−10	+30	–	–
C	−5	+2	+2	+2	+2
D	–	−15	−15	+20	+20
E	−20	+10	−20	+20	+20
F	−8	−4	+15	+10	–

There is only $20,000 of capital available at T_0 and only $5,000 at T_1, plus the cash inflows from the projects undertaken at T_0. In each time period thereafter, capital is freely available. The appropriate discount rate is 10%.

Required:

Formulate the linear programme.

Solution

Since our objective is to maximise the total NPV from the investments the first (additional) stage will be to calculate those NPVs at a discount rate of 10%.

Project	NPV @ 10%
	$000
A	+8.77
B	+5.70
C	+1.34
D	+2.65
E	+1.25
F	+8.27

We now progress as for a standard linear programme:

1 **Define the unknowns**

   The linear programme will then select the combination of projects, which will maximise total NPV.

   Therefore:

   Let a = the proportion of project A undertaken

   Let b = the proportion of project B undertaken

   Let c = the proportion of project C undertaken

   Let d = the proportion of project D undertaken

   Let e = the proportion of project E undertaken

   Let f = the proportion of project F undertaken

   And

   Let z = the NPV of the combination of projects selected.

2 **Formulate the objective function**

   The objective function to be maximised is:

   $z = 8.77a + 5.70b + 1.34c + 2.65d + 1.25e + 8.27f$.

3 **Express the constraints in terms of inequalities including the non-negativities**

Time 0	$10a + 10b + 5c + 20e + 8f \le 20$
Time 1	$20a + 10b + 15d + 4f \le 5 + 2c + 10e$
Also	$0 \le a, b, c, d, e, f \le 1$

4 Interpret the results

The linear programme when solved will give values for a, b, c, d, e and f. These will be the proportions of each project which, should be undertaken to maximise the NPV – an amount given by z.

Further details on interpretation

The objective function (z) is the maximum NPV earned. This will be the sum of the NPVs earned from each product. Since they may each be done only in part, the full NPV from each one is multiplied by the proportion of it to be undertaken (a, b, c etc.) and these are then summed together to give the objective function.

The main constraints simply say that you cannot spend any more money than you have available.

– The first constraint relates to the limited capital available at T_0.

– How much of the T_0 capital for each project will actually be needed, depends on the proportions of each project undertaken. The full T_0 amounts are therefore multiplied by the proportions to be undertaken, and the sum of those amounts must not exceed the $20,000 available.

– The second constraint relates to the limited capital available at T_1.

– Here the financial situation is eased because projects C and E have positive cash inflows at T_1 and these flows can be used to fund investment needs at that time.

– The funds required by projects using limited cash (A, B, D, and F) are therefore multiplied by the proportions to be undertaken. This amount must be less than what is available – the $5,000 plus the funds brought it by whatever proportions of C and E we end up choosing to do.

The third constraint is a summarised one. It shows that none of the projects can be done more than once (i.e. must be ≤1) and that is not possible to do a negative amount of any project (they must be ≥ 0). This second non-negative rule is essential. If it were not included, a computer model may well compute that effectively 'undoing' a project frees up cash and include it in a solution!

Illustration 3 – Multi-period capital rationing

Jacqui Co is considering investing in three projects over the next two years.

The level of investment required for each project is as follows:

$000	T_0	T_1	T_2
Project A	500	200	0
Project B	600	200	400
Project C	1,000	100	500

After these amounts have been invested, all three projects have several years of positive cash inflows, and all three projects have positive NPVs as follows:

$000	**NPV**
Project A	3,050
Project B	2,885
Project C	7,560

Jacqui Co faces a capital rationing constraint at each of T_0, T_1 and T_2, where spending limits are

- $2,000,000 at T_0

- $300,000 at T_1

- $700,000 at T_2

Required:

On the assumption that none of the projects can be deferred and all of the projects can be scaled down but not scaled up, formulate an appropriate capital rationing model that maximises the net present value for Jacqui Co.

(Finding a solution for the model is not required.)

Solution

Define the unknowns:

Let a = the proportion of project A undertaken

Let b = the proportion of project B undertaken

Let c = the proportion of project C undertaken

and

Let z = the NPV of the combination of projects selected.

> **Formulate the objective function**
>
> The objective function to be maximised is:
>
> $z = 3{,}050a + 2{,}885b + 7{,}560c$
>
> **Express the constraints in terms of inequalities including the non-negativities**
>
> | | |
> |---|---|
> | T_0 | $500a + 600b + 1{,}000c \leq 2{,}000$ |
> | T_1 | $200a + 200b + 100c \leq 300$ |
> | T_2 | $400b + 500c \leq 700$ |
> | Also | $0 \leq a, b, c \leq 1$ |

10 The impact of corporate reporting on investment appraisal

The main approach to evaluating capital investment projects and financing options, for a profit-maxi miser, is their impact on shareholder value. However, the impact on the reported financial position and performance of the firm must also be considered. In particular, you may need to examine the implications for:

- the share price
- gearing
- ROCE
- earnings per share (EPS).

Timing differences between cash flows and profits

For NPV purposes, the timing of the cash flows associated with a project is taken account of through the discounting process. It is therefore irrelevant if the cash flows in the earlier years are negative, provided overall the present value of the cash inflows outweighs the costs.

However, the impact on reported profits may be significant. Major new investment will bring about higher levels of depreciation in the earlier years, which are not yet matched by higher revenues. This will reduce reported profits and the EPS figure.

This reduction could impact:

- the share price – if the reasons for the fall in profit are not understood
- key ratios such as:
  - ROCE
  - asset turnover
  - profit margins
- the meeting of loan covenants.

11 Chapter summary

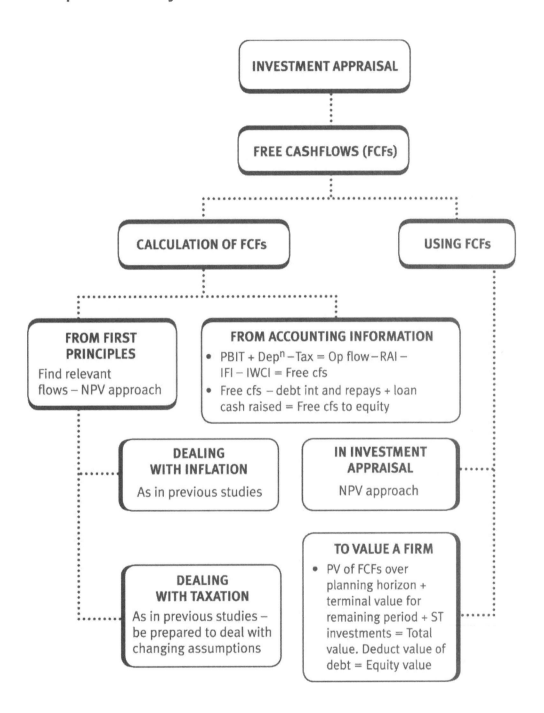

INVESTMENT APPRAISAL

FREE CASHFLOWS (FCFs)

CALCULATION OF FCFs

USING FCFs

FROM FIRST PRINCIPLES

Find relevant flows – NPV approach

FROM ACCOUNTING INFORMATION

- PBIT + Dep^n – Tax = Op flow – RAI – IFI – IWCI = Free cfs
- Free cfs – debt int and repays + loan cash raised = Free cfs to equity

DEALING WITH INFLATION

As in previous studies

IN INVESTMENT APPRAISAL

NPV approach

DEALING WITH TAXATION

As in previous studies – be prepared to deal with changing assumptions

TO VALUE A FIRM

- PV of FCFs over planning horizon + terminal value for remaining period + ST investments = Total value. Deduct value of debt = Equity value

Test your understanding answers

Test your understanding 1 – NPV with inflation revision

	$(000) T₀	$(000) T₁	$(000) T₂	$(000) T₃	$(000) T₄	$(000) T₅
Contribution (infl. @ 8%)		4,536	4,899	5,291	5,714	6,171
Marketing (infl. @ 3%)		(1,442)	(1,485)	(1,530)	(1,576)	(1,623)
Operating cash flows		3,094	3,414	3,761	4,138	4,548
New investment	(7,000)					
Asset replacement (infl. @ 4%)	(1,300)	(1,352)	(1,406)	(1,462)	(1,520)	
Working capital injection (W1)	(454)	(36)	(39)	(42)	(46)	617
Free cash flows	(8,754)	1,706	1,969	2,257	2,572	5,165
PV factor @ 11% (W2)	1.000	0.901	0.812	0.731	0.659	0.593
PV of free cash flows	(8,754)	1,537	1,599	1,650	1,695	3,063

The NPV = +$790,000 which suggests that the project is worthwhile.

(W1) Working capital injection

	T₀	T₁	T₂	T₃	T₄	T₅
Increased revenues		4,536	4,899	5,291	5,714	6,171
Working capital required 10% in advance	454	490	529	571	617	
Working capital injection	(454)	(36)	(39)	(42)	(46)	617

(W2) Cost of capital

$(1 + i) = (1 + r)(1 + h) = (1 + 0.06)(1 + 0.047) = 1.11$, giving $i = 11\%$

Test your understanding 2 – NPV with taxation revision

Working – Tax allowable depreciation (TAD)

Time		$
T₀	Initial investment	10,000
T₁	TAD @ 25%	(2,500)
		____
	Written down value	7,500
T₂	TAD @ 25%	(1,875)
		____
	Written down value	5,625
T₃	TAD @ 25%	(1,406)
		____
	Written down value	4,219
	Sale proceeds	(2,500)
		____
T₄	Balancing allowance	1,719

Note:

- Total TAD = 2,500 + 1,875 + 1,406 + 1,719 = 7,500 = fall in value of the asset

NPV calculation

Time	T_0	T_1	T_2	T_3	T_4	T_5
Net trading inflows		4,000	4,000	4,000	4,000	
TAD (from working)		2,500	1,875	1,406	1,719	
Taxable profit		1,500	2,125	2,594	2,281	
Tax payable (30%)			(450)	(638)	(778)	(684)
Add back TAD		2,500	1,875	1,406	1,719	
Initial investment	(10,000)					
Scrap proceeds					2,500	
Free cash flows	(10,000)	4,000	3,550	3,362	5,722	(684)
Discount factor @ 10%	1.000	0.909	0.826	0.751	0.683	0.621
Present value	(10,000)	3,636	2,932	2,525	3,908	(425)
					NPV	2,576

Test your understanding 3

It is useful to set out the cash flows in a table:

Time	0	1	2	3	4	5
	−$2,000	+$500	+$500	+$600	+$600	+$440

(a) **Net present value approach**

Year	Cash flow $	PV factor @ 12%	Present value $
0	−2,000	1.000	−2,000
1	+500	0.893	+446
2	+500	0.797	+398
3	+600	0.712	+427
4	+600	0.636	+382
5	+440	0.567	+249
			−98

Since the net present value at 12% is negative, the project should be rejected.

(b) **Internal rate of return approach**

Calculating IRR requires a trial and error approach. Since we have already calculated in (a) that NPV at 12% is negative, we must decrease the discount rate to bring the NPV towards zero – try 8%.

Year	Cash flow	PV factor @ 12% $	Present value	PV factor @ 8% $	Present value
0	−2,000	1.000	−2,000	1.000	−2,000
1	+500	0.893	+446	0.926	+463
2	+500	0.797	+398	0.857	+428
3	+600	0.712	+427	0.794	+476
4	+600	0.636	+382	0.735	+441
5	+440	0.567	+249	0.681	+300
			−98		+108

See above: NPV is + $108.

Thus, the IRR lies between 8% and 12%. We may estimate it by interpolation, as before.

IRR = 8% + [108/(108 − (−98))] × (12% − 8%)

= 10.1%

The project should be rejected because the IRR is less than the cost of borrowing, which is 12%, i.e. the same conclusion as with NPV analysis above.

Test your understanding 4

PVR = 22,340 (this is the present value of the year 1 – 4 cash flows).

PVI = 20,000

$1 + MIRR = (1 + r_e) \times (PVR/PVI)^{1/n} = 1.08 \times (22,340/20,000)^{1/4}$

= 1. 1103, giving MIRR = 11% per year.

Test your understanding 5

Workings:

$m	T0	T1	T2	T3	T4	T5	T6
Net cash flow	(127)	37	52	76	69	44	29
DF @ 10%	1	0.909	0.826	0.751	0.683	0.621	0.564
PV @ 10%	(127)	33.6	43.0	57.1	47.1	27.3	16.4

Discounted payback period

$m	T0	T1	T2	T3	T4	T5	T6
PV @ 10%	(127)	33.6	43.0	57.1	47.1	27.3	16.4
Cumulative PV	(127)	(93.4)	(50.4)	6.7	53.8	81.1	97.5

So discounted payback period = 2 years + (50.4/57.1) = 2.9 years

Duration

$m	T0	T1	T2	T3	T4	T5	T6
PV @ 10%	(127)	33.6	43.0	57.1	47.1	27.3	16.4
PV × Year		33.6	86.0	171.3	188.4	136.5	98.4

So duration = (33.6 + 86.0 + 171.3 + 188.4 + 136.5 + 98.4)/(33.6 + 43.0 + 57.1 + 47.1 + 27.3 + 16.4)

= 714.2/224.5

= 3.2 years

Test your understanding 6 – Single period capital rationing

(i) When projects are independent and divisible, the PI method can be used.

Project	PI (NPV/Investment)	Ranking
A	6.67	1
B	3.33	4
C	5.83	2
D	5.00	3

So, first do Project A (cost $9m), then do half of project C (cost $6m/2 = $3m) to use the $12m of capital.

Total NPV = $60m (from A) + $17.5m (from half of C) = **$77.5m**

(ii) If projects are indivisible, a trial and error approach has to be used.

Choices for $12m investment are:

Either do A, or B, or (C + D).

By inspection, the best option is A, with an NPV of **$60m**.

(iii) If projects are mutually exclusive, pick the one with the highest positive NPV, i.e. A, with an NPV of **$60m**.

International operations and international investment appraisal

Chapter learning objectives

Study guide section	Study guide outcome	
A4: Management of international trade and finance	(a)	Advise on the theory and practice of free trade and the management of barriers to trade.
	(b)	Demonstrate an up to date understanding of the major trade agreements and common markets and, on the basis of contemporary circumstances, advise on their policies and strategic implications for a given business.
	(c)	Discuss how the actions of the World Trade Organisation, the International Monetary Fund, The World Bank and Central Banks can affect a multinational organisation.
	(d)	Discuss the role of international financial institutions within the context of a globalised economy, with particular attention to the principal Central Banks (the Fed, Bank of England, European Central Bank and the Bank of Japan).

A4: Management of international trade and finance (continued)	(e)	Assess the role of the international financial markets with respect to the management of global debt, the financial development of the emerging economies and the maintenance of global financial stability.
	(f)	Discuss the significance to the organisation, of latest developments in the world financial markets such as the causes and impact of the recent financial crisis; the removal of barriers to the free movement of capital; and the international regulations on money laundering.
	(g)	Demonstrate an awareness of new developments in the macroeconomic environment, assessing their impact upon the organisation, and advising on the appropriate response to those developments both internally and externally.
A5: Strategic business and financial planning for multinationals	(a)	Advise on the development of a financial planning framework for a multinational organisation taking into account: (i) Compliance with national regulatory requirements (for example the London Stock Exchange admission requirements) (ii) The mobility of capital across borders and national limitations on remittances and transfer pricing (iii) The pattern of economic and other risk exposures in the different national markets (iv) Agency issues in the central coordination of overseas operations and the balancing of local financial autonomy with effective central control.

B5: International investment and financing decisions

(a) Assess the impact upon the value of a project of alternative exchange rate assumptions.

(b) Forecast project or organisation free cash flows in any specified currency and determine the project's net present value or organisation value under differing exchange rate, fiscal and transaction cost assumptions.

(c) Evaluate the significance of exchange controls for a given investment decision and strategies for dealing with restricted remittance.

(d) Assess the impact of a project upon an organisation's exposure to translation, transaction and economic risk.

PER

One of the PER performance objectives (PO09 – Evaluate Investment and Financing Decisions) is to be able to review the financial and strategic consequences of undertaking a particular investment decision.

Working through this chapter should help you understand how to demonstrate that objective.

1 Introduction

In the previous chapter, we looked closely at the investment decision – one of the main decisions faced by the financial manager.

In all cases so far, our considerations have been restricted to organisations operating in a single, domestic market. For example, none of our investment appraisals involved foreign projects and hence foreign currency denominated cash flows.

This chapter first introduces the concepts of international trade and multinational companies, and then looks at the additional complexities when making investment decisions in an international context.

2 Multinational companies and international trading

A multinational company (MNC) is defined as one that generates at least 25% of its sales from activities in countries other than its own.

From this definition we can see that many companies are multinationals. Increasingly, in the modern business environment, organisations are trading with customers and suppliers in many different countries. It is useful to consider why this happens, and what the advantages and disadvantages of international trading are.

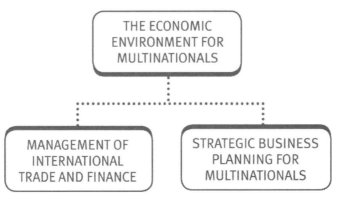

International trading

Practical reasons for international trading

- Choice – The diversity of goods available in a domestic economy is increased through the import of goods that could be uneconomic or impossible to produce at home.

- Competition – International trade will increase competition in domestic markets, which is likely to lead to both a reduction in price, together with increasing pressure for new products and innovation.

- Economies of scale – By producing both for the home and international markets companies can produce at a larger scale and therefore take advantage of economies of scale.

- Specialisation – If a country specialises in producing the goods and services at which it is most efficient, it can maximise its economic output.

Illustration 1

Imagine the impact on a country's consumers if international trade did not take place. No bananas, no tropical fruits at any time of the year, vegetables only when they are in season. Less obviously, some countries would be chronically short of many basic metals and materials. Many countries are also increasingly dependent on energy imports. Overall, world economic output would be far lower as countries would be forced to allocate resources to inefficient methods of production.

The theory of comparative advantage

The main theoretical justification for international trade is the law of comparative advantage.

The law of comparative advantage states that two countries can gain from trade when each specialises in the industries in which each has the lowest opportunity cost.

Comparative advantage between countries – Illustration

Imagine a global economy with two countries and two products. Each country needs both products and at present all needs are met by domestic production. Each country has the same resources available to it and they are split equally between the two products.

Suppose the current situation with regard to production is as follows:

	Units of X per day	Units of Y per day
Country A	1,200	720
Country B	960	240
Total daily production	2,160	960

As the situation currently stands, country A has an absolute advantage in production of both X and Y.

Given this what are the benefits of A trading with B?

To answer this question we need to consider the opportunity costs incurred by producing X and Y.

- If country A were to focus on making X only, it would give up 720 units of Y to produce an extra 1,200 units of X, i.e. the opportunity cost of 1 unit of X is $720/1{,}200 = 0.6$ units of Y.

- If country B were to focus on making X only, it would give up 240 units of Y to produce an extra 960 units of X, i.e. the opportunity cost of 1 unit of X is $240/960 = 0.25$ units of Y.

- The opportunity cost of producing X is lower for country B than it is for country A. It follows that B has a comparative advantage in production of X and should specialise in this product.

If country B is to make product X, it follows that country A should make product Y. An analysis of opportunity costs supports this conclusion.

- If country A were to focus on making Y only, it would give up 1,200 units of X to make 720 units of Y, i.e. the opportunity cost of 1 unit of Y is 1,200/720 = 1.67 units of X.

- If country B were to focus on making Y only, it would give up 960 units of X to make 240 units of Y, i.e. the opportunity cost of 1 unit of Y is 960/240 = 4 units of X.

- Since country A has the lowest opportunity cost for production of Y, it should specialise in production of this product.

The impact of this decision by each country to specialise in production of the good for which they have the lowest opportunity cost on world output is shown below:

Specialisation based on lowest opportunity cost

	Units of X per day	Units of Y per day
Country A	0	1,440
Country B	1,920	0
Total daily production	1,920	1,440

Trade barriers

There are a number of ways that a country can seek to restrict imports. Trade barriers include:

- Quotas – imposition of a maximum number of units that can be imported e.g. quotas on the number of cars manufactured outside of Europe that can be imported into the EU.

- Tariffs – imposition of an import tax on goods being imported into the country to make them uncompetitive on price.

- Exchange controls – domestic companies wishing to buy foreign goods will have to pay in the currency of the exporter's country. To do this they will need to buy the currency involved by selling their domestic currency. If the government controls the sale of the domestic currency it can control the level of imports purchased.

- Administrative controls – a domestic government can subject imports to excessive levels of administration, paperwork and red tape to slow down and increase the cost of importing goods into the home economy.

- Embargoes – the prohibition of commerce and trade with a certain country.

Multinational companies have to find ways of overcoming these barriers, for example by investing directly and manufacturing within a country rather than importing into it.

Trade agreements and common markets

In many parts of the world, governments have created trade agreements and common markets to encourage free trade. However, the World Trade Organisation (WTO) is opposed to these trading blocs and customs unions (e.g. the European Union) because they encourage trade between members but often have high trade barriers for non-members.

Example of trade agreements and common markets

Bi-lateral trade agreements

These are agreements between two countries to eliminate quotas and tariffs on the trade of most (if not all) goods between them.

e.g. The Closer Economic Relations (CER) agreement between Australia and New Zealand.

Multi-lateral trade agreements

These are similar to bi-lateral agreements except more than two countries are involved.

e.g. The US-Mexico-Canada Agreement (USMCA) (which replaced NAFTA on 1 July 2020).

Free trade areas

If the members of a multi-lateral free trade agreement are all in the same geographical area then it is sometimes described as a free trade area.

e.g. The ASEAN Free Trade Area (AFTA) is an agreement by the Association of Southeast Asian Nations (Brunei, Indonesia, Malaysia, Philippines, Singapore, Thailand, Vietnam, Laos, Myanmar and Cambodia).

Customs unions

A customs union is a free trade area with a common external tariff. The participant countries set up common external trade policy, but in some cases they use different import quotas.

e.g. Mercosur is a customs union between Brazil, Argentina, Uruguay and Paraguay in South America (Venezuela is currently suspended).

Single markets (economic communities)

A single market is a customs union with common policies on product regulation, and freedom of movement of all the four factors of production (goods, services, capital and labour).

e.g. The Economic Community of West African States (ECOWAS).

Economic unions

An economic and monetary union is a single market with a common currency.

e.g. The largest economic and monetary union at present is the Eurozone. The Eurozone consists of the European Union member states that have adopted the Euro.

The World Trade Organisation (WTO)

The World Trade Organisation (WTO) was set up to continue to implement the General Agreement on Tariffs and Trade (GATT), and its main aims are to reduce the barriers to international trade. It does this by seeking to prevent protectionist measures such as tariffs, quotas and other import restrictions. It also acts as a forum for negotiation and offering settlement processes to resolve disputes between countries.

The WTO encourages free trade by applying the most favoured nation principle between its members, where reduction in tariffs offered to one country by another should be offered to all members.

Whereas the WTO has had notable success, some protectionist measures between groups of countries are nevertheless allowed and some protectionist measures, especially non-tariff based ones, have been harder to identify and control.

Advantages of reducing protectionist measures

A country (say X) can benefit from reducing protectionist measures because its actions would make other nations reduce their protectionist measures against it.

Normally countries retaliate against each other when they impose protectionist measures. A reduction in these may allow X to benefit from increased trade and economic growth. Such a policy may also allow X to specialise and gain competitive advantage in certain products and services, and compete more effectively globally. Its actions may also gain political capital and more influence worldwide.

Disadvantages of reducing protectionist measures

Possible drawbacks of reducing protectionist policies mainly revolve around the need to protect certain industries.

It may be that these industries are developing and in time would be competitive on a global scale. However, inaction to protect them now would damage their development irreparably. Protection could also be given to old, declining industries, which, if not protected, would fail too quickly due to international competition, and would create large scale unemployment making such inaction politically unacceptable.

Certain protectionist policies are designed to prevent 'dumping' of goods at a very cheap price, which hurt local producers.

International Financial Institutions

International Monetary Fund (IMF)

The IMF was founded in 1944 at an international conference at Bretton Woods in the USA but did not really begin to fully function until the 1950s. The so called Bretton Woods System that the IMF was to supervise was to have two main characteristics: stable exchange rates and a multilateral system of international payments and credit.

IMF objectives and functions:

- Promoting international financial cooperation and establishing a system of stable exchange rates and freely convertible currencies.

- Providing a source of credit for members with balance of payments deficits while corrective policies were adopted.

- Managing the growth of international liquidity.

The Bank for International Settlements

The Bank for International Settlements (BIS) is an intergovernmental organisation (IGO) whose membership consists of central banks and national monetary authorities.

Objectives:

- to foster international monetary and financial stability, and

- to foster financial cooperation, and

- to serve as a bank for central banks.

World Bank

The International Bank for Reconstruction and Development (IBRD), also known as the World Bank, was the second institution created at the Bretton Woods meeting in 1944. Its membership and decision making processes are similar to those of the IMF. The original purpose of the IBRD was to help finance the reconstruction of economies damaged by the war. However, it soon shifted the focus of its lending to countries of the developing world. The bank now comprises three principal constituent elements:

- The IBRD proper whose function is to lend long-term funds for capital projects in developing economies at a commercial rate of interest. The main source of these funds is borrowing by the IBRD itself.

- The International Development Association (IDA) which was established in 1960 to provide 'soft' loans to the poorest of the developing countries. The IDA:

   (a) is mainly financed by 20 donor countries providing funds every three years; funding therefore depends on the generosity or otherwise of these countries

   (b) provides loans on concessionary terms, normally interest free loans repayable over 50 years.

- The International Finance Corporation which promotes the private sector in developing countries by lending or by taking equity.

The World Bank is clearly an important source of capital funds for the developing countries. However, it has been criticised in recent years over the nature of its lending conditions. For example criticisms have been levelled about conditions that tie farmers into growing cash crops (e.g. oil seed rape) in countries that have a historical propensity for famine (e.g. parts of Eastern Africa).

Principal Central Banks

The Fed

The Federal Reserve System, also known as 'The Fed,' is the central bank of the United States.

Functions and objectives:

- In its role as a central bank, the Fed is a bank for other banks and a bank for the federal government.

- It was created to provide the US with a safer, more flexible, and more stable monetary and financial system.

- Over the years, its role in banking and the economy has expanded. The Federal Reserve System is a network of 12 Federal Reserve Banks and a number of branches under the general oversight of the Board of Governors. The Reserve Banks are the operating arms of the central bank.

ECB

The **European Central Bank (ECB)** is one of the world's most important central banks, responsible for monetary policy covering the member countries of the Eurozone.

The ECB was established on June 1, 1998 and its headquarters are located in Frankfurt, Germany.

Objectives of the ECB:

- The primary objective of the ECB, and the wider ESCB, is 'to maintain price stability' within the euro area, i.e. to keep inflation low.

- In addition, and without prejudice to the objective of price stability, the bank has to support the economic policies of the European Union. These are designed to foster a high level of employment and sustainable and non-inflationary economic growth.

Bank of Japan

The Bank of Japan is based in Tokyo.

Objectives and functions:

According to its charter, the missions of the Bank of Japan are

- issuance and management of banknotes

- implementation of monetary policy

- providing settlement services and ensuring the stability of the financial system

- treasury and government securities-related operations

- international activities

- compilation of data, economic analyses and research activities.

The Bank of England

The Bank of England's Monetary Policy Committee sets interest rates in the UK.

Another of the Bank's main roles is to act as 'lender of last resort' to other UK banks.

The role of the international financial markets

The global financial system is the worldwide framework of legal agreements, institutions, and both formal and informal economic entities that together facilitate international flows of financial capital for purposes of investment and trade financing. The system has evolved substantially since its emergence in the late 19th century during the first modern wave of economic globalisation, marked by the establishment of central banks, multilateral treaties, and intergovernmental organizations aimed at improving the transparency, regulation, and effectiveness of international markets.

The world economy became increasingly financially integrated throughout the 1980s and 1990s as nations liberalised capital accounts and deregulated financial sectors.

With greater exposure to volatile capital flows, a series of financial crises in Europe, Asia, and Latin America had contagious effects on other countries. In the 2000s, financial institutions became increasingly large with a more sophisticated range of investment activities.

During 2007 and 2008, the United States experienced a financial crisis characteristic of earlier systemic crises, which quickly propagated among other nations. It became known as the global financial crisis, or 'credit crunch' (see more details below), and is recognized as the catalyst for the worldwide Great Recession. Following revelations of Greece's falsified fiscal data in 2009, financial markets began to adjust to the realisation that Greece was no longer in compliance with the European Economic and Monetary Union. The crisis spread to other European nations experiencing sovereign debt problems and became known as the Eurozone crisis.

A country's decision to operate with an open economy and globalise its financial capital carries monetary implications captured by the balance of payments, which can indicate the degree to which a nation is living within its means and can reveal the composition of a nation's wealth as well as its economic competitiveness. Globalised financial capital also carries exposure to systemic risks unique to international finance, such as political deterioration, regulatory changes, foreign exchange controls, and legal uncertainties for foreign investments and property rights.

Numerous groups and individuals participate in the global financial system. Economic entities such as general consumers and international businesses undertake functions such as consumption, production, and investment. Governments and intergovernmental organisations also participate as economic entities, undertaking roles as investors and as purveyors of international trade, economic development, and crisis management.

Regulatory bodies such as governments and multilateral institutions establish financial regulations and legal procedures, while independent self-regulatory associations attempt to coordinate standard practices and facilitate industry supervision.

Professional associations, policy think tanks, and research institutes undertake an observational role by collecting and analysing data, publishing reports and policy recommendations, and facilitating public discourse on global financial affairs.

The global credit crunch and toxic assets

During the 'Credit Crunch' of 2008, the phrase 'toxic assets' was used by the international media to describe the range of financial products traded by banks and other financial institutions in order to earn income and lay off risk.

To understand the problem of toxic assets it is first necessary to understand how banks have traditionally moved to lay off risk through a process of securitisation using 'Collateralised Debt Obligations' (CDOs).

Securitisation through CDOs

When banks lend money to borrowers (for mortgages, car loans etc), they invariably try to lay off their risk by a process of securitisation. This involves selling the asset from the bank's statement of financial position to a company called a 'Special Purpose Vehicle' (SPV). This sale generates cash for the bank in the short term which can then be lent again, in an expanding cycle of credit formation.

CDOs are 'packages' of many securitised loans which are put together by an SPV and sold to investors. The investors decide what level of risk they are prepared to tolerate and invest in an appropriate grade of CDO accordingly. The CDOs are then traded between investors (usually banks).

The Credit Crunch

During the late 2000s, it became apparent that the banks had pursued borrowers so aggressively that many of the loans sold to SPVs in the securitisation process were likely not to be repaid (so called 'sub-prime' loans). This in turn meant that it had become very difficult to trace which CDOs represented loans which were sound, and which were likely to be defaulted. Even some CDOs which were sold as AAA grade investments were found to be unexpectedly risky.

Consequently, suspicion grew in the financial markets that some banks' statements of financial position were carrying large amounts of CDOs which were not worth what they appeared to be.

This meant that inter-bank lending reduced dramatically, as banks viewed each other with suspicion.

These CDOs are known as toxic assets.

The main problem is the uncertainty about which loans (and CDOs) are sound and which aren't. In practice, until time passes and some of the loans are repaid, it will be impossible to tell which banks' statements of financial position are most badly affected.

The impact on business in general

As a consequence of the credit crunch, the banks have been more reluctant to lend and have set more stringent lending criteria. This has meant that many businesses have struggled to refinance their debts.

Various financial stimulus packages introduced by governments in 2009 – 2011 helped to encourage banks to lend, and therefore enabled businesses to source finance to fund growth.

Numerical example of securitisation (and tranching)

Smithson Bank has made a number of loans to customers with a current value of $500 million. The loans have an average term to maturity of four years. The loans generate a steady income to the bank of 9% per year. The company will use 95% of the loan pool as collateral for a collateralised loan obligation structured as follows:

- 70% of the collateral value to support a tranche of A-rated fixed rate loan notes offering investors 7% per year.

- 20% of the collateral value to support a tranche of B-rated fixed rate loan notes offering investors 10% per year.

- 10% of the collateral value to support a tranche of subordinated certificates (unrated).

Required:

Calculate the maximum rate of interest that Smithson Bank can afford to pay to investors in the subordinated certificates.

Solution

In order to estimate the returns an annual cash account should be created showing the cash flow receivable from the pool of assets and the cash payments against the various liabilities created by the securitisation process.

Receipts	$m	Payments	$m
$500m × 9%	45	To A class $332.5m (W1) × 7%	(23.275)
		To B class $95m (W2) × 10%	(9.500)
	45		(32.775)
		Excess (45 – 32.775) could be paid to investors in the subordinated certificates	12.225

The payment of $12.225m to the subordinated loan holders would represent an effective return of

$12.225m/($500m × 95% × 10%) = 25.7%

This is therefore the maximum rate that the bank can afford to pay.

(W1) A class total $500m × 95% × 70% = $332.5m

(W2) B class $500m × 95% × 20% = $95m

Student Accountant article

The article 'Securitisation and tranching' in the Technical Articles section of the ACCA website provides further details on this topic.

The Eurozone debt crisis

The global financial crisis which started in 2007-2008 caused problems with the liquidity of banks and, as a result, lending and economic growth faltered. However, many of the loans made to both governments and private organisations had assumed certain levels of growth and when these failed to materialise, problems arose with repaying and servicing the debts.

In particular, several countries within the Eurozone (notably Ireland, Portugal and Greece) had to be bailed out by the other members of the European Union.

As the crisis developed, the loss of confidence in the countries affected led to rises in the bond yields required on their government debt.

Given the amount of debt their governments had, bond yields quickly achieved levels at which the governments could no longer afford to service their debt.

This loss of confidence was fuelled by downgrades from the credit rating agencies, media speculation and speculators betting against the Euro and/or certain countries.

Free movement of capital and money laundering

The removal of barriers to the free movement of capital

The free movement of goods, services and capital across national barriers has long been considered a key factor in establishing stable and independent world economies.

However, removing barriers to the free movement of capital also increases the opportunities for international money laundering and terrorist financing.

Money laundering is a process in which assets obtained or generated by criminal activity are moved or concealed to obscure their link with the crime.

The international fight against money laundering and terrorist financing

Ever since the second world war, organisations such as the international monetary fund (IMF) have been working to establish a multilateral framework for trade and finance.

However, terrorist activities are sometimes funded from the proceeds of illegal activities, and perpetrators must find ways to launder the funds in order to use them without drawing the attention of authorities.

The international community has made the fight against money laundering and terrorist financing a priority. Among the goals of this effort are:

- protecting the integrity of the international financial system
- cutting off the resources available to terrorists
- making it harder for criminals to profit from their crimes.

The IMF is especially concerned about the possible consequences of money laundering on its members' economies, which could include risks to the soundness and stability of financial institutions and financial systems and increased volatility of international capital flows.

Outcomes of the fight against money laundering and terrorist financing

One of the results of this activity is to create a wide definition of the offence of money laundering to include:

- possessing, dealing with, or concealing the proceeds of a crime
- attempting or conspiring to commit such an offence
- failing to inform the national financial intelligence unit (FIU) of knowledge or suspicion of such an offence.

Furthermore, the international efforts to combat money laundering and terrorist financing have resulted in:

- the establishment of an international task force on money laundering (the international Financial Action Task Force on money laundering (FATF))
- the issue of specific recommendations to be adopted by nation states
- the enactment of legislation by many countries on matters covering:
  - the criminal justice system and law enforcement
  - the financial system and its regulation
  - international co-operation.

The implications for the financial manager

The regulatory framework recommended by the FATF and implemented in countries throughout the world, places significant responsibilities on accountants and other professional advisors.

The rules are designed to ensure:

- all customers are properly identified as legitimate and no anonymous accounts are permitted
- any suspect financial activities are immediately reported to the appropriate authorities
- records of all due diligence investigations and financial transactions are kept for the proscribed number of years
- adequate and appropriate policies and procedures are established to forestall and prevent operations related to money laundering or terrorist financing including staff training
- sanctions for non-compliance are in place.

The laws implemented by most countries have had a significant impact on professional accountants who are obliged to:

- undertake customer due diligence (CDD) procedures before acting for a client

- keep records of transactions undertaken and of the verification procedures carried out on clients

- report suspicions to the relevant financial intelligence unit (FIU) e.g. the Serious Organised Crime Agency (SOCA) in the UK.

Professional accountants are not in breach of their professional duty of confidence if, in good faith, they report any knowledge or suspicions of money laundering to the appropriate authorities.

Penalties for non-compliance can be imposed by the regulator (such as the financial services authority in the UK) on any firm or individual. In addition, the ACCA may take its own disciplinary action against its members. It is therefore essential for all accountants to:

- monitor developments in legislation

- stay abreast of the requirements

- implement all recommended protocols.

Strategic issues for MNCs

National governance requirements

Different countries have different governance requirements. These national governance requirements will impact on the behaviour of multinational organisations.

Individual countries have imposed their own restrictions from time to time by, for example, reserving certain shareholdings for their own nationals or by limiting the transference of profits or royalties. But even governments have to tread carefully lest the subject of their attentions abandons the market altogether.

The mobility of capital

One of the drivers of globalisation has been the increased level of mobility of capital across borders.

Implications of an increased mobility of capital:

- Lower costs of capital.

- Ability of MNCs to switch activities between countries.

- Ability of MNCs to circumnavigate national restrictions.

- Potentially increased exposure to foreign currency risk.

'Local risk'

Local risk for multinationals includes the following:

- Economic risk is the possibility of loss arising to a firm from changes in the economy of a country.

- Political risk is the possibility of loss arising to a firm from actions taken by the government or people of a country.

Examples of political risk:

Confiscation political risk

This is the risk of loss of control over the foreign entity through intervention of the local government or other force.

For example:

- Countries vulnerable to changes of regime

- Invasion by powerful neighbours

- Transition to local ownership

- Confiscation is a very real possibility.

Commercial political risk

Example: The Portuguese revolution of 1974 was followed by several years of left-wing military rule in which wages were compulsorily raised and prices controlled at unrealistic falling real levels. Subsidiaries of foreign parents found their margins squeezed and little sympathy from the authorities. Those that which happened to be suppliers to the government were hit hardest and also had to face serious attempts by the unions to take control of the management. Many such subsidiaries were either abandoned by their shareholders or sold at knockdown prices to local interests. It was interference with the commercial processes of supply and demand that drove their parents out, not confiscation. What drove their parents out was not confiscation but interference with the commercial processes of supply and demand.

Financial political risk

This risk takes many forms:

- Restricted access to local borrowings.

- Restrictions on repatriating capital, dividends or other remittances. These can take the form of prohibition or penal taxation.

- Financial penalties on imports from the rest of the group such as heavy interest-free import deposits.

Exchange control risk

One form of exchange control risk is that the group may accumulate surplus cash in the country where the subsidiary operates, either as profits or as amounts owed for imports to the subsidiary, which cannot be remitted out of the country. This can be mitigated by using FOREX hedging.

A good example is the French regulation under which intra-group trade debts of a French subsidiary to its associated companies, if not made within 12 months of import, become unremittable as 'capital invested in the subsidiary'. Often the French subsidiary delays payment by more than 12 months because of a shortage of cash created by other French official actions or policies.

Control and agency issues

Within the hierarchy of firms (in a group) goal incongruence may arise when divisional managers in overseas operations promote their own self-interest over those of other divisions and of the organisation generally.

In order to motivate local management and to obtain the benefit of their local knowledge, decision making powers should be delegated to them. However, given the wide geographical spread of divisions, it is difficult for group management to control the behaviour of the local managers.

This gives rise to agency costs, and a difficult balance between local autonomy and effective central control.

Agency issues have already been discussed in terms of the relationship between shareholders and managers of a business.

In any large business there will also be agency relationships between the Board of Directors and the managers of individual business units. The managers of individual business units may well have goals which are not congruent with the main company Board, or the managers of the other business units. For example, the manager of a particular business unit will often make decisions which are in the best interests of that division, without considering how the decision impacts the other business units or the company as a whole.

In a multinational company, these agency relationships may be more problematic, because of the different cultures, languages and time zones which may hamper communication between the parties.

In order to minimise the agency problems which might arise in a multinational company, it is important that the company implements suitable corporate governance procedures, and attempts to align the goals of all the managers by using appropriate managerial compensation packages.

3 Investment appraisal for international projects

NPV analysis

The appraisal of projects involving international investments uses the same NPV model we have used in the last chapter. It includes basics such as:

- identifying relevant cash flows

- calculating a project's corporation tax liability, including the calculation of tax relief on capital expenditure

- dealing with inflation and distinguishing money and real flows.

However, international investment appraisal includes additional challenges:

- Forecasting future exchange rates.

- Double taxation.

- Inter-company flows (e.g. management charges or royalties).

- Remittance restrictions.

Impact of a project on the firm's risk exposure

When a firm starts trading in a different country, it is exposed to three types of risk: transaction, economic and translation risk. These terms are defined in detail in Chapter 10: Hedging foreign exchange risk.

Undertaking a new, foreign currency, project affects the firm's exposure to these risks as follows:

Transaction risk

Individual receipts and payments which arise during the new project's life will be subject to transaction risk, in that the value of the transactions will initially be calculated using the forecast rate of exchange which may differ from the actual rate on the transaction date. Firms can use hedging methods (see Chapter 10) to eliminate this transaction risk.

Economic risk

The project NPV is initially calculated using forecast exchange rates. A change in these forecasts over the life of the project will increase or decrease the project NPV, and hence the gain to shareholders.

Translation risk

Undertaking a foreign project often involves setting up a foreign based subsidiary, whose financial statements will have to be translated back into the home currency for the purposes of group accounting (consolidation). A change in exchange rates from one year to the next will cause the value of the subsidiary to fluctuate when its results are translated.

4   Forecasting foreign exchange rates

The relationship between interest, inflation, spot and forward rates

The overall relationship between spot rates, interest rates, inflation rates and the forward and expected future spot rates was covered in Financial Management (FM).

A feature of exam questions covering international investment decisions is often the need to calculate the relevant exchange rates over a number of years, and a summary of the key relationships is therefore given in the four-way equivalence table follows.

Note:

F_0 = forward rate

S_0 = spot rate

S_1 = expected future spot rate

i_b = interest rate for base currency

i_c = interest rate for counter currency

h_b = inflation rate for base currency

h_c = inflation rate for counter currency

DIFFERENCE IN INTEREST RATES $$\frac{(1+i_c)}{(1+i_b)}$$	EQUAL International Fisher Effect	EXPECTED DIFFERENCE IN INFLATION RATES $$\frac{(1+h_c)}{(1+h_b)}$$
EQUAL Interest rate parity theory		**EQUAL** Purchasing power parity theory
DIFFERENCE BETWEEN FORWARD AND SPOT RATES $$\frac{F_0}{S_0}$$	EQUAL Expectations theory	EXPECTED CHANGE IN SPOT RATES $$\frac{S_1}{S_0}$$

Illustration of parity calculations

The current exchange rate is given as ($... to £1) 1.7025 – 1.7075.

Expected inflation rates are:

Year	USA	UK
1	5%	2%
2	3%	4%
3	4%	4%

Use the relationships above to work out the expected spot rate for the next three years.

Solution

Using the PPPT formula:

$$S_1 = S_0 \times \frac{(1 + h_c)}{(1 + h_b)}$$

$$S_1 = S_0 \times \frac{(1 + \text{USA inflation})}{(1 + \text{UK inflation})}$$

and the midpoint of the quoted spread as the exchange rate today:

$$\left(\frac{1.7075 + 1.7025}{2}\right) = 1.7050$$

The calculations for the next three years are:

Year 1 $1.7050 \times \left(\frac{1.05}{1.02}\right) = 1.7551$

Year 2 $1.7551 \times \left(\frac{1.03}{1.04}\right) = 1.7382$

Year 3 $1.7382 \times \left(\frac{1.04}{1.04}\right) = 1.7382$

Note that the exchange rate at the end of one year becomes the basis of the next year's calculation.

Test your understanding 1

The spot exchange rate is €1.5325 to £1.

Expected inflation rates are:

Year	Europe	UK
1	3%	1%
2	1%	4%
3	2%	3%

Required:

Use the relationships above to work out the expected spot rate for the next three years.

Cross rate calculation

Cross rates

You may not be given the exchange rate you need for a particular currency, but instead be given the relationship it has with a different currency. You will then need to calculate a **cross rate**.

For example, if you have a rate in $/£ and a rate in €/£, you can derive a cross rate for $/€ by dividing the $/£ rate by the €/£ rate.

Cross rates example

A UK company has a Greek subsidiary which is to purchase materials costing $100,000. The NPV of the overseas cash flows is being calculated in euros, but you have not been provided with the euro/dollar exchange rate. Instead you have the following information:

$/£1   1.90

€/£1   1.45

Required:

Calculate the value of the purchase in euros.

Solution

The solution could be calculated in two stages:

1   Convert the purchase into £:

      $100,000/1.90 = £52,632

2   Convert the £ value into euros

      £52,632 × 1.45 = €76,316

However an easier alternative, particularly if there are a number of transactions to convert, is to calculate a cross rate:

The $/€ rate will be 1.90/1.45 = 1.3103

The value of the transaction is therefore:

$100,000/1.3103 = €76,318

Changing inflation rates

When finding exchange rates it might first be necessary to calculate the inflation rates expected in a foreign country.

Illustration 2

Inflation is currently 80% in Brazil, although the government hopes to reduce it each year by 25% of the previous year's rate.

What will the inflation rate be in Brazil over the next four years?

Solution

Year 1	80% × 0.75	= 60%
Year 2	60% × 0.75	= 45%
Year 3	45% × 0.75	= 34%
Year 4	34% × 0.75	= 26%
OR	80% × $(0.75)^4$	= 25.3% (more accurate)

You should also comment in your answer that it is unlikely the government will achieve this reduction each year.

Test your understanding 2

The current rate of inflation in Costovia is 65%. Government action is helping to reduce this rate each year by 10% of the previous rate. The Costovian peso/ US dollar exchange rate is currently 144 pesos to 1 US dollar, and the inflation rate in the US over the next three years is expected to be 4%, 3.5% and 3% respectively.

Required:

Calculate the exchange rate for the Costovian peso against the US dollar for the next three years.

5 The impact of taxation, intercompany cash flows and remittance restrictions

Taxation

The level of taxation on a project's profits will depend on the relationship between the tax rates in the home and foreign country.

There are three possible tax scenarios for an exam question.

The home country may have a tax rate that is:

- lower than
- the same as
- higher than the foreign country.

The question will always assume a double-tax treaty => project always taxed at the **higher** rate.

Illustration 3

What will be the rate of tax on a project carried out in the US by a UK company in each of the following scenarios?

	UK tax		US tax
(a)	33%	<	40%
(b)	33%	=	33%
(c)	33%	>	25%

Solution

- Scenario (a) – no further UK tax to pay on the project's $ profits. Profits taxed at 40% in the US.

- Scenario (b) – no further UK tax to pay on the project's $ profits. Profits taxed at 33% in the US.

- Scenario (c) – project's profits would be taxed at 33% : 25% in the US and a further 8% tax payable in the UK.

Inter-company cash flows

Inter-company cash flows, such as transfer prices, royalties and management charges, can also affect the tax computations.

 Although complex in reality, in the exam:

- Assume inter-company cash flows are allowable for tax (and state it) unless the question says otherwise.

- If an inter-company cash flow is allowable for tax relief overseas, there will be a corresponding tax liability on the income in the home country.

- Assume that the tax authorities will only allow 'arm's length'/open-market prices for tax relief and will not allow an artificially high or low transfer price.

 Transfer pricing

The transfer price is the price charged by one part of a company when supplying goods or services to another part of the company, e.g. overseas subsidiary.

Transfer prices are particularly problematical. By manipulating the transfer prices charged it may be possible to minimise the global taxation cost for the group, i.e. to report low profits in countries with high taxes and high profits in countries with low rates.

For instance, suppose we have two companies within a group that are based in different countries.

Company A sells components to Company B, whilst B sells marketing services to Company A.

- Company A will report low income therefore limiting its tax charge.

  Company B will be reporting high income as it pays less tax.

By manipulating the transfer price the overall tax charge can be lowered. However, the government of country A will not look favourably on this action.

This objective is therefore frustrated in many countries, as the relevant tax authorities require the transfer price to be set on an arm's length basis, i.e. the market price.

If a question tells you that a company is going to considerably increase its transfer price, you could incorporate the new price in your NPV calculations. However it is essential that you then state in your report that the policy may be unsuccessful, as most governments require the transfer price to be set on an arm's length basis, i.e. the market price.

Therefore it is preferable, for exam purposes, to assume that the tax authorities will only allow 'arm's length'/open-market prices for tax relief and will not allow an artificially high or low transfer price.

A second problem may also arise. Although the above may decrease the taxation, the profits will end up in country B. If the currency of country B is weak relative to the holding company, then loss from the depreciation of the currency may be more than the tax saving.

The issues of double taxation and the tax treatment of inter-company flows can be shown with an example:

Illustration 4

A project carried out by a US subsidiary of a UK company is due to earn revenues of $100m in the US in Year 2 with associated costs of $30m. Royalty payments of $10m will be made by the US subsidiary to the UK. Assume tax is paid at 25% in the US and 33% in the UK; and assume a forecast $/£ spot rate of $1.50/£1.

Required:

Forecast the project's cash flows in Year 2.

Solution

Year 2	$m	
Revenues	100	
Costs	(30)	
Royalties	(10)	
	─────	
Pre-tax profit	60	
25% US tax	(15)	$10m
	─────	÷1.50
Remit to parent	45	= £6.7m
@ $/£ Spot	÷1.50	
	─────	
£ Cash flow	30	
Royalties	6.7	
UK tax	(5.4)*	
	─────	
After tax cash flow	£31.3m	
	─────	

UK tax computation

UK tax on $ profits = 33% − 25% = 8%

8% UK tax on $ profits	$60m ÷ 1.50	= £40m
	£40m × 0.08	= £3.2m
33% UK tax on royalties:	£6.7m × 0.33	= £2.2m
UK tax payable		= £5.4m*

Remittance restrictions

Remittance restrictions occur where a foreign government places a limit on the foreign profits that can be repatriated back to the parent company. This restriction may change the extra tax payable by the parent company.

Illustration 5

A UK company is appraising a new US project.

The forecast pre-tax US profit is as follows ($m):

Year	0	1	2	3
		3	4	6

In any one year, only 50% of profits generated can be remitted back to the parent. The blocked profits can be released back to the parent in the year after the end of the project.

The US tax rate is 15% and the UK tax rate is 25%. Assume that the exchange rate will be £1 = $1.30 for the foreseeable future.

Required:

Calculate the additional UK tax payable each year.

Solution

Profits remitted to parent:

Year	1	2	3	4
US$ profit before tax	3	4	6	
US tax (15%)	(0.450)	(0.600)	(0.900)	
US$ profit after tax	2.550	3.400	5.100	
Blocked funds (50%)	(1.275)	(1.700)	(2.550)	
Remitted to parent ($m)	**1.275**	**1.700**	**2.550**	**5.525**
Amount remitted (£m)	0.981	1.308	1.962	4.250
Extra tax payable	(0.115)	(0.154)	(0.231)	(0.500)
(10%×50%×US$ PBT/1.30)				

Exchange controls and how to deal with them

Exchange controls

Foreign exchange controls are various forms of controls imposed by governments on the purchase/sale of foreign currencies by residents or on the purchase/sale of local currency by non-residents. Common foreign exchange controls include:

- Banning the use of foreign currency within the country.

- Banning locals from possessing foreign currency.

- Restricting currency exchange to government-approved exchangers.

- Fixed exchange rates.

- Restrictions on the amount of currency that may be imported or exported.

Countries with foreign exchange controls are also known as 'Article 14 countries' after the provision in the International Monetary Fund agreement allowing exchange controls for transitional economies. Such controls used to be common in most countries, particularly poorer ones, until the 1990s when free trade and globalisation started a trend towards economic liberalisation. Today, countries that still impose exchange controls are the exception rather than the rule.

Strategies to deal with exchange controls

Multinational companies have several options if they want to get round the problem posed by exchange controls, such as:

- management charges – levied by the parent company for costs incurred in the management of the foreign operations.

- transfer pricing – on goods/services supplied by one member of a group to another.

- royalty payments – imposed when the foreign subsidiary is granted the right to make certain patented goods.

- loans – if the parent lends money to the foreign subsidiary, the interest rate can be set at a level to ensure that the required amount of money is transferred to the parent from the subsidiary.

Working capital

It is normally assumed that the working capital requirement for the foreign project will increase by the annual rate of inflation in that country.

Working capital calculation

Four million pesos in working capital are required immediately for a project running in South America. The inflation rates for the next six years in the South American country are expected to be:

Year	1	2	3	4	5	6
	6%	4%	5%	4%	3%	4%

Required:

Identify the working capital flows for the NPV calculation:

Solution

All cash flows in $000s

Year	0	1	2	3	4	5	6	7
Working capital	4,000							
Inflation	1	1.06	1.04	1.05	1.04	1.03	1.04	
Total w/c	4,000	4,240	4,410	4,631	4,816	4,960	5,158	
W/c injection	(4,000)	(240)	(170)	(221)	(185)	(144)	(198)	5,158

Working capital released

Test your understanding 3

Four million pesos are required in working capital immediately. The inflation rate in the South American country is expected to remain constant for the next six years at a rate of 6%.

Required:

Identify the working capital flows for the NPV calculation, assuming the working capital is released at t = 7.

6   NPV analysis for foreign projects

There are two methods for calculating the NPV of foreign projects:

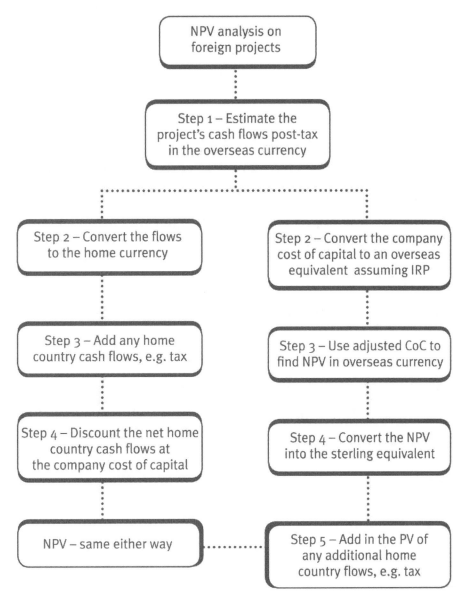

The simpler 4-step method is the more conventional one which is used in the majority of cases.

Test your understanding 4 – Standard method for foreign NPV

A manufacturing company based in the United Kingdom is evaluating an investment project overseas – in REBMATT a politically stable country. It will cost an initial 5.0 million REBMATT dollars (RM$) and it is expected to earn post-tax cash flows as follows:

Year	1	2	3	4
Cash flow RM$'000	1,500	1,900	2,500	2,700

The following information is available:

- Real interest rates in the two countries are the same. They are expected to remain the same for the period of the project.

- The current spot rate is RM$ 2 per £1.

- The risk-free rate of interest in REBMATT is 7% and in the UK 9%.

- The company requires a UK return from this project of 16%.

Required:

Calculate the £ net present value of the project using the standard method i.e. by discounting annual cash flows in £.

The alternative method for foreign NPV

In the previous Test your understanding, the NPV could have been calculated by discounting cash flows in REBMATT $ as follows:

Calculate the adjusted discount rate using the interest rate parity formula:

$$\frac{1 + i_{1st}}{1 + i_{2nd}} = \frac{spot}{forward\ spot} = \frac{spot}{expected\ future\ spot}$$

$$\frac{1 + 0.16}{1 + i_\$} = \frac{2.000}{1.9633}$$

$$1 + i_\$ = \frac{(1 + 0.16) \times 1.9633}{2.000}$$

$$i_\$ = 13.87\%$$

Year	Cash flow RM $	DF 13.87%	PV(000)
0	(5,000)	1.000	(5,000)
1	1,500	0.878	1,317
2	1,900	0.771	1,465
3	2,500	0.678	1,695
4	2,700	0.594	1,604
			RM $1,081

PV = **1,081/2.000 = £541,000.**

The difference between the two results is due to rounding.

Free cash flows in foreign currency

In an exam question, you may be told specifically what the foreign currency free cash flows are for a new project. Alternatively, you may be expected to estimate the free cash flows from given accounting information. This is covered in more detail in Chapter 13: Business valuation, but a simple introductory illustration is shown below.

Illustration of how to estimate free cash flow

Wine Co is considering international expansion by taking over House Co, a manufacturing company based in a foreign country (whose currency is the Foreign Dollar, F$).

According to the most recent accounts of House Co, its revenue and EBIT are F$356m and F$70m respectively. Capital expenditure in the most recent year was F$33m and the depreciation charge was F$24m. If Wine Co takes over House Co, it expects growth in revenue and profitability to be 3% per year, and capital expenditure and depreciation to stay constant. The tax rate in the foreign country is 30% per year.

The current exchange rate is F$2 = H$1 (H$ is the home currency, the Home Dollar), and this is expected to stay constant for the foreseeable future.

Required:

Estimate the free cash flow, in H$, for the first year after the takeover.

Solution

	Current F$m	Year 1 F$m
EBIT (3% increase)	70	72.1
Less: Tax (30%)	(21)	(21.6)
Add back depreciation	24	24
Operating cash flow	73	74.5
Less: Capital Expenditure	(33)	(33)
Free cash flow in F$m	40	41.5
Exchange rate (F$ ...=H$1)		2
Free cash flow in H$m		20.75

Standard proforma for the conventional approach

Year	0 FC	1 FC	2 FC	3 FC	4 FC	5 FC
Sales/receipts payments:		X	X	X	X	
Variable costs		(x)	(x)	(x)	(x)	
Wages/materials		(x)	(x)	(x)	(x)	
Incremental fixed costs		(x)	(x)	(x)	(x)	
Untaxed royalties/mgt charges etc		(x)	(x)	(x)	(x)	
Tax allowable depn		(x)	(x)	(x)	(x)	
Taxable profits		X	X	X	X	
Foreign tax @ say 20%		(x)	(x)	(x)	(x)	
Add: Tax allowable depn		X	X	X	X	
Initial outlay	(x)					
Realisable value					X	
Working capital	(x)	(x)	(x)	(x)	(x)	X
Net foreign CF	(x)	X	X	X	X	X

Year	0 FC	1 FC	2 FC	3 FC	4 FC	5 FC
Exchange rate (based on PPPT)	X	X	X	X	X	X
Home currency CF	(x)	X	X	X	X	X
Domestic tax on foreign taxable profits @ 30% – 20% = 10%		(x)	(x)	(x)	(x)	
Untaxed royalties/mgt charges etc		X	X	X	X	
Domestic tax on royalties etc. @ 30%		(x)	(x)	(x)	(x)	
Net home currency CF	(x)	X	X	X	X	X
DF (say 16%)	1	0.862	0.743	0.641	0.552	0.476
Home currency PV	(x)	X	X	X	X	X
Home currency NPV			x/(x)			

Performing the calculation

It will be necessary to do a number of subsidiary workings in order to reach the final NPV figure, so remember the basic rules:

- Lay out your table clearly and remember you will need one column more than the length of the project if tax is lagged by a year.

- Make sure all workings are clearly referenced.

- State any assumptions and be prepared to comment on them further in any written report that follows.

The following is a guideline order of approach for the conventional approach:

1   Calculate all the relevant flows in the foreign currency.

2   If tax is payable on the foreign flows, deduct it.

3   Convert the net flows into the domestic currency – you may well need to predict future exchange rates to do so.

4   Consider whether any restrictions are placed on remittances and whether these will impact the additional tax payable by the parent.

5   Add any other domestic cash flows to the remitted amounts from overseas.

6   Discount the total net cash flows in the domestic currency at an appropriate cost of capital.

Student Accountant articles

Read the pair of articles 'International project appraisal' in the Technical Articles section of the ACCA website to see more worked examples covering this topic.

Test your understanding 5 – Introductory question

Foreign NPV

Parrott Co is a UK based company. It is considering a 3 year project in Farland.

The project will require an initial investment of 81 m Farland Florins (FFI) and will have a residual value of 10m FFI.

The project's pre-tax net FFI inflows are expected to be:

Year 1   35m

Year 2   80m

Year 3   50m

The UK parent company will charge the overseas project with £2m of management charges each year.

The current spot rate is 5FFI – £1. UK inflation is expected to be 4% per year, and Farland inflation is expected to be 7% per year.

Farland tax is 20% and is paid immediately. Any losses are carried forward and netted off the first available profits for tax purposes. Tax allowable depreciation will be granted on a straight line basis, and any residual value will be taxable at 20%. UK tax is 30% and is payable 1 year in arrears.

Parrott Co recently undertook a similar risk project in the UK and used 11% as a suitable discount rate.

Required:

Calculate the NPV of the project in £.

Test your understanding 6 – Exam standard question

Foreign NPV

Puxty plc is a specialist manufacturer of window frames. Its main UK manufacturing operation is based in the south of England, from where it distributes its products throughout the UK.

The directors are now considering whether they should open up an additional manufacturing operation in France – which they believe there will be a good market for their products.

A suitable factory has been located just outside Paris that could be rented on a 5-year lease at an annual charge of €3.8m, payable each year in advance. The manufacturing equipment would cost €75m, of which €60m would have to be paid at the start of the project, with the balance payable 12 months later.

At the start of each year the French factory would require working capital equal to 40% of that year's sales revenues. It is expected that the factory will be able to produce and sell 80,000 window units per year although, in the first year, because of the need to 'run in' the machinery and its new workforce, output is only expected to be 50,000 window units. Each window is likely to be sold for €750, a price that represents a 150% mark-up on cash production costs.

The French factory would be set up as a wholly-owned subsidiary of Puxty plc. In France, 25% straight-line depreciation on cost is an allowable expense against company tax. Corporation tax is payable at 40% at each year-end without delay and any unused losses can be brought forward for set off against the following year's profits. No UK tax would be payable on the after-tax French profits.

All amounts in € are given in current terms. Annual inflation in France is expected to run at 6% per year in the foreseeable future. All € cash flows involved are expected to increase in line with this inflation rate, with the exception of the factory rental and the cost of the manufacturing equipment, both of which would remain unchanged.

The French factory would be producing windows to a special design patented by Puxty. To protect its patent rights, Puxty plc will charge its French subsidiary a fixed royalty of £20 per window. This cost would be allowable against the subsidiary's French tax liability.

The current €.../£1 spot rate is 1.5. Inflation in the UK is expected to be 4% per year over the period. There are no remittance restrictions between France and the UK.

Puxty plc is an all-equity financed company that is quoted on the London Stock Exchange. Its shares have a beta value of 1.25. The current annual return on UK Government Treasury Bills is 10% and the expected return on the market is 18%. In the UK Corporation Tax is payable at 35%, one year in arrears.

Puxty operates on a 5-year planning horizon. At the end of five years, assume that working capital would be fully recovered and the production equipment would have a scrap value, at that time, of €70m before tax. Proceeds on asset sales are taxed at 40%. Assume all cash flows arise at the end of the year to which they relate, unless otherwise stated.

Required:

Evaluate the proposed investment in France and recommend what investment decision should be made by Puxty plc. State clearly any assumptions you make and work all calculations rounded to nearest 10,000 (either € or £) – i.e. €0.01 m or £0.01m.

Note that in the CBE you can use the NPV spreadsheet function to save time here.

7 Chapter summary

This chapter has looked at the additional considerations when appraising an international investment.

As discussed earlier in the Text, the investment decision cannot be made without also considering the impact on financing and dividends.

These issues are covered in the next two chapters.

Test your understanding answers

Test your understanding 1

Using the formula:

$$\text{Future Spot} = \text{Spot} \times \frac{(1 + h_c)}{(1 + h_b)}$$

the calculations for the next three years are:

Year 1 $1.5325 \times \left(\frac{1.03}{1.01}\right) = 1.5628$

Year 2 $1.5628 \times \left(\frac{1.01}{1.04}\right) = 1.5177$

Year 3 $1.5177 \times \left(\frac{1.02}{1.03}\right) = 1.5030$

Test your understanding 2

Step 1 – Find the inflation rate in Costovia over the next three years:

Year 1: $65\% \times 0.9 = 58.5\%$

Year 2: $58.5\% \times 0.9 = 52.7\%$

Year 3: $52.7\% \times 0.9 = 47.4\%$

Step 2 – Find the exchange rates:

Using the formula:

$$\text{Future Spot} = \text{Spot} \times \frac{(1 + h_c)}{(1 + h_b)}$$

The calculations for the next three years are:

Year 1: $144 \times (1.585/1.04) = 220$

Year 2: $220 \times (1.527/1.035) = 325$

Year 3: $325 \times (1.474/1.03) = 465$

Test your understanding 3

Year	0	1	2	3	4	5	6	7
Working capital	4,000							
Inflation	1.00	1.06	1.06	1.06	1.06	1.06	1.06	
Total money	4,000	4,240	4,494	4,764	5,050	5,353	5,674	
Movement	(4,000)	(240)	(254)	(270)	(286)	(303)	(321)	5,674

Working capital released

Test your understanding 4 – Standard method for foreign NPV

Calculation of exchange rates

Using the interest rate parity theory:

Year 1 $2.00 \times 1.07/1.09 = 1.9633$

Year 2 $1.9633 \times 1.07/1.09 = 1.9273$

Year 3 $1.9273 \times 1.07/1.09 = 1.8919$

Year 4 $1.8919 \times 1.07/1.09 = 1.8572$

Year	0	1	2	3	4
Cash flow (RM$000)	(5,000)	1,500	1,900	2,500	2,700
Exchange rate	2.000	1.9633	1.9273	1.8919	1.8572
Cash flow £	(2,500)	764	986	1,321	1,454
PV factor 16%	1.000	0.862	0.743	0.641	0.552
PV	(2,500)	659	733	847	803

NPV = £542,000

Test your understanding 5 – Introductory question

FFI(millions)	T₀	T₁	T₂	T₃	T₄
Net inflow		35	80	50	
Mgt charge (W2)		(10.3)	(10.6)	(10.9)	
Tax allowable depn		(27)	(27)	(27)	
		(2.3)	42.4	12.1	
Tax (20%) (W3)		–	(8.0)	(2.4)	
Tax allowable depn		27	27	27	
Capital expenditure	(81)				
Residual value				10	
Tax on residual value				(2)	
Net FFI cash flow	(81)	24.7	61.4	44.7	
Exchange rate (W1)	5	5.14	5.29	5.45	
Net £ cash flow	(16.2)	4.8	11.6	8.2	
Extra UK tax (W4)				(0.8)	(0.4)
Management charge		2	2	2	
Tax on mgt charge			(0.6)	(0.6)	(0.6)
	(16.2)	6.8	13.0	8.8	(1.0)
DF @ 11%	1	0.901	0.812	0.731	0.659
PV	(16.2)	6.1	10.6	6.4	(0.7)

So, NPV = £6.2m, so accept the project.

Workings:

(W1) Exchange rates

Using Purchasing Power Parity,

future exchange rate = spot × (1.07/1.04)

Year 1 rate = 5 × (1.07/1.04) = 5.14

Year 2 rate = 5.14 × (1.07/1.04) = 5.29

Year 3 rate = 5.29 × (1.07/1.04) = 5.45

(W2) Management charges

Convert into FFI using the exchange rates from (W1) above.

Year 1: £2m × 5.14 = 10.3m FFI

Year 2: £2m × 5.29 = 10.6m FFI

Year 3: £2m × 5.45 = 10.9m FFI

(W3) Farland tax

Tax is 20% in the same year.

However, the loss of 2.3m FFI in year 1 is carried forward and netted off the profit of 42.4m FFI in year 2 to give year 2 tax of 20% × (42.4 – 2.3) = 8.0m FFI

(W4) UK tax

From (W3) above, the taxable profit in year 2 is 42.4 – 2.3 = 40.1m FFI. At the year 2 exchange rate of 5.29 (W1) this amounts to £7.6m.

Hence, the extra UK tax payable is 10% × £7.6m = £0.8m, one year later (in year 3).

The taxable profit in year 3 is 12.1m + 10m (residual value) = 22.1m FFI. At the year 3 exchange rate of 5.45 (W1) this amounts to £4.1m.

Hence the extra UK tax payable is 10% × £4.1m = £0.4m, one year later (in year 4).

Test your understanding 6 – Exam standard question

Cash flow analysis (€m)

	0	1	2	3	4	5	6
Revenues (W1)	–	39.75	67.42	71.46	75.75	80.29	–
Operating costs (W2)	–	(15.90)	(26.97)	(28.58)	(30.30)	(32.12)	–
Rental charges	(3.80)	(3.80)	(3.80)	(3.80)	(3.80)	–	–
Royalties (W3)	–	(1.53)	(2.50)	(2.54)	(2.59)	(2.64)	–
Tax charge (W5)	–	(0.00)	(6.07)	(7.12)	(8.12)	(16.69)	–
Equipment outlay	(60.00)	(15.00)	–	–	–	–	–
Scrap value	–	–	–	–	–	70.00	–
Tax on scrap	–	–	–	–	–	(28.00)	–
Working capital (W6)	(15.90)	(11.07)	(1.61)	(1.72)	(1.82)	32.12	–
Net €m c/f	(79.70)	(7.55)	26.47	27.70	29.12	102.96	–
€/£ (W4)	1.50	1.53	1.56	1.59	1.62	1.65	–
£m c/f	(53.13)	(4.93)	16.97	17.42	17.98	62.40	–
£m royalties (W3)	–	1.00	1.60	1.60	1.60	1.60	–
UK royalty tax 35%	–	–	(0.35)	(0.56)	(0.56)	(0.56)	(0.56)
Net £m c/f	(53.13)	(3.93)	18.22	18.46	19.02	63.06	(0.56)
20% Discount (W7)	1	0.833	0.694	0.579	0.482	0.402	0.335
	(53.13)	(3.27)	12.64	10.69	9.17	25.35	(0.19)

NPV: + £1.26m.

Workings

(W1) €m Sales revenues

$50{,}000 \times 750 \ (1.06) = 39.75$ Year 1

$80{,}000 \times 750 \ (1.06)^2 = 67.42$ Year 2

$80{,}000 \times 750 \ (1.06)^3 = 71.46$ Year 3

$80{,}000 \times 750 \ (1.06)^4 = 75.75$ Year 4

$80{,}000 \times 750 \ (1.06)^5 = 80.29$ Year 5

(W2) €m Production costs

$39.75 \div 2.5 = 15.9$ Year 1

$67.42 \div 2.5 = 26.97$ Year 2

$71.46 \div 2.5 = 28.58$ Year 3

$75.75 \div 2.5 = 30.30$ Year 4

$80.29 \div 2.5 = 32.12$ Year 5

(W3) €m Royalty payments

$50,000 \times £20 = £1$ m $\times 1.53 = €1.53m =$ Year 1
(exchange rate calculations – see (W4)).

$80,000 \times £20 = £1.6m \times 1.56 = €2.50m =$ Year 2

$80,000 \times £20 = £1.6m \times 1.59 = €2.54m =$ Year 3

$80,000 \times £20 = £1.6m \times 1.62 = €2.59m =$ Year 4

$80,000 \times £20 = £1.6m \times 1.65 = €2.64m =$ Year 5

(W4) €/£ Exchange rate

$$S_1 = S_0 \times \frac{(1 + h_c)}{(1 + h_b)}$$

Year 1 = $1.50 \times 1.06/1.04 = 1.53$

Year 2 = $1.53 \times 1.06/1.04 = 1.56$

Year 3 = $1.56 \times 1.06/1.04 = 1.59$

Year 4 = $1.59 \times 1.06/1.04 = 1.62$

Year 5 = $1.62 \times 1.06/1.04 = 1.65$

(W5) Basic €m tax calculations

	Years				
	1	**2**	**3**	**4**	**5**
Revenues	39.75	67.42	71.46	75.75	80.29
Less:					
Operating costs	(15.90)	(26.97)	(28.58)	(30.30)	(32.12)
Depreciation	(18.75)	(18.75)	(18.75)	(18.75)	–
Rental charges	(3.80)	(3.80)	(3.80)	(3.80)	(3.80)
Royalties	(1.53)	(2.50)	(2.54)	(2.59)	(2.64)
Taxable cash flow	(0.23)	15.40	17.79	20.31	41.73
Loss b/f*		(0.23)			
Tax at 40% (no lag)	**0.00**	**6.07**	**7.12**	**8.12**	**16.69**

*No other business in France means no profits available to set off the loss in that year. Instead it is carried forward for set off in the following year.

(W6) €m Working capital requirement

Revenue × 40% Needed – Previous balance = Injection

39.75 × 0.4 = 15.90 – 0 = 15.90 Year 0

67.42 × 0.4 = 26.97 – 15.90 = 11.07 Year 1

71.46 × 0.4 = 28.58 – 26.97 = 1.61 Year 2

75.75 × 0.4 = 30.30 – 28.58 = 1.72 Year 3

80.29 × 0.4 = 32.12 – 30.30 = 1.82 Year 4

Recovery 32.12 Year 5

(W7) £ discount rate

Using the CAPM equation:

$R_j = R_f + \beta(R_m - R_f)$

The discount rate can be found as: 10% + (18% – 10%) × 1.25 = 20%.

Conclusion

As the French manufacturing project generates a positive NPV it should be undertaken, provided the directors are happy with the estimates they have made.

Assumptions

Royalties are allowable against French tax.

Royalties are subject to UK tax.

Further information that might be useful to the analysis would include:

- Details as to how the estimates of the project's cash flows were made.

- Details about where the company derived its estimate of the future French inflation rate and the future rate of depreciation of the euro.

- Details of how the estimate of the machinery's five-year scrap value was made.

- An analysis about whether or not country risk might be a significant factor.

- How sensitive is the NPV calculation to changes in some of the key estimates.

The financing decision

Chapter learning objectives

Study guide section	Study guide outcome	
A2: Financial strategy formulation	(b)	Recommend the optimum capital mix and structure within a specified business context and capital asset structure.
A4: Management of international trade and finance	(f)	Discuss the significance to the organisation, of latest developments in the world financial markets such as the growth and impact of dark pool trading systems.
B3: Impact of financing on investment decisions and adjusted present values	(a)	Identify and assess the appropriateness of the range of sources of finance available to an organisation including equity, debt, hybrids, lease finance, venture capital, business angel finance, private equity, asset securitisation and sale, Islamic finance and initial coin offerings. Including assessment on the financial position, financial risk and the value of an organisation.
	(b)	Discuss the role of, and developments in, Islamic financing as a growing source of finance for organisations; explaining the rationale for its use, and identifying its benefits and deficiencies.

B3: Impact of financing on investment decisions and adjusted present values (continued)	(h) Assess the impact of financing and capital structure upon the organisation with respect to:(i) Modigliani and Miller propositions, before and after tax (ii) Static trade-off theory (iii) Pecking order propositions (iv) Agency effects.
B5: International investment and financing decisions	(e) Assess and advise on the costs and benefits of alternative sources of finance available within the international equity and bond markets.

One of the PER performance objectives (PO10 – Manage and Control Working Capital) is to be able to source finance to improve organisational liquidity.

PER

Working through this chapter should help you understand how to demonstrate that objective.

One of the PER performance objectives (PO09 – Evaluate Investment and Financing Decisions) is to be able to identify and raise an appropriate source of finance for a specific business need.

PER

Working through this chapter should help you understand how to demonstrate that objective.

KAPLAN PUBLISHING

1 Introduction

As discussed at the beginning of Chapter 2: Investment appraisal, the financial manager often has to decide what type of finance to raise in order to fund the investment in a new project i.e. there is a very close link between the investment decision and the financing decision.

This chapter starts by looking at the 'financial system' and then it covers the key practical and theoretical considerations that influence the basic long-term financing decision i.e. should debt or equity finance be used?

Then, the chapter explains the main features of the key debt and equity financing sources, incorporating both domestic and international financing options.

2 The financial system

It is important to understand the financial system before we look at specific financing options:

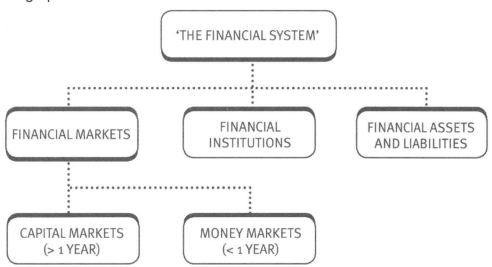

Collectively the financial system does the following:

1   Channels funds from lenders to borrowers.

2   Provides a mechanism for payments – e.g. direct debits, cheque clearing system.

3   Creates liquidity and money – e.g. banks create money through increasing their lending.

4   Provides financial services such as insurance and pensions.

5   Offers facilities to manage investment portfolios – e.g. to hedge risk.

Details of the financial system

The financial system

'The financial system' is an umbrella term covering the following:

- Financial markets – e.g. stock exchanges, money markets.
- Financial institutions – e.g. banks, building societies, insurance companies and pension funds.
- Financial assets and liabilities – e.g. mortgages, bonds, bills and equity shares.

Financial markets

The financial markets can be divided into different types, depending on the products being issued/bought/sold:

- Capital markets which consist of stock-markets for shares and bond markets.
- Money markets, which provide short-term (< 1 year) debt financing and investment.
- Commodity markets, which facilitate the trading of commodities (e.g. oil, metals and agricultural produce).
- Derivatives markets, which provide instruments for the management of financial risk, such as options and futures contracts.
- Insurance markets, which facilitate the redistribution of various risks.
- Foreign exchange markets, which facilitate the trading of foreign exchange.

Within each sector of the economy (households, firms and governmental organisations) there are times when there are cash surpluses and times when there are deficits.

- In the case of surpluses the party concerned will seek to invest/deposit/lend funds to earn an economic return.
- In the case of deficits the party will seek to borrow funds to manage their liquidity position.

In our syllabus, we focus on the long-term financing options. Short-term financing options (e.g. money market instruments) are not normally used to finance long-term capital investment projects such as the ones appraised in the previous chapters.

3 The basic long-term financing decision – Debt or equity

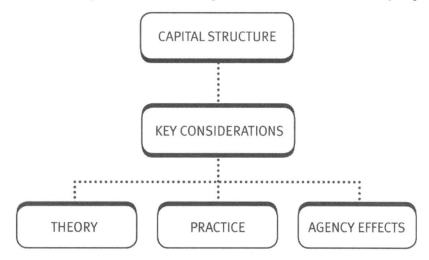

Practical considerations

The following diagram summarises the main practical factors that must be considered when choosing between debt and equity finance.

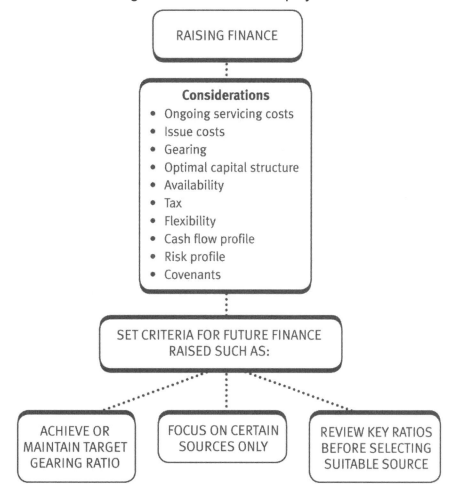

More detail on practical considerations

Ongoing servicing costs

Debt is usually cheaper than equity due to lower risk faced by the providers of finance and the tax relief possible on interest payments. However, some debt, such as an unsecured overdraft, may be more expensive than equity.

Issue costs

The costs of raising debt are usually lower than those for issuing new shares (e.g. prospectus costs, stock exchange fees, stamp duty).

Gearing

Debt and preference shares give rise to fixed payments that must be made before ordinary shareholder dividends can be paid. These methods of finance thus increase shareholder risk.

Optimal capital structure

This was previously covered in Financial Management (FM), and is discussed further below. You will remember that firms have to make a trade-off between the benefits of cheap debt finance on the one hand and the costs associated with high levels of gearing (such as the risk of bankruptcy) on the other. If the correct balance can be achieved, the cost of finance will fall to a minimum point, maximising NPVs and hence the value of the firm.

Availability of sources of finance

Not all firms have the luxury of selecting a capital structure to maximise firm value. More basic concerns, such as persuading the bank to release further funds, or the current shareholders to make a further investment, may override thoughts about capital structure.

Tax position

The tax benefits of debt only remain available whilst the firm is in a tax paying position.

Flexibility

Some firms operating in high risk industries use mainly equity finance to gain the flexibility not to have to pay dividends should returns fall.

Cash flow profile

Cash flow forecasts are central to financing decisions – e.g. ensuring that two sources of finance do not mature at the same time.

Risk profile

Business failure can have a far greater impact on directors than on a well-diversified investor. It may be argued that directors have a natural tendency to be cautious about borrowing.

Covenants

There may be restrictions imposed on the level of gearing, either by the company's Articles of Association (the internal regulations that govern the way the company must be run), or by previous loan agreements.

Theoretical considerations

The main capital structure theories assess the way in which a change in gearing/capital structure impacts on the firm's weighted average cost of capital (WACC).

Note: Although the detailed calculation of WACC is not covered until later in this Text (Chapter 6: The weighted average cost of capital), you will be aware from your previous studies that the WACC is a vitally important concept in financial management. If the financial manager can find a way of reducing the WACC, projects will have higher NPVs and consequently the wealth of the firm's shareholders will be increased.

The theories consider the relative sizes of the following two opposing forces:

First, debt is (usually) cheaper than equity:

- Lower risk.
- Tax relief on interest.

so we might expect that increasing proportion of debt finance would **reduce WACC**.

BUT:

Second, increasing levels of debt makes equity more risky:

- Fixed commitment paid before equity – finance risk.

so increasing gearing (proportion of finance in the form of debt) increases the cost of equity and that would **increase WACC**.

The theories attempt to answer the question:

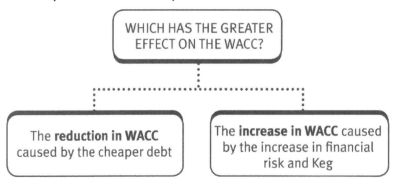

The traditional view

Also known as the intuitive view, the traditional view has no theoretical basis but common sense. It concludes that a firm should have an optimal level of gearing, where WACC is minimised, BUT it does not tell us where that optimal point is. The only way of finding the optimal point is by trial and error.

The traditional view explained

At low levels of gearing:

> Equity holders see risk increases as marginal as gearing rises, so the cheapness of debt issue dominates resulting in a lower WACC.

At higher levels of gearing:

> Equity holders become increasingly concerned with the increased volatility of their returns (debt interest paid first). This dominates the cheapness of the extra debt so the WACC starts to rise as gearing increases.

At very high levels of gearing:

> Serious bankruptcy risk worries equity and debt holders alike so both k_e and k_d rise with increased gearing, resulting in the WACC rising further.

This can be shown diagrammatically:

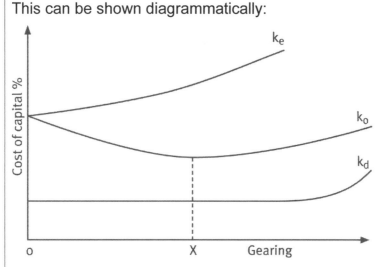

where:

k_e is the cost of equity

k_d is the cost of debt, and

k_o is the overall or weighted average cost of capital.

Conclusion:

There is an optimal level of gearing – point X.

Problem:

There is no method, apart from trial and error, available to locate the optimal point.

Modigliani and Miller's theory (with tax)

Modigliani and Miller's 'with tax theory' concluded that because of the tax advantages of issuing debt finance (tax relief on debt interest) firms should increase their gearing as much as possible. The theory is based on assumptions such as perfect capital markets.

Modigliani and Miller's theory explained

The starting point for the theory is that:

- as investors are rational, the required return of equity is directly linked to the increase in gearing – i.e. as gearing increases, k_e increases in direct proportion.

However, this is adjusted to reflect that:

- debt interest is tax deductible so the overall cost of debt to the company is lower than in MM – no tax

- lower debt costs imply less volatility in returns for the same level of gearing, giving smaller increases in k_e

- the increase in k_e does not offset the benefit of the cheaper debt finance and therefore the WACC falls as gearing is increased.

Conclusion:

Gearing up reduces the WACC, and the optimal capital structure is 99.9% gearing.

This is demonstrated in the following diagrams:

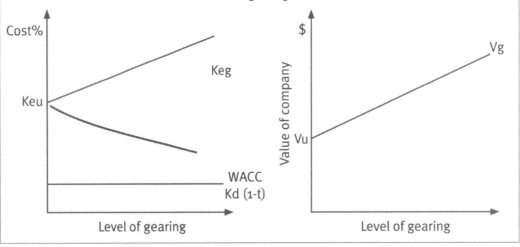

In practice firms are rarely found with the very high levels of gearing as advocated by Modigliani and Miller. This is because of:

- bankruptcy risk
- agency costs
- tax exhaustion
- the impact on borrowing/debt capacity
- differences in risk tolerance levels between shareholders and directors
- restrictions in the Articles of Association
- increases in the cost of borrowing as gearing increases.

As a result, despite the theories, gearing levels in real firms tend to be based on more practical considerations.

Key practical arguments against M+M

Bankruptcy risk

As gearing increases so does the possibility of bankruptcy. If shareholders become concerned, this will reduce the share price and increase the WACC of the company.

Agency costs: restrictive conditions

In order to safeguard their investments lenders/debentures holders often impose restrictive conditions in the loan agreements that constrains management's freedom of action.

E.g. restrictions:

- on the level of dividends

- on the level of additional debt that can be raised

- on management from disposing of any major fixed assets without the debenture holders' agreement.

Tax exhaustion

After a certain level of gearing companies will discover that they have no tax liability left against which to offset interest charges.

$$k_d(1 - t) \text{ simply becomes } k_d.$$

Borrowing/debt capacity

High levels of gearing are unusual because companies run out of suitable assets to offer as security against loans. Companies with assets, which have an active second-hand market, and low levels of depreciation such as property companies, have a high borrowing capacity.

Difference risk tolerance levels between shareholders and directors

Business failure can have a far greater impact on directors than on a well-diversified investor. It may be argued that directors have a natural tendency to be cautious about borrowing.

Test your understanding 1

X Co, an unquoted manufacturing company, has been experiencing a growth in demand, and this trend is expected to continue. In order to cope with the growth in demand, the company needs to buy further machinery and this is expected to cost 30% of the current company value.

In the past, a high proportion of earnings has been distributed by way of dividends so few cash reserves are available. 51% of the shares in X Co are still owned by the founding family.

A decision must now be taken about how to raise the funds. The firm has already raised some loan finance and this is secured against the company land and buildings.

Required:

Suggest the issues that should be considered by the board in determining whether debt would be an appropriate source of finance.

Real world issues – Static trade-off theory

Static trade-off theory

It is possible to revise M and M's theory to incorporate bankruptcy risk and so to arrive at the same conclusion as the traditional theory of gearing – i.e. that an optimal gearing level exists.

Given this, firms will strive to reach the optimum level by means of a trade-off.

Static trade-off theory argues that firms in a stable (static) position will adjust their current level of gearing to achieve a target level:

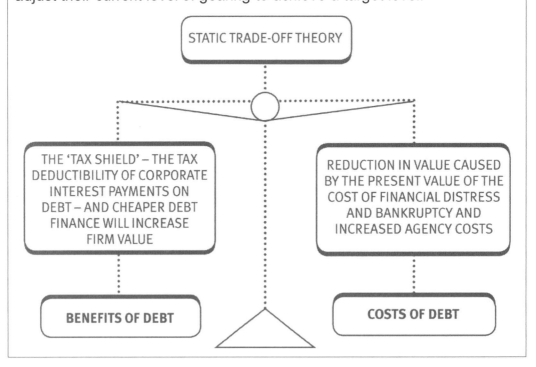

STATIC TRADE-OFF THEORY

THE 'TAX SHIELD' – THE TAX DEDUCTIBILITY OF CORPORATE INTEREST PAYMENTS ON DEBT – AND CHEAPER DEBT FINANCE WILL INCREASE FIRM VALUE

REDUCTION IN VALUE CAUSED BY THE PRESENT VALUE OF THE COST OF FINANCIAL DISTRESS AND BANKRUPTCY AND INCREASED AGENCY COSTS

BENEFITS OF DEBT

COSTS OF DEBT

Above target debt ratio the value of the firm is not optimal:

- Financial distress and agency costs exceed the benefits of debt.

- Firms decrease their debt levels.

Below the target debt ratio can still increase the value of the firm because:

- marginal value of the benefits of debt are still greater than the costs associated with the use of debt

- firms increase their debt.

NB: Research suggests that this theory is not backed up by empirical evidence.

Real world issues – Pecking order theory

Pecking order theory

Pecking order theory tries to explain why firms do not behave the way the static trade-off model would predict. It states that firms have a preferred hierarchy for financing decisions:

The implications for investment are that:

- the value of a project depends on how it is financed

- some projects will be undertaken only if funded internally or with relatively safe debt but not if financed with risky debt or equity

- companies with less cash and higher gearing will be more prone to under-invest.

If a firm follows the pecking order:

- its gearing ratio results from a series of incremental decisions, not an attempt to reach a target

  - High cash flow $\Rightarrow$ Gearing ratio decreases

  - Low cash flow $\Rightarrow$ Gearing ratio increases

- there may be good and bad times to issue equity depending on the degree of information asymmetry.

Real world issues – A compromise approach

A compromise approach

The different theories can be reconciled to encourage firms to make the correct financing decisions:

1   Select a long run target gearing ratio.

2   Whilst far from target, decisions should be governed by static trade-off theory.

3   When close to target, pecking order theory will dictate source of funds.

More on pecking order v static trade off

Pecking order theory was developed to suggest a reason for this observed inconsistency in practice between the static trade-off model and what companies actually appear to do.

Issue costs

Internally generated funds have the lowest issue costs, debt moderate issue costs and equity the highest. Firms issue as much as they can from internally generated funds first then move on to debt and finally equity.

Asymmetric information

Myers has suggested asymmetric information as an explanation for the heavy reliance on retentions. This may be a situation where managers, because of their access to more information about the firm, know that the value of the shares is greater than the current market value based on the weak and semi-strong market information.

In the case of a new project, managers forecast maybe higher and more realistic than that of the market. If new shares were issued in this situation there is a possibility that they would be issued at too low a price, thus transferring wealth from existing shareholders to new shareholders. In these circumstances there might be a natural preference for internally generated funds over new issues. If additional funds are required over and above internally generated funds, then debt would be the next alternative.

If management is against making equity issues when in possession of favourable inside information, market participants might assume that management would be more likely to favour new issues when they are in possession of unfavourable inside information. This leads to the suggestion that new issues might be regarded as a signal of bad news! Managers may therefore wish to rely primarily on internally generated funds supplemented by borrowing, with issues of new equity as a last resort.

Myers and Majluf (1984) demonstrated that with asymmetric information, equity issues are interpreted by the market as bad news, since managers are only motivated to make equity issues when shares are overpriced. Bennett Stewart (1990) puts it differently: 'Raising equity conveys doubt. Investors suspect that management is attempting to shore up the firm's financial resources for rough times ahead by selling over-valued shares.'

Asquith and Mullins (1983) empirically observed that announcements of new equity issues are greeted by sharp declines in stock prices. Thus, equity issues are comparatively rare among large established companies.

Real world issues – Gearing drift

Dealing with 'gearing drift'

Profitable companies will tend to find that their gearing level gradually reduces over time as accumulated profits help to increase the value of equity. This is known as 'gearing drift'.

Gearing drift can cause a firm to move away from its optimal gearing position. The firm might have to occasionally increase gearing (by issuing debt, or paying a large dividend or buying back shares) to return to its optimal gearing position.

Real world issues – Signalling to investors

Signalling to investors

In a perfect capital market, investors fully understand the reasons why a firm chooses a particular source of finance.

However, in the real world it is important that the firm considers the signalling effect of raising new finance. Generally, it is thought that raising new finance gives a positive signal to the market: the firm is showing that it is confident that it has identified attractive new projects and that it will be able to afford to service the new finance in the future.

Investors and analysts may well assess the impact of the new finance on a firm's statement of profit or loss and balance sheet (statement of financial position) in order to help them assess the likely success of the firm after the new finance has been raised.

Consider the following example, which shows the impact on key financial ratios of using different sources of finance:

A company is considering a number of funding options for a new project. The new project may be funded by $10m of equity or debt. Below are the financial statements under each option.

Statement of financial position (Balance sheet) extract

	Equity finance $m	Debt finance $m
Long term liabilities		
Debentures (10%)	0.0	10.0
Capital		
Share capital (50¢)	11.0	3.5
Share premium	4.0	1.5
Reserves	5.0	5.0
	20.0	10.0

Statement of profit or loss extract

	$m
Revenue	100.0
Gross profit	20.0
Less expenses (excluding finance charges)	(15.0)
Operating profit	5.0

Corporation tax is charged at 30%.

Required:

(a) Calculate ROCE and return on equity (ROE) and compare the financial performance of the company under the two funding options.

(b) What is the impact on the company's performance of financing by debt rather than equity?

Solution

		Equity finance = $5m/$20m ×	Debt finance = $5m/$20m ×
(a)	Return on capital employed		
		100 = 25%	100 = 25%

Working

	$m	$m
PB FC & T	5.0	5.0
Finance charges	0.0	(1.0)
PBT	5.0	4.0
Tax (@ 30%)	(1.5)	(1.2)
PAT	3.5	2.8

Return on equity	= $3.5m/$20m × 100 = 17.5%	= $2.8m/$10m × 100 = 28%

The financial performance of the two funding options is exactly the same for ROCE. This should not be a surprise given that ROCE is an indication of performance before financing, or underlying performance.

(b) When considering the ROE we see that the geared option achieves a higher return than the equity option. This is because the debt (10%) is costing less than the return on capital (25%). The excess return on that part funded by debt passes to the shareholder enhancing their return. The only differences between ROCE and ROE will be due to taxation and gearing.

4 Agency effects

Agency costs have a further impact on a firm's practical financing decisions.

Where gearing is high, the interests of management and shareholders may conflict with those of creditors.

Management may for example:

- gamble on high-risk projects to solve problems
- pay large dividends to secure company value for themselves
- hide problems and cut back on discretionary spending
- invest in higher risk business areas than the loan was designated to fund.

In order to safeguard their investments lenders/debentures holders often impose restrictive conditions in the loan agreements that constrains management's freedom of action: these may include restrictions:

- on the level of dividends

- on the level of additional debt that can be raised

- on acceptable working capital and other ratios

- on management from disposing of any major asset without the debenture holders' agreement.

These effects may:

- encourage use of retained earnings

- restrict further borrowing

- make new issues less attractive to investors.

 More on agency effects

In a situation of high gearing, shareholder and creditor interests are often at odds regarding the acceptability of investment projects.

Shareholders may be tempted to gamble on high-risk projects as if things work out well they take all the 'winnings' whereas if things turn out badly the debenture holders will stand part of the losses, the shareholders only being liable up to their equity stake.

There are further ways in which managers (appointed by shareholders) can act in the interests of the shareholders rather than the debt holders:

Dividends

We have seen how shareholders may be reluctant to put money into an ailing company. On the other hand they are usually happy to take money out. Large cash dividends will secure part of the company's value for the shareholders at the expense of the creditors.

Playing for time

In general, because of the increasing effect of the indirect costs of bankruptcy, if a firm is going to fail, it is better that this happens sooner rather than later from the creditors' point of view. However, managers may try to hide the extent of the problem by cutting back on research, maintenance, etc. and thus make 'this year's' results better at the expense of 'next year's'.

Changing risks

The company may change the risk of the business without informing the lender. For example, management may negotiate a loan for a relatively safe investment project offering good security and therefore carrying only modest interest charges and then use the funds to finance a far riskier investment. Alternatively management may arrange further loans which increase the risks of the initial creditors by undercutting their asset backing. These actions will once again be to the advantage of the shareholders and to the cost of the creditors.

It is because of the risk that managers might act in this way that most loan agreements contain restrictive covenants for protection of the lender, the costs of these covenants to the firms in terms of constraints upon managers' freedom of action being a further example of **agency costs**.

Covenants used by suppliers of debt finance may place restrictions on:

- issuing new debt – with a superior claim on assets
- dividends – growth to be linked to earnings
- merger activity – to ensure post-merger asset backing of loans is maintained at a minimum prescribed level
- investment policy.

Contravention of these agreements will usually result in the loan becoming immediately repayable, thus allowing the debenture holders to restrict the size of any losses.

5 Specific financing options

Recap of basic financing options

The basic choice for a business wanting to raise new finance is between equity finance and debt finance.

Equity finance

This is finance raised by the issue of shares to investors.

Equity holders (shareholders) receive their returns as dividends, which are paid at the discretion of the directors. This makes the returns potentially quite volatile and uncertain, so shareholders generally demand high rates of return to compensate them for this high risk.

From the business's point of view therefore, equity is the most expensive source of finance, but it is more flexible than debt given that dividends are discretionary (subject to the issues discussed in Chapter 5: The dividend decision).

Debt finance

Short term debt finance

In the short term, businesses can raise finance through overdrafts or short term loans.

Overdrafts are very flexible, can be arranged quickly, and can be repaid quickly and informally if the company can afford to do so. However, if the bank chooses to, it can withdraw an overdraft facility at any time, which could leave a company in financial trouble.

A short term loan is a more formal arrangement, which will be governed by an agreement which specifies exactly what amounts should be paid and when, and what the interest rate will be.

Long term debt finance

Long term debt finance tends to be more expensive than short term finance, unless the debt is secured, when the reduction in risk brings down the cost. Long term debt tends to be used as an alternative to equity for funding long term investments. It is cheaper than equity finance, since the lender faces less risk than a shareholder would, and also because the debt interest is tax deductible. However, the interest is an obligation which cannot be avoided, so debt is a less flexible form of finance than equity.

Specific equity financing options

The main options for companies wishing to raise equity finance are:

*   rights issue to existing shareholders – this option is the simplest method, providing the existing shareholders can afford to invest the amount of funds required. The existing shareholders' control is not diluted.

*   public issue of shares – gaining a public listing increases the marketability of the company's shares, and makes it easier to raise further equity finance from a large number of investors in the future. Becoming a listed company in the first place (an initial public offering, or IPO) is an expensive and time-consuming process, and once listed, the company has to face a higher level of regulation and public scrutiny. Also, since the company's shares are likely to become widely distributed between many investors, the threat of takeover increases when a company becomes listed.

- private placing – 'private equity finance' is the name given to finance raised from investors organised through the mediation of a venture capital company or private equity business. These investors do not operate through the formal equity market, so raising private equity finance does not expose the company to the same level of scrutiny and regulation that a stock market listing would. Private equity is often perceived as a relatively high risk investment, so investors usually demand higher rates of return than they would from a stock market listed company. Business Angels are a source of private equity finance for small companies.

Stock Exchange listing requirements

If a company decides to raise equity finance from the local capital market, it must comply with the listing requirements of the capital market. For illustration, the listing requirements for the London Stock Exchange are given below:

Track record requirements

The company must be able to provide a revenue earnings record for at least 75% of its business for the previous 3 years. Also, any significant acquisitions in the 3 years before flotation must be disclosed.

Market capitalisation

The shares must be worth at least £700,000 at the time of listing.

Share in public hands

At least 25% of the shares must be in public hands.

Future prospects

The company must show that it has sufficient working capital for its current needs and for the next 12 months. More generally, a description of future plans and prospects must be given.

Audited historical financial information

This must be provided for the last 3 full years, and any published later interim period.

Corporate governance

The Chairman and Chief Executive roles must be split, and half the Board should comprise non-executive directors. There must be an independent audit committee, remuneration committee and nomination committee. The company must provide evidence of a high standard of financial controls and accounting systems.

Acceptable jurisdiction and accounting standards

The company must be properly incorporated and must use IFRS and equivalent accounting standards.

Other considerations

A sponsor/underwriter will need to make sure that the company has established procedures which allow it to comply with the listing and disclosure rules.

Regulations in other countries

Companies must meet an exchange's requirements to have their stocks and shares listed and traded there, but requirements vary by stock exchange. The above points all refer to the London stock exchange. Some examples of other major global stock exchange requirements are:

New York Stock Exchange: To be listed on the New York Stock Exchange (NYSE) a company has to already have 1.1 million publicly-traded shares outstanding with a collective market value of at least $100 million.

NASDAQ Stock Exchange: To be listed on the NASDAQ a company must already have 1.25 million publicly-traded shares with a collective market value of $45 million.

Both the NYSE and the Nasdaq require a minimum security listing price of $4 per share.

Delisting

Delisting is the removal of a listed security from the exchange on which it trades.

Stock is removed from an exchange because the company for which the stock is issued, whether voluntarily or involuntarily, is not in compliance with the listing requirements of the exchange. The reasons for delisting include violating regulations and/or failing to meet financial specifications set out by the stock exchange.

Companies that are delisted are not necessarily bankrupt, and may continue trading over the counter.

In order for a stock to be traded on an exchange, the company that issues the stock must meet the listing requirements set out by the exchange.

Listing requirements include minimum share prices, certain financial ratios, minimum sales levels, and so on. If listing requirements are not met by a company, the exchange that lists the company's stock will probably issue a warning of non-compliance to the company.

If the company's failure to meet listing requirements continues, the exchange may delist the company's stock.

Alternatively, a company may choose to delist its own stock, or indeed the stock of a company that it has taken over.

A listing on the stock exchange brings with it extra scrutiny of the company's affairs, and attracts a wide range of investors, some of whom may have very different objectives (say short term gain) from the original shareholders.

Faced with this scrutiny and conflict, the company may choose to delist its own shares from the exchange and return to private ownership.

Dark pool trading systems

Definition

Dark pool trading relates to the trading volume in listed stocks created by institutional orders that are unavailable to the public. The bulk of dark pool trading is represented by block trades facilitated away from the central exchanges.

It is also referred to as the 'upstairs market', or 'dark liquidity', or just 'dark pool'.

The dark pool gets its name because details of these trades are concealed from the public, clouding the transactions like murky water. Some traders that use a strategy based on liquidity feel that dark pool trading should be publicised, in order to make trading more 'fair' for all parties involved. Indeed, some stock exchanges have prohibited dark pool trading.

The problem with dark pool trading

If an institutional investor looking to make a large block order (thousands or millions of shares) makes a trade on the open market, investors across the globe will see a spike in volume.

This might prompt a change in the price of the security, which in turn could increase the cost of purchasing the block of shares. When thousands of shares are involved, even a small change in share price can translate into a lot of money. If only the buyer and seller are aware of the transaction, both can skip over market forces and get a price that's better suited to them both.

The rise in popularity of dark pool trading raises questions for both investors and regulators. With a significant proportion of trades occurring without the knowledge of the everyday investor, information asymmetry becomes an issue of greater importance.

More on private equity and venture capital

Private equity is an asset class consisting of equity securities and debt in operating companies that are not publicly traded on a stock exchange.

A private equity investment will generally be made by a private equity firm, a venture capital firm or an angel investor. Each of these categories of investor has its own set of goals, preferences and investment strategies; however, all provide working capital to a target company to nurture expansion, new-product development, or restructuring of the company's operations, management, or ownership.

Among the most common investment strategies in private equity are: leveraged buyouts, venture capital, growth capital, distressed investments and mezzanine capital.

In a typical leveraged buyout transaction, a private equity firm buys majority control of an existing or mature firm, to try to improve its results before selling it or listing it on the stock market.

This is distinct from a venture capital or growth capital investment, in which the investors (typically venture capital firms or angel investors) invest in young, growing or emerging companies, and rarely obtain majority control.

Specific debt financing options

A company seeking to raise long term debt finance will be constrained by its size, its debt capacity and its credit rating.

Small and medium sized enterprises (SMEs) may make use of private lending through family, friends and other small business investors. The usual starting point is to approach a bank, which will make a lending decision based on the company's business plan.

Alternatively, companies often elect to lease assets rather than purchasing them. Leasing is often viewed as a type of debt financing, because it requires a company to commit to a fixed stream of payments for a number of years, in a similar way to repaying loan capital and interest. The main consideration with lease financing is that (depending on the terms of the specific lease) the ownership of the asset often stays with the lessor. While this can be attractive in that maintenance costs are reduced, it does mean that the company doesn't actually own the asset so cannot claim the tax depreciation allowances or benefit from an increase in asset value.

Larger companies have the following additional options:

- Bond issue – this is an attractive way of raising large amounts of debt finance, at a low rate of interest. There are however significant issue costs and there is a risk that the issue might not be fully subscribed (unless it is underwritten). Bonds may be issued in the domestic, or an overseas, capital market.

- Debenture issue – debentures are asset backed securities (i.e. lower risk for investors).

- Convertible bond issue – convertibles carry the right of conversion to equity at some future date. This makes the bond more attractive to a potential investor.

- Mezzanine finance – the most risky type of debt from the lender's point of view. The holder of mezzanine debt is ranked after all the other debt holders on a liquidation, and the debt is unsecured. A high coupon rate has to be paid to compensate the investor for this risk.

- Syndicated loan – for large amounts of debt finance, where one bank is not prepared to take the risk of lending such a large amount, a loan may be raised from a syndicate of banks. Rates of interest tend to be slightly higher than those in the bond market, but transaction costs are low and loans can be arranged much quicker than a bond issue.

 Cryptocurrency and initial coin offerings (ICOs)

Cryptocurrency definition

A cryptocurrency is a digital or virtual currency that uses cryptography for security. A cryptocurrency is difficult to counterfeit because of this security feature.

The defining feature of a cryptocurrency, and arguably its most attractive feature, is its organic nature. It is not issued by any central authority, so it is theoretically immune to government interference or manipulation.

Initial Coin Offering (ICO) definition

An Initial Coin Offering (ICO) is the cryptocurrency equivalent to an IPO (Initial Public Offering) in the mainstream investment world.

When a company is looking to create a new coin, app, or service, it can launch an ICO and ask interested investors to buy in to the offering. In exchange for their support, investors receive a new cryptocurrency token specific to the ICO.

These tokens are similar to shares of a company sold to investors in an IPO-type transaction. Investors hope that the tokens will perform well in the future, providing them with a good return on investment. The company holding the ICO uses the investor funds to invest in a new product, or start a new digital currency.

ICOs are similar to IPOs and also to crowdfunding. Like IPOs, a stake of the company is sold to raise money during an ICO operation. However, while IPOs deal with investors, ICOs deal with supporters that are keen to invest in a new project much like a crowdfunding event. But ICOs differ from crowdfunding in that the backers of the former are motivated by a prospective return in their investments, while the funds raised in the latter campaign are basically donations. For these reasons, ICOs are sometimes referred to as crowdsales.

Advantages and disadvantages of ICOs

ICOs are decentralised i.e. there is no single authority governing them.

Also, ICOs are largely unregulated, meaning that government organisations do not oversee them.

This means that ICOs are much freer in terms of structure than IPOs, and they are often used to bypass the rigorous and regulated capital-raising process required by venture capitalists or banks.
The most successful ICOs over the past several years have produced tremendous returns and the number of ICOs is growing rapidly. In fact, in the first quarter of 2018, ICOs brought in more funds than in the whole of 2017.

However, this investor enthusiasm can also lead to problems. Because they are largely unregulated, some ICOs have been accused of being little more than scams, preying on under-informed but enthusiastic and wealthy investors.

6 Islamic finance

Islamic finance has the same purpose as other forms of business finance except that it operates in accordance with the principles of Islamic law (Sharia). The basic principles covered by Islamic finance include:

- Sharing of profits and losses.
- No interest (riba) allowed.
- Finance is restricted to Islamically accepted transactions i.e. no investment in alcohol, gambling etc.

Therefore, ethical and moral investing is encouraged. Instead of interest being charged, returns are earned by channelling funds into an underlying investment activity, which will earn profit. The investor is rewarded by a share in that profit, after a management fee is deducted by the bank. The main Islamic finance products are:

- Murabaha (trade credit)
- Ijara (lease finance)
- Sukuk (debt finance)
- Mudaraba (equity finance)
- Musharaka (venture capital)
- Salam and Istisna (forward contracts).

Student Accountant articles

Two articles in the Technical Articles section of the ACCA website cover the topic of Islamic finance.

More details on Islamic finance

The Islamic economic model has developed over time based on the rulings of Sharia on commercial and financial transactions. The Islamic finance framework seen today is based on the principles developed within this model. These include:

- An emphasis on fairness such that all parties involved in a transaction can make informed decisions without being misled or cheated. Equally reward should be based on effort rather than for simple ownership of capital.

- The encouragement and promotion of the rights of individuals to pursue personal economic wellbeing, but with a clear distinction between what commercial activities are allowed and what are forbidden (for example, transactions involving alcohol, pork related products, armaments, gambling and other socially detrimental activities). Speculation is also prohibited (so instruments such as options and futures are not allowed). Ethical and moral investing is encouraged.

- The strict prohibition of interest (riba). Instead interest is replaced with cash flows from productive sources, such as returns from wealth generating investment activities.

How returns are earned

Riba is defined as the excess paid by the borrower over the original capital borrowed i.e. the equivalent to interest on a loan. Its literal translation is 'excess'. Within the conventional banking system, a bank get access to funds by offering interest to depositors. It will then apply those funds by lending money, on which it charges interest. The bank makes a profit by charging more interest on the money it lends than it pays to its depositors.

This process is outlawed under Islamic finance. In an Islamic bank, the money provided by depositors is not lent, but is instead channelled into an underlying investment activity, which will earn profit. The depositor is rewarded by a share in that profit, after a management fee is deducted by the bank. For example, in an Islamic mortgage transaction, instead of loaning the buyer money to purchase the item, a bank might buy the item itself from the seller, and resell it to the buyer at a profit, while allowing the buyer to pay the bank in instalments. However, the bank's profit cannot be made explicit and therefore there are no additional penalties for late payment. In effect, the interest is replaced with cash flows from productive sources, such as returns from wealth generating investment activities and operations. These include profits from trading in real assets and cash flows from the transfer of the right to use an asset (for example, rent).

Sharia boards (SBs)

Sharia Boards (SBs) ensure that all products and services offered by Islamic banks and other Islamic financing institutions (IFIs) are compliant with the principles of Sharia rules.

They review and oversee all new product offerings made by the IFIs and make judgments on an individual case-by-case basis, regarding their acceptability with Sharia rulings. Additionally, SBs often oversee Sharia compliant training programmes for an IFI's employees and participate in the preparation and approval of the IFIs' annual reports.

SBs are normally made up of a mixture of Islamic scholars and finance experts to ensure that fair and reasonable judgments are made. Where necessary, the finance experts can explain the products to the Islamic scholars. The Islamic scholars often sit on several SBs of a number of different IFIs. SBs are, in turn, supervised by the International Association of Islamic Bankers (IAIB).

SBs face several challenges when making judgments. Sharia law can be open to different interpretations, leading to different outcomes on the acceptability of the same products by different SBs and Islamic scholars.

Furthermore, precedents set by SBs are not binding, and changes in SBs' personnel over time may shift the balance of the SB's collective opinions and judgments on the acceptability of existing and new products.

SBs need considerable resources to operate effectively, and IFIs need to ensure that their SB members are well informed about the developments and trends in global financial markets.

Specific Islamic financing methods

Islamic sources of finance

In Islamic Banking there are broadly 2 categories of financing techniques:

- 'Fixed Income' modes of finance – murabaha, ijara, sukuk, salam, istisna

- Equity modes of finance – mudaraba, musharaka.

Each of these is discussed in more detail below.

Murabaha

Murabaha is a form of trade credit or loan. The key distinction between a murabaha and a loan is that with a murabaha, the bank will take actual constructive or physical ownership of the asset. The asset is then sold onto the 'borrower' or 'buyer' for a profit but they are allowed to pay the bank over a set number of instalments. The period of the repayments could be extended but no penalties or additional mark-up may be added by the bank. Early payment discounts are not welcomed (and will not form part of the contract) although the financier may choose (not contract) to give discounts.

Ijara

Ijara is the equivalent of lease finance; it is defined as when the use of the underlying asset or service is transferred for consideration. Under this concept, the Bank makes available to the customer the use of assets or equipment such as plant, office automation, or motor vehicles for a fixed period and price. Some of the specifications of an Ijara contact include:

- The use of the leased asset must be specified in the contract.

- The lessor (the bank) is responsible for the major maintenance of the underlying assets (ownership costs).

- The lessee is held for maintaining the asset in good shape.

Sukuk

Within other forms of business finance, a company can issue tradable financial instruments to borrow money. Key features of these debt instruments are that they

- don't give voting rights in the company.

- give right to profits before distribution of profits to shareholders.

- may include securities and guarantees over assets.

- include interest based elements.

All of the above are prohibited under Islamic law. Instead, Islamic bonds (or sukuk) are linked to an underlying asset, such that a sukuk-holder is a partial owner in the underlying assets and profit is linked to the performance of the underlying asset. So for example a sukuk-holder will participate in the ownership of the company issuing the sukuk and has a right to profits (but will equally bear their share of any losses).

Sukuk is about the finance provider having ownership of real assets and earning a return sourced from those assets. This contrasts with conventional bonds where the investor has a debt instrument earning the return predominately via the payment of interest (riba). Riba or excess is not allowed under Sharia law.

There has been considerable debate as to whether sukuk instruments are akin to conventional debt or equity finance. This is because there are two types of sukuk:

Asset based – raising finance where the principal is covered by the capital value of the asset but the returns and repayments to sukuk holders are not directly financed by these assets.

Asset backed – raising finance where the principal is covered by the capital value of the asset but the returns and repayments to sukuk holders are directly financed by these assets.

Salam

Salam contracts are similar to forward contracts, where a commodity (or service) is sold today for future delivery. Cash is received immediately from the bank and the quantity, quality, and the future date and time of delivery are determined immediately. The sale will probably be at a discount so that the bank can make a profit.

In turn, the bank would probably sell the contract to another buyer for immediate cash and profit, in a parallel Salam arrangement. Salam contracts are prohibited for commodities such as gold, silver and other money-type assets.

Istisna

Istisna contracts are often used for long-term, large construction projects of property and machinery. Here, the bank funds the construction project for a client that is delivered on completion to the bank's client. The client pays an initial deposit, followed by instalments, to the bank, the amount and frequency of which are determined at the start of the contract.

Mudaraba

Mudaraba is a special kind of partnership where one partner gives money to another for investing it in a commercial enterprise. The investment comes from the first partner (who is called 'rab ul mal'), while the management and work is an exclusive responsibility of the other (who is called 'mudarib'). The Mudaraba (profit sharing) is a contract, with one party providing 100% of the capital and the other party providing its specialist knowledge to invest the capital and manage the investment project. Profits generated are shared between the parties according to a pre-agreed ratio. In a Mudaraba only the lender of the money has to take losses. This arrangement is therefore most closely aligned with equity finance.

Musharaka

Musharaka is a relationship between two or more parties, who contribute capital to a business, and divide the net profit and loss pro rata. It is most closely aligned with the concept of venture capital. All providers of capital are entitled to participate in management, but are not required to do so. The profit is distributed among the partners in pre-agreed ratios, while the loss is borne by each partner strictly in proportion to their respective capital contributions.

Advantages and limitations of using Islamic finance

Advantages of using Islamic finance

Corporations, individuals and IFIs engaged in raising and issuing funding based on Islamic finance virtues may be viewed as belonging in stakeholder-type partnerships that are engaged in deriving benefits from ethical, fair business activity. The result of these partnerships is one of mutual interest, trust and co-operation. The ethical stance and fair dealing of Islamic finance virtues means that partnerships, business activity and profit creation comes from benefiting the community as a whole.

Since the virtues of Islamic finance and enterprise prohibit speculation and short-term opportunism, it encourages all parties to take a longer term view of success from the partnership. It focuses all the parties' attention on creating a successful outcome to the venture. This should result in a more stable financial environment. Indeed, literature in this area suggests that had banks and other financial institutions conducted their business activity based on Islamic finance principles, the negative impact of the banking and sovereign debt financial crises would have been much reduced.

IFIs or conventional financial institutions with products based on Islamic finance principles gain access to Muslim funds across the world and provide finance for organisations and individuals who need them. It is estimated that Islamic financial assets have exceeded $1,600bn worldwide. As the world emerges from the global financial crisis and business activity increases, this should increase. Furthermore, access to Islamic finance is not restricted to Muslim communities only. The wider business community could have access to new sources of finance. This may be particularly attractive to corporations focused on ethical investments that Islamic finance virtues stipulate.

Limitations of using Islamic financing methods

Because of the prohibitions of riba and on speculation, IFIs may be slower to react to market demand and changes. They may lack sufficient flexibility in their product offering when compared to conventional financial institutions and may be less able to take advantage of short-term opportunities.

Moral hazard and principal-agent issues may be more pronounced between IFIs and organisations and individuals to whom they lend funds. This is because Islamic finance virtues stipulate close relationships from partnership-like arrangements. However, information asymmetry between the IFI and the borrower of funds will always exist. Therefore, costs related to increased level of due diligence and negotiating are probably higher for IFIs.

Costs related to developing new financial products may also be higher for IFIs because not only will the products have to comply with normal financial laws and regulations but also with Sharia rules. As stated above, the resources required by SBs can be considerable.

Added to this, because these financial products need to go through stages of compliance and layers of complications before they are approved, the approval process can take time. The pace of innovation of new Islamic financial products may be considerably slower than that of conventional products. This may make the IFI less able to compete with conventional financial institutions and may make it restrict its activities to smaller, niche markets. Some Islamic financial products may not be compatible with international financial regulation – for example, a diminishing Musharaka contract may not be an acceptable mortgage instrument in law, although it could be constructed as such. The need to ensure that such products comply with regulations may increase legal and insurance costs.

The interpretation of Sharia rulings may allow certain Islamic finance products to be acceptable in some markets, but not in others. This has led to some Islamic scholars, who are experts in Sharia and finance, to criticise a number of product offerings. For example, some Murabaha contracts have been criticised because their repayments have been based on prevailing interest rates rather than on economic or profit conditions within which the asset will be used. Some Sukuk bonds have faced similar criticisms in that their repayments have been based on prevailing interest rates, they have been credit-rated and their redemption value is based on a nominal value rather than on a market value, and thereby, perhaps, making them too close to conventional bonds and their repayments too similar to riba. On the other hand, the opposite argument could be that in order to make Islamic financial products competitive in all markets, their valuations need to be comparable. Therefore, benchmarking them using conventional means is necessary.

So far the discussion on limitations has focused on IFIs, as providers of Islamic finance. It is also important to consider the drawbacks and challenges that corporations may face when using Islamic finance.

From the above discussion, the costs related to developing and gaining approval for Islamic financial products is likely to be passed down to customers and possibly make these products more expensive. In addition to this, access to new products and flexibility within existing products may be limited, due to the more complicated approval process that is necessary. These more expensive and less flexible sources of finance may make the corporation using them less competitive when compared to rivals who have access to cheaper, more flexible sources of finance.

The partnership nature of Islamic finance contracts may also cause agency type issues within corporations. These may be more prevalent in joint venture type situations or where the diverse range of stakeholders may make it more difficult for corporations to determine and act upon the importance of various stakeholder groups. For example, in the case of a Musharaka contract, where the IFI and the organisation are both involved in the management of a project, dealing with other stakeholder groups may be more challenging.

Before the global financial crisis, trading in asset backed and securitised Sukuk products, issued by corporations, has been limited (a notable exception was Sukuk products denominated in Malaysian ringgits). Furthermore, since the financial crisis, issuance in new Sukuk products has reduced somewhat.

Using Islamic finance may also increase the cost of capital for a corporation. For example, it may be more difficult to demonstrate that repayments for Mudaraba, Musharaka and Sukuk contracts are like debt, and therefore they may not attract a tax-shield. However, an equivalent organisation which raises the same finance using conventional debt finance may be able to lower its cost of capital due to tax-shields and therefore increase the value of its investment.

7 Financing foreign projects – Introduction

Foreign currency denominated finance

Large companies can borrow money in foreign currencies as well as their own domestic currency from banks or capital markets at home or abroad. Often large companies set up foreign subsidiaries to invest in foreign projects and arrange the financing.

The main reason for wanting to borrow in a foreign currency is to fund a foreign investment project or foreign subsidiary. The foreign currency borrowing provides a hedge of the value of the project or subsidiary to protect against changes in value due to currency movements. The foreign currency borrowing can be serviced from cash flows arising from the foreign currency investment.

In the developed countries of the world, companies can choose which currency they prefer for both bank borrowings and bonds.

In most developing countries, companies will need to raise finance in an international currency such as US dollars.

Financing options for international investments

The main options are:

- use the investment's own free cash flows
- use finance raised in the parent entity's home country (denominated in either the parent's currency or the currency of the subsidiary)
- use finance raised in the subsidiary's country
- use finance raised in a completely separate country.

More detail on the financing of international investment projects

Using free cash flows

A foreign subsidiary or project could rely upon its own internally generated funds.

This would avoid many of the problems of international financing, but is unlikely to result in the necessary level of expansion to meet high growth objectives, and is not suitable for new foreign ventures whose cash flows may be low at first.

Finance raised by the parent

Funds could be raised by the parent company and transferred to subsidiary entities by way of a combination of equity and loans. The main advantage of this method is that the parent company is more likely to have a better reputation and creditworthiness than the subsidiary and therefore have better access to funds at finer rates. A centralised treasury function at the parent may also have the expertise to and financial backing to be able to choose to access funds from a wider range of sources, including more complex products. Indeed, it may be possible to extend funds to a foreign subsidiary as part of a larger bond issue or bank debt arrangement.

However, if exchange controls exist this method can become difficult and expensive.

If the borrowing is denominated in the parent's domestic currency, this will in no way reduce foreign exchange risk through matching. However, if the funds are denominated in the subsidiary's currency, the foreign currency borrowing can be designated as a hedge of the net investment in the foreign subsidiary for hedge accounting purposes to reduce the impact of fluctuations in value due to currency movements. Interest payable on the foreign currency borrowing can also be set against income from the subsidiary, again reducing currency exposure to some extent.

General disadvantages of this method (whether the funds are denominated in the domestic or the foreign currency) are:

- The entity will also be more exposed to political risk. If the investment is lost, perhaps through a war or expropriation by a foreign government, the liability will still remain intact.

- Also, if the investment is a subsidiary entity, failure of the subsidiary would leave the parent entity with the liability in the same way.

Finance raised by the subsidiary

Finance raised by the subsidiary is likely to be denominated in the subsidiary's currency.

This method will result in a reduction in risk. Foreign exchange risk will again be reduced, since the exposure of the parent company to the net worth of the subsidiary will be reduced by the amount of the foreign currency borrowing. However, complete elimination of the risk through matching will not be possible due to the likelihood of thin capitalisation rules in the foreign country which may restrict the proportion of debt capital allowed. The currency exposure of the parent to annual reported foreign currency profits from the subsidiary would also be reduced by the extent of the interest charges paid by the foreign subsidiary on the borrowings.

Political risk can also be reduced since, if the investment is lost, the liability will be eliminated as well.

Difficulties may be experienced with this method of finance if the subsidiary company does not have sufficient history or reputation to be able to raise bank debt or the country concerned does not have a well-developed capital market.

On the other hand, financing in the subsidiary's country can make such investments more acceptable to that country since it is then seen that not all of the profits made are sent to the parent entity's country.

Most governments take steps to encourage international investors since they are beneficial to that country's economy, creating employment and wealth. Such encouragement often takes the form of grants, subsidies and cheap or guaranteed finance. These incentives should be taken into account when considering international investments and their financing.

Finance raised in a third currency

Finance can today be raised in a variety of different currencies, from a variety of capital markets in many different countries.

The main reason for raising money in other currencies is that interest rates may be substantially lower than in the entity's home country or in the country where an investment is intended.

However, if the interest cost is lower, then it is likely that the currency borrowed is strong, and will therefore appreciate with respect to other currencies (as per the interest rate parity theory introduced earlier). The expected exchange loss on the borrowings would therefore offset any benefit through a lower interest rate.

Specific foreign currency financing options

There is a variety of sources of foreign currency denominated finance available:

Short-term funding:

- Eurocurrency loans.

- Syndicated loans.

- Short-term syndicated credit facilities.

- Multiple option facilities.

- Euronotes.

Long-term funding:

- Syndicated loans.

- Eurobonds.

Short term funding options

Eurocurrency loans

Multinational companies and large companies, which are heavily engaged in international transactions, may require funds in a foreign currency.

A Eurocurrency loan is a loan by a bank to a company denominated in currency of a country other than that in which they are based.

> e.g. A UK company acquiring a dollar loan from a UK bank operating in the Eurocurrency market has acquired a Eurodollar loan.

Loans can take a variety of forms:

- Straight loans.

- Lines of credit.

- Revolving loans.

Borrowers looking to eurocurrency loans must have first class credit ratings and wish to deal in large sums of money.

A variety of factors will influence the decision over whether to borrow in the domestic currency or in a foreign currency. The most important are:

- the currency required

- cost and convenience

- the size of loans.

The currency required

Companies may have needs for foreign currency funds for either trading or financing purposes and the Eurocurrency market may be a more convenient or cheaper source of such funds than in the domestic market of the country whose currency is needed.

Cost and convenience

Eurocurrency loans may be:

- cheaper if interest rates are lower; even if interest rate differentials are small this may be significant for large loans

- quicker to arrange

- unsecured and large companies can rely on their credit ratings rather than the security that can offer.

The size of loans

The Eurocurrency markets hold very large funds and for companies wishing to obtain very large loans this may be a viable alternative to domestic banking sources.

As well as conventional Eurocurrency loans, the international money markets have developed alternative short-term credit instruments.

Syndicated loans

For large loans a single bank may not be willing (due to risk exposure) or able to lend the whole amount.

A syndicated loan is a loan made to a borrower by two or more participants but is governed by a single loan agreement. The loan is structured by an arranger and each syndicate participant contributes a defined percentage of the loan and receives the same percentage of the repayments.

The syndicated loan market is made up of international lenders and was originally limited to global firms for acquisitions and other major investments. This is for the following reasons:

- Cost – being international, loans can often be raised avoiding national regulation and are thus cheaper.

- Speed – the market is very efficient so large loans can often be put together quickly if necessary.

- By diversifying lending sources borrowers may be able to eliminate foreign exchange rate risk.

However, the market has expanded rapidly with smaller and medium sized firms borrowing funds – syndicated loans as small as USD 10 million are now commonplace.

Syndicated credits

Similar to syndicated loans, syndicated credits allow a borrower to borrow funds when it requires, but can choose not take up the full amount of the agreed facility. These are expensive funds used commonly

- to fund takeovers
- to refinance debts incurred during a takeover.

Multiple option facilities

Recently developed financial instruments, these are designed to give the borrower a choice of available funds.

Commonly this will combine

- a panel of banks to provide a credit standby at a rate of interest linked to a "reference rate" (see more information below)
- another panel of banks to bid to provide loans when the borrower needs cash.

These funds can be in a variety of forms and denominated in a variety of currencies.

Reference rates

The most common reference rate, LIBOR (the London Inter Bank Offered Rate), was phased out in 2021 after being discredited in a manipulation scandal. Other common reference rates are:

- SOFR – the Secured Overnight Financing Rate
- ESTER – the Euro Short Term Rate
- SONIA – the Sterling Over Night Index Average rate.

Euronotes

Euronotes have the following features:

- Firms issue promissory notes which promise to pay the holder a fixed sum of money on a specific date or range of dates in the future.
- The Eurobond market acts as both a primary and secondary market often underwritten by banks through revolving underwriting facilities.
- Can be are short or medium term issued in single or multiple currencies. The medium-term notes bridge the gap between the short-term issues and the longer-term Eurobonds.

Eurobonds

The most important source of longer term funding is the Eurobond.

Eurobonds are:

- long term (3–20 years)
- issued and sold internationally
- denominated in a single currency
- fixed or floating interest rate bonds.

They are suitable for organisations that require:

- large capital sums for long periods
- borrowing not subject to domestic regulations.

However, a currency risk may arise if the investment the bonds are funding generates net revenues in a currency different from that the bond is denominated in.

More details on Eurobonds

In addition to short-term credit, companies and government bodies may wish to raise long-term capital. For this there is an international capital market corresponding to the international money market but dealing in longer-term funding with a different range of financial instruments. The most important of these is the Eurobond.

Eurobonds are long-term loans, usually between 3 and 20 years duration, issued and sold internationally and denominated in a single currency, often not that of the country of origin of the borrower. They may be fixed or floating interest rate bonds. The latter were introduced since inflation, especially if unpredictable, made fixed rate bonds less attractive to potential borrowers.

Eurobonds are suitable sources of finance for organisations that require:

- large capital sums for long periods, e.g. to finance major capital investment programmes
- borrowing not subject to domestic regulations especially exchange controls which may limit their ability to export capital sums.

However, Eurobonds involves the borrower in currency risk. If the capital investment generates revenue in a currency other than that in which the bond is denominated and exchange rates change the borrower will:

- suffer losses if the currency in which the bond is denominated strengthens against the currency in which the revenues are denominated
- make gains if the currency in which the bond is denominated weakens against the currency in which the revenues are denominated.

8   Chapter summary

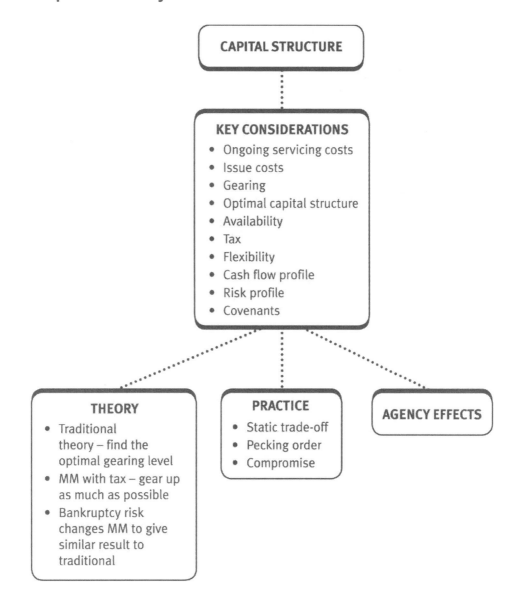

Test your understanding answers

 Test your understanding 1

Issues to raise would include:

- Retained earnings – often a preferred source of funds for smaller firms, these cannot be easily used here as the family shareholders expect significant dividends. This means that outside finance must be considered.

- High level of required funding relative to the size of the firm – could be perceived by potential investors as increasing business risk even though the expansion is in the same industry. This would increase required returns of equity investors before the increase in debt funding is even considered.

- Assets for loan security – since land and buildings are already mortgaged, the machinery will have to be used as security.

- Gearing levels – the company is already geared but it is not clear whether the current level is optimum. Raising further debt finance, subject to the taxation considerations below, should reduce the overall cost of capital, but such a significant sum is likely to be seen as high risk.

- Taxation – the high levels of investment will attract tax allowable depreciation. Depending on the current tax position of the firm and the treatment of this TAD, the company may find itself in a non-tax-paying position. This would negate the benefits of the cheaper debt finance.

- Agency costs – lenders often impose restrictive covenants on the company. This is particularly likely where such a significant level of funds is to be raised. A company largely in family control may be reluctant to have such restrictions.

- Risk profile – the family members may be reluctant to take on further debt. The risk of bankruptcy mentioned above, is of greater concern to undiversified family owners than to the typically well diversified outside investor.

- Control – since the family retain voting control, the choice may be between debt finance and a rights issue, unless they are willing to give up control. If they do not have the funds to inject, a loan may be the only choice.

- Consideration should be given to alternatives such as leasing the machinery, or seeking venture capital funding (although that too may also require a loss of absolute family control).

5

The dividend decision

Chapter learning objectives

Study guide section	Study guide outcome
A2: Financial strategy formulation	(c) Recommend appropriate distribution and retention policy.
A6: Dividend policy in multinationals and transfer pricing	(a) Determine a corporation's dividend capacity and its policy given: (i) The corporation's short- and long-term reinvestment strategy (ii) The impact of capital reconstruction programmes such as share repurchase agreements and new capital issues on free cash flow to equity. (iii) The availability and timing of central remittances (iv) The corporate tax regime within the host jurisdiction.
	(b) Advise, in the context of a specified capital investment programme, on an organisation's current and projected dividend capacity.
	(c) Develop organisational policy on the transfer pricing of goods and services across international borders and be able to determine the most appropriate transfer pricing strategy in a given situation reflecting local regulations and tax regimes.

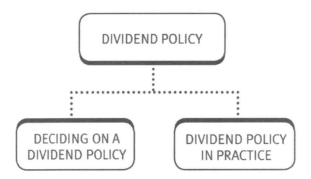

1 Introduction

In the previous chapters we have seen that the dividend decision is one of three key inter-related decisions that must be made by the financial manager (alongside the investment decision and the financing decision).

This chapter covers the main theoretical and practical considerations when deciding upon a firm's dividend policy.

2 Dividend policy – The theory

Dividend irrelevancy theory (Modigliani and Miller)

In an efficient market, dividend irrelevancy theory suggests that, provided all retained earnings are invested in positive NPV projects, existing shareholders will be indifferent about the pattern of dividend pay-outs.

However, practical influences, including market imperfections, mean that changes in dividend policy, particularly reductions in dividends paid, can have an adverse effect on shareholder wealth:

- Reductions in dividend can convey 'bad news' to shareholders (dividend signalling).

- Changes in dividend policy, particularly reductions, may conflict with investor liquidity requirements (selling shares to 'manufacture dividends' is not a costless alternative to being paid the dividend).

- Changes in dividend policy may upset investor tax planning (e.g. income v capital gain if shares are sold). Companies may have attracted a certain clientele of shareholders precisely because of their preference between income and growth.

As a result, most companies prefer to predetermine dividend policy.

More details on Modigliani and Miller's theory

The classic view of the irrelevance of the source of equity finance

This view was developed by Modigliani and Miller and may now be regarded as the classic position:

- Their argument is that the source of equity finance is in itself irrelevant.

- Since ultimately it represents a sacrifice of consumption (or other investment opportunities) by the investor at identical risk levels, it makes no difference whether dividends are paid to the investor, or equity is raised as new issues, or profits are simply retained.

- The only differences would arise due to institutional frictional factors, such as issue costs, taxation and so on.

- If both new equity and retained earnings have the same cost then it should be irrelevant, in terms of shareholder wealth, where equity funds come from.

- Provided any cash retained is invested at the shareholders' required return, a cut in dividend of any size should not adversely affect the investor – the cash lost now is exactly compensated by an increase in the value of their shares. If the funds were actually invested at higher than the expected return for the level of risk, this would in fact increase shareholders' wealth.

- It theoretically makes no difference whether the new investment is funded by retention of dividend or new equity raised.

- The key issue is thus the investment policy not the dividend policy.

Arguments for the relevance of dividend policy

It was shown above that in theory the level of dividend is irrelevant.

In a perfect capital market it is difficult to challenge the dividend irrelevance position. However, once these assumptions are relaxed, certain practical influences emerge and the arguments need further review.

Dividend signalling

In reality, investors do not have perfect information concerning the future prospects of the company. Many authorities claim, therefore, that the pattern of dividend payments is a key consideration on the part of investors when estimating future performance.

Preference for current income

Many investors require cash dividends to finance current consumption. This does not only apply to individual investors needing cash to live on but also to institutional investors, such as pension funds and insurance companies, who require regular cash outflows to meet day to day outgoings such as pension payments and insurance claims. This implies that many shareholders will prefer companies who pay regular cash dividends and will therefore value their shares more highly.

Resolution of uncertainty

One argument often put forward for high dividend pay-out is that income in the form of dividend is more secure than income in the form of capital gain. This, therefore, leads investors to place more value on high pay-out shares (sometimes referred to as the 'Bird in the Hand' theory).

Taxation

In many situations, income in the form of dividend is taxed in a different way from income in the form of capital gains. This distortion in the personal tax system can have an impact on investors' preferences.

From the corporate point of view, this further complicates the dividend decision, as different groups of shareholders are likely to prefer different pay-out patterns.

3   Dividend policy – Practical issues

Practical influences on dividend policy

Before developing a particular dividend policy, a company must consider the following:

- legal position
- levels of profitability and free cash flow
- expectations of shareholders
- optimal gearing position – paying a large dividend reduces the value of equity in the firm, so can help a firm move towards its optimal gearing position

- inflation

- control

- tax

- liquidity/cash management in the short and long term

- other sources of finance and the necessary servicing costs.

These factors limit the 'dividend capacity' of the firm.

Dividend capacity

 This can be simply defined as the ability at any given time of a firm's ability to pay dividends to its shareholders. This will clearly have a direct impact on a company's ability to implement its dividend policy (i.e. can the company actually pay the dividend it would like to?).

Legally, the firm's dividend capacity is determined by the amount of accumulated distributable profits.

However, more practically, the dividend capacity can be calculated as the Free Cash Flow to Equity (after reinvestment), since in practice, the level of cash available will be the main driver of how much the firm can afford to pay out.

 Legal position in relation to dividends

Many countries will place legal restrictions on the amount of dividend that can be paid out relative to a company's earnings.

In addition, governments have operated policies of dividend restraint over various periods.

Profitability

Profit is obviously an essential requirement for dividends. All other things being equal, the more stable the profit the greater the proportion that can be safely paid out as dividends. If profits are volatile it is unwise to commit the firm to a higher dividend pay-out ratio.

Inflation

In periods of inflation, paying out dividends based on historic cost profits can lead to erosion of the operating capacity of the business. For example, insufficient funds may be retained for future asset replacement. Current cost accounting recalculates profit taking into consideration inflation, asset values and capital maintenance. Firms would then ensure that the dividend is limited to the CCA profit.

Growth

Rapidly growing companies commonly pay very low dividends, the bulk of earnings being retained to finance expansion.

Control

The use of internally generated funds does not alter ownership or control. This can be advantageous particularly in family owned firms.

Liquidity

Sufficient liquid funds need to be available to pay the dividend.

Tax

The personal tax position of investors may put them in a position of preferring either dividend income or capital gains though growing share prices. If the clientele of investors in the company have a clear preference for one or the other, the company should be wary of altering dividend policy and upsetting investors.

Other sources of finance

If a firm has limited access to other sources of funds, retained earnings become a very important source of finance. Dividends will therefore tend to be small. This situation is commonly experienced by unquoted companies that have very limited access to external finance.

4 Real world dividend policies

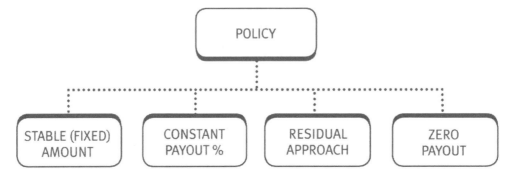

In practice, there are a number of commonly adopted dividend policies:

- stable dividend policy
- constant pay-out ratio
- zero dividend policy
- residual approach to dividends.

Stable dividend policy

Paying a constant or constantly growing dividend each year:

- offers investors a predictable cash flow
- reduces management opportunities to divert funds to non-profitable activities
- works well for mature firms with stable cash flows.

However, there is a risk that reduced earnings would force a dividend cut with all the associated difficulties.

Constant pay-out ratio

Paying out a constant proportion of equity earnings:

- maintains a link between earnings, reinvestment rate and dividend flow but
- cash flow is unpredictable for the investor
- gives no indication of management intention or expectation.

Zero dividend policy

All surplus earnings are invested back into the business. Such a policy:

- is common during the growth phase
- should be reflected in increased share price.

When growth opportunities are exhausted (no further positive NPV projects are available):

- cash will start to accumulate
- a new distribution policy will be required.

Residual dividend policy

A dividend is paid only if no further positive NPV projects available. This may be popular for firms:

- in the growth phase
- without easy access to alternative sources of funds.

However:

- cash flow is unpredictable for the investor
- gives constantly changing signals regarding management expectations.

Ratchet patterns

Most firms adopt a variant on the stable dividend policy – a **ratchet pattern** of payments. This involves paying out a stable, but rising dividend per share:

- Dividends lag behind earnings, but can then be maintained even when earnings fall below the dividend level.

- Avoids 'bad news' signals.

- Does not disturb the tax position of investors.

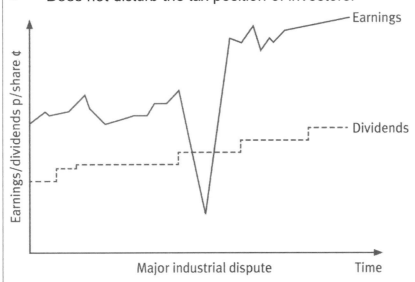

Scrip dividends

A scrip dividend is where a company allows its shareholders to take their dividends in the form of new shares rather than cash.

Do not confuse a scrip issue (which is a bonus issue of shares designed to reduce the share price to make the shares more affordable to smaller investors) with a scrip dividend.

- The advantage to the shareholders of a scrip dividend is that they can painlessly increase their shareholdings in the company without having to pay broker's commissions or stamp duty on a share purchase.

- The advantage to the company is that it does not have to find the cash to pay a dividend and in certain circumstances it can save tax.

Some companies give shareholders the choice between cash and scrip dividends. In such cases the terms of the choice are usually designed so that the shareholder who chooses the scrip sees their wealth increase with a fall in wealth if cash is chosen. Such an arrangement is called 'an enhanced scrip'. A scrip dividend effectively converts retained profits into permanent share capital.

There can be a number of advantages to 'paying' a scrip dividend rather than cash:

- Preservation of cash for re-investment.

- Unless significant, a scrip issue will not dilute the share price.

- More shares reduce the company's gearing and hence increase its borrowing capacity.

- Shareholders get more shares without incurring transaction costs.

- Shareholders may get a tax advantage if dividends in the form of shares rather than cash.

One major disadvantage in these scrip dividend plans is that shareholders receive no cash with which to pay taxes on the dividends.

Test your understanding 1

A Co, a listed company, has produced either trading losses or only small profits over the last few years and so has not recently paid any dividends. However following recent management changes and a company restructuring, the company is earning good profits and the directors are looking to formalise the future dividend policy at a forthcoming board meeting.

Particular concerns have been expressed by some directors:

- Director X has referred to the need to provide investors with stability, not reduce dividends and only increase them when it is clear that the increase can be maintained.

- Director Y has commented on the relationship between dividend payments and share price. The director believes that the dividend pay-out should therefore be as high as possible, with the company borrowing to pay them if necessary.

Required:

Make notes on the relevant matters to raise at the board meeting including comments on the specific concerns raised.

5 Share buyback schemes

If a company wishes to return a large sum of cash to its shareholders, then it might consider a share buyback (or repurchase) rather than a one-off special dividend.

These are schemes through which a company 'buys back' its shares from shareholders and cancels them. The company's Articles of Association must allow it.

It often occurs when the company:

- has no positive NPV projects
- wants to increase the share price [cosmetic exercise]
- wants to reduce the cost of capital by increasing its gearing
- wants to give a positive signal to the market. In the real world, since the directors have more information than the investors about the firm's financial position, buying the shares gives a signal to investors that the shares currently represent good value for money.

 Advantages and disadvantages of a share buyback

Advantages for the company might include:

- Giving flexibility where a firm's excess cash flows are thought to be only temporary. Management can make the distribution in the form of a share repurchase rather than paying higher cash dividends that cannot be maintained.
- Increasing EPS through a reduction in the number of shares in issue.
- Effective use of surplus funds where growth of business is poor, outlook is poor (i.e. adjusting the equity base to a more appropriate level).
- Buying out dissident shareholders.
- Creation of a 'market' where no active market exist for its shares (e.g. if the company is unquoted).
- Altering capital structure to reduce the cost of capital.
- Reducing likelihood of a takeover.

For the shareholders, advantages might include:

- Giving a choice, as they can sell or not sell. With cash dividend shareholders must accept the payment and pay the taxes.
- Saving transaction costs.

But constraints might include:

- Getting approval by general meeting (arguments about the price at which repurchase is to take place).
- The company may pay too high a price for the shares.
- The shareholders may feel they have received too small a price for their shares.

- Premiums paid are set first against share premium and then against distributable profits (if against distributable profits, this will reduce future dividend capacity).

- Might be seen as a failure of the current management/company to make better use of the funds through reinvesting them in the business.

- Shareholders may not be indifferent between dividends and capital gains due to their tax circumstances.

6 Dividend policy in multinational companies

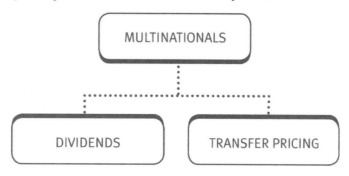

Objectives of a firm's dividend policy

As discussed earlier, when deciding how much cash to distribute to shareholders, the company directors must keep in mind that the firm's objective is to maximise shareholder value.

The dividend pay-out policy should be based on investor preferences for cash dividends now or capital gains in future from enhanced share value resultant from re-investment into projects with a positive NPV.

Many types of multinational company shareholder (for example, institutions such as pension funds and insurance companies) rely on dividends to meet current expenses and any instability in dividends would seriously affect them.

An additional factor for multinationals is that they have more than one dividend policy to consider:

- Dividends to external shareholders.

- Dividends between group companies, facilitating the movement of profits and funds within the group.

Alternative dividend policies used by MNCs

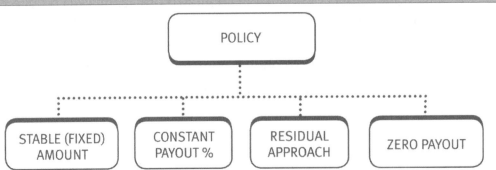

Probably the most common policy adopted by multinationals for external shareholders is a variant on stable dividend policy. Most companies go for a stable, but rising, dividend per share:

- Dividends lag behind earnings, but are maintained even when earnings fall below the dividend level, as happens when production is lost for several months during a major industrial dispute. This was referred to as a 'ratchet' pattern of dividends.

- This policy has the advantage of not signalling 'bad news' to investors. Also if the increases in dividend per share are not too large it should not seriously upset the firm's clientele of investors by disturbing their tax position.

A policy of a constant pay-out ratio is seldom used by multinationals because of the tremendous fluctuations in dividend per share that it could bring:

- Many firms, however, might work towards a long-run target pay-out percentage smoothing out the peaks and troughs each year.

- If sufficiently smoothed the pattern would be not unlike the ratchet pattern demonstrated above.

The residual approach to dividends contains a lot of financial common sense:

- If positive NPV projects are available, they should be adopted, otherwise funds should be returned to shareholders.

- This avoids the unnecessary transaction costs involved in paying shareholders a dividend and then asking for funds from the same shareholders (via a rights issue) to fund a new project.

- The major problem with the residual approach to dividends is that it can lead to large fluctuations in dividends, which could signal 'bad news' to investors.

7 Dividend capacity

Dividend capacity for a multinational company

As for any company, dividend capacity is a major determinant of dividend policy for multinationals. Key factors include:

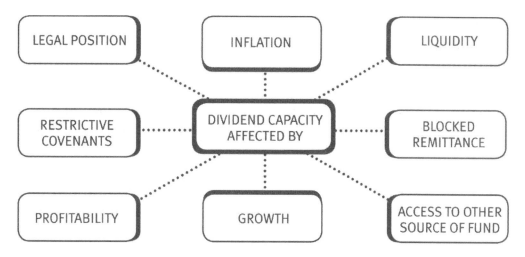

The additional factor that was not discussed earlier is 'remittance blocking'.

If, once a foreign direct investment has taken place, the government of the host country imposes a restriction on the amount of profit that can be returned to the parent company, this is known as a 'block on the remittance of dividends':

- Often done through the imposition of strict exchange controls.

- Limits the amount of centrally remitted funds available to pay dividends to parent company shareholders (i.e. restricts dividend capacity).

How the parent company might try to avoid such a block on remittances

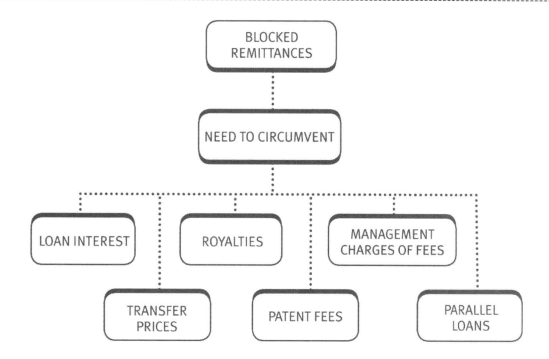

Blocked remittances may be avoided by one of the following methods:

- Increasing transfer prices paid by the foreign subsidiary to the parent company (see below).

- Lending the equivalent of the dividend to the parent company.

- Making payments to the parent company in the form of royalties, payments for patents, and/or management fees and charges.

- Charging the subsidiary company additional head office overheads.

- Parallel loans (currency swaps), whereby the foreign subsidiary lends cash to the subsidiary of another a company requiring funds in the foreign country. In return the parent company would receive the loan of an equivalent amount of cash in the home country from the other subsidiary's parent company.

The government of the foreign country might try to prevent many of these measures being used.

Free cash flow to equity for a MNC

Free cash flow to equity (FCFE)

- The gross free cash flow to equity of a multinational company can be defined as:

  Operating cash flow + dividends from joint ventures – net interest paid – tax.

- To determine the potential dividend capacity of the business, account needs to be taken of any capital re-investment. This is known as the net free cash flow to equity and can be defined as:

  Gross free cash flow to equity – capital expenditure +/– disposals/acquisitions + new capital issued.

Example showing FCFE for a MNC

What is the 20X6 net free cash flow to equity (i.e. the potential dividend capacity) for the following business? [All figures are taken from the company's cash flow statement]

	20X6	20X5
	$m	$m
Capital expenditure	500	400
Acquisition of new subsidiary company	325	0
Disposal of old subsidiary	250	100
Equity dividends paid	75	70
Taxation paid	275	200
Operating cash inflow	1,000	800
Interest paid	315	295
Dividend from joint venture	150	80
New ordinary shares issued	100	100

Solution

Gross FCFE = $(1,000 + 150 – 315 – 275) = $560m

Net FCFE [potential dividend capacity] = $(560 – 500 – 325 + 250 + 100) = $85m

This potential can then be compared to the actual dividend to determine whether there has been an over or under distribution.

 FCFE – Reinvestment and capital reconstruction

Reinvestment strategy

A company's reinvestment strategy will have two strands:

- Short-term reinvestment – working capital requirements that will come from operating cash flow (for example, an investment in inventory).

- Long-term reinvestment – capital expenditure programmes:

  - Generally positive purpose (for example, an expansion plan) and positive expected NPV.

  - Sometimes negative purpose (for example, compliance with new legal requirements on emissions in a factory) and negative expected NPV.

Any reinvestment of profits earned will restrict the capacity of a company to pay a dividend.

Management will require to show that the proposed reinvestment strategy will provide a return to shareholders (i.e. increase their wealth) more than an immediate pay-out in the form of dividends or share repurchase.

In these circumstances, a company may decide to give its shareholders a 'pay-out' using a scrip dividend, preserving the cash in the business for reinvestment and at the same time rewarding its shareholders with a non-cash return in the form of additional shares.

Capital reconstruction programmes

The nature of the capital reconstruction will determine its impact on both current and future free cash flow.

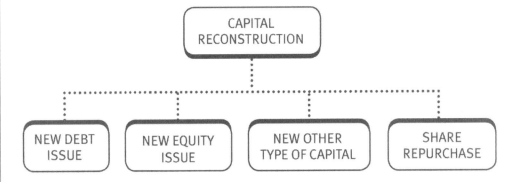

Share repurchase scheme

- Reduces immediate free cash flow to give shareholders an alternative to a straight cash dividend.

- Potentially increases future free cash flows as there will be fewer shares to pay future dividends on but the company may decide to keep the absolute dividend pay-out the same as before, simply paying out a higher dividend per share than before the repurchase.

New issue of debt for reinvestment purposes (i.e. working capital or capital expenditure)

- Reduces future free cash flow by interest costs and debt repayments.

New issue of debt to pay current cash dividend or share repurchase

- Provides immediate cash to pay dividend or share repurchase.

- Reduces future free cash flow by interest costs and debt repayments.

New issue of equity for reinvestment purposes (i.e. working capital or capital expenditure)

- Increases the number of shares on which dividends may have to be paid in the future but the company may decide to keep the absolute dividend pay-out the same as before, simply paying out a lower dividend per share than before the new issue.

Other

There may be other forms of capital issue, such as:

- special types of ordinary shares, perhaps with enhanced dividend rights or fixed dividend rights, both payable before 'normal' ordinary shares

- preference shares with a first dividend claim on the after tax profit.

Any negative impact that required payments for the type of finance have on free cash flow will reduce the company's dividend capacity.

8   Transfer pricing

Large diversified groups will be split into numerous smaller profit centres, each preparing accounts for its own sphere of activities and paying tax on its profits. Multinational groups are likely to own individual companies established in different countries throughout the world.

Multinational transfer pricing is the process of deciding on appropriate prices for the goods and services sold intra-group across national borders.

Revision of basic transfer pricing

Basic principles

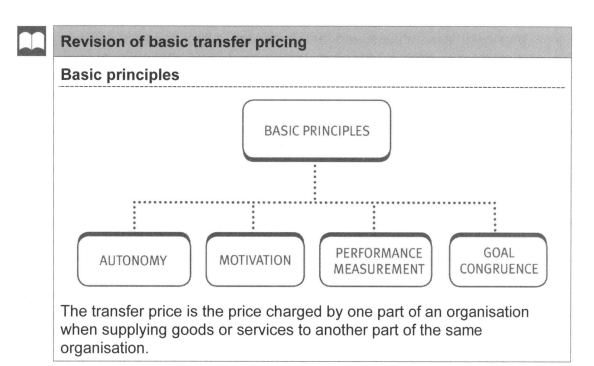

The transfer price is the price charged by one part of an organisation when supplying goods or services to another part of the same organisation.

Remember the objectives of a good 'domestic' transfer pricing system:

- Maintain divisional autonomy.
- Maintain motivation for managers.
- Assess divisional performance objectively.
- Ensure goal congruence.

Multinational aspects

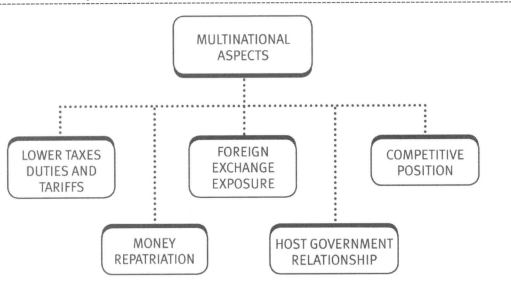

The setting of transfer prices is vital for multinational groups.

When considering a multinational firm, additional (and in most cases overriding) international transfer pricing objectives are to

- pay lower taxes, duties, and tariffs. A detailed knowledge of different tax regimes is outside the syllabus, but be aware that multinational firms will be keen to transfer profits if possible from high tax countries to low tax ones

- repatriate funds from foreign subsidiary companies to head office

- be less exposed to foreign exchange risks

- build and maintain a better international competitive position

- enable foreign subsidiaries to match or undercut local competitors' prices

- have good relations with governments in the countries in which the multinational firm operates.

In particular, international transfer pricing requires careful consideration of multiple currency effects and multiple tax and legal regimes.

Illustration 1

Examples in practice of the objectives of international transfer pricing might include:

- reduction of overall corporate income taxes, primarily by manipulating the transfer price to divert taxable income from high tax countries to low tax countries

- minimisation of import duties by setting a low transfer price into a country with import duties will reduce the level of duty paid

- avoidance of exchange controls or other restrictions such as dividend remittance restrictions by setting a low transfer price to the parent company as an alternative to a dividend payment

- improvement of the appearance of the financial performance of a subsidiary by increasing profits through transfer pricing thus helping to:

  - satisfy any earnings criteria set by lenders to the subsidiary

  - make the acquisition of a new loan easier.

Transfer pricing (especially international transfer pricing) is not simply buying and selling products between divisions. The term is also used to cover, inter alia:

- head office general management charges to subsidiaries for various services

- specific charges made to subsidiaries by, for example, head office human resource or information technology functions

- royalty payments

  - between parent company and subsidiaries

  - among subsidiaries.

- interest rate on borrowings between group companies.

The basics of transfer pricing

A general rule for transfer pricing

Transfer price per unit = Standard variable cost in the producing division plus the opportunity cost to the company as a whole of supplying the unit internally.

The opportunity cost will be either the contribution forgone by selling one unit internally rather than externally, or the contribution forgone by not using the same facilities in the producing division for their next best alternative use.

The application of this general rule means that the transfer price equals:

- **the standard variable cost of the producing division**, if there is no outside market for the units manufactured and no alternative use for the facilities in that division

- **the market price**, if there is an outside market for the units manufactured in the producing division and no alternative more profitable use for the facilities in that division.

Transfer pricing systems

A transfer pricing system should:

- be reasonably easy to operate and to understand

- be flexible in terms of a changing organisation structure

- allow divisional autonomy to be maintained, since continued autonomy should motivate divisional managers to give their best performance

- allow divisional performance to be assessed objectively

- ensure that divisional managers make decisions that are in the best interests both of the divisions and of the whole company.

There are broadly three types of transfer prices:

- Market-based prices.

- Cost-related prices.

- Negotiated prices and dual prices.

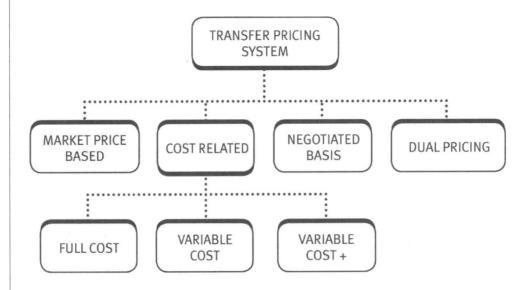

The basics of transfer pricing were covered in detail in Performance Management (PM).

Application to multinational companies

Choice of transfer price basis for the multinational company

Basis	Comments
Market based	<ul><li>Encouraged by tax and customs authorities in both multinational company and local subsidiary jurisdictions.</li><li>The profit split between the group companies is fair and therefore the authorities in each country receive their appropriate share of corporate tax and duties.</li><li>Prices for the same goods in different countries could vary significantly.</li><li>Exchange rate changes could have significant impact.</li><li>Local taxes could have significant impact.</li><li>Strategically, subsidiary will want to set its prices in accordance with local supply and demand conditions.</li></ul>
Full cost	<ul><li>Acceptable to tax and customs authorities in both multinational company and local subsidiary jurisdictions.</li><li>The authorities in each country receive their appropriate share of corporate tax and duties as the transfer price approximates to the 'correct' cost of the goods.</li></ul>
Variable cost	<ul><li>Unacceptable to tax and customs authorities in the supplying company's jurisdiction.</li><li>All profits allocated to the receiving company and thus no corporate tax payable by supplying company.</li></ul>
Negotiated	<ul><li>Could result in sub-optimal decision as no advantage taken of different corporate tax rates and duties.</li></ul>

Tax considerations

Local regulations and tax regimes

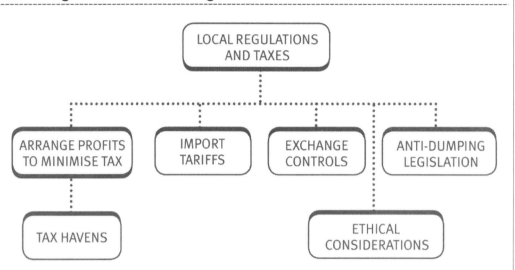

Transfer pricing and tax authorities

One common approach to setting international transfer prices adopted by multinational companies is to seek to minimise the group's overall total tax liability. The objective is to set transfer prices in order to report:

* low profits in countries with high tax rates
* high profits in countries with low tax rates.

Illustration of a tax minimising strategy

If the taxation on corporate profits is:

* 35% in Wyland
* 25% in Exland.

A multinational company operating in both of these countries may try to 'manipulate' its results so that the majority of the profit is made by its subsidiary/division in Exland thereby saving corporate tax.

The aim is to minimise profits in Wyland and maximise profit in Exland. It could do this via:

* increasing or decreasing transfer prices between the subsidiaries/divisions as appropriate
* invoice services provided by the Exland subsidiary/division to the Wyland subsidiary/division.

This objective is frustrated in many countries whose governments require that transfer prices are set on an arm's length basis [i.e. using the prevailing market price]. The principle is still useful however as a broad objective and particularly valuable when transferring goods for which no external market price exists or when operating in countries without an arm's length transfer price requirement.

Alternatively many multinational businesses sited in high tax jurisdictions create marketing/promotional/distribution subsidiaries in low tax jurisdictions and transfer products to them at low transfer prices. Overall corporate tax will be reduced, as the profit from selling these products to the final customer will be taxed in the lower jurisdiction.

If transfer prices are set on the basis of minimising tax, this can have consequences for the whole company:

- Autonomy will be compromised if the parent company fixes transfer prices throughout the group to minimise total tax.

- This can have adverse motivational consequences.

 Tax havens, import tariffs and local regulations

The use of tax havens

A tax haven is a country that has a series of unique characteristics, the primary one being relatively low tax compared to other countries. Bank secrecy and strict privacy laws are also other common features of tax havens.

There are many tax havens throughout the world. Well-known examples are:

- Cayman Islands
- Luxembourg
- Liechtenstein
- Bahamas
- Jersey (the Channel Islands).

From the perspective of a multinational company, tax havens may provide opportunities to reduce corporate taxes by the quite legal use of subsidiaries in offshore tax havens like the Cayman Islands. Where tax regimes differ around the globe organisations can make use of differing tax rules to keep a larger proportion of their profits.

A defining feature of the tax haven is that normally little production takes place but many organisations are registered there. Many companies seek to lower their taxes by, for example, setting up foreign units and using internal lending so that profits are taken primarily in tax havens and costs are incurred in high tax countries.

Inevitably tax authorities in higher tax countries have sought to close tax loopholes, and potentially such changes could result in a heavily increased tax burden for multinationals and hence represents a significant risk to their post-tax earnings. However, advantages still exist. A tax haven will be most attractive with the following criteria:

- Low rate of corporation tax.

- Low withholding tax on dividends paid to overseas holding companies.

- Comprehensive tax treaties with other countries.

- Stable economy with low political risk.

- Lack of exchange controls.

- Good communications with the rest of the world.

- Developed legal framework so that rights can be safeguarded.

Import tariffs

An import tariff is a schedule of duties imposed by a country on imported goods. The tariff can be levied on a percentage of the value of the import, or as an amount per unit of import.

For example, if the government of Zedland imposes an import tariff of 10% on the value of all goods imported, a multinational company with a subsidiary/division in Zedland that imports goods from another subsidiary in another country may decide to minimise costs by minimising the transfer price.

That decision might, however, conflict with the objective of minimising corporate taxation if the subsidiary then sold the goods to the final customer and corporate taxation rate in Zedland was very high.

Local regulations

There are other potential local rules and regulations that will impact on the transfer pricing policy of a multinational company.

Exchange controls

Foreign exchange controls are various forms of controls imposed by a government on the purchase/sale of foreign currencies by residents or on the purchase/sale of local currency by non-residents. A common exchange control is a restriction on the amount of currency that may be imported or exported.

Profits made and cash flows earned in a foreign country are of no value to a multinational group if they cannot be repatriated to the home country for distribution to shareholders. Under exchange controls, capital invested into a country may often be repatriated, whereas remittance of the profits is strictly limited.

Charging management fees, royalties, fees for research and development, technical know-how and so on, will impact upon the profitability in a subsidiary abroad. Provided that even those fees and so on can be remitted, and do not become restricted also by the exchange controls, this is a way of releasing funds from a country, which has such controls.

Most governments are naturally well aware of these possibilities and respond by limiting repatriations in general. For example, a proportion of profit made may have to be retained and reinvested in the host country. Such 'blocked funds' may even have to be invested in government bonds, the cash from which may then be sent to the group but only upon maturity.

Anti-dumping legislation

'Dumping' is the practice of selling goods/services in an overseas/foreign market at a price lower than the price or cost in the home market. It might be without motive or it might have an economic purpose such as trying to put competitors out of business. Anti-dumping legislation is designed to minimise the impact of this practice.

For example, many governments take action to protect domestic industries by preventing multinational companies from transferring goods cheaply into their countries. Forcing the use of market price based transfer pricing can do this.

Ethical issues in transfer pricing

There are a number of potential ethical issues for the multinational company to consider when formulating its transfer pricing strategy:

- Social responsibility, reducing amounts paid in customs duties and tax.

- Bypassing a country's financial regulation via remittance of dividends.

- Not operating as a 'responsible citizen' in foreign country.

- Reputational loss.

- Bad publicity.

- Tax evasion.

Summary – Deciding on a transfer pricing strategy

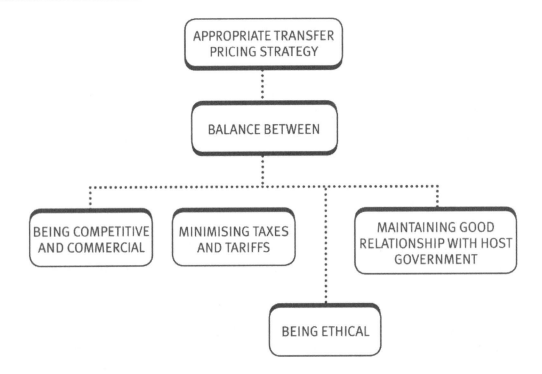

Comprehensive example

Colsan Co ['Colsan'] is a UK-based multinational company with two overseas subsidiaries. Colsan wishes to minimise its global tax bill, and part of its tax strategy is to try to take advantage of opportunities provided by transfer pricing.

Colsan has subsidiaries in Fraland and Serland

Taxation and excise duty rates	UK	Fraland	Serland
Corporate tax on profits	30%	45%	20%
Withholding tax on dividends	–	10%	–
Import tariffs on all goods (not tax allowable)	–	–	5%

The Fraland subsidiary produces 100,000 sofa frames per year, which are then sent to Serland for the upholstery to be added, and the furniture completed. The frames are sold to the Serland subsidiary at a transfer price equal to variable cost (which is £50) plus 50%. Annual fixed costs in Fraland are £1.5m.

The Serland subsidiary incurs additional variable costs of £72 per unit and sells the completed furniture for £200 per unit in Serland. Annual fixed costs in Serland are £1.7m.

All transactions between the companies are in £ (British pounds). Each year, the Fraland subsidiary remits 60% of its profit after tax and the Serland subsidiary remits 100% of its profit after tax to Colsan.

Required:

If Colsan instructs the Fraland subsidiary to sell the frames to the Serland subsidiary at full cost

- **Determine the potential effect of this on the group tax and tariff payments.**

- **Outline the consequences of this strategy.**

Assume that bilateral tax agreements exist which allow Fraland and Serland tax paid to be credited against Colsan's UK tax liability.

Potential effect 1 [under the current scheme]	Fraland	Serland
	£000	£000
Sales	7,500	20,000
Variable costs	(5,000)	(7,200)
Cost from Fraland	–	(7,500)
Fixed costs	(1,500)	(1,700)
Profit before tax	1,000	3,600
Local corporate tax [45% in Fraland, 20% in Serland]	(450)	(720)
Profit after local corporate tax	550	2,880
Import tariff [5% in Serland]	–	(375)
Gross remittance to UK [60% before withholding tax in Fraland, 100% in Serland]	330	2,505
With-holding tax [10% in Fraland]	(33)	–
With-holding tax [10% in Fraland]	(33)	–
Net remitted to UK	297	2,505
Retained locally	220	0
UK corporate tax:		
Taxable profit	1,000	3,600
UK corporate tax @ 30%	300	1,080
Less: local corporate tax [allowed under bi-lateral agreement]	(300)	(720)
Additional UK corporate tax payable	0	360
Sales	6,500	20,000
Variable costs	(5,000)	(7,200)
Cost from Fraland	–	(6,500)
Fixed costs	(1,500)	(1,700)
Profit before tax	0	4,600
Local corporate tax [45% in Fraland, 20% in Serland]	0	(920)
Profit after local corporate tax	0	3,680
Import tariff [5% in Serland]	–	(325)
Gross remittance to UK [60% before withholding tax in Fraland, 100% in Serland]	0	3,355
With-holding tax [10% in Fraland]	0	–
Net remitted to UK	0	3,355
Retained locally	0	0
UK corporate tax:		
Taxable profit	0	4,600
UK corporate tax @ 30%	0	1,380
Less: local corporate tax		
[allowed under bi-lateral agreement]	0	(920)
Additional UK corporate tax payable	0	460

Summary of potential effects	Under the current scheme	Under the proposed scheme	Difference
	£000	£000	£000
Net amount remitted to UK	2,802	3,355	553
Retained locally in Fraland	220	0	(220)
Taxes payable:			
In UK [additional tax]	360	460	(100)
In Fraland	483	0	483
In Serland	1,095	1,245	(150)
Total taxes payable	1,938	1,705	233

The proposed new scheme may be unacceptable to:

- The tax authorities in Fraland, where £483,000 in corporate taxes would be lost. The tax authorities might insist on an arms-length transfer price for transfers between Fraland and Serland.

- The subsidiary in Fraland, which would no longer make a profit, or have retentions available for future investment in Fraland. Dependent on how performance in Fraland was evaluated, this might adversely affect rewards and motivation for the employees in Fraland.

9 Chapter summary

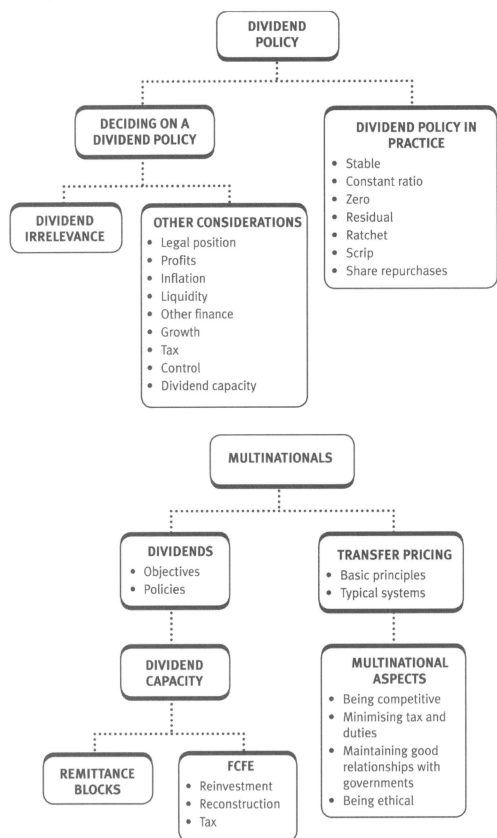

Test your understanding answers

Test your understanding 1

Notes would need to cover:

Theoretical position on dividends

Provided a company invests in positive NPV projects, the pattern of dividend payments is not relevant to an investor. The company should therefore use the funds available to invest in all positive NPV opportunities and any remaining funds should be distributed as dividends. Dividends are a **residual decision**.

Information content

In practice however, investors treat the level of dividends as a signal about the financial wellbeing of the company, and believe that high dividends signal confidence about the future.

This contrasts directly with the theory which would suggest a confident company would be retaining dividends to invest in all the positive NPV projects.

Clientele effect

Certain types of investor have a preference for certain types of income, and constantly changing the level of dividend pay-out will make it difficult for investors to plan their cash and tax positions.

Liquidity

Whilst it is theoretically possible for a firm to borrow to pay dividends, taking out loan finance will alter the gearing level of the firm, which itself will be the subject of policy and cannot be altered arbitrarily.

Cost of finance

If the firm needs funds for future investments, retained earnings are the cheapest source of funds available.

Policy

A suitable policy would therefore be one that:

- leaves sufficient funds for investment and avoids the need to incur transaction costs raising funds in the near future

- has a fairly constant dividend pattern.

Director X

This is the policy many companies do adopt in practice. The problem is that it ignores the availability of funds, and the investment projects that may require them.

Director Y

Director Y is correct that the value of a share is, in part, dependent on the dividend stream. In theory, as mentioned above, it should not matter if a dividend is missed, provided the funds are invested in positive NPV projects. However, it is true that in practice, if shareholders are unhappy about the cut, and sell their shares the price fall.

The weighted average cost of capital (WACC)

Chapter learning objectives

Study guide section	Study guide outcome
B3: Impact of financing on investment decisions and adjusted present value	(c) Calculate the cost of capital of an organisation, including the cost of equity and cost of debt, based on the range of equity and debt sources of finance. Discuss the appropriateness of using the cost of capital to establish project and organisational value, and discuss its relationship to such value.
	(e) Assess an organisation's debt exposure to interest rate changes using the simple Macaulay duration and modified duration methods.
	(f) Discuss the benefits and limitations of duration including the impact of convexity.
	(g) Assess the organisation's exposure to credit risk, including: (i) Explain the role of, and the risk assessment models used by the principal rating agencies (ii) Estimate the likely credit spread over risk free (iii) Estimate the organisation's current cost of debt capital using the appropriate term structure of interest rates and the credit spread.

One of the PER performance objectives (PO09 – Evaluate Investment and Financing Decisions) is to be able to advise on the cost of different sources of finance.

PER

Working through this chapter should help you understand how to demonstrate that objective.

1 The weighted average cost of capital (WACC)

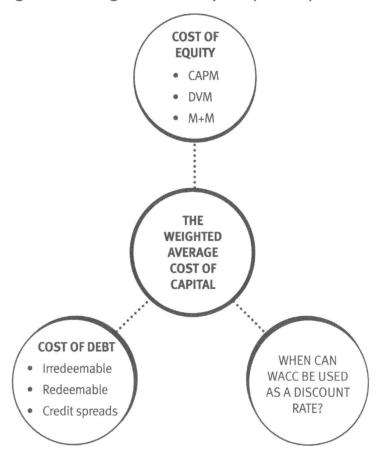

Overview of the WACC

A key consideration in financial management is the firm's WACC. The WACC is derived by finding a firm's cost of equity and cost of debt and averaging them according to the market value of each source of finance. The formula for calculating WACC is given on the exam formula sheet as:

$$\text{WACC} = \left[\frac{V_e}{V_e + V_d}\right] k_e + \left[\frac{V_d}{V_e + V_d}\right] k_d (1 - T)$$

> ### Explanation of terms
>
> V_e and V_d are the market values of equity and debt respectively.
>
> k_e and k_d are the returns required by the equity holders and the debt holders respectively.
>
> T is the corporation tax rate
>
> k_e is the cost of equity
>
> $k_d(1 - T)$ is the cost of debt

This chapter reviews the basic techniques for deriving cost of equity and cost of debt from the Financial Management (FM) syllabus, and adds some more advanced techniques too.

2   The cost of equity

Methods of calculating the cost of equity (k_e)

The three main methods of calculating k_e are:

- the Capital Asset Pricing Model (CAPM)

- the Dividend Valuation Model (DVM)

- Modigliani and Miller's Proposition 2 formula.

The formulae for these methods are all given on the exam formula sheet.

The Capital Asset Pricing Model (CAPM)

The CAPM derives a required return for an investor by relating return to the level of systematic risk faced by an investor – note that the CAPM is based on the assumption that all investors are well-diversified, so only systematic risk is relevant.

The CAPM formula is:

Required return $(k_e) = R_f + \beta_i (E(R_m) - R_f)$

where:

R_f = risk free rate

$E(R_m)$ = expected return on the market

N.B. $(E(R_m) - R_f)$ is called the equity risk premium

β_i = beta factor = systematic risk of the firm or project compared to market.

The portfolio effect

The CAPM model is based upon the assumption that investors are well diversified, so will have eliminated all the unsystematic (specific) risk from their portfolios. The beta factor is a measure of the level of systematic risk (general, market risk) faced by a well-diversified investor – see more details on beta factors below.

The risk reduction through diversifying is known as the portfolio effect.

 The beta factor

The beta factor indicates the level of systematic risk faced by an investor.

A beta > 1 indicates above average risk, while beta < 1 means relatively low risk.

Beta factors are derived by statistically analysing returns from a particular share over a period compared to the overall market returns. If the returns on the individual share are more volatile than the overall market, the firm's beta will be greater than 1.

 Illustration of the use of the CAPM formula

Gillespie Co has a beta factor of 1.73. The current return on a risk free asset is 3% per year and the equity risk premium is 12%.

Hence, using CAPM, Gillespie Co's cost of equity (return required by the shareholders) is 3% + (1.73 × 12%) = 23.76%.

Which beta factor to use?

To calculate the current cost of equity of a firm, the current beta factor can be used.

However, if the firm's current beta factor cannot be derived easily, a proxy beta may be used.

A proxy beta is usually found by identifying a quoted company with a similar business risk profile and using its beta. However, when selecting an appropriate beta from a similar company, account has to be taken of the gearing ratios involved.

The beta values for companies reflect both:

- business risk (resulting from operations)
- finance risk (resulting from their level of gearing).

There are therefore two types of beta:

- 'Asset' or 'ungeared' beta, β_a, which reflects purely the systematic risk of the business area.

- 'Equity' or 'geared' beta, β_e, which reflects the systematic risk of the business area and the company specific gearing ratio.

In the exam, you will often have to degear the proxy equity beta (using the gearing of the quoted company) and then regear to reflect the gearing position of the company in question.

The formula to regear and degear betas is:

$$\beta_a = \left[\frac{V_e}{(V_e + V_d(1-T))} \beta_e \right] + \left[\frac{V_d(1-T)}{(V_e + V_d(1-T))} \beta_d \right]$$

However, β_d (beta value for debt) is often assumed to be zero, because of the low risk of being a debt holder, so this equation often simplifies to give

$$\beta_a = \left[\frac{V_e}{(V_e + V_d(1-T))} \beta_e \right]$$

Test your understanding 1

The directors of Moorland Co, a company which has 75% of its operations in the retail sector and 25% in manufacturing, are trying to derive the firm's cost of equity. However, since the company is not listed, it has been difficult to determine an appropriate beta factor. Instead, the following information has been researched:

Retail industry – quoted retailers have an average equity beta of 1.20, and an average gearing ratio of 20:80 (debt: equity).

Manufacturing industry – quoted manufacturers have an average equity beta of 1.45 and an average gearing ratio of 45:55 (debt: equity).

The risk free rate is 3% and the equity risk premium is 6%. Tax on corporate profits is 30%. Moorland Co has gearing of 50% debt and 50% equity by market values. Assume that the risk on corporate debt is negligible.

Required:

Calculate the cost of equity of Moorland Co using the CAPM model.

Arbitrage pricing theory

Arbitrage pricing theory (APT) is an alternative pricing model to CAPM, developed by Stephen Ross in 1976. It attempts to explain the risk-return relationship using several independent factors rather than a single index.

CAPM is a single index model in that the expected return from a security is a function of only one factor, its beta value:

Expected return = $R_f + ß (E(R_m) - R_f)$

However APT is a multi-index model in that the expected return from a security is a linear function of several independent factors:

Expected return = $a + ß_1 f_1 + ß_2 f_2 + ...$

where a, $ß_1$, $ß_2$, ... are constants

f_1, f_2, ... are the various factors that influence security returns

For example, f_1 could be the return on the market (as in CAPM), f_2 could be an industry index specific to the sector in which the company operates, f_3 could be an interest rate index, etc.

Ross showed that, if shares are assumed to form an efficient market, an equilibrium is reached when:

Expected return = $R_f + ß_1 (R_1 - R_f) + ß_2 (R_2 - R_f) + ...$

where R_f = the risk free rate

$ß_i$ = constants expressing the security's sensitivity to each factor

R_i = the expected return on a portfolio with unit sensitivity to factor i and zero sensitivity to any other factor.

Research undertaken to date suggests that there are a small number of factors, or economic forces, that systematically affect the returns on assets. These are:

* inflation or deflation

* long run growth in profitability in the economy

* industrial production

* term structure of interest rates

* default premium on bonds

* price of oil.

Each factor must be independent of the other factors. APT assumes that the process of arbitrage would ensure that two assets offering identical returns and risks will sell for the same price. Intuitively, APT appears to improve on CAPM, as return is determined by a number of independent factors. The main practical difficulties are in determining what those factors are, as the model does not specify them, and forecasting their value. There have been few tests of APT, probably because of the difficulties in determining which variables to include in the model and how to weigh them.

APT has gained in popularity as empirical tests of CAPM in practice have raised significant doubts as to CAPM's validity. However it is fair to say that empirical testing of APT has to date been only limited, so its effectiveness remains to be proved. CAPM is certainly simpler than APT, being a single index rather than a multi-index model, so CAPM will remain popular for some time.

The dividend valuation model (DVM)

Theory: The value of the company/share is the present value of the expected future dividends discounted at the shareholders' required rate of return.

Assuming a constant growth rate in dividends, g:

$P_0 = D_0(1 + g)/(k_e - g)$

(this formula is given on the formula sheet)

Explanation of terms

D_0 = current level of dividend

P_0 = current share price

g = estimated growth rate

If we need to derive k_e the formula can be rearranged to:

$k_e = [D_0 (1 + g)/P_0] + g$

Illustration of the DVM formula

Cocker Co has just paid a dividend of 14 cents per share. In recent years, annual dividend growth has been 3% per year, and the current share price is $1.48.

Using the DVM formula, the cost of equity is $[0.14 \times 1.03/1.48] + 0.03 = 12.7\%$.

Deriving g in the DVM formula

There are two ways of estimating the likely growth rate of dividends:

*   Extrapolating based on past dividend patterns.

*   Assuming growth is dependent on the level of earnings retained in the business.

Estimating dividend growth from past dividend patterns

This method assumes that the past pattern of dividends is a fair indicator of the future.

The formula for extrapolating growth can therefore be written as:

$$g = \sqrt[n]{\frac{D_0}{\text{Dividend n yrs ago}}} - 1 = \left(\frac{D_0}{\text{Dividend n years ago}}\right)^{\left(\frac{1}{n}\right)} - 1$$

where:

n = number of years of dividend growth

This method can only be used if:

*   recent dividend pattern is considered typical

*   historical pattern is expected to continue.

As a result, this method will usually only be appropriate to predict growth rates over the short term.

Illustration of the calculation

A company currently pays a dividend of 32 cents; five years ago the dividend was 20 cents.

Estimate the annual growth rate in dividends.

Solution

Since growth is assumed to be constant, the growth rate, g, can be assumed to have been the same in each of the 5 years, i.e. the 20 cents will have become 32 after 5 years of constant growth.

$20 \times (1 + g)^5 = 32$

or $(1 + g)^5 = 32/20 = 1.6$

$1 + g = 1.6^{1/5} \approx 1.1$, so g = 0.1 or 10%.

Estimating growth using the earnings retention model (Gordon's growth model)

This model is based on the assumption that:

- growth is primarily due to the reinvestment of retained earnings

The formula is therefore:

$g = r \times b$

where:

b = earnings retention rate

r = rate of return to equity

What is r?

At FM level, r was considered to be the Accounting Rate of Return on equity calculated as:

r = PAT/opening shareholders' funds

However, at AFM level we need to re-examine this assumption. The weakness of the ARR as a measure of return is that:

- it ignores the level of investment in intangible assets

- in the long run, the return on new investment tends to the cost of equity.

Hence, if a short term growth rate is required, the ARR provides a fair approximation for use in the growth model. However, if a long term growth rate is needed, k_e should be used as the percentage return. To avoid a recursion problem, this should be derived using CAPM.

Modigliani and Miller's Proposition 2 formula

Modigliani and Miller's gearing theory was covered in the earlier chapter on the financing decision.

As part of their theory, they derived a formula which can be used to derive a firm's cost of equity:

$k_e = k_e^i + (1 - T)(k_e^i - k_d)(V_d / V_e)$

(this formula is given on the formula sheet)

Explanation of terms

V_e and V_d are the market values of equity and debt respectively.

k_d is the (pre-tax) return required by the debt holders.

T is the corporation tax rate.

k_e^i is the cost of equity in an equivalent ungeared firm.

k_e is the cost of equity in the geared firm.

Test your understanding 2

Moondog Co is a company with a 20:80 debt: equity ratio. Using CAPM, its cost of equity has been calculated as 12%.

It is considering raising some debt finance to change its gearing ratio to 25:75 debt to equity. The expected return to debt holders is 4% per year, and the rate of corporate tax is 30%.

Required:

Calculate the theoretical cost of equity in Moondog Co after the refinancing.

3 The cost of debt

Methods of calculating cost of debt

The company's cost of debt is found by taking the return required by debt holders/lenders (k_d) and adjusting it for the tax relief received by the firm as it pays debt interest.

Note on exam terminology

In exam questions you may be given the cost of debt or you may have to calculate it – see below for calculations.

If you are given the 'cost of debt', be aware that the cost of debt is normally quoted pre-tax because this is the rate at which the companies will pay interest on their borrowings (even though the 'true' cost to them will be net of tax because interest is payable before tax and therefore companies benefit from the 'tax shield').

It can be assumed, therefore, that cost of debt will mean pre-tax cost of debt (k_d) unless it is clearly stated otherwise.

Using the DVM to estimate cost of debt

In Financial Management (FM), the cost of debt was generally estimated using the principles of the dividend valuation model. As seen above, the basic theory of the DVM is:

> The value of a share = the present value of the future dividends discounted at the shareholders' required rate of return.

Using the same logic

> The value of a bond = the present value of the future receipts (interest and redemption amount) discounted at the lenders' required rate of return.

This theory gives rise to two alternative calculations of k_d $(1-T)$, for irredeemable debt and redeemable debt.

Irredeemable debt

k_d $(1-T) = I$ $(1-T)/MV$

where

I = the annual interest paid

T = corporation tax rate

MV = the current bond price

Test your understanding 3

Mackay Co has some irredeemable, 5% coupon bonds in issue, which are trading at $94.50 per $100 nominal. The tax rate is 30%.

Required:

Calculate Mackay Co's post-tax cost of debt.

Redeemable debt

k_d $(1-T)$ = the Internal Rate of Return (IRR) of:

- the bond price
- the interest (net of tax)
- the redemption payment.

Test your understanding 4

Dodgy Co's 6% coupon bonds are currently priced at $89%. The bonds are redeemable at par in 5 years. Corporation tax is 30%.

Required:

Calculate the post-tax cost of debt.

Pre-tax cost of debt (or 'yield' to the debt holder)

In both the previous examples, the focus was on finding the post-tax cost of debt, which is a key component in the company's WACC calculation.

In order to compute the pre-tax cost of debt (sometimes called the yield to the investor, yield to maturity, or gross redemption yield) the method is very similar.

For **irredeemable debt**, the pre-tax cost of debt is simply I/MV.

For **redeemable debt**, the pre-tax cost of debt is the IRR of the bond price, the GROSS interest (i.e. pre-tax) and the redemption payment.

In both cases, the only difference from the above calculations is that interest is now taken pre-tax in the formulae.

Student Accountant article

The examiner's article 'Bond valuation and bond yields' in the Technical Articles section of the ACCA website covers the calculation of bond yields in more detail.

Credit spread

An alternative technique used in AFM for deriving cost of debt is based on an awareness of **credit spread** (sometimes referred to as the 'default risk premium'), and the formula:

$k_d (1-T) = $ (Risk free rate + Credit spread) $(1-T)$

The credit spread is a measure of the credit risk associated with a company. Credit spreads are generally calculated by a credit rating agency and presented in a table like the one below.

Credit risk, rating agencies and spread

What is credit risk?

Credit or default risk is the uncertainty surrounding a firm's ability to service its debts and obligations.

It can be defined as the risk borne by a lender that the borrower will default either on interest payments, the repayment of the borrowing at the due date or both.

The role of credit rating agencies

If a company wants to assess whether a firm that owes them money is likely to default on the debt, a key source of information is a credit rating agency.

They provide vital information on creditworthiness to:

- potential investors
- regulators of investing bodies
- the firm itself.

The assessment of creditworthiness

A large number of agencies can provide information on smaller firms, but for larger firms credit assessments are usually carried out by one of the international credit rating agencies. The three largest international agencies are S&P Global Ratings, Moody's and Fitch.

Certain factors have been shown to have a particular correlation with the likelihood that a company will default on its obligations:

- The magnitude and strength of the company's cash flows.
- The size of the debt relative to the asset value of the firm.
- The volatility of the firm's asset value.
- The length of time the debt has to run.

Using this and other data, firms are scored and rated on a scale, such as the one shown here:

Fitch/S&P	Grade	Risk of default
AAA	Investment	Highest quality – zero risk
AA	Investment	High quality – v little risk
A	Investment	Strong – minimal risk
BBB	**Investment**	**Medium grade – low but clear risk**
BB	Junk	Speculative – marginal
B	Junk	Significant risk exposure
CCC	Junk	Considerable risk exposure
CC	Junk	Highly speculative – v high risk
C	Junk	In default – v high likelihood of failure

Calculating credit scores

The credit rating agencies use a variety of models to assess the creditworthiness of companies.

In the popular Kaplan Urwitz model, measures such as firm size, profitability, type of debt, gearing ratios, interest cover and levels of risk are fed into formulae to generate a credit score.

These scores are then used to create the rankings shown above. For example a score of above 6.76 suggests an AAA rating.

Credit spread

There is no way to tell in advance which firms will default on their obligations and which won't. As a result, to compensate lenders for this uncertainty, firms generally pay a spread or premium over the risk free rate of interest, which is proportional to their default probability.

The yield on a corporate bond is therefore given by:

Yield on corporate bond = Yield on equivalent treasury bond
+ credit spread

Table of credit spreads for industrial company bonds:

Rating	1 yr	2 yr	3 yr	5 yr	7 yr	10 yr	30 yr
AAA	5	10	15	22	27	30	55
AA	15	25	30	37	44	50	65
A	40	50	57	65	71	75	90
BBB	65	80	88	95	126	149	175
BB	210	235	240	250	265	275	290
B+	375	402	415	425	425	440	450

Examples of calculations of yield

Simple illustration

The current return on 5-year treasury bonds is 3.6%. C Co has equivalent bonds in issue but has an A rating. What is the expected yield on C's bonds?

Solution

From the table the credit spread for an A rated, 5-year bond is 65.

This means that 0.65% must be added to the yield on equivalent treasury bonds.

So yield on C's bonds = 3.6% + 0.65% = 4.25%.

More advanced illustration

The current return on 8-year treasury bonds is 4.2%. X Co has equivalent bonds in issue but has a BBB rating. What is the expected yield on X's bonds?

Solution

From the table the credit spread for a BBB rated, 7-year bond is 126. The spread for a 10-year bond is 149.

This would suggest an adjustment of

$$126 + \frac{(149 - 126)}{3}$$

= 126 + 7.67 = 133.67

So 1.34% must be added to the yield on equivalent treasury bonds.

So yield on X's bonds = 4.2% + 1.34% = 5.54%.

Test your understanding 5

The current 4-year risk free return is 2.6%. F Co has 4-year bonds in issue but has an AA rating.

Required:

(a) **calculate the expected yield on F's bonds**

(b) **find F's post-tax cost of debt associated with these bonds if the rate of corporation tax is 30%.**

(Use the information in the table of credit spreads above).

Test your understanding 6

Landline Co has an A credit rating.

It has $30m of 2 year bonds in issue, which are trading at $90%, and $50m of 10 year bonds which are trading at $108%.

The risk free rate is 2.5% and the corporation tax rate is 30%.

Required:

Calculate the company's post-tax cost of debt capital.

(Use the information in the table of credit spreads above).

More details on the 'risk free rate' – The spot yield curve

In all the previous examples, the risk free rate has been given as a single figure, based on the return required on government bonds.

However, in reality the return required will usually be higher for longer dated government bonds, to compensate investors for the additional uncertainty created by the longer time period.

Therefore, you might be given a 'spot yield curve' for government bonds, instead of a single 'risk free rate'. Then to calculate the yield curve for an individual company's bonds, add the given credit spread to the relevant government bond yield.

Test your understanding 7

The spot yield curve for government bonds is:

Year	%
1	3.50
2	3.65
3	3.80

The following table of credit spreads (in basis points) is presented by S&P Global Ratings:

Rating	1 year	2 year	3 year
AAA	14	25	38
AA	29	41	55
A	46	60	76

Required:

Estimate the individual yield curve for Stone Co, an A rated company.

Estimating the spot yield curve

There are several different methods used to estimate a spot yield curve, and the iterative process based on bootstrapping coupon paying bonds is perhaps the simplest to understand. Discussion of other methods of estimating the spot yield curve, such as using multiple regression techniques and observation of spot rates of zero coupon bonds, is beyond the scope of the AFM syllabus.

The following example demonstrates how the iterative process works:

Illustration of how to calculate the spot yield curve for government bonds

A government has three bonds in issue that all have a par value of $100 and are redeemable in one year, two years and three years respectively. Since the bonds are all government bonds, let's assume that they are of the same risk class. Let's also assume that coupons are payable on an annual basis.

Bond A, which is redeemable in a year's time, has a coupon rate of 7% and is trading at $103.

Bond B, which is redeemable in two years, has a coupon rate of 6% and is trading at $102.

Bond C, which is redeemable in three years, has a coupon rate of 5% and is trading at $98.

To determine the spot yield curve, each bond's cash flows are discounted in turn to determine the annual spot rates for the three years, as follows:

Bond A: $103 = \$107/(1 + r_1)$

so $r_1 = 107/103 - 1 = 0.0388$ or 3.88%

Bond B: $102 = (\$6/1.0388) + [106/(1 + r_2)^2]$

so $r_2 = [106/(102 - 5.78)]^{1/2} - 1 = 0.0496$ or 4.96%

Bond C: $98 = (\$5/1.0388) + (\$5/1.0496^2) + [105/(1 + r_3)^3]$

so $r_3 = [105/(98 - 4.81 - 4.54)]^{1/3} - 1 = 0.0580$ or 5.80%

The annual spot yield curve is therefore

Year	%
1	3.88
2	4.96
3	5.80

Student Accountant article

The examiner's article 'Bond valuation and bond yields' in the Technical Articles section of the ACCA website covers the calculation of bond yield curves in more detail.

Using the CAPM to calculate cost of debt

The CAPM can be used to derive a required return as long as the systematic risk of an investment is known. Earlier in the chapter we saw how to use an equity beta to derive a required return on equity. We also said that the risk on debt is usually relatively low, so the debt beta is often zero. However, if the debt beta is not zero (for example if the company's credit rating shows that it has a credit spread greater than zero) the CAPM can also be used to derive k_d as follows:

$$kd = R_f + \beta_{debt} (E(R_m) - R_f)$$

Then, the post-tax cost of debt is kd (1–T) as usual.

Test your understanding 8 – WACC

An entity has the following information in its balance sheet (statement of financial position):

	$000
Ordinary shares (50c nominal)	2,500
Debt (8%, redeemable in 5 years)	1,000

The entity's equity beta is 1.25 and its credit rating according to S&P Global Ratings is A. The share price is $1.22 and the debenture price is $110 per $100 nominal.

Extract from S&P Global Ratings credit spread tables:

Rating	1 yr	2 yr	3 yr	5 yr	7 yr	10 yr	30 yr
AAA	5	10	15	22	27	30	55
AA	15	25	30	37	44	50	65
A	40	50	57	65	71	75	90

The risk free rate of interest is 6% and the equity risk premium is 8%. Tax is payable at 30%.

Required:

Calculate the entity's WACC.

Application of duration to debt

In Chapter 2, we saw how to calculate the Macaulay Duration and the Modified Duration of an investment project. The methods can also be used to measure the sensitivity of a bond's price to a change in interest rates.

The bigger the duration, the greater the risk associated with the bond.

Illustration of duration calculation for a bond

Tyminski Co has some 10% coupon bonds in issue. They are redeemable at par in 5 years, and are trading at $97.25%. The yield (pre-tax cost of debt) is 10.743%.

The Macaulay Duration is calculated first, as follows:

Step 1: Calculate the present value of each future receipt from the bond, using the pre-tax cost of debt as the discount rate.

($)	t_1	t_2	t_3	t_4	t_5
Receipt	10	10	10	10	110
PV @ 10.743%	9.03	8.15	7.36	6.66	66.05

Step 2: Calculate the sum of (time to maturity × PV of receipt)
$(1 \times 9.03) + (2 \times 8.15) + (3 \times 7.36) + (4 \times 6.66) + (5 \times 66.05) = 404.30$

Step 3: Divide this by the total PV of receipts (i.e. the bond price) to give the Macaulay Duration.

Macaulay Duration = 404.30/97.25 = 4.157 years

The longer the Macaulay Duration, the more volatile the bond.

Modified Duration

Note that the Modified Duration can then be simply calculated as:

Macaulay Duration/(1 + discount rate)

= 4.157/1.10743

= 3.754

The size of the Modified Duration identifies how much the value of the bond will change if there is a change in interest rates. A higher modified duration means that the fluctuations in the value of the bond will be greater, hence the value of 3.754 means that the value of the bond will change by 3.754 times the change in interest rates multiplied by the original value of the bond.

The relationship is only an approximation because duration assumes that the relationship between the change in interest rates and the corresponding change in the value of the bond or loan is linear. In fact, the relationship between interest rates and bond price is in the form of a curve which is convex to the origin (i.e. non-linear). Therefore duration can only provide a reasonable estimation of the change in the value of a bond or loan due to changes in interest rates, when those interest rate changes are small.

Benefits and limitations of duration

Benefits

- Duration allows bonds of different maturities and coupon rates to be compared. This makes decision making regarding bond finance easier and more effective.

- If a portfolio of bonds is constructed based on weighted average duration, it is possible to identify the change in value of the portfolio as interest rates change.

- Managers may be able to reduce interest rate risk by changing the overall duration of the bond portfolio (e.g. by adding shorter maturity bonds to reduce duration).

Limitations

The main limitation of duration is that it assumes a linear relationship between interest rates and bond price. In reality, the relationship is likely to be curvilinear. The extent of the deviation from a linear relationship is known as **convexity**. The more convex the relationship between interest rates and bond price, the more inaccurate duration is for measuring interest rate sensitivity.

Further information on convexity

The sensitivity of bond prices to changes in interest rates is dependent on their redemption dates. Bonds which are due to be redeemed at a later date are more price-sensitive to interest rate changes, and therefore are riskier.

Duration measures the average time it takes for a bond to pay its coupons and principal and therefore measures the redemption period of a bond. It recognises that bonds which pay higher coupons effectively mature 'sooner' compared to bonds which pay lower coupons, even if the redemption dates of the bonds are the same.

This is because a higher proportion of the higher coupon bonds' income is received sooner. Therefore these bonds are less sensitive to interest rate changes and will have a lower duration.

Duration can be used to assess the change in the value of a bond when interest rates change using the following formula:

$\Delta P = [-D \times \Delta i \times P]/[1 + i]$,

where P is the price of the bond, D is the duration and i is the redemption yield.

However, duration is only useful in assessing small changes in interest rates because of **convexity**. As interest rates increase, the price of a bond decreases and vice versa, but this decrease is not proportional for coupon paying bonds, the relationship is non-linear. In fact, the relationship between the changes in bond value to changes in interest rates is in the shape of a convex curve to origin, see below.

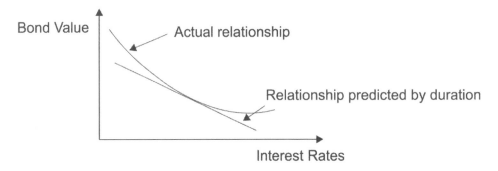

Duration, on the other hand, assumes that the relationship between changes in interest rates and the resultant bond is linear.

Therefore duration will predict a lower price than the actual price and for large changes in interest rates this difference can be significant. Duration can only be applied to measure the approximate change in a bond price due to interest changes, only if changes in interest rates do not lead to a change in the shape of the yield curve. This is because it is an average measure based on the gross redemption yield (yield to maturity). However, if the shape of the yield curve changes, duration can no longer be used to assess the change in bond value due to interest rate changes.

4   How do lenders set their interest rates?

Link to credit spreads

The table of credit spreads shown above showed the premium over risk free rate which a company would have to pay in order to satisfy its lenders. Another way of looking at the issue of yield on a bond is to look at it from the perspective of the lender.

Overview of the method

Lenders set their interest rates after assessing the likelihood that the borrower will default. The basic idea is that the lender will assess the likelihood (using normal distribution theory) of the firm's cash flows falling to a level which is lower than the required interest payment in the coming year. If it looks likely that the firm will have to default, the interest rate will be set at a high level to compensate the lender for this risk.

Introduction to normal distribution theory

The exam formula sheet contains a normal distribution table. Normal distributions have several applications in the AFM syllabus.

A normal distribution is often drawn as a 'bell shaped' curve, with its peak at the mean in the centre, as shown:

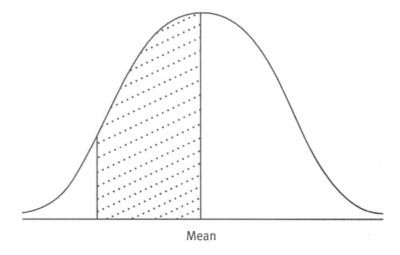

Mean

The figure from the normal distribution table gives the size of an area (shaded on the diagram) between the mean and a point z standard deviations away.

Example of a simple normal distribution

The height of adult males is normally distributed with a mean of 175 cm and a standard deviation of 5cm.

What is the probability of a man being shorter than 168cm?

Solution

168cm is 7cm away from the mean.

This represents 7/5 = 1.40 standard deviations.

From tables, 0.4192 of the normal curve lies between the mean and 1.40 standard deviations.

Hence, the probability of a man being shorter than 168cm is 0.5 – 0.4192 = 0.0808 (approximately 8%).

Illustration of how lenders set their interest rates

Villa Co has $2m of debt, on which it pays annual interest of 6%.

The company's operating cash flow in the coming year is forecast to be $140,000, and currently the company has $12,000 cash on deposit.

Required:

Given that the annual volatility (standard deviation) of the company's cash flows (measured over the last 5 years) has been 25%, calculate the probability that Villa Co will default on its interest payment within the next year (assuming that the company has no other lines of credit available).

Solution

The key here is that Villa Co will have expected cash of $140,000 + $12,000 = $152,000, and its interest commitment will be 6% on $2m, i.e. $120,000.

We need to calculate the probability that the cash available will fall by $152,000 – $120,000 = $32,000 over the next year.

Assuming that the annual cash flow is normally distributed, a volatility (standard deviation) of 25% on a cash flow of $140,000 represents a standard deviation of 0.25 × $140,000 = $35,000.

Thus, our fall of $32,000 represents 32,000/35,000 = 0.91 standard deviations.

From the normal distribution tables, the area between the mean and 0.91 standard deviations = 0.3186.

Hence, there must be a 0.5 – 0.3186 = 0.1814 chance of the cash flow being insufficient to meet the interest payment.

i.e. the probability of default is approximately 18%.

5   The use of WACC as a discount rate in project appraisal

Link to project appraisal

When evaluating a project, it is important to use a cost of capital which is appropriate to the risk of the new project. The existing WACC will therefore be appropriate as a discount rate if **both**:

1   the new project has the same level of business risk as the existing operations. If business risk changes, required returns of shareholders will change (to compensate them for the new level of risk), and hence WACC will change.

2   undertaking the new project will not alter the firm's gearing (financial risk). The values of equity and debt are key components in the calculation of WACC, so if the values change, clearly the existing WACC will no longer be applicable.

If one or both of these factors do not apply when undertaking a new project, the existing WACC cannot be used as a discount rate. The next chapter explores the alternative methods available in these situations.

6 Chapter summary

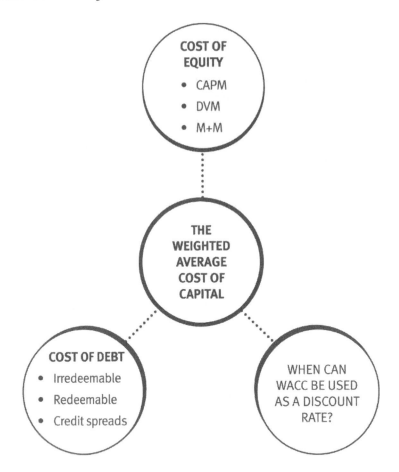

Test your understanding answers

 Test your understanding 1

In order to use CAPM we shall need to derive a suitable equity beta for Moorland Co.

This will be done by first finding a suitable asset beta (based on the asset betas of the 2 parts of the business) and gearing up to reflect Moorland Co's 50:50 gearing level.

Retail industry

The asset beta of retail operations can be found from the industry information as follows: (assuming the debt beta is zero)

$$\beta_a = \beta_e \times \frac{V_e}{V_e + V_d(1-T)}$$

$$= 1.20 \times (80/(80 + 20(1 - 0.30)))$$

$$= 1.02$$

Manufacturing industry

Similarly, the asset beta for manufacturing operations is:

$$\beta_a = \beta_e \times \frac{V_e}{V_e + V_d(1-T)}$$

$$= 1.45 \times (55/(55 + 45(1 - 0.30)))$$

$$= 0.92$$

Moorland Co asset beta

Hence, the asset beta of Moorland will be a weighted average of these two asset betas:

β_a (Moorland) = $(0.75 \times 1.02) + (0.25 \times 0.92) = 1.00$

Moorland Co equity beta

So, regearing this asset beta now gives:

$$1.00 = \beta_e \times [50/(50 + 50(1 - 0.30))]$$

So, $\beta_e = 1.00/0.59 = 1.69$

Moorland Co cost of equity

Using CAPM:

$k_e = R_F + \beta (E(R_M) - R_F) = 3\% + (1.69 \times 6\%) = 13.1\%$

Test your understanding 2

Using M+M's Proposition 2 equation, we can degear the existing k_e and then regear it to the new gearing level:

Degearing:

$k_e = k_e^i + (1 - T)(k_e^i - kd)(V_d/V_e)$

$12\% = k_e^i + (1 - 0.30)(k_e^i - 4\%)(20/80)$

Now we need to rearrange this formula:

$0.12 = k_e^i + (1-0.30)(k_e^i - 0.04)(20/80)$

$0.12 = k_e^i + (0.7)(k_e^i - 0.04)(0.25)$

$0.12 = k_e^i + (0.175)(k_e^i - 0.04)$

$0.12 = k_e^i + 0.175\ k_e^i - 0.007$

$0.12 = 1.175\ k_e^i - 0.007$

$0.127 = 1.175\ k_e^i$

$(0.127/1.175) = k_e^i$

So rearranging carefully gives $k_e^i = 0.108$ (10.8%)

Now regearing:

$k_e = 10.8\% + (1 - 0.30)(10.8\% - 4\%)(25/75)$

$k_e = 12.4\%$

Test your understanding 3

Mackay Co's post-tax cost of debt is $5(1 - 0.30)/94.50 = 3.7\%$

Test your understanding 4

To calculate IRR, we discount at 2 rates (5% and 10% here) and then interpolate:

PV at 5% = 89 – (6(1 – 0.30) × 5 yr 5% annuity factor) – (100 × 5 yr 5% discount factor) = –7.58

PV at 10% = 89 – (6(1 – 0.30) × 5 yr 10% annuity factor) – (100 × 5 yr 10% discount factor) = 10.98

Hence IRR (post-tax cost of debt) is approximately

$= 5\% + (-7.58/(-7.58 - 10.98) \times (10\% - 5\%))$

$= 7.04\%$

Test your understanding 5

From the table the credit spread for an AA rated, 3-year bond is 30. The spread for a 5-year bond is 37.

This would suggest an adjustment of:

30 + (37 − 30)/2 = 33.5 basis points

The yield is therefore found by adding 0.335% to the risk free rate.

So yield on F's bonds =

2.6% + 0.335% = 2.935%

The cost of debt = 2.935 × (1 − 0.3) = 2.05%.

Test your understanding 6

The overall cost of debt will be the weighted average of the costs of the two types of debt (weighted according to market values).

2 year bonds

Market value = $30m × 0.90 = $27m

kd = 2.5% + 50 credit spread (from table) = 3.00%

10 year bonds

Market value = $50m × 1.08 = $54m

kd = 2.5% + 75 credit spread (from table) = 3.25%

Overall cost of debt

Therefore the weighted average cost of debt (given that the ratio of market values is 1:2) is

[((1/3) × 3.00%) + ((2/3) × 3.25%)] × (1 − 0.30) = 2.22%

Test your understanding 7

The individual yield curve for Stone Co is found by adding the government spot yield curve figures to the credit spreads for an A rated company:

Year	Spot yield (%)	Credit spread (%)	Individual yield curve (%)
1	3.50	0.46	3.96
2	3.65	0.60	4.25
3	3.80	0.76	4.56

This shows that (for example) the yield on a 2 year Stone Co bond will be 4.25%.

Test your understanding 8 – WACC

$$WACC = \left[\frac{V_e}{V_e + V_d}\right] k_e + \left[\frac{V_d}{V_e + V_d}\right] k_d (1-T)$$

Workings:

From CAPM, $k_e = R_f + ß_i (E(R_m) - R_f) = 6\% + (1.25 \times 8\%) = 16\%$

$V_e = \$2,500,000 \times 1.22/0.50 = \$6.1m$

k_d (yield on debt) = risk free rate + credit spread = 6% + 65 basis points = 6.65%

Hence, post-tax cost of debt = 6.65% (1 – 0,30) = 4.66%

$V_d = \$1,000,000 \times 110/100 = \$1.1m$

Therefore, WACC = (6.1/7.2) × 16% + (1.1/7.2) × 4.66% = 14.3%

Chapter

7

Risk adjusted WACC and adjusted present value

Chapter learning objectives

Study guide section	Study guide outcome
B1: Discounted cash flow techniques	(a) Evaluate the potential value added to an organisation arising from a specified capital investment project or portfolio using the net present value (NPV) model. Project modelling should include explicit treatment and discussion of: (v) Risk adjusted discount rates.
B3: Impact of financing on investment decisions and adjusted present values	(d) Calculate and evaluate project specific cost of equity and cost of capital, including their impact on the overall cost of capital of an organisation. Demonstrate detailed knowledge of business and financial risk, the capital asset pricing model and the relationship between equity and asset betas.

B3: Impact of financing on investment decisions and adjusted present values (continued)

(i) Apply the adjusted present value technique to the appraisal of investment decisions that entail significant alterations in the financial structure of the organisation, including their fiscal and transactions cost implications.

(j) Assess the impact of a significant capital investment project upon the reported financial position and performance of the organisation taking into account alternative financing strategies.

One of the PER performance objectives (PO09 – Evaluate Investment and Financing Decisions) is to be able to advise on the cost of different sources of finance.

PER   Working through this chapter should help you understand how to demonstrate that objective.

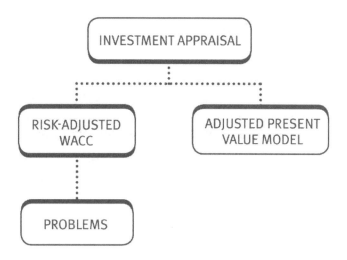

1 Introduction

Alternatives to the use of existing WACC as a discount rate in project appraisal

We have now established that the existing WACC should only be used as a discount rate for a new investment project if the business risk and the capital structure (financial risk) are likely to stay constant. Alternatively,

If the business risk of the new project differs from the entity's existing business risk

A risk adjusted WACC can be calculated, by recalculating the cost of equity to reflect the business risk of the new project. This often involves the technique of 'degearing' and 'regearing' beta factors, covered later in this chapter.

If the capital structure (financial risk) is expected to change when the new project is undertaken

The simplest way of incorporating a change in capital structure is to recalculate the WACC using the new capital structure weightings. This is appropriate when the change in capital structure is not significant, or if the new investment project can be effectively treated as a new business, with its own long term gearing level.

Alternatively, if the capital structure is expected to change significantly, the Adjusted Present Value method of project appraisal could be used. This approach separates the investment element of the decision from the financing element and appraises them independently. APV is generally recommended when there are complex funding arrangements (e.g. subsidised loans).

2 The risk adjusted WACC

Basic principle

If the business risk of the new project is different from the business risk of a company's existing operations, the company's shareholders will expect a different return to compensate them for this new level of risk.

Hence, the appropriate WACC which should be used to discount the new project's cash flows is not the company's existing WACC, but a 'risk adjusted' WACC which incorporates this new required return to the shareholders (cost of equity).

Calculating a risk-adjusted WACC

1   Find the appropriate equity beta from a suitable quoted company.

2   Adjust the available equity beta to convert it to an asset beta – degear it.

3   Readjust the asset beta to reflect the project (i.e. its own) gearing levels – regear the beta.

4   Use this beta in the CAPM equation to find k_e.

5   Use this k_e to find the WACC.

6   Evaluate the project.

> **Test your understanding 1**
>
> B Co is a hot air balloon manufacturer whose equity: debt ratio is 5:2.
>
> The company is considering a waterbed-manufacturing project. B Co will finance the project to maintain its existing capital structure.
>
> S Co is a waterbed-manufacturing company. It has an equity beta of 1.59 and a $V_e{:}V_d$ ratio of 2:1.
>
> The yield on B Co's debt, which is assumed to be risk free, is 11%. B Co's equity beta is 1.10. The average return on the stock market is 16%. The corporation tax rate is 30%.
>
> **Required:**
>
> **Calculate a suitable cost of capital to apply to the project.**

Using the risk-adjusted WACC

The risk-adjusted WACC calculated above reflects the business risk of the project and the current capital structure of the business, so it is wholly appropriate as a discount rate for the new project.

Two other issues also need to be considered:

- The method used to gear and degear betas is based on the assumption that debt is perpetual. This overvalues the tax shield where debt is finite.

- Issue costs on equity are ignored.

Theoretical points re: risk adjusted WACC

The degearing and regearing procedure is a product of the M&M 1963 position. To use these equations debt must be perpetual and risk free. If it is not perpetual, to ignore that it is for a shorter period will overvalue the tax shield on debt.

The value $V_e + V_d$ used in the WACC equation should represent market values of debt and equity after the project has been adopted (i.e. the equity value should include the NPV of the project).

By using the ratio of the company before the project we have assumed that the project has a zero NPV – this is unlikely to be the case. If the project has a positive NPV the calculation will assume that borrowing is proportional to the present value of future cash flows rather than the initial value of the asset.

3 The adjusted present value (APV) technique

Basic principle

The APV method evaluates the project and the impact of financing separately. Hence, it can be used if a new project has a different financial risk (debt-equity ratio) from the company, i.e. the overall capital structure of the company changes.

APV consists of two different elements:

APV	=	Base case NPV	+	Financing impact
(3) Value of a geared project	=	(1) Value of an all equity financed project	+	(2) Present value of financing side effects

The investment element (base case NPV)

The project is evaluated as though it were being undertaken by an all equity company with all financing side effects ignored. The financial risk is quantified later in the second part of the APV analysis. Therefore:

* ignore the financial risk in the investment decision process

* use a beta that reflects just the business risk, i.e. ß asset.

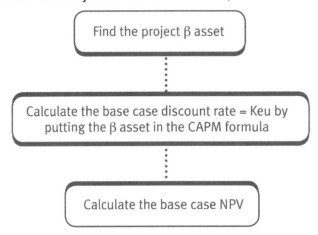

Find the project β asset

Calculate the base case discount rate = Keu by putting the β asset in the CAPM formula

Calculate the base case NPV

Once the base case NPV is identified, the PV of the financing package is evaluated.

The financing impact

Financing cash flows consist of:

* issue costs

* tax reliefs.

As all financing cash flows are low risk they are discounted at either:

* the k_d or

* the risk free rate.

Examples of exam tricks on APV

APV tricks

In exam questions, you may see the following tricks when calculating the 'financing impact' part. All these tricks are covered in the next 'Test your understanding' questions:

Grossing up

A firm will know how much finance is required for the investment. Issue costs of finance will usually be quoted on top. It will therefore be necessary to gross up the funds to be raised.

Grossing up illustration

The finance required for a planned investment is $2m (net of issue costs). Issue costs are 3%. And the finance raised will also have to cover the issue costs.

What are the issue costs and what sum will need to be raised altogether?

Solution

The $2m is 97% of the amount to be raised:

Therefore, ($2m/0.97) = $2,061,856 will be needed.

Issue costs are 3%

3% × $2,061,856 = $61,856

Issue costs can be calculated in one stage as:

$2m × 3/97 = $61,856

PV of debt issue costs

As always, calculations involving debt must take account of the tax effects.

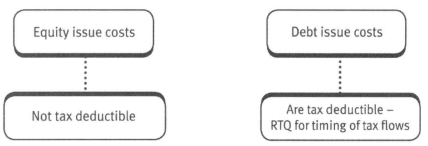

Method:

Issue costs at T_0	(X)
Tax relief at the CT rate (issue costs × CT rate)	X
PV of the tax relief (RTQ for timing of tax flows)	X
	—
PV of the issue costs	**(X)**
	—

(issue costs – PV of tax relief)

PV of the tax relief on interest payments

The PV of the tax relief on interest payments is also known as the PV of the tax shield.

The method adopted depends on the information given:

Simple scenario: Bonds – interest paid at a fixed amount each year

Annual tax relief = Total loan × interest rate × tax rate	X
Annuity factor for n years	X
Year one discount factor (if tax is delayed one year)	X
PV of the tax shield	**X**

More complex scenario: Bank loans – repayments are for equal amounts

The repayments will be made up of both interest and capital elements.

Step 1

Find the amount of the repayment

Annual amount = (Amount of the loan/Relevant annuity factor)

Step 2

Compute the annual interest charge.

Illustration of the more complex scenario

$400,000 is to be borrowed for 3 years and repaid in equal instalments. The risk free rate is 10% and all debt is assumed to be risk free. Calculate the present value of the tax relief on the debt interest if the corporation tax rate is 30%. Assume that tax is delayed 1 year.

Solution

Equal annual repayment = 400,000/3yr AF@10% = 400,000/2.487 = $160,836.

Year	Opening balance	Interest at 10%	Repayment	Closing balance
	$	$	$	$
1	400,000	40,000	160,836	279,164
2	279,164	27,916	160,836	146,244
3	146,244	14,624	160,836	32 (diff due to rounding)

The tax relief on the interest can now be calculated:

Year	Interest cost	Tax relief @ 30%	Timing of tax	10% DCF	PV
	$	$			$
1	40,000	12,000	Year 2	0.826	9,912
2	27,916	8,375	Year 3	0.751	6,290
3	14,624	4,387	Year 4	0.683	2,932
PV of tax relief =					19,134

Calculation of APV (in detail)

The base case NPV is used as a starting point. The costs and benefits of the financing are then added to find a final adjusted present value:

Base case NPV	X
PV of the issue costs	
Equity	(X)
Debt	(X)
PV of the tax shield	X
	——
Adjusted Present Value	X

A fully worked example now follows.

Test your understanding 2

Rounding Co is a company currently engaged in the manufacture of baby equipment. It wishes to diversify into the manufacture of snowboards.

The investment details

The company's equity beta is 1.27 and is current debt to equity ratio is 25:75, however the company's gearing ratio will change as a result of the new project.

Firms involved in snowboard manufacture have an average equity beta of 1.19 and an average debt to equity ratio of 30:70.

Assume that the debt is risk free, that the risk free rate is 10% and that the expected return from the market portfolio is 16%.

The new project will involve the purchase of new machinery for a cost of $800,000 (net of issue costs), which will produce annual cash inflows of $450,000 for 3 years. At the end of this time it will have no scrap value.

Corporation tax is payable in the same year at a rate of 33%. The machine will attract tax allowable depreciation of 25% per year on a reducing balance basis, with a balancing allowance at the end of the project life when the machine is scrapped.

The financing details:

The new investment will be financed as follows:

Bonds (redeemable in three years' time):	40%
Rights issue of equity:	60%

The issue costs are 4% on the gross equity issued and 2% on the gross debt issued. Assume that the debt issue costs are tax deductible.

Required:

Calculate the adjusted present value of the project.

Additional factors regarding the APV method

Additional factors – Subsidised/cheap loans

If a loan is cheap, the interest cost is lower. However, the benefit is reduced since the tax shield will also be lower:

PV of the cheap loan (opportunity benefit):

PV of the interest saved	X
Less: PV of the tax relief lost	(X)
PV of the cheap loan	X

Example: A Co requires $1 million in debt finance for 5 years.

It has borrowed $700,000 in the form of 10% bonds redeemable in 5 years and the remainder under a government subsidised loan scheme at 6%. The tax rate is 30%. Assume that tax is delayed one year.

Calculate the PV of the tax shields and the PV of the cheap loan.

(a) **PV of the tax shields**

Although the cheap loan has a cost of 6% it has the same risk as a normal loan, therefore the appropriate discount rate is 10% per year.

	Normal loan	Cheap loan
Annual tax relief = Total loan × interest rate × tax rate		
$700,000 \times 0.10 \times .30 =$	21,000	
$300,000 \times 0.06 \times .30 =$		5,400
Annuity factor for 5 years @10%	3.791	3.791
Discount factor for 1 year @10%	0.909	0.909
PV of the tax shield	**72,366**	**18,609**

(b) PV of the cheap loan

		0	1	2	3	4	5	6
Annuity	PV of the interest saved		X	X	X	X	X	
Deferred annuity	PV of the tax relief lost	•	•	(X)	(X)	(X)	(X)	(X)

	Interest saved	Tax relief lost
Annual amount		
300,000 × (10% – 6%) =	12,000	
12,000 × .30 =		3,600
Annuity factor for 5 years	3.791	3.791
Present value factor –		0.909
PV of the cheap loan	**45,492**	**(12,406)**

The APV calculation is therefore amended as follows:

Base case NPV	X/(X)
PV of the issue costs:	
Equity	(X)
Debt	(X)
PV of the tax shield:	
Normal loan	X
Cheap loan	X
PV of the cheap loan:	
Interest saved	X
Tax relief lost	(X)
Adjusted present value	X/(X)

Additional factors – Debt capacity

Debt finance benefits a project because of the associated tax shield. If a project brings about an increase in the borrowing capacity of the firm, it will increase the potential tax shield available.

An occasional exam trick is to give both the amount of debt actually raised and the increase in debt capacity brought about by the project. It is this theoretical debt capacity on which the tax shield should be based.

A project's debt capacity denotes its ability to act as security for a loan. It is the tax relief available on such a loan, which gives debt capacity its value.

When calculating the present value of the tax shield (tax relief on interest) it should be based on the project's theoretical debt capacity and not on the actual amount of the debt used.

The tax benefit from a project accrues from each pound of debt finance that it can support, even if the debt is used on some other project. We therefore use the theoretical debt capacity to match the tax benefit to the specific project.

For example, if a question stated that actual debt raised is $800,000 but you are told in the question 'The investment is believed to add $1 million to the company's debt capacity.' The present value of the tax shield is based on the $1 million – the theoretical amount.

Test your understanding 3

Blades Co is considering diversifying its operations away from its main area of business (food manufacturing) into the plastics business. It wishes to evaluate an investment project, which involves the purchase of a moulding machine that costs $450,000. The project is expected to produce net annual operating cash flows of $220,000 for each of the three years of its life. At the end of this time its scrap value will be zero.

The assets of the project can support debt finance of 40% of its initial cost. Blades is considering borrowing this amount from two different sources.

First, a local government organisation has offered to lend $90,000, with no issue costs, at a subsidised interest rate of 3% per year. The full $90,000 would be repayable after 3 years.

The rest of the debt would be provided by the bank, at Blades' normal interest rate. This bank loan would be repaid in three equal annual instalments.

The balance of finance will be provided by a placing of new equity.

Issue costs will be 5% of funds raised for the equity placing and 2% for the bank loan. Debt issue costs are allowable for corporation tax.

The plastics industry has an average equity beta of 1.368 and an average debt: equity ratio of 1:5 at market values. Blades' current equity beta is 1.8 and 20% of its long-term capital is represented by debt which is generally regarded to be risk free.

The risk free rate is 10% per year and the expected return on an average market portfolio is 15%.

Corporation tax is at a rate of 30%, payable in the same year. The machine will attract a 70% initial tax allowable depreciation allowance and the balance is to be written off evenly over the remainder of the asset life and is allowable against tax. The firm is certain that it will earn sufficient profits against which to offset these allowances.

Required:

Calculate the adjusted present value and determine whether the project is worthwhile.

Advantages and disadvantages of APV

The APV technique has practical advantages and theoretical disadvantages.

Advantages	Disadvantages
• Step-by-step approach gives clear understanding of the elements of the decision	• Based on M&M's with-tax theory. Therefore ignores: – Bankruptcy risk – Tax exhaustion – Agency costs
• Can evaluate any type of financing package	• Based on M&M's with-tax theory. Therefore assumes: – Debt is risk free and irredeemable
• More straightforward than adjusting the WACC which can be very complex	

International CAPM and APV

A recap of the basics

The APV method of investment appraisal has been introduced in this chapter in the context of domestic investments. There are essentially three steps to the technique:

Step 1: Estimate the base case NPV assuming that the project is financed entirely by equity.

Step 2: Estimate the financial 'side effects' of the actual method of financing.

Step 3: Add the values from steps 1 and 2 to give the APV.

If the APV is positive, accept the project.

We now examine the applicability of the method in appraising international investments.

Mechanics of the International APV method

The normal procedure of determining the relevant cash flows and discounting at a rate of return commensurate with the project's risk should be followed as before, but taking account of the international factors as discussed earlier.

The steps therefore become:

Step 1: The base case NPV assumes that the project is financed entirely by equity, so the discount rate must be the cost of equity allowing for the project risk but excluding financial risk – using the international CAPM equation with an ungeared 'world' β **(see below)**.

Step 2: Adjustments should be made for

- tax relief on debt interest and issue costs

- subsidies from foreign governments

- projects financed by loans raised locally

- restriction on remittances.

Step 3: Add the values from steps 1 and 2 to give the APV.

This is basically the same approach as for domestic appraisal, with a little more care needed in identifying the appropriate appraisal rates and adjustments.

International CAPM

In the domestic context you should recall that the CAPM could be used to derive the return required as

$R_j = R_f + \beta(R_m - R_f)$

where R_j is the required return from the investment

R_f is the risk free rate of return

R_m is the expected return from the whole market

β is a measure of the systematic risk of the investment

However, where a company operates

- internationally

- in integrated markets.

investors should therefore consider applying the international cost of capital to investment appraisal, rather than a domestic CAPM.

The logic:

1   A company involved in international operations, will, in addition to the usual risk, be exposed to:

     –   currency risk

     –   political risk.

     These are mainly unsystematic and can be diversified away by holding an internationally diversified portfolio.

2   For example, a fully diversified UK investor can achieve further risk reduction by investing in other countries. Part of the systematic risk of the UK market is in fact unsystematic risk from an international viewpoint.

The international CAPM equation will therefore read:

$R_j = R_f + \beta_w (R_w - R_f)$

where

R_j is the required return

R_w is the expected return from the whole world portfolio

β_w is a measure of the project's world systematic risk, i.e. how returns on the investment correlate with those on the world market.

In the UK, for example, the return from the whole market could be estimated from looking at domestic stock market indexes such as the FTSE All-Share index, which covers about 600 of the top shares listed in the UK.

This basic CAPM model is valid for:

•   a company or investor with domestic investments only, or

•   investments in a country with segmented markets, as opposed to integrated markets.

Integrated capital markets exist if investors can invest in any country that does not impose restrictions on capital movements. Segmented markets are associated with a closed economy, or markets where switching investments from country to country is not easily achieved, such as in many service industries.

It is argued that:

- Investors can diversify their risk more effectively in an integrated market, because more investments are available and returns on domestic and foreign assets are not perfectly correlated.

- The cost of capital is lower if markets are integrated than in a closed economy. Companies whose shareholders are international investors should therefore consider applying the international cost of capital to investment appraisal, rather than a domestic CAPM.

This can be done by looking at the international CAPM.

In practice it is impossible to hold a share of the whole world portfolio, but significant international diversification can be achieved by:

- direct holdings in overseas companies

- holdings in unit trusts specialising in overseas companies

- investing in multinational companies.

You should appreciate that in principle risk reduction can be achieved either by investing directly in an international portfolio of shares or investing in local companies with significant overseas activities.

Implications of the international capital asset pricing model (or IAPM) are that:

- When setting a cost of capital, a company should assess the nature of its investors and their investment portfolios.

- If markets are segmented, investments that are profitable for an international/foreign company might not be profitable for a domestic company, because the international company will have a lower cost of capital.

However, the validity of the international capital asset pricing model rests on the assumption that capital markets are fully integrated and investors are 'world' investors. In practice, this is not necessarily the case. Countries and capital markets are not fully integrated, since there are costs to foreign investment and domestic investors often have better access to information than foreign investors.

In conclusion, although the international capital asset pricing model can in theory be applied, there remain valid reasons for measuring the cost of equity on the basis of a domestic market portfolio and the basic CAPM.

4   Chapter summary

Beta revisited

Asset beta − reflects pure systematic business risk

Equity beta − reflects business and gearing risk

Betas can be geared and ungeared:

$$\beta \text{ asset} = \beta \text{ equity} \times \frac{V_e}{V_e + V_d (1-T)}$$

INVESTMENT APPRAISAL

Problems with the risk-adjusted WACC

- Can't cope if gearing ratio changed by project
- Over-values tax shield where debt not permanent
- Ignore costs of raising finance.

Adjusted present value model

Two-part approach:

- Find base NPV:
  PV of project flows using asset beta in the CAPM
- Find PV of financing:
  PV of issue costs on equity
  PV of issue costs on debt
  PV of tax relief

Test your understanding answers

Test your understanding 1

Step 1

B Co has selected an appropriate equity beta for waterbed-manufacturing of 1.59.

Step 2

Based on new industry information:

- the ß equity (1.59)

- gearing ratio of the new industry (2:1)

de-gear the equity beta of the company in the new industry and find the business risk asset beta of the new project/industry.

$$\beta_a = \beta_e \times \frac{V_e}{V_e + V_d\,(1-T)}$$

$$= 1.59 \times (2/(2 + 1(1 - 0.3)))$$

$$= 1.18$$

Step 3

Calculate the equity beta of the new project, by re-gearing:

- incorporate the financial risk of our company using our gearing ratio (5:2)

$$\beta_a = \beta_e \times \frac{V_e}{V_e + V_d\,(1-T)}$$

$$1.18 = \beta_e \times [5/(5 + 2(0.70))]$$

$$1.18 = 0.78\,\beta_e$$

$$\beta_e = 1.18/0.78 = 1.51$$

Now proceed as usual

Calculate the cost of equity of the project based on CAPM:

$k_e = R_F + \beta\,(E(R_M) - R_F) = 11\% + 1.51\,(16\% - 11\%) = 18.55\%$

Find the cost of debt:

$k_d = I\,(1 - T)$

$k_d = 11\%\,(1 - 0.3) = 7.70\%$

Calculate the WACC of the project.

(Use our company's D:E ratio)

$WACC = 18.55\% \times 5/7 + 7.70 \times 2/7 = 15.45\%$

We have calculated a discount rate, which reflects the systematic risk of this particular project.

Test your understanding 2

The investment element

Estimate the base case NPV.

Firstly compute the asset beta of the project. This is achieved by degearing the equity beta from the snowboard industry average.

$\beta_a = \beta_e \times [V_e/(V_e + V_d(1 - T))]$

$\beta_a = 1.19 \times (70/(70 + 30(1 - 0.33)))$

$\beta_a = 0.92$

The next task is to determine the base case discount rate for the project.

$E(R_i) = R_f + (E(R_m) - R_f) \beta_a$

$= 10\% + (16\% - 10\%) 0.92$

$= 15.52\%$ – round to the nearest % point so we can use the tables.

Therefore we will use **16%**.

1   **Base case NPV calculation**

Time	0	1	2	3
	$000	$000	$000	$000
Receipts		450	450	450
Corporation tax @ 33%		(149)	(149)	(149)
Tax relief on TAD (W1)		66	50	149
Initial outlay	(800)			
	———	———	———	———
Net cash flow	(800)	367	351	450
Discount rate (16%)	1	0.862	0.743	0.641
	———	———	———	———
Present value	(800)	316	261	288
Base case NPV	**65,000**			

Tax allowable depreciation computation (W1)

	W.D.A.	Tax relief at 33%	Timing
Investment	800		
Y1 TAD	(200)	66	Time 1
	600		
Y2 TAD	(150)	50	Time 2
	450		
Y3 Proceeds	0		
Balancing allowance	450	149	Time 3

2 The financing impact

Lay out the financing package:

	$	Issue costs
Equity – 60% × 800,000	480,000	4%
Debt – 40% × 800,000	320,000	2%
	800,000	

A PV of issue costs on equity

The question states that the $800k is net of issue costs therefore we need to gross up.

Equity issue cost: $480,000 × 4/96 = ($20,000)

B PV of issue costs on debt

Debt issue cost: $320,000 × (2/98) ($6,531)

Issue costs of debt at T_0	($6,531)
Tax relief at 33%	$2,155
PV of the issue costs on debt	**($4,376)**

C PV of the tax shield

Total amount raised by loan – don't forget to add the issue costs

= $320,000 + $6,531 = **$326,531**

Annual tax relief = $326,531 × 0.10 × 0.33	10,776
	×
Annuity factor for 3 years	2.487
PV of the tax shield	**$26,800**

3   The APV calculation

Base cost NPV	65,000
Less: PV of issue costs:	
Equity	(20,000)
Debt	(4,376)
Plus PV of tax shield	26,800
Therefore adjusted present value is	$67,424

Based upon these estimates the project appears financially viable.

Test your understanding 3

Step 1: Base case net present value

First compute the ungeared (asset) beta for this project type (based on the equity beta for the plastics industry).

$$\beta_a = \beta_e \times \frac{V_e}{V_e + V_d\,(1-T)}$$

$$= 1.368 \times [5/(5 + 1(1 - 0.30))]$$

$$= 1.2$$

Required return of project
$$= 10\% + (15\% - 10\%)\,1.2$$

$$= 16\% \text{ per year}$$

Then discount the project cash flows at 16%

Time	0	1	2	3
	$000	$000	$000	$000
Equipment	(450)			
TAD (W1)		94.5	20.25	20.25
Operating cash flows		220.00	220.00	220.00
Tax on operating cash flows		(66.00)	(66.00)	(66.00)
	(450)	248.5	174.25	174.25
16% factors	1	0.862	0.743	0.641
PV	(450)	214.21	129.47	111.69
Base case NPV =	$5,370			

Workings

(W1) – Tax allowable depreciation

	Tax @ 30% $	$
Cost of machine	450,000	
First year allowance (70%)	315,000	94,500
	135,000	
TAD allowances (straight line) (for each of next two years)	67,500	20,250

Step 2: Adjusted present value (the financing side effects)

Lay out the financing package:

	$
Capital requirements:	
Equity (60%)	270,000
Subsidised debt	90,000
Bank loan	90,000
	450,000

		$
Issue costs:		
(i) Equity 5/95 × 270,000	14,210	
(ii) Debt 2/98 × 90,000	1,837	
Issue costs on debt at T_0		($1,837)
Tax relief at 30%		$551
PV of the issue costs on debt		**($1,286)**

(iii) Tax relief on loan interest

Gross value of bank loan = $90,000 + $1,837 (issue costs) = $91,837

Annual repayments = $91,837/2.487 = $36,927

Loan schedule

Year	Opening balance	Interest	Repayment	Closing balance
	$	$	$	$
1	91,837	**9,184**	36,927	64,094
2	64,094	**6,409**	36,927	33,576
3	33,576	**3,358**	36,927	7 (rounding diff)

Subsidised loan interest will be 3% of $90,000 each year for 3 years, i.e. $2,700 per year.

Tax relief at 30% on interest:

Year	Cash	10% factor	PV
	$		$
1	30% × (9,184 + 2,700)	0.909	3,241
2	30% × (6,409 + 2,700)	0.826	2,257
3	30% × (3,358 + 2,700)	0.751	1,365
			6,863

(iv) Interest saving on subsidised loan

Saving = $90,000 × (10% – 3%) = $6,300 per year

Present value of saving (post-tax) = $6,300 × (1 – 0.30) × 2.487 = $10,968

Step 3: Adjusted present value

	$
Base case NPV	5,370
Issue costs – equity	(14,210)
Issue costs – debt	(1,286)
Tax shield	6,863
Value of subsidy	10,968
The project APV is	7,705

The project will increase shareholder wealth by $7,705, so the project funded in this way is acceptable.

Option pricing

Chapter learning objectives

Study guide section	Study guide outcome	
B2: Application of option pricing theory in investment decisions and valuation	(a)	Apply the Black-Scholes Option Pricing (BSOP) model to financial product valuation and to asset valuation: (i) Determine and discuss, using published data, the five principal drivers of option value (value of the underlying, exercise price, time to expiry, volatility and risk free rate (ii) Discuss the underlying assumptions, structure, applications and limitations of the BSOP model.
	(b)	Evaluate embedded real options within a project, classifying them into one of the real option archetypes.
	(c)	Assess, calculate and advise on the value of options to delay, expand, redeploy and withdraw using the BSOP model.
B4: Valuation and the use of free cash flows	(d)	Explain the use of the BSOP model to estimate the value of equity of an organisation and discuss the implications of the model for a change in the value of equity.

B4: Valuation and the use of free cash flows (continued)	(e)	Explain the role of BSOP model in the assessment of default risk, the value of debt and its potential recoverability.
E1: The role of the treasury function in multinationals	(b)	Discuss the operations of the derivatives market, including: (iv) Risks such as delta, gamma, vega, rho and theta, and how these can be managed.

PER

One of the PER performance objectives (PO09 – Evaluate Investment and Financing Decisions) is to be able to evaluate projects, financial securities and instruments – and advise on their costs and benefits to the organisation.

Working through this chapter should help you understand how to demonstrate that objective.

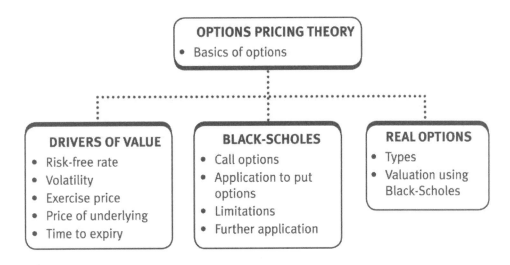

1 The principles of option pricing theory

Option terminology

An option	The right but not an obligation, to buy or sell a particular good at an exercise price, at or before a specified date.
Call option	The right but not an obligation to buy a particular good at an exercise price.
Put option	The right but not an obligation to sell a particular good at an exercise price.
Exercise/strike price	The fixed price at which the good may be bought or sold.
American option	An option that can be exercised on any day up until its expiry date.
European option	An option that can only be exercised on the last day of the option.
Premium	The cost of an option.
Traded option	Standardised option contracts sold on a futures exchange (normally American options).
Over the counter (OTC) option	Tailor-made option – usually sold by a bank (normally European options).

Option value

The key aspect to an option's value is that the buyer has a choice whether or not to use it. Thus the option can be used to avoid downside risk exposure without foregoing upside exposure.

The value of an option is made up of two components. These are illustrated below for a call option:

The intrinsic value

The intrinsic value looks at the exercise price compared with the price of the underlying asset.

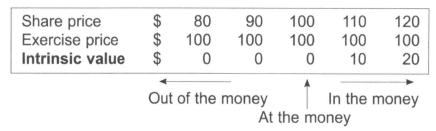

Share price	$	80	90	100	110	120
Exercise price	$	100	100	100	100	100
Intrinsic value	$	0	0	0	10	20

Out of the money ← | → In the money

At the money

- The value of the call option will increase as the share price increases. Conversely a lower exercise price would also give a higher option value.

- An option can never have a negative intrinsic value. If the option is out of the money, then the intrinsic value is zero.

- On the expiry date, the value of an option is equal to its intrinsic value.

The time value

- Time to expiry.

  - As the period to expiry increases, the chance of a profit before the expiry date grows, increasing the option value.

- Volatility of the share price.

  - The holder of a call option does not suffer if the share price falls below the exercise price, i.e. there is a limit to the downside.

  - However the option holder gains if the share price increases above the exercise price, i.e. there is no limit to the upside.

  - Thus the greater the volatility the better, as this increases the probability of a valuable increase in share price.

- Risk-free interest rate.

  - As stated above, the exercise price has to be paid in the future, therefore the higher the interest rates the lower the present value of the exercise price. This reduces the cost of exercising and thus adds value to the current call option value.

  - Alternatively, since having a call option means that the share purchase can be deferred, owning a call option becomes more valuable when interest rates are high, since the money left in the bank will be generating a higher return.

Summary of the determinants of call option prices:

Increase in	Value of a call
Share price	Increase
Exercise price	Decrease
Time to expiry	Increase
Volatility	Increase
Interest rate	Increase

Test your understanding 1

Complete the following table for put options.

Summary of the determinants of call option prices:

Increase in	Call	Put
Share price	Increase	
Exercise price	Decrease	
Time to expiry	Increase	
Volatility	Increase	
Interest rate	Increase	

Test your understanding 2

A pension fund manager is concerned that the value of the stock market will fall.

Required:

Suggest an option strategy the manager could use to protect the fund value.

The drivers of option value in practice – Introduction

As discussed above, the main drivers of option value are as follows:

- value of the underlying asset
- exercise price
- time to expiry
- volatility
- risk-free rate.

Determining these figures in practice is discussed below:

Value of the underlying asset

- For quoted underlying assets a value can be looked up on the market. Most markets give prices for buying and selling the underlying asset. A mid-price is usually used for option pricing.

  For example, if a price is quoted as 243–244 cents, then a mid-price of 243.5 cents should be used.

- In the case of unquoted underlying assets a separate exercise must be undertaken to value them.

  For example, suppose an unquoted company has issued share options to employees as part of their remuneration package. To value these call options (e.g. for disclosure or taxation purposes) one must first value the shares using, e.g. P/E ratios.

Exercise price and time to expiry

Both the exercise price and expiry date are stated in the terms of the option contract.

Volatility

- Volatility represents the standard deviation of day-to-day price changes in a security, expressed as an annualised percentage. Two measures of volatility are commonly used in options trading: historical and implied.

- Historical volatility can be measured by observing price changes of a security over a period of time. It is not necessarily a forecast of future volatility, but can be used to determine the option price.

- Implied volatility can be calculated by taking current quoted options prices and working backwards.

A common approach to calculating historical volatility is as follows: (N.B. This is presented for illustration only. You would never be asked to calculate the standard deviation in the AFM exam.)

1   Calculate the daily return using (current price/previous day's price) or P_n/P_{n-1}.

2   Take the log of each 'return' to convert into a continuous return.

3   Calculate the standard deviation of the logs to get a daily volatility.

4   Annualise the result.

Volatility calculation

Day	Price	P_n/P_{n-1}	$\ln(P_n/P_{n-1})$ 'x'	x^2
Monday	100			
Tuesday	101	1.010000	0.009950	0.000099
Wednesday	105	1.039604	0.038840	0.001509
Thursday	103	0.980952	−0.019231	0.000370
Friday	104	1.009709	0.009662	0.000093
Sum			0.039221	0.002071
Average			0.009805	0.000518

In order to calculate the volatility (standard deviation) we need to use these two final figures.

Volatility = square root of (the average value of x^2 less the square of the average value of x)

$= \sqrt{(0.000518 - 0.009805^2)}$

= 0.0205 or approximately 2%

Assuming 260 trading days on the market, Annualised volatility = daily volatility × $\sqrt{260}$ = 0.33 or 33%.

The method for calculating the continuous return in the above example may be unfamiliar to you. The basic idea is that instead of dividing a time period into years or weeks or days for discounting purposes we can discount continuously. To get the same answer either way, we need to set continuous rate = ln (1 + discrete rate)

For example, if the discrete rate is 10% per year, then a continuous rate is given by:

Continuous rate = ln 1.10 = 0.0953 or 9.53%.

Discount factors using continuous rates are given by $DF = e^{-it}$ where i is the continuous rate and t the time period.

Risk-free rate

- The risk-free rate is the minimum return required by investors from a risk-free investment.

- Treasury bills or other short-term (usually three months). Government borrowings are regarded as the safest possible investment and their rate of return is often given in a question to be used as a figure for the risk-free rate.

2   The Black-Scholes option pricing model

Introduction

The **Black-Scholes** model values call options before the expiry date and takes account of all five factors that determine the value of an option.

Using the Black-Scholes model to value call options

Value of a call option = $P_a N(d_1) - P_e N(d_2)e^{-rt}$

Where $\quad d_1 = \dfrac{\ln(Pa/Pe) + (r + 0.5s^2)t}{s\sqrt{t}}$

$\qquad d_2 = d_1 - s\sqrt{t}$ calculate d_1 and d_2 to two decimal places

Note: The formula is daunting, but fortunately you do not need to learn it, as it will be given in the examination paper. You need to be aware only of the variables which it includes, to be able to plug in the numbers.

The key:

P_a = current price of underlying asset (e.g. share price)

P_e = exercise price

r = risk-free rate of interest

t = time until expiry of option in years

s = volatility of the share price (as measured by the standard deviation expressed as a decimal)

N(d) = equals the area under the normal curve up to d (see normal distribution tables)

e = the exponential constant (approx. 2.71828)

ln = the natural logarithm (logarithm base 'e')

$P_e e^{-rt}$ = present value of the exercise price calculated by using continuous discounting factors.

Measures of volatility
Standard deviation and variance
The measure of volatility used in the Black-Scholes model is the annual standard deviation (s), expressed as a decimal.
Past exam questions have occasionally quoted volatility in terms of the 'variance', which is the square of the standard deviation. In this case, take the square root of the given variance figure to give the volatility in the correct terms for the Black-Scholes formula.

Alternatively, monthly, or weekly, standard deviations may be quoted. To convert from a monthly standard deviation to an annual figure

- square the monthly standard deviation

- multiply by 12

- take the square root of the result.

This will now be the annual standard deviation figure as required.

Normal distribution tables

Recap of normal distributions

Extract from standard normal distribution table

	0.00	0.01	0.02	0.03	0.04	0.05	0.06	0.07	0.08	0.09
0.0	.0000	.0040	.0080	.0120	.0159	.0199	.0239	.0279	.0319	.0359
0.1	.0398	.0438	.0478	.0517	.0557	.0596	.0636	.0675	.0714	.0753
0.2	.0793	.0832	.0871	.0910	.0948	.0987	.1026	.1064	.1103	.1141
0.3	.1179	.1217	.1255	.1293	.1331	.1368	.1406	.1443	.1480	.1517
0.4	.1554	.1591	.1628	.1664	.1700	.1736	.1772	.1808	.1844	.1879
0.5	.1915	.1950	.1985	.2019	.2054	.2088	.2123	.2157	.2190	.2224
0.6	.2257	.2291	.2324	.2357	.2389	.2422	.2454	.2486	.2518	.2549
0.7	.2580	.2611	.2642	.2673	.2704	.2734	.2764	.2794	.2823	.2852
0.8	.2881	.2910	.2939	.2967	.2995	.3023	.3051	.3078	.3106	.3133
0.9	.3159	.3186	.3212	.3238	.3264	.3289	.3315	.3340	.3365	.3389
1.0	.3413	.3438	.3461	.3485	.3508	.3531	.3554	.3577	.3599	.3621
1.1	.3643	.3665	.3686	.3708	.3729	.3749	.3770	.3790	.3810	.3830
1.2	.3849	.3869	.3888	.3907	.3925	.3944	.3962	.3980	.3997	.4015
1.3	.4032	.4049	.4066	.4082	.4099	.4115	.4131	.4147	.4162	.4177
1.4	.4192	.4207	.4222	.4236	.4251	.4265	.4279	.4292	.4306	.4319
1.5	.4332	.4345	.4357	.4370	.4382	.4394	.4406	.4418	.4430	.4441
1.6	.4452	.4463	.4474	.4485	.4495	.4505	.4515	.4525	.4535	.4545
1.7	.4554	.4564	.4573	.4582	.4591	.4599	.4608	.4616	.4625	.4633
1.8	.4641	.4649	.4656	.4664	.4671	.4678	.4686	.4693	.4699	.4706
1.9	.4713	.4719	.4726	.4732	.4738	.4744	.4750	.4756	.4762	.4767

This table can be used to calculate $N(d_1)$, the cumulative normal distribution function needed for the Black-Scholes model of option pricing.

- If $d_1 > 0$, add 0.5 to the relevant number above.

- If $d_1 < 0$, subtract the relevant number above from 0.5.

For example if d_1 is 1.05, $N(d_1) = 0.3531 + 0.5 = 0.8531$.

Note: $N(d) = $ Is the area under the normal curve up to d in the shaped area of the figure below.

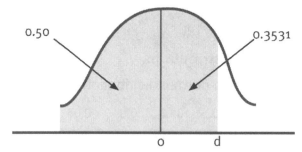

Illustration of the Black-Scholes model

The current share price of B Co shares	=	$100		
The exercise price	=	$95		
The risk-free rate of interest	=	10%	=	0.1
The standard deviation of return on the shares	=	50%	=	0.5
The time to expiry	=	3 months	=	0.25

Required:

Calculate the value of the above call option.

Solution

Step 1: Calculate d_1 and d_2.

$$d_1 = \frac{\ln(P_a/P_e) + (r + 0.5s^2)t}{s\sqrt{t}}$$

$$d_1 = \frac{\ln(100/95) + (0.1 + 0.5 \times 0.5^2)0.25}{0.5 \times \sqrt{0.25}}$$

$d_1 = 0.43$

$d_2 = d_1 - s\sqrt{t} = 0.43 - 0.5 \times \sqrt{0.25} = 0.18$

Step 2: Use normal distribution tables to find the value of N(d₁) and N(d₂).

$N(d_1) = 0.5 + 0.1664 = 0.6664$

$N(d_2) = 0.5 + 0.0714 = 0.5714$

Step 3: Plug these numbers into the Black-Scholes formula.

Value of a call option $= P_a N(d_1) - P_e N(d_2)e^{-rt}$

$= 100 \times 0.6664 - 95 \times 0.5714 \times e^{-(0.1 \times 0.25)}$

$= \$13.70$

Note: This can be split between the intrinsic value of $5 (100 – 95) and the time value which is $8.70.

Test your understanding 3

Suppose that the risk-free rate is 5% and the standard deviation of the return on the share in the past has been estimated as 34.64%.

Required:

Estimate the value of a six-month call option at an exercise price of $1.48 (current share price = $1.64).

Note that in the CBE you'll need to be familiar with the LN, EXP and NORMSDIST spreadsheet functions to calculate the option value.

Using the Black-Scholes model to value put options

If you have calculated the value of a call option using Black-Scholes, then the value of a corresponding put option can be found using the put call parity formula.

The put call parity equation is on the examination formula sheet:

Put call parity $P = c - P_a + P_e \times e^{-rt}$

Step 1: Value the corresponding call option using the Black-Scholes model.

Step 2: Then calculate the value the put option using the put call parity equation.

Black-Scholes model: value put options

Returning to the earlier example of B Co, where the current share price is $100, exercise price is $95, the risk-free rate of interest is 10%, the standard deviation of shares return is 50% and the time to expiry is three months, calculate the value of a put option.

Solution

*   **Step 1:** We have already calculated the value of the call option at $13.70.

*   **Step 2:** Using put call parity equation:

Put call parity $P = c - P_a + P_e \times e^{-rt}$

Value of a put = 13.70 − 100.00 + 92.65

= $6.35

Test your understanding 4

Using the information given in TYU3, calculate the value of the corresponding put option.

Underlying assumptions and limitations

The model assumes that:

*   The options are European calls.

*   There are no transaction costs or taxes.

*   The investor can borrow at the risk-free rate.

*   The risk-free rate of interest and the share's volatility is constant over the life of the option.

*   The future share-price volatility can be estimated by observing past share price volatility.

*   The share price follows a random walk and that the possible share prices are based on a normal distribution.

*   No dividends are payable before the option expiry date.

In practice these unrealistic assumptions can be relaxed and the basic model can be developed to reflect a more complex situation.

Delta and delta hedges

The figure $N(d_1)$ is known as delta. Delta measures the change in option value which would result from a \$1 change in the value of the underlying asset (e.g. share).

An investor can eliminate the risk of his or her shareholding by constructing a 'delta hedge'.

- An investor who holds a number of shares and sells (an option writer) a number of call options in the proportion dictated by the delta (the hedge ratio) ensures a hedged portfolio. **N.B.** A hedged portfolio is one where the gains and losses cancel out against each other.

- Number of option calls to sell = Number of shares held/$N(d_1)$.

- Alternatively, if you have already written call options, then a delta hedge can be constructed by buying shares.

- Number of shares to hold = Number of call options sold × $N(d_1)$.

Because share prices change continuously in the real world, the value of delta also changes continuously. Therefore, the investor who wants to maintain a risk neutral position will have to continuously adjust the balance of options and shares in his or her portfolio. This process is known as 'dynamic delta hedging'.

 Example of a delta hedge

Assuming a call option currently has a delta of 0.5, let use it to construct a hedged portfolio for an investor who holds 100 shares.

The investor in shares will find out how many call options she will have to (write) sell.

So if you had 100 shares we would need to sell (100 shares/0.5) = 200 calls to construct a delta hedge. The number of options will exceed the number of shares unless the delta is 1, then they would be an equal number of each.

The call option writers (the seller of the call options) will find out how many shares they will have to buy.

If the share price increases by 10 cents, the call options increase by 5 cents. However as we have sold the call option our portfolio decreases by 5 cents for every call option sold.

The Comfort Table:	Delta	Number of shares purchased	Number of call options sold	Overall gain or loss is zero. Delta neutral
Current position	0.5	100	200	
Share price increases by 10c		$10	(−5c × 200) − $10 =	0

However, the difficulty is that the delta value is not at a constant. It changes as the share price changes.

Suppose that the 10 cents move in the share price caused the delta to move to 0.7. The option writer will need to buy 200 calls × 0.7 = 140 shares in order to hedge the position, i.e. 40 extra shares.

The portfolio will need rebalancing as the delta value changes. The frequency of this depends on the rate of change of delta, measured by gamma.

Gamma, vega, rho and theta

Delta measures the sensitivity of the option value to changes in the value of the underlying asset (explained in detail above).

Sensitivities to other factors in the Black Scholes formula are denoted by other Greek letters as follows:

Gamma – measures the rate of change of delta as the underlying asset's price changes.

Vega – measures the sensitivity of an option's value to a change in the implied volatility of the underlying asset.

Rho – measures the sensitivity of the option value to changes in the risk free rate of interest.

Theta – measures the rate of decline in the value of the option caused by the passage of time.

More details on 'The Greeks'

Collectively, delta, gamma, vega, rho and theta are known as 'The Greeks'.

The importance of the delta value has been illustrated above i.e. it is useful when setting up a delta hedge. The importance of the other Greeks is explained below.

Gamma

A high gamma value indicates that the delta value is quite volatile.

This means that it will be quite difficult for an option writer to maintain a delta hedge, since the volatile delta value will require the option writer to be constantly changing the number of options written.

Therefore, gamma is a measure of how easy risk management will be.

Vega

The vega determines the sensitivity of an option's value to a change in the implied volatility of the underlying asset. Implied volatility is what the market is implying the volatility of the underlying asset will be in the future, based on the price changes in an option. The option price may change independently of whether or not the underlying asset's value changes, due to new information being presented to the markets. Implied volatility is the result of this independent movement in the option's value, and this determines the vega.

The vega only impacts the time value of an option and as the vega increases, so will the value of the option.

Rho

Interest rates tend to change slowly and by small amounts, so the impact of interest rates on option prices (measured by rho) is generally not particularly significant.

However, note that rho is positive for call options (an increase in interest rates leads to an increase in option price) but negative for puts (an increase in interest rates leads to a decrease in option price).

Also, longer term options have larger rhos than short term options, because the more time there is until expiry of the option, the more significant a change in interest rates is.

Theta

An option price has two components, the intrinsic value and the time value. However, when the option expires, the time premium reduces to zero. Therefore, theta measures how much value is lost over time.

Theta is usually expressed as an amount lost per day (e.g. theta could be −$0.06, indicating that 6 cents of value is lost per day. Theta usually increases as the expiry date approaches.

3 Identifying real options in investment appraisal

Introduction

- Flexibility adds value to an investment.

- Financial options are an example where this flexibility can be valued.

- Conventional investment-appraisal techniques typically undervalue flexibility within projects with high uncertainty.

- Real options theory attempts to classify and value flexibility in general by taking the ideas of financial options pricing and developing them.

More detail on valuing flexibility

- Flexibility adds value to an investment:

  - For example, if an investment can be staggered, then future costs can be avoided if the market turns out to be less attractive than originally expected.

  - The core to this value lies in reducing downside risk exposure but keeping upside potential open – i.e. in making probability distributions asymmetric.

- Financial options are an example where this flexibility can be valued.

  - A call option on a share allows an investor to 'wait and see' what happens to a share price before deciding whether to exercise the option and will thus benefit from favourable price movements without being affected by adverse movements.

- Conventional investment-appraisal techniques typically undervalue flexibility within projects with high uncertainty.

  - High uncertainty within a NPV context will result in a higher discount rate and a lower NPV. However, with such uncertainty any embedded real options will become more valuable.

- Real options theory attempts to classify and value flexibility in general by taking the ideas of financial options pricing and developing them:

  - A financial option gives the owner the right, but not the obligation, to buy or sell a security at a given price. Analogously, companies that make strategic investments have the right, but not the obligation, to exploit these opportunities in the future.

  - As with financial options most real options involve spending more up front (analogous to the option premium) to give additional flexibility later.

Different types of real option

There are many different classifications of real options. For the purposes of the AFM syllabus, we use the following four generic headings:

Options to delay/defer

The key here is to be able to delay investment without losing the opportunity, creating a call option on the future investment.

 Illustration 1 – Identifying real options in investment appraisal

For example, establishing a drugs patent allows the owner of the patent to wait and see how market conditions develop before producing the drug, without the potential downside of competitors entering the market.

(**Note:** Drugs patents was the subject of a past examination question on this area. However, there is some debate whether or not patents are real options. This debate is outside the scope of the syllabus.)

Options to switch/redeploy

It may be possible to switch the use of assets should market conditions change.

 Illustration 2 – Identifying real options in investment appraisal

For example, traditional production lines were set up to make one product. Modern flexible manufacturing systems (FMS) allow the product output to be changed to match customer requirements.

Similarly a new plant could be designed with resale and/or other uses in mind, using more general-purpose assets than dedicated to allow easier switching.

 Illustration 3 – Identifying real options in investment appraisal

For example, when designing a plant management can choose whether to have higher or lower operating gearing. By having mainly variable costs, it is financially more beneficial if the plant does not have to operate every month.

Options to expand/follow-on

It may be possible to adjust the scale of an investment depending on the market conditions.

Options to abandon

If a project has clearly identifiable stages such that investment can be staggered, then management have to decide whether to abandon or continue at the end of each stage.

Illustration 4 – Identifying real options in investment appraisal

When looking to develop their stadiums, many football clubs face the decision whether to build a one- or a two-tier stand:

- A one-tier stand would be cheaper but would be inadequate if the club's attendance improved greatly.

- A two-tier stand would allow for much greater fan numbers but would be more expensive and would be seen as a waste of money should attendance not improve greatly.

Some clubs (e.g. West Bromwich Albion in the UK) have solved this problem by building a one-tier stand with stronger foundations and designed in such a way (e.g. positioning of exits, corporate boxes, etc.) that it would be relatively straightforward to add a second tier at a later stage without knocking down the first tier.

Such a stand is more expensive than a conventional one-tier stand but the premium paid makes it easier to expand at a later date when (if!) attendance grows.

Illustration 5 – Identifying real options in investment appraisal

Amazon.com undertook a substantial investment to develop its customer base, brand name and information infrastructure for its core book business.

This in effect created a portfolio of real options to extend its operations into a variety of new businesses such as CDs, DVDs, etc.

Test your understanding 5

Comment on a strategy of vertical integration in the context of real options.

Test your understanding 6

A film studio has three new releases planned for the Christmas period but does not know which will be the biggest hit for allocating marketing resources. It thus decides to do a trial screening of each film in selected cinemas and allocates the marketing budget on the basis of the results.

Required:

Comment on this plan using real option theory.

4 Valuing real options

Introduction

Valuing real options is a complex process and currently a matter of some debate as to the most suitable methodology. Within the AFM syllabus you are expected to be able to apply the Black-Scholes model to real options.

Using the Black-Scholes model to value real options

The **Black-Scholes** equation is well suited for simple real options, those with a single source of uncertainty and a single decision date. To use the model we need to identify the five key input variables as follows:

Exercise price

For most real options (e.g. option to expand, option to delay), the capital investment required can be substituted for the exercise price. These options are examples of call options.

For an option to abandon, use the salvage value on abandonment. This is an example of a put option.

Value of the underlying asset (share price in the earlier calculations)

The value of the underlying asset is usually taken to be the PV of the future cash flows from the project (i.e. excluding any initial investment).

This could be the value of the project being undertaken for a call option (e.g. option to expand, option to delay), or the value of the cash flows being foregone for a put option (option to abandon).

Time to expiry

This is straightforward if the project involves a single investment.

Volatility

The volatility of the underlying asset (here the future operating cash flows) can be measured using typical industry sector risk.

Risk-free rate

Many writers continue to use the risk-free rate for real options. However, some argue that a higher rate be used to reflect the extra risks when replacing the share price with the PV of future cash flows.

Illustration 6 – Valuing real options

A UK retailer is considering opening a new store in Germany with the following details (note that all figures have been converted into the domestic currency):

- Estimated cost
- £12m
- Present value of net receipts
- £10m
- NPV
- –£2m

These figures would suggest that the investment should be rejected. However, if the first store is opened then the firm would gain the option to open a second store (an option to expand or follow-on).

Suppose this would have the following details:

- Timing (t)
- 5 years' time
- Estimated cost (P_e)
- £20m
- Present value of net receipts (P_a)
- £15m
- Volatility of cash flows (s)
- 28.3%
- Risk-free rate (r)
- 6%

The value of the call option on the second store is then calculated as normal using **Black-Scholes**:

Step 1: Compute d_1 and d_2

$$d_1 = \frac{\ln (P_a/P_e) + (r + 0.5s^2)t}{s\sqrt{t}}$$

$$d_1 = \frac{\ln (15/20) + (0.06 + 0.5 \times 0.283^2)5}{0.283 \times \sqrt{5}}$$

$d_1 = 0.33$

$d_2 = d_1 - s\sqrt{T} = 0.33 - 0.283 \times \sqrt{5} = -0.30$

Step 2: Compute N(d₁) and N(d₂).

$N(d_1) = 0.5 + 0.1293 = 0.6293$

$N(d_2) = 0.5 - 0.1179 = 0.3821$

Step 3: Use formula.

$$\text{Value of a call option} = P_a\, N(d_1) - P_e N(d_2) e^{-rt}$$

$$= 15 \times 0.6293 - 20 \times 0.3821 \times e^{-(0.06 \times 5)}$$

$$= \pounds 3.8m$$

Summary

	£m
Conventional NPV of first store	(2)
Value of call option on second store	3.8
Strategic NPV	**1.8**

The project should thus be accepted.

Test your understanding 7

An online DVD and CD retailer is considering investing $2m on improving its customer information and online ordering systems. The expectation is that this will enable the company to expand by extending its range of products. A decision will be made on the expansion in 1 years' time, when the directors have had chance to analyse customer behaviour and competitors' businesses in more detail, to assess whether the expansion is worthwhile.

Preliminary estimates of the expansion programme have found that an investment of $5m in 1 years' time will generate net receipts with a present value of $4m in the years thereafter. The project's cash flows are expected to be quite volatile, with a standard deviation of 40%.

The current risk free rate of interest is 5%.

Required:

Advise the firm whether the initial investment in updating the systems is worthwhile.

Further numerical example – Option to abandon

The real options considered in the above examples were call options (i.e. there was an option to buy into a project). All options to delay/defer and options to expand/follow-on are call options.

By contrast, an option to abandon is a put option, in that now the business has an option to sell the assets used in the project.

(Note that calculations involving options to switch/redeploy are beyond the AFM syllabus. These real options will only be tested in discussion questions in AFM.)

Numerical example

ABC Co is considering investing in the following project:

$000	T_0	T_1	T_2	T_3	T_4
PV of cash flows	(100)	12	15	30	35

So the NPV of the project is –$8,000, and the project would be rejected.

However, if the company had the option to abandon the project after 2 years (i.e. at T_2) and to receive $70,000 for the sale of the assets, consider the value of this option to abandon, and the impact on the decision. (Assume that the risk free rate is 5% and that the volatility associated with the project cash flows is 20%).

It is critical that we can correctly identify the five variables to input into the Black-Scholes model.

For the option to abandon, these are as follows:

P_a = PV of CF foregone if we abandon = $30,000 + $35,000 = $65,000

s = standard deviation of the project cash flows = 20%

P_e = abandonment proceeds = $70,000

t = time until abandonment = 2 years

r = risk free interest rate = 5%

Calculate Black Scholes figures

d_1 = 0.23

d_2 = –0.05

$N(d_1)$ = 0.5910

$N(d_2)$ = 0.4801

Calculating the main formula gives a call option value of $8,006

Therefore, using put-call parity, the put option value is $6,342

In this case the project, even when considering the possibility of abandonment after two years, is still not acceptable.

It has a strategic NPV of –$8,000 (basic NPV) + $6,342 (value of real option) = –$1,658.

Using real options when making financial strategy decisions

Manics Co is considering investing in the following project:

$m	T_0	T_1	T_2	T_3-T_8
Free cash flows	(500)	120	(200)	160

At a discount rate of 10%, the NPV of the project is positive (approximately $19.7m NPV).

This is a very small positive NPV, so some of the directors have expressed concerns about the sensitivity of the project to possible changes in the forecast cash flows.

However, the financial manager feels that the project is being unfairly under-valued, so he has prepared some further analysis of the project.

The key to the financial manager's concern is that he feels that the large cash outflow at the end of year 2 is discretionary and does not have to be made (in particular if circumstances have changed and the project is not proving to be as successful as had been hoped).

He has therefore split the original project into two: an initial investment of $500m which will produce net cash inflows of $120m for the following 8 years, and a further investment of $320m after two years which will increase the net cash inflows by $40m to $160m per year for the remaining six years.

The project is now being viewed as an initial expansion costing $500m – phase 1 – followed by an option to expand further after two years – phase 2.

If separate NPV calculations are carried out for each of these phases (again using 10% as the discount rate), the results below are obtained:

Phase 1: NPV = $140.2m positive

Phase 2: NPV = $120.5 negative

Note that the overall NPV is $140.2m – $120.5m = $19.7m as before.

This extra analysis provides some interesting insight. Given that there is no obligation for the company to carry out phase 2, the overall NPV must be at least $140.2m, which far exceeds the initial NPV calculated of $19.7m.

Although phase 2 does not currently seem worthwhile, the option to carry out this phase can only add value as an option can never have a negative value.

If the cash flows expected from phase 2 were to become favourable, the company will have the ability to carry out phase 2 and reap the benefit.

Hence, the overall NPV will be $140.2m plus the value of the option to carry out phase 2.

The financial manager has therefore used the BSOP model to value the option to expand (real option), as shown below.

The inputs required for the Black Scholes option pricing (BSOP) formula are:

P_e = the investment required after two years to carry out phase 2 = $320m

P_a = the PV of the net cash inflows currently forecast to arise from phase two = $144.0m (this must exclude the P_e)

t = the time until phase 2 will begin = 2 years

The s and r figures (volatility and risk free rate respectively) have not been presented yet in this example, but they will both be given within any exam question.

Assume that s is 50% and r is 5% here.

Using these inputs the option value can now be calculated:

d_1 = –0.63

d_2 = –1.34

$N(d_1)$ = 0.2643

$N(d_2)$ = 0.0901

Value of the call option = $12.0m

Hence, the total NPV for the project with the option to expand

= $140.2m + $12.0m = $152.2m

As a result of the financial manager's further analysis, a project which initially seemed fairly marginal has been shown to be extremely attractive.

The directors who were expressing concerns about the sensitivity associated with the project will presumably be much happier now to proceed with the project.

The attractiveness of the project arises because phase 1 of the project is itself attractive and the company can potentially benefit if the phase 2 expansion finally becomes worthwhile.

Student Accountant article

The articles 'Investment appraisal and real options' and 'Using real options when making financial strategy decisions' in the Technical Articles section of the ACCA website provide further details on real options, including some good examples of calculations.

5 Other uses of the Black-Scholes model

Use of the Black-Scholes model in equity valuation

The model can also be used to value the equity of a company.

The basic idea is that, because of limited liability, shareholders can walk away from a company when the debt exceeds the asset value. However, when the assets exceed the debts, those shareholders will keep running the business, in order to collect the surplus.

Therefore, the value of shares can be seen as a call option owned by shareholders – we can use Black-Scholes to value such an option.

Five factors to input into the Black-Scholes model

It is critical that we can correctly identify the five variables to input into the Black-Scholes model.

For equity valuation, these are as follows:

P_a = fair value of the firm's assets

s = standard deviation of the assets' value

P_e = amount owed to bank (see below for more details)

t = time until debt is redeemed

r = risk free interest rate

Note that the value of P_e will not just be the redemption value of the debt. The amount owed to the bank incorporates all the interest payments as well as the ultimate capital repayment.

In fact, the value of P_e to input into the Black-Scholes model should be calculated as the theoretical redemption value of an equivalent zero coupon debt.

Deriving Pe

A company has $100 of debt in issue carrying 5% interest and with five years to maturity. The company's current (pre-tax) cost of debt capital is 8%.

Required:

Calculate the theoretical redemption value of an equivalent zero coupon debt.

Solution

Year	Cash flow ($)	DF (8%)	PV
1	5	0.926	4.63
2	5	0.857	4.29
3	5	0.794	3.97
4	5	0.735	3.68
5	105	0.681	71.51
			———
			88.08
			———

The repayment value on a zero coupon bond of the same current market value is calculated by finding the unknown future value which, when discounted at 8% over five years, gives a present value of $88.08.

i.e. $88.08 = \text{Value}/1.08^5$

Value = $129.42

Numerical example of BSOP and equity valuation

Sparks is a company in the electronics industry and is looking to expand through acquisition.

A target company, EBMS, has been identified and the directors of Sparks are looking to value the entire equity capital of EBMS.

From discussions with the directors of EBMS, the assets of EBMS have been valued at $1,450m which the directors of EBMS consider to be their fair value in use in the business. The volatility of the asset value has been agreed at 10% per year.

EBMS currently has 4% bonds in issue with a book value of $900m which are redeemable in 3 years' time at a premium of 25% over par. Interest is payable annually.

Short dated Government bonds are currently yielding on average 4.25% and SOFR is 0.75% above this. EBMS currently has a BBB credit rating and the following data on credit risk premiums (in basis points) has been obtained from commercial rating sources:

1 year 75

2 year 95

3 year 120

5 year 135

The directors of Sparks always try to obtain as many different valuations as possible when evaluating a potential acquisition and wish to use option pricing theory in addition to the more usual methods.

Required:

Using the Black Scholes option pricing model, derive a value for the total equity of EBMS.

Solution

The basic process is to recognise that the equity represents a call option to purchase the company from the bond holders in three years' time.

First, calculate the exercise price. This is the redemption value of the debt BUT including the interest element also. This requires calculating the fair value of the debt and then converting it to a zero coupon bond with the same fair value and time to maturity to obtain a redemption value incorporating interest as well.

Required yield = risk free rate + credit risk premium = 4.25 + 1.20 = 5.45%

Fair value calculation:

Year	Cash flow ($)	DF(5.45%)	PV
1	4	0.9483	3.79
2	4	0.8993	3.60
3	4	0.8528	3.41
4	125	0.8528	106.60
			117.40

Fair Value per $100 is $117.40

For a 3 year zero coupon bond to have the same fair value, the redemption premium would need to be:

Premium in 3 years = $117.40 \times (1 + 5.45\%)^3 = \$137.66$

Therefore, theoretical exercise price = 137.66/100 × $900m = $1,238.94m

The variables can now be assigned:

Exercise Price   1238.94

Asset Value   1450

Risk free rate   0.0425

Time to maturity   3

Volatility   0.1

Calculate Black Scholes figures

d_1 = 1.73

d_2 = 1.56

$N(d_1)$ = 0.9582

$N(d_2)$ = 0.9406

Calculating the main formula gives an option value of $363.5m.

This can be broken down into:

Intrinsic value $211.06m (1,450 – 1,238.94)

Time value $152.44m

Therefore, the equity value is $363.5m which is $152.44m more than the current net assets value of the business.

Use of the Black-Scholes model in debt valuation

The Black-Scholes model can also be used in debt valuation.

The value of a (risky) bond issued by a company can be calculated as the value of an equivalent risk-free bond minus the value of a put-option over the company's assets.

Therefore, if the value of equity has already been calculated as a call option over the company's assets (as explained above), the value of debt can then be calculated using the put-call parity equation.

Calculation of credit spreads

For any bond the lender's required/expected return will be made up of two elements:

- The risk free rate of return

- A premium ('the credit spread') based on the expected probability of default and the expected loss given default – covered in more detail in the next chapter (when looking at cost of debt).

Option pricing theory (OPT) can be used to calculate these credit spreads and the risk of default.

How to use OPT to calculate credit spreads

Overview of the method

A key concept in this context is that shareholders can be viewed as having a call option on the company's assets. By redeeming the debt, shareholders effectively acquire the assets of the company. Default hands the assets to the lenders.

Shareholders exercise this option if the value of the firm's assets is at least equal to the redemption value. If not, then the option is allowed to lapse, the company is handed over to the debt holders and the shareholders walk away.

Not defaulting thus corresponds to the call option being in the money at expiry.

(A corresponding view is that the lenders have sold a put option under which the company is sold to them for more than it's worth – they give up the full redemption value in exchange for the company assets.)

Calculations in this area are not examinable in the AFM syllabus.

6 Chapter summary

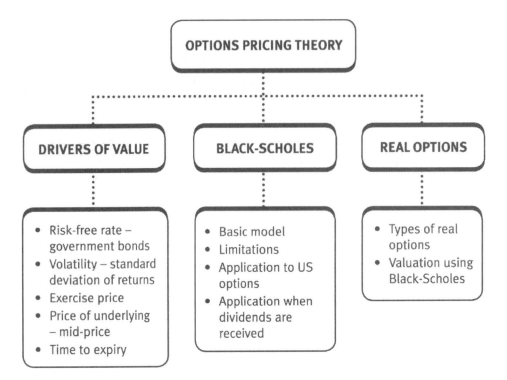

Test your understanding answers

Test your understanding 1

Summary of the determinants of option prices.

Increase in	Call	Put
Share price	Increase	Decrease
Exercise price	Decrease	Increase
Time to expiry	Increase	Increase
Volatility – s	Increase	Increase
Interest rate	Increase	Decrease

Comments:

- Share price and exercise price – opposite of call option.

- Time and volatility – same argument as for call.

- Interest rate – a higher interest rate reduces the present value of deferred receipts making the option less valuable as an alternative to selling now.

Test your understanding 2

Buying put options would allow the manager to limit the downside exposure.

Test your understanding 3

Value of a call option = $P_a N(d_1) - P_e N(d_2)e^{-rt}$

Step 1: Compute d_1 and d_2.

Where $d_1 = \dfrac{\ln(P_a/P_e) + (r + 0.5s^2)t}{s\sqrt{t}}$

$d_2 = d_1 - s\sqrt{t}$ calculate d_1 and d_2 to two decimal places

$d_1 = [\ln(164/148) + (0.05 + (0.5 \times 0.3464^2))0.5]/0.3464 \times \sqrt{0.5} = 0.64$

$d_2 = 0.64 - (0.3464 \times \sqrt{0.5}) = 0.40$

Step 2: Compute N(d₁) and N(d₂).

$N(d_1) = 0.5 + 0.2389 = 0.7389$

$N(d_2) = 0.5 + 0.1554 = 0.6554$

Step 3: Use formula.

Value of a call option
$$= P_a N(d_1) - P_e N(d_2) e^{-rt}$$
$$= 164 \times 0.7389$$
$$\quad - 148 \times 0.6554 \times e^{-(0.05 \times 0.5)}$$
$$= 26.6 \text{ cents}$$

Test your understanding 4

Put call parity p $\quad = c - P_a + P_e e^{-rt}$

Value of a put $\quad = 26.6 - 164 + 144.32$

$\quad\quad = 6.9 \text{ cents}$

Test your understanding 5

- Vertical integration is usually evaluated in terms of cost, quality and barriers to entry.

- By outsourcing, the company can switch between different types of supply and different suppliers.

- Vertical integration loses this flexibility, effectively giving up a switching option.

Test your understanding 6

The studio has effectively acquired a learning option allowing better subsequent decisions. The feedback generates a range of call options on future marketing investment.

Test your understanding 7

The value of the follow-on call option is calculated using **Black-Scholes**:

Step 1: Compute d_1 and d_2.

$$d_1 = \frac{\ln(P_a/P_e) + (r + 0.5s^2)t}{s\sqrt{t}}$$

$$d_1 = \frac{\ln(4/5) + (0.05 + 0.5 \times 0.4^2)1}{0.4 \times \sqrt{1}}$$

$$d_1 = -0.23$$

$$d_2 = d_1 - s\sqrt{t} = -0.23 - 0.4 \times \sqrt{1} = -0.63$$

Step 2: Compute $N(d_1)$ and $N(d_2)$.

$$N(d_1) = 0.5 - 0.0910 = 0.4090$$

$$N(d_2) = 0.5 - 0.2357 = 0.2643$$

Step 3: Use formula.

Value of a call option

$$= Pa\,N(d_1) - P_e e^{-rt}\,N(d_2)$$

$$= 4 \times 0.4090 - 5 \times e^{-(0.05 \times 1)} \times 0.2643$$

$$= 1.636 - 4.756 \times 0.2643$$

$$= \$0.38m.$$

Summary

	$m
Investment in upgrading customer database and online ordering	(2)
Value of follow-on call option	0.38
Strategic NPV	**(1.62)**

The project should thus be rejected.

An introduction to risk management

Chapter learning objectives

Study guide section		Study guide outcome
A2: Financial strategy formulation	(d)	Explain the theoretical and practical rationale for the management of risk.
	(e)	Assess the organisation's exposure to business and financial risk including operational, reputational, political, economic, regulatory and fiscal risk.
	(f)	Develop a framework for risk management, comparing and contrasting risk mitigation, hedging and diversification strategies.
	(g)	Establish capital investment monitoring and risk management systems.
B1: Discounted cash flow techniques	(a)	Evaluate the potential value added to an organisation arising from a specified capital investment project or portfolio using the net present value (NPV) model. Project modelling should include explicit treatment and discussion of: (iv) Probability analysis and sensitivity analysis when adjusting for risk and uncertainty in investment appraisal.

(b) Outline the application of Monte Carlo simulation to investment appraisal. Candidates will not be expected to undertake simulations in an examination context but will be expected to demonstrate an understanding of (i) The significance of the simulation output and the assessment of the likelihood of project success (ii) The measurement and interpretation of project value at risk.

E1: The role of the treasury function in multinationals

(b) Discuss the operations of the derivatives market (ii) Key features such as standard contracts, tick sizes, margin requirements, and margin trading.

One of the PER performance objectives (PO11 – Identify and Manage Financial Risk) is to be able to identify, measure, and advise on the financial risks to the organisation.

PER   Working through this chapter should help you understand how to demonstrate that objective.

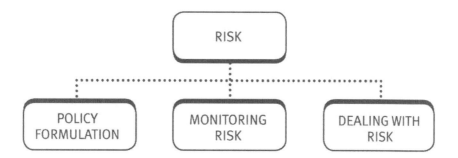

1 Risk policy formulation

An important part of the financial manager's role and responsibility is considering how risk is to be managed.

The control and mitigation of risk costs money and takes up management time, so it is critical that we can understand the benefits of risk management and compare these to the costs to assess whether a risk management strategy is worthwhile.

Strategic Business Leader (SBL) covered managing and controlling risk in some detail. This section initially introduces an overview of risk management in relation to capital investment projects, then explains some specific examples of risks. More detailed techniques for risk management, such as the use of derivatives and Value at Risk (VaR), are covered later in the chapter.

Student Accountant article

Read the examiner's 'Risk Management' article in the Technical Articles section of the ACCA website for more details on why companies need to manage risk.

The theory of risk management

Risk management is about decisions made to change the volatility of returns a corporation is exposed to, for example changing a company's exposure to floating interest rates by swapping them to fixed rates for a fee.

Since business is about generating higher returns by undertaking risky projects, important management decisions revolve around which projects to undertake, how they should be financed and whether the volatility of a project's returns (its risk) should be managed.

The volatility of returns of a project should be managed if it results in increasing the value to a corporation. Given that the market value of a corporation is the net present value (NPV) of its future cash flows discounted by the return required by its investors, then higher market value can either be generated by increasing the future cash flows or by reducing investors' required rate of return (or both).

A risk management strategy that increases the NPV at a lower comparative cost would benefit the corporation.

Risk and stakeholder conflict

- Shareholders will invest in companies with a risk profile that matches that required for their portfolio.

- Management should thus be wary of altering the risk profile of the business without shareholder support.

- An increase in risk will bring about an increase in the required return and may lead to current shareholders selling their shares and so depressing the share price.

- Inevitably management will have their own attitude to risk. Unlike the well-diversified shareholders, the directors are likely to be heavily dependent on the success of the company for their own financial stability and be more risk averse as a consequence.

Risk and policy decisions

The financial manager will need to make policy decisions in the following areas:

- Type of business area

- Operating gearing

- Financial gearing

- Accuracy of forecasts.

Risk and policy decisions

Type of business area

Based on the risk appetite of the firm, decisions must be taken about those types of activity suitable for investment. This will involve decisions about the acceptability of:

- economic volatility of the industry

- degree of seasonality

- intensity of competitor action.

Operating gearing

The level of operating gearing of the firm is the proportion of fixed costs to variable in the cost structure. Whilst some industries are destined to have higher levels of operating gearing than others (compare the travel industry with manufacturing for example), policy decisions about what level is acceptable will drive choices about factors such as:

- outsourcing v providing internally

- leasing v buying

- full-time staff v freelance providers.

Financial gearing

More fully discussed elsewhere, increasing debt levels can reduce the cost of finance but increases the risks of bankruptcy as the same time. Directors must decide what level of gearing they are prepared to accept.

Accuracy of forecasts

The success of any planned investment programme will rely heavily on the accuracy of forecasts of future cash flows (in and out) and an NPV assessment also relies on an accurate calculation of the discount rate. The sensitivity of these forecasts can be calculated, and the probability of the variation assessed, but in the end the directors must decide what level of risk they are willing to accept in order to accept or reject the project.

2 The risk framework

All projects are risky. When a capital investment programme commences, a framework for dealing with this risk must be in place.

This framework must cover:

- risk awareness
- risk assessment and monitoring
- risk management (i.e. strategies for dealing with risk and planned responses should unprotected risks materialise).

Risk awareness

In appraising most investment projects, reliance will be placed on a large number of estimates. For all material estimates, a formal risk assessment should be carried out to identify:

- potential risks that could affect the forecast
- the probability that such a risk would occur.

Risks may be:

- strategic
- tactical
- operational.

Once the potential risks have been identified, a monitoring process will be needed to alert management if they arise.

Different types of risk

Strategic risks are those affecting the overall direction and outcome of the project, such as changes in macroeconomic factors or changes in corporate policies.

Tactical risks affect the way the various parts of the project are interlinked, the way resources are acquired or the way in which the business functions involved in the project are run.

Operational risks are those affecting the day to day running of the project.

Examples of risk for an investment project

Some strategic, tactical and operational risks that would affect the estimates on a typical investment project might be:

Strategic:

- brand awareness in the new sector

- risk of recession

- political changes.

Tactical – changes to forecasts based on:

- supply chain changes

- major payment timings

- intended sales of machinery

- contractor overruns on time or amounts spent.

Operational – changes occurring because:

- production breakdown

- breakdown of the supply chain

- failure of the distribution network

- failure to recruit staff with the necessary skills.

Risk assessment and monitoring

A useful way to manage risk is to identify potential risks (usually done in either brainstorming meetings or by using external consultants) and then categorise them according to the likelihood of occurrence and the significance of their potential impact.

Decisions about how to manage the risk are then based on the assessment made.

These assessments may be time consuming and the executive will need to decide:

- how they should be carried out
- what criteria to apply to the categorisation process and
- how often the assessments should be updated.

The essence of risk is that the returns are uncertain. As time passes, so the various uncertain events on which the forecasts are based will occur. Management must monitor the events as they unfold, reforecast predicted results and take action as necessary. The degree and frequency of the monitoring process will depend on the significance of the risk to the project's outcome.

Specific risk assessment and monitoring methods

Internal audit

Many companies set up internal audit departments to assist them in their responsibility to monitor and manage risk.

It is not the job of the internal audit department to monitor results and perform risk assessments, but they can provide valuable support in the creation and successful running of such monitoring systems.

Information systems

Information systems play a key part in effective risk monitoring. Once risk factors have been identified, information systems must be put in place to ensure that any changes affecting project estimates are:

- recorded
- brought to the attention of the responsible manager
- dealt with in an appropriate way.

This will usually include:

- management information systems (MIS)

- executive information systems (EIS).

These systems are expensive to set up and the executive team must decide on the extent to which they wish to use them and the scope required.

The difference between them is:

- Management information systems – feeding back operational data to allow for action to prevent or mitigate risk.

- Executive information systems – bringing senior executives up-to-date with external information such as competitor action, currency fluctuations and economic forecasts as well as providing summarised operational data.

3   Risk management

Strategies for dealing with risk

Risk can be either accepted or dealt with. Possible solutions for dealing with risk include:

- mitigating the risk – reducing it by setting in place control procedures

- hedging the risk – taking action to ensure a certain outcome

- diversification – reducing the impact of one outcome by having a portfolio of different ongoing projects.

More on mitigation, hedging and diversification

Mitigation

- All companies should have in place a comprehensive system of controls. These controls play an essential role in good corporate governance and mitigate risk by working to prevent, or detect and correct potential risks before they become a problem.

- Management would be expected to implement controls over most material risks subject to the following:

    - The cost of the control should not be disproportionate to the potential loss.

    - For non-routine events it may be more practical to devise a specific strategy for dealing with the risk should it arise.

Hedging the risk

- Hedging is a strategy, usually some form of transaction, designed to minimise exposure to an unwanted business risk, commonly arising from fluctuations in exchange rates, commodity prices, interest rates etc.

- It will often involve the purchase or sale of a derivative security (such as options or futures) in order to reduce or neutralise all or some portion of the risk of holding another security. This is dealt with in detail later in this chapter.

- A perfect hedge will eliminate the prospects of any future gains or losses and put the company into a risk-free position in respect of the hedged risk.

- This strategy may be chosen where the downside risk would have serious negative consequences for the firm, and the costs of hedging (including the chance to participate in any upside) are outweighed by the benefits of certainty.

Diversification

- This involves reducing the impact of one outcome by having a portfolio of different ongoing projects.

- Within the context of a single project, this may take the form of selling to a number of different customers to reduce reliance on a single one or sourcing from a number of different suppliers.

- For businesses operating internationally, it may involve locating key parts of the business in different countries.

- Diversification would be chosen wherever reliance on a single source of resource has been identified as a potential risk.

The 4T approach to risk management

A company can adopt four possible approaches to a risk, known as the **4T** approach:

- Tolerate it.

- Transfer it.

- Terminate it.

- Treat it (i.e. by mitigating it, hedging or diversifying).

Potential risks are often categorised according to the likelihood of occurrence and the significance of their potential impact. An appropriate response can then be adopted.

This method was covered in Strategic Business Leader (SBL) and is summarised here:

		Impact/consequence	
		Low	High
Likelihood	**High**	Treat	Terminate
	Low	Tolerate	Transfer

Appropriate responses would be matched to the risk as shown above.

Tolerate

Accept that the risk might occur but do not put in place any systems to manage it. For example, a power failure may cause a serious production stoppage but few firms would consider acquiring a back-up generator. However a call centre, heavily reliant on its computer system, may decide that it would be worthwhile.

Transfer

The risk is passed on elsewhere. This can be achieved by activities such as:

- insuring against the risk (for example against the risk of fire)

- taking out fixed price contracts (such as with construction companies or suppliers)

- outsourcing production (buying in from a range of providers rather than relying on own production).

Terminate

This can mean deciding against the activity altogether, but in the context of a project, would mean identifying at what point it would be better to 'bail out' rather than proceed with the project – i.e. when the NPV of the revised future cash flows is negative.

Treat

A risk is treated when controls are in place to reduce either:

- the likelihood or
- the consequences

of the event occurring.

Illustration of the 4T approach

(a) A leisure company has just approved a large-scale investment project for the development of a new sports centre and grounds in a major city. The forecast NPV is approximately $6m, assuming a time horizon of five years, steady growth in business and constant returns in perpetuity thereafter.

Required:

Explain what the company would need to do, to ensure that the risks associated with the project are properly managed?

(b) A number of specific risks have been identified:

1   A potential lawsuit may be brought for death or injury of a member of the public using the equipment. No such event has ever occurred in the company's other centres.

2   The loss of several weeks' revenue from pool closure for repairs following the appearance of cracks in the infrastructure. This has occurred in several of the other centres in the past few years.

3   Income fraud as a result of high levels of cash receipts.

4   Loss of playing field revenue from schools and colleges because of poor weather.

Required:

Suggest how these risks could be best managed.

Solution

(a) (i)   Risk awareness – The potential risks associated with the project at strategic, tactical and operational levels should be identified. The fact that the company has carried out such projects before should make this task relatively straightforward.

(ii)   Risk monitoring – Information systems should be put into place to ensure that all material risk factors are continuously monitored. The impact of any changes likely to the affect the success of the project can then be identified and action taken as necessary. The forecast growth and return figures are undoubtedly critical to the success of the project and the underlying assumptions such as economic predictions, local demographics, competitor activity and recreational trends should be carefully monitored and assessed.

(iii)   Risk management – Risks identified can be categorised according to the likelihood of occurrence and the significance of the impact, in order to decide how best to manage them.

(b)   The identified risks could be mapped as shown below:

		Impact/consequence	
		Low	High
Likelihood	High	**3** Fraud – Treat	**2** Pool closure – Can't terminate so have to prevent
	Low	**4** Weather – Tolerate	**1** Lawsuit – Transfer

1   The risk of a lawsuit should be dealt with my taking out indemnity insurance. The risk is then transferred to the insurance company.

2   The risk of pool closure is serious and since a provision of a pool is clearly essential for the sports centre, the risk must be treated instead. This would mean putting in place a series of controls over the building process to prevent later cracks from occurring.

3   The risk of fraud is exactly the type of risk that a good internal control system would be designed to prevent.

4   Bad weather will always be a risk when dealing with outdoor activities and is probably best accepted and the lost revenues factored into the initial forecasts.

4 Specific types of risk

Political risk

Political risk is the risk that a company will suffer a loss as a result of the actions taken by the government or people of a country. It arises from the potential conflict between corporate goals and the national aspirations of the host country.

This is obviously a particular problem for companies operating internationally, as they face political risk in several countries at the same time.

Sources, measurement and management – Political risk

Sources of political risk

Whilst governments want to encourage development and growth there are also anxious to prevent the exploitation of their countries by multinationals.

Whilst at one extreme, assets might be destroyed as the result of war or expropriation, the most likely problems concern changes to the rules on the remittance of cash out of the host country to the holding company.

Exchange control regulations, which are generally more restrictive in less developed countries for example:

- rationing the supply of foreign currencies which restricts residents from buying goods abroad

- banning the payment of dividends to foreign shareholders such as holding companies in multinationals, who will then have the problem of blocked funds.

Import quotas to limit the quantity of goods that subsidiaries can buy from its holding company to sell in its domestic market.

Import tariffs could make imports (from the holding company) more expensive than domestically produced goods.

Insist on a minimum shareholding, i.e. that some equity in the company is offered to resident investors.

Company structure may be dictated by the host government – requiring, for example, all investments to be in the form of joint ventures with host country companies.

Discriminatory actions

Super-taxes imposed on foreign firms, set higher than those imposed on local businesses with the aim of giving local firms an advantage. They may even be deliberately set at such a high level as to prevent the business from being profitable.

Restricted access to local borrowings by restricting or even barring foreign-owned enterprises from the cheapest forms of finance from local banks and development funds. Some countries ration all access for foreign investments to local sources of funds, to force the company to import foreign currency into the country.

Expropriating assets whereby the host country government seizes foreign property in the national interest. It is recognised in international law as the right of sovereign states provided that **prompt consideration at fair market value in a convertible currency** is given. Problems arise over the exact meaning of the terms prompt and fair, the choice of currency, and the action available to a company not happy with the compensation offered.

Measurement of political risk

When considering measurement, distinctions are sometimes made between macro and micro political risk.

Micro political risks are ones that are specific to an industry, company or project within a host country. For example, the tobacco industry has faced increasing global opposition since the 1970s, nowhere more so than in the USA. There are increasing threats that tobacco will be classified as a drug and that companies supplying tobacco may face continuing litigation. This has been a consequence of a change in the social and political climate in the USA and elsewhere.

By contrast Iran at the moment presents political risks for almost any organisation who may wish to operate there in terms of the threat of loss of assets or personnel. This therefore represents macro political risk.

Different methods may be appropriate to measuring different types of risk. Traditional methods for assessing political risk range from comparative techniques such as rating and mapping systems to the analytical techniques of special reports, expert systems and probability determination, through to use of econometric techniques of model building. More recently, option-pricing techniques (using real options) have been applied to the evaluation of political risk associated with foreign direct investment.

Some examples of methods used to measure political risk are indicated below:

- 'Old hands' – Experts on the country provide advice upon the risk of investment in a specific country. Experts may include those with existing businesses, academics, diplomats or journalists. The value of the advice depends on how directly it can be applied to the investment under consideration.

- 'Grand tours' – The home firm may send a selection of employees to the potential investment country to act as an inspection team. The employees meet government officials, business people and local leaders to gain an understanding of the country first hand. However, this technique is generally considered inferior to the use of advice from well-established experts as outlined above.

- Surveys – Commercially produced country political risk indices are available. These are produced by groups of experts using Delphi techniques via the ranking of key risk variables. The experts individually answer a comprehensive questionnaire. Their answers are then collected, aggregated and returned to the experts, who have the chance to change their minds having seen the answers of their peers.

- Quantitative measures – Measures such as GNP and ethnic fractionalisation are combined to give countries an overall score. Commercially produced indices are available. One is the business environment risk index (BERI). This index gives each country a score out of 100, where a low score indicates unacceptable business conditions. Also, the Economist Intelligence Unit (EIU)'s Country Risk Model allows users to quantify the risk of cross-border transactions such as bank loans, trade finance, and investments in securities. Often some form of sensitivity or simulation analysis is incorporated to examine the effect of different possible scenarios. A general risk index offers a cost effective overview of potential investment climates but cannot take account of the variations in risk on individual projects. It should also be borne in mind that the scoring systems are essentially subjective.

Management of political risk

There are a number of ways of managing the political risk associated with an investment.

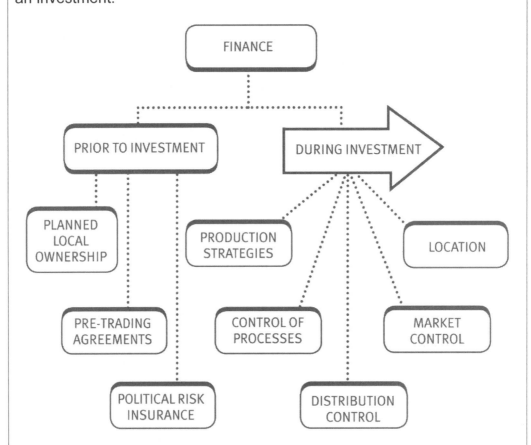

- **Planned local ownership**

  Target dates can be set on which proportions of company ownership will pass to the local nationals. These should be spread into the long term so that local authorities can see the eventual benefits that will be gained through allowing successful foreign investments.

- **Pre-trading/concession agreements**

  Prior to making the investments, agreements should be secured with the local government or other authority regarding rights, responsibilities, remittance of funds and local equity investments. This attempts to solve anticipated problems and prevent misunderstandings at some later date.

  The biggest problem with this policy is that host governments in developing countries are very volatile; consequently, agreements made with previous administrations can be repudiated by the new government.

Wells (1977) argues that the terms of concession agreements will normally change even with the same host government as:

The terms and conditions required to entice a company to invest in a particular country are different from the terms and conditions required to a company remain, once it has committed and developed its investment. (Remember sunk costs)

If the multinational is more successful than both parties anticipated in the beginning of the investment, thus the government may want their share of the windfall.

The agreement will cover transfer of capital, transfer of remittances, transfer of products, access to local capital markets, transfer pricing, taxation and social and economic obligations.

- **Political risk insurance**

  It may be possible to transfer the risk by taking out insurance. In the UK, the Export Credits Guarantee Department (ECGD) provides protection against various threats including expropriation and nationalisation, currency inconvertibility, war and revolution.

During investment

Political risk can be managed on a continuous basis through consideration of the following areas:

- **Production strategies**

  The decision here is to find the balance between:

  - contracting out to local sources (local sourcing) and losing control

  - producing directly in the host country (increasing investment in host country)

  - importing from outside the host country (foreign sourcing).

  By using local materials and labour it becomes in the interest of the country for the company to succeed. However, following success the locals may then have the knowledge to continue operations alone. Chrysler in Peru imported 50% of components from abroad and thus avoided expropriation of its plant because the plant was worthless without the foreign sourced Chrysler parts.

- **Control of patents and processes**

  Coca Cola is a prime example of how control of patents reduces political risk. The secret ingredient in Coca Cola has never been divulged. Therefore, Coca Cola can quite happily set up bottling plants worldwide, as the plants are worthless to any host government as they would not be able to create 'the taste of Coca Cola'. Patents can be enforced internationally.

- **Distribution control**

  Control and development of such items as pipelines and shipping facilities will deter expropriation of assets.

- **Market control**

  Securing markets through copywriting, patents and trademarks deters political intervention as the local markets come to depend on 'protected' goods.

- **Location**

  Oil companies frequently mine oil in a politically unstable area but refine it in western Europe. Expropriation of assets would not therefore benefit the less stable countries.

Financing decisions

Political risk may be mitigated by choosing the right location for raising funds:

- **Local finance**

  As the foreign investment grows, further finance can be raised locally to maintain the authorities' interest in the success of the business – any damaging intervention would also damage the local institutions. Also the wealthier locals who provide this finance often have considerable power. As a result there is less likelihood of others expropriating the assets. However, the cost of such funds may be relatively more expensive and many governments restrict the ability of multinational to borrow from local money and capital markets.

- **Borrow worldwide**

  A multinational also has the option of financing worldwide, using institutions from several countries. This discourages expropriation because if the host government intervenes in the company's operations, default on the loans may cause a diplomatic backlash from a number of countries, not just the multinational's own parent country. However, it is important to take account of the new risks associated with, for example, foreign exchange and tax, that may be introduced where funds are borrowed overseas.

Economic risk

Economic risk is the variations in the value of the business (i.e. the present value of future cash flows) due to unexpected changes in exchange rates. It is the long-term version of transaction risk which is covered in detail in the hedging chapters.

In a broader sense, economic risk can also be defined as the risk facing organisations from changes in economic conditions, such as economic growth or recession, government spending policy and taxation policy, unemployment levels and international trading conditions.

It affects:

- the affordability of exports and therefore competitiveness
- the affordability of imports and therefore profitability
- the value of repatriated profits.

Examples and management of economic risk

Economic risk is the possibility that the value of the company (the present value of all future post-tax cash flows) will change due to unexpected changes in future exchange rates. The size of the risk is difficult to measure as exchange rates can change significantly and unexpectedly. Such changes can affect firms in many ways:

- Consider the example of a US firm, which operates a subsidiary in a country that unexpectedly devalues its currency. This could be 'bad news' in that every local currency unit of profit earned would now be worth less when repatriated to the US. On the other hand it could be 'good news' as the subsidiary might now find it far easier to export to the rest of the world and hence significantly increase its contribution to parent company cash flow. The news could, alternatively, be neutral if the subsidiary intended to retain its profits to reinvest in the same country abroad.

- An exporter may suffer different forms of economic risk:

  Direct: If the firm's home currency strengthens, foreign competitors are able to gain sales at their expense because their products become more expensive (unless the firm reduces margins) in the eyes of customers both abroad and at home.

  Indirect: Even if the home currency does not move vis-à-vis the customers' currency the firm may lose competitive position. For example, suppose a South African firm is selling into Hong Kong and its main competitor is a New Zealand firm. If the New Zealand dollar weakens against the Hong Kong dollar, the South African firm has lost some competitive position.

  Although economic exposure is difficult to measure it is of vital importance to firms as it concerns their long-run viability. Economic exposure is really the long-run equivalent of transaction exposure, and ignoring it could lead to reductions in the firm's future cash flows or an increase in the systematic risk of the firm, resulting in a fall in shareholder wealth.

Managing economic risk

Note that the recommended methods of mitigating economic exposure, are also suggested as ways of mitigating political exposure:

- Diversification of production and supply.

- Diversification of financing.

If a firm manufactures all its products in one country and that country's exchange rate strengthens, then the firm will find it increasingly difficult to export to the rest of the world. Its future cash flows and therefore its present value would diminish.

However, if it had established production plants worldwide and bought its components worldwide (a policy which is practised by many multinationals, e.g. Ford) it is unlikely that the currencies of all its operations would revalue at the same time. It would therefore find that, although it was losing exports from some of its manufacturing locations, this would not be the case in all of them. Also if it had arranged to buy its raw materials worldwide it would find that a strengthening home currency would result in a fall in its input costs and this would compensate for lost sales.

Diversification of financing

When borrowing internationally, firms must be aware of foreign exchange risk. When, for example, a firm borrows in Swiss francs it must pay back in the same currency. If the Swiss franc then strengthens against the home currency this can make interest and principal repayments far more expensive. However, if borrowing is spread across many currencies it is unlikely they will all strengthen at the same time and therefore risks can be reduced. Borrowing in foreign currency is only truly justified if returns will then be earned in that currency to finance repayment and interest.

International borrowing can also be used to hedge off the adverse economic effects of local currency devaluations. If a firm expects to lose from devaluations of the currencies in which its subsidiaries operate it can hedge off this exposure by arranging to borrow in the weakening currency. Any losses on operations will then be offset by cheaper financing costs.

Regulatory risk

Regulatory risk is the potential for laws related to a given industry, country, or type of security to change and affect:

- how the business as a whole can operate

- the viability of planned or ongoing investments.

Regulations might apply to:

- businesses generally (for example, competition laws and antimonopoly regulations)

- specific industries (for example, catering and health and safety regulations, publishing and copyright laws).

Managing regulatory risk

Managing regulatory risk

| Identify applicable regulations | Understand impact of regulations | Develop regulatory risk plan | Ensure all projects comply with plan | Monitor and keep abreast of developments |

Whilst larger companies may have the resources to set up a permanent regulatory team, smaller firms may:

- incorporate the role within the internal audit department

- consult a firm specialising in regulatory risk.

In practice, research suggests that many firms do not commit sufficient resources to this area and are exposed to a high degree of regulatory risk.

Associated with regulatory risk is compliance risk.

Compliance risk is the risk of losses, such as fines or even temporary closure, resulting from non-compliance with laws or regulations.

Measures to ensure compliance with rules and regulations should be an integral part of an organisation's internal control system.

Fiscal risk

Fiscal risk from a corporate perspective is the risk that the government will have an increased need to raise revenues and will increase taxes, or alter taxation policy accordingly. Changes in taxation will affect the present value of investment projects and thereby the value of the company.

Managing fiscal risk

The primary requirement of a fiscal risk management strategy is an awareness of the huge impact tax can make to the viability of a project. Tax should be factored in to the calculations for all significant investment appraisal projects.

It is important not only to ensure that the tax rules being applied are up-to-date, but that any potential changes in the tax rules are also considered. Investment projects may be intended to run for many years and future changes (particularly those intended to close 'loop holes' in the taxation system) could wipe out the expected benefits from the project.

Many larger firms will maintain a full time taxation team within the finance function to deal with the tax implications of investment plans. Smaller companies are more likely to employ external tax experts. In either case, a relevant tax expert should always be involved in the analysis of the project and its sensitivity to the taxation assumptions should be carefully modelled.

Test your understanding 1

M Co is a mineral extraction company based in the UK but with plants based in many countries worldwide. Following recent discovery of mineral reserves in Mahastan in Central Asia, M Co has acquired a licence to extract the minerals from the recently elected Mahastani government and plans to commence work on the plant there within the next six months.

In the past ten years, Mahastan has seen significant unrest, following the deposing of the previous dictator in a military coup. However, the recent election of the newly fledged democracy is hoped to be the beginning of a new era of stability in the region. The currency of Mahastan is the puto. It is not traded internationally and the preferred currency for international business is the US dollar. There are currently no double tax treaties between Mahastan and the rest of the world, but the prime minister has signalled her intention to develop them within her first term of office to encourage inward investment.

Required:

Assess the exposure of M Co to political, economic, regulatory and fiscal risk and suggest how these risks may be mitigated.

Other types of risk

It is important to read the financial press to keep abreast of recent developments in risk management.

Risk management is a constantly evolving process. Financial managers need to understand the threats from emerging risks such as:

- global terrorist risk

- computer virus risks

- spreadsheet risk – for example, Fannie Mae's $1.136 billion underestimate of total stockholder equity in 2003 was the result of errors in a spreadsheet used in the implementation of a new accounting standard.

Policies will need to be kept up to date, so that these newer risks are managed properly.

5 Incorporating risk into investment appraisal

Overview of methods

The input variables in an investment appraisal are all estimates of likely future outcomes. There are several methods of incorporating risk into an investment appraisal, for example:

- expected values (probability analysis)

- use of the CAPM model to derive a discount rate

- sensitivity analysis, and simulation.

These methods have all been covered in Financial Management (FM), but some more details on probability analysis, sensitivity and simulation follow below.

Probability analysis

If the outcome from an investment is uncertain, but the probability associated with each of the possible outcomes is known, an expected value calculation can be used.

The expected value is calculated as the sum of (each outcome multiplied by its associated probability).

For example, if sales are expected to be either $1,000,000 or $1,500,000 with probabilities of 35% and 65% respectively, the expected sales can be calculated as:

$$(\$1,000,000 \times 0.35) + (\$1,500,000 \times 0.65) = \$1,325,000$$

The main problem with the expected value calculation is that the value might not correspond to any of the possible outcomes, so although the calculation gives a useful long-run average figure, it is not useful for one-off calculations.

More on the use of probability analysis

Probability analysis can be applied to potential cash flows of a project (as demonstrated in the simple example above regarding the sales figure). However, it can also be applied to other uncertain estimates, such as units of activity or even cost of capital.

After probabilities have been used to calculate an expected value figure for one or more of these variables, the project can then be appraised as normal, using methods such as NPV.

If several uncertain variables have been estimated using probability analysis, it is important to note that the potential for inaccuracy in the final NPV calculation is increased. Then, techniques such as sensitivity analysis and simulation (see below) come into play.

Conditional probabilities

In complex cases of uncertainty, conditional probabilities may be useful. Here, the probability of one outcome is dependent (conditional) on another outcome. The expected value is now found by multiplying the relevant probabilities together.

Example:

There is a 60% chance that sales levels will be high ($3 million) in year 1, and hence a 40% chance that year 1 sales will be low ($1 million).

If sales in year 1 are high, the sales in year 2 will be either $5 million (30% probability) or $4 million (70% probability).

If sales in year 1 are low, the sales in year 2 will be either $0.5 million (80% probability) or $1.5 million (20% probability).

Solution

The expected sales in year 1, which should be entered in year 1 of the investment appraisal, is:

$(0.60 \times 3m) + (0.40 \times 1 m) = \$2.2$ million

Then, the expected sales in year 2, which should be entered in year 2 of the investment appraisal, is:

$(0.60 \times [(0.30 \times 5m) + (0.70 \times 4m)]) + (0.40 \times [(0.80 \times 0.5m) + (0.20 \times 1.5m)]) = \$2.86$ million

Student Accountant article

The article 'Conditional probability' in the Technical Articles section of the ACCA website provides further details on this topic.

Sensitivity analysis

Sensitivity analysis measures the change in a particular variable which can be tolerated before the NPV of a project reduces to zero.

It can be calculated as

(NPV of project)/(PV of cash flows affected by the estimate) × 100%

Illustration of sensitivity analysis

AVI Co is evaluating a new investment project as follows:

$000	t	t	t	t	t_4
Sales		1,000	1,000	1,000	1,000
Costs		600	600	600	600
		———	———	———	———
		400	400	400	400
Tax (30%)		(120)	(120)	(120)	(120)
		———	———	———	———
Net		280	280	280	280
CapEx	(600)				
Tax relief on depreciation (30%)		45	45	45	45
		———	———	———	———
Free cash flow	(600)	325	325	325	325
		———	———	———	———
DF @ 10%	1	0.909	0.826	0.751	0.683

NPV = $430,000

Sensitivity to sales

= (NPV/PV of cash flows affected by the estimate of sales) × 100%

= [430/(1,000 × (1 − 0.30) × 3.170)] × 100%

= 19.4%

i.e. if sales were to fall by 19.4% (to $806,000 per year) then the NPV would be zero.

Sensitivity to tax rate

= (NPV/PV of cash flows affected by the estimate of tax rate) × 100%

= [430/((45 − 120) × 3.170)] × 100%

= 181%

i.e. if the tax rate were to rise by 181% (from 30% to 30 × 2.82 = 84.6%) then the NPV would fall to zero.

Sensitivity to discount rate

This cannot be calculated using the standard formula. Instead, the IRR of the project is calculated and the difference between the existing cost of capital and the IRR indicates the sensitivity to the discount rate.

Interpretation of sensitivity calculations

AVI Co would initially be inclined to accept the project due to its positive NPV. However, before making a final decision, the sensitivities would be considered. Any factors with small percentage sensitivities will have to be carefully assessed, because if the estimates of these factors turn out to be incorrect, the result may be a negative NPV.

Simulation

The main problem with sensitivity analysis is that it only allows us to assess the impact of one variable changing at a time. Simulation addresses this problem by considering how the NPV will be impacted by a number of variables changing at once.

Simulation employs random numbers to select specimen values for each variable in order to estimate a 'trial value' for the project NPV. This is repeated a large number of times until a distribution of net present values emerge.

By analysing this distribution, the firm can decide whether to proceed with the project. For example, if 95% of the generated NPVs are positive, this might reassure the firm that the chances of suffering a negative NPV are small.

Monte Carlo simulation assumes that the input variables are uncorrelated. However, more sophisticated modelling can incorporate estimates of the correlation between variables.

More details on Monte Carlo simulation

The assessment of the volatility (or standard deviation) of the net present value of a project entails the simulation of the financial model using estimates of the distributions of the key input parameters and an assessment of the correlations between variables.

Some of these variables are normally distributed but some are assumed to have limit values and a most likely value. Given the shape of the input distributions, simulation employs random numbers to select specimen values for each variable in order to estimate a 'trial value' for the project NPV.

This is repeated a large number of times until a distribution of net present values emerge.

By the central limit theorem the resulting distribution will approximate normality and from this project volatility can be estimated.

In its simplest form, Monte Carlo simulation assumes that the input variables are uncorrelated. However, more sophisticated modelling can incorporate estimates of the correlation between variables.

Other refinements such as the Latin Hypercube technique can reduce the likelihood of spurious results occurring through chance in the random number generation process.

The output from a simulation will give the expected net present value for the project and a range of other statistics including the standard deviation of the output distribution.

In addition, the model can rank order the significance of each variable in determining the project net present value.

Example of Monte Carlo simulation

The MP Organisation is an independent film production company. It has a number of potential films that it is considering producing, one of which is the subject of a management meeting next week. The film which has been code named CA45 is a thriller based on a novel by a well-respected author.

The expected revenues from the film have been estimated as follows: there is a 30% chance it may generate total sales of $254,000; 50% chance sales may reach $318,000 and 20% chance they may reach $382,000.

Expected costs (advertising, promotion and marketing) have also been estimated as follows: there is a 20% chance they will reach approximately $248,000; 60% chance they may get to $260,000 and 20% chance of totalling $272,000.

In a Monte Carlo simulation, these revenues and costs could have random numbers assigned to them:

Sales Revenue	Probability	Assign Random Numbers (assume integers)
$254,000	0.30	00 – 29
$318,000	0.50	30 – 79
$382,000	0.20	80 – 99
Costs		
$248,000	0.20	00 – 19
$260,000	0.60	20 – 79
$272,000	0.20	80 – 99

A computer could generate 20-digit random numbers such as 98125602386617556398. These would then be matched to the random numbers assigned to each probability and values assigned to 'Sales Revenues' and 'Costs' based on this. The random numbers generated give 5 possible outcomes in our example:

Random number	Sales revenue in $000	Random Number	Costs in $000	Profit
98	382	12	248	134
56	318	02	248	70
38	318	66	260	58
17	254	55	260	(6)
63	318	98	272	46

After the computer simulation has been run many times, a frequency distribution of the profits (in the final column of the above table) can be drawn, to give a sense of what the likely outcome will be.

After so few runs (only 5 in the above example), it is difficult to see a pattern yet, but if similar results were to be obtained over many many simulations, only 20% of the combinations (1 in 5) would give a loss.

Simulation cannot give a definitive answer on whether to undertake the project or not, but an analysis of the results will enable the decision maker to assess the risk associated with the project, for example the risk of making a loss in the above example.

Illustration 1 – Monte Carlo simulation

A business is choosing between two projects, project A and project B. It uses simulation to generate a distribution of profits for each project.

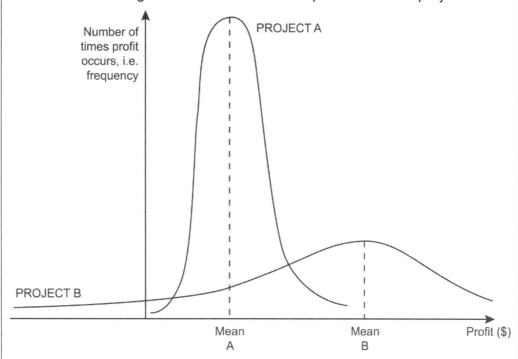

Required:

Which project should the business invest in?

Solution

Project A has a lower average profit but is also less risky (less variability of possible profits).

Project B has a higher average profit but is also more risky (more variability of possible profits).

There is no correct answer. All simulation will do is give the business the above results. It will not tell the business which is the better project.

If the business is willing to take on risk, they may prefer project B since it has the higher average return.

However, if the business would prefer to minimise its exposure to risk, it would take on project A. This has a lower risk but also a lower average return.

6 Value at Risk (VaR)

The meaning of VaR

Value at risk (VaR) is a measure of how the market value of an asset or of a portfolio of assets is likely to decrease over a certain time, the **holding period** (usually one to ten days), under 'normal' market conditions.

VaR is measured by using normal distribution theory.

It is typically used by security houses or investment banks to measure the market risk of their asset portfolios.

VaR = amount at risk to be lost from an investment under usual conditions over a given holding period, at a particular 'confidence level'.

Confidence levels are usually set at 95% or 99%,

e.g. for a 95% confidence level, the VaR will give the amount that has a 5% chance of being lost.

Illustration 2

A bank has estimated that the expected value of its portfolio in two weeks' time will be $50 million, with a standard deviation of $4.85 million.

Required:

Using a 95% confidence level, identify the value at risk.

Solution

A 95% confidence level will identify the reduced value of the portfolio that has a 5% chance of occurring.

From the normal distribution tables, 1.65 is the normal distribution value for a one-tailed 5% probability level. Since the value is below the mean, − 1.65 will be needed.

$z = (x - \mu)/\sigma$

$(x - 50)/4.85 = -1.65$

$x = (-1.65 \times 4.85) + 50 = 42$

There is thus a 5% probability that the portfolio value will fall to $42 million or below.

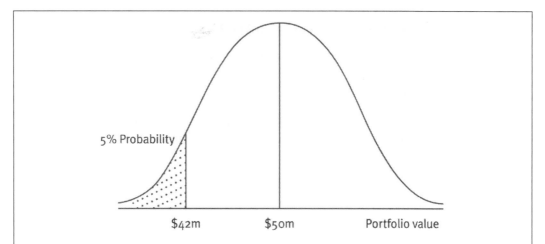

A bank can try to control the risk in its asset portfolio by setting target maximum limits for value at risk over different time periods (one day, one week, one month, three months, and so on).

Link between Monte Carlo Simulation and VaR

In the above Illustration, the expected portfolio value in two weeks' time was presented as a normal distribution with a mean of $50m.

This distribution may well have been created by running a Monte Carlo simulation on the likely outcome over the next two weeks.

Alternatively, the future expected value may have been forecasted by using historical data.

Test your understanding 2

A five year project has an NPV of $1 million. The project's cash flows are normally distributed and the annual standard deviation associated with the cash flows is $0.3 million. Company policy is to accept only those projects where there is at least a 90% certainty that the net present value will be positive.

Required:

Calculate the value at risk of the project, and advise whether it should be undertaken.

7 Introduction to hedging methods

The use of derivative products

Hedging methods relating to currency risk and interest rate risk are covered in separate later chapters. Many of the hedging methods use 'derivatives' (e.g. futures contracts) to reduce the firm's exposure to risk.

This section introduces some basic terms relating to derivatives.

The operation of the derivatives market

- A derivative is an asset whose performance (and hence value) is derived from the behaviour of the value of an underlying asset (the 'underlying').

- The most common underlying assets are commodities (e.g. tea, pork bellies), shares, bonds, share indices, currencies and interest rates.

- Derivatives are contracts that give the right and sometimes the obligation, to buy or sell a quantity of the underlying or benefit in some other way from a rise or fall in the value of the underlying.

- Derivatives include the following:

  - Forwards

  - Forward rate agreements ('FRAs')

  - Futures

  - Options

  - Swaps.

- Forwards, FRAs and futures effectively fix a future price. Options give you the right without the obligation to fix a future price.

- The legal right is an asset with its own value that can be bought or sold.

- Derivatives are not fixed in volume of supply like normal equity or bond markets. Their existence and creation depends on the existence of counter-parties, market participants willing to take alternative views on the outcome of the same event.

- Some derivatives (especially futures and options) are traded on exchanges where contracts are standardised and completion guaranteed by the exchange. Such contracts will have values and prices quoted. Exchange-traded instruments are of a standard size thus ensuring that they are marketable.

- Other transactions are over the counter ('OTC'), where a financial intermediary puts together a product tailored precisely to the needs of the client. It is here where valuation issues and credit risk may arise.

Futures contracts

Introduction

- A futures contract is an exchange traded forward agreement to buy or sell an underlying asset at some future date for an agreed price.

- There are two ways of closing a position:

    - Deliver the underlying on the maturity date – RARE.

    - If futures contracts have been bought, then equivalent contracts can be sold before maturity, resulting in the company having a net profit or loss (and no obligation to deliver).

- Hedging is achieved by combining a futures transaction with a market transaction at the prevailing spot rate.

Illustration 3 – TAL

TAL Inc is a sugar grower looking to **sell** 3,000 tonnes of white sugar in August and wants to fix the price via futures.

Suppose that the quoted futures price today on the ICE Futures Europe exchange for white sugar for August delivery is $221.20 per tonne and that each contract is for 50 tonnes.

TAL would agree to **sell** 60 futures contracts at a price of $221.20.

Suppose the market price in August (on the final day of the contract) has risen to $230. The futures price would also equal $230.

TAL thus has two transactions:

- TAL would sell its sugar in the open market (i.e. not via the futures contract) for $230/tonne.

- Separately TAL would buy 60 futures contracts for August delivery for $230 per tonne, making a loss on the futures of $8.8 per tonne.

This gives an overall (fixed) net receipt of $221.2 per tonne.

Note: Futures do not always give a perfect hedge because of

1   Basis risk.

2   The size of contracts not matching the commercial transaction.

Tick sizes

- A 'tick' is the standardised minimum price movement of a futures or options contract.

- Ticks are useful for calculating the profit or loss on a contract.

Illustration 4 – TAL continued

For the sugar futures contract in the above example, a tick is $0.01 per tonne. Given that a contract is for 50 tonnes, each tick is worth $0.50 per contract.

The overall movement of $8.80 per tonne would be expressed as 880 ticks.

The total loss on the contracts would thus be:

60 contracts × 880 ticks × $0.50 per tick = $26,400

As detailed below, this amount would not be collected in one amount when the position is closed but instead daily 'marking to market' occurs.

The margin system

Margins

A potential problem of dealing in futures is that having made a profit, the other party 'to the contract' has therefore made a loss and defaults on paying you your profit. This is termed 'counter party credit risk'.

- However the buyer and seller of a contract do not transact with each other directly but via members of the market.

- Therefore the market's Clearing House is the formal counter party to every transaction.

- This effectively reduces counter party default risk for those dealing in futures.

- As the Clearing House is acting as guarantor for all deals it needs to protect itself against this enormous potential credit risk. It does so by operating a margining system, i.e. an initial margin and the daily variation margin.

The initial margin

- When a futures position is opened the Clearing House requires that an initial margin be placed on deposit in a margin account to act as a security against possible default.

- The objective of the initial margin is to cover any possible losses made from the first day's trading.

- The size of the initial margin depends on the future market, the level of volatility of the interest rates and the risk of default.

- Some investors use futures for speculation rather than hedging. The margin system allows for highly leveraged 'bets'.

Maintenance margin, margin call and the variation margin

- When the hedge is set up, the Clearing House specifies an amount ('the maintenance margin') which represents the minimum amount that the client must keep in the margin account.

- At the end of each day the Clearing House calculates the daily profit or loss on the futures position. This is known as 'marking to market'. The daily profit or loss is added or subtracted to the margin account balance.

- If this causes the amount in the margin account to fall below the specified maintenance margin, a 'margin call' is made to the investor, requiring the investor to deposit extra funds (the 'variation margin') to top-up the margin account.

- An inability to pay the variation margin causes default and the contract is closed, thus protecting the Clearing House from the possibility that the investor might accumulate further losses without providing cash to cover them.

Numerical example

Peter Ng is a wealthy speculator who believes that oil prices will fall over the next three months. Oil futures are quoted with the following details:

- Futures price for 3 month delivery = $68.20 per barrel.

- Contract size = 1,000 barrels.

- Tick size = 1 cent per barrel.

- Initial margin = 10% of contract.

Peter decides to set his level of speculation at 10 contracts.

Required:

(a) **Calculate Peter's initial margin.**

(b) **Assuming that the initial margin calculated in part (a) is the same as the maintenance margin on Peter's account, calculate the required variation margin cash flow the next day if the futures price moves to $68.35.**

Solution

(a) Initial margin = 10% × 10 contracts × 1,000 barrels × $68.20 = $68,200.

(b) Price has increased so Peter will make a loss of $0.15 per barrel or 15 ticks. This equates to a total loss (which will need to be paid in to top-up the margin account).

Loss = 10 contracts × 15 ticks × $10 per tick = $1,500.

8 Chapter summary

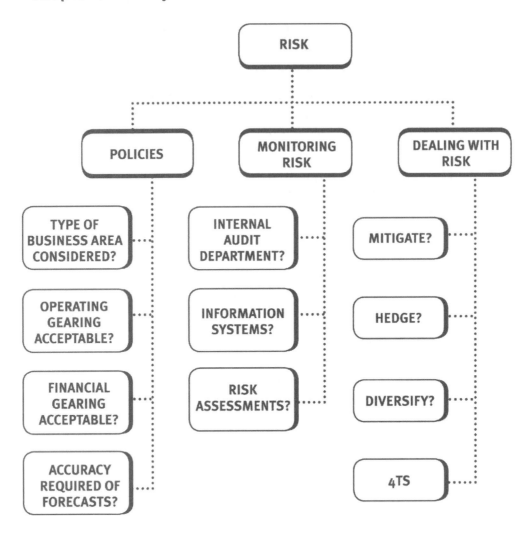

Test your understanding answers

Test your understanding 1

Political risks

Possible ramifications would include:

- revocation of the licence

- significant increase in the licence fee

- company subject to regulations designed to prevent the company taking profits earned from the country:
    - imposition of punitive taxes
    - restrictive exchange controls

- seizure of control of the plant

- expropriation of the extracted minerals

- total disruption to operations from further coup attempts.

Economic risks

In terms of exchange risk, the primary risk will be caused by changes in value between the UK currency and the US dollar. Although some payments (such as employee wages) will presumably be made in putos and M Co will therefore be subject to some risk associated with fluctuations between the puto and the dollar, it is unlikely to have any significant impact on the long term viability of the project.

Regulatory risk

As M Co is based in the UK, which can be expected to have a fairly stringent set of regulations covering mineral extraction, it is not anticipated that the Mahastan project will present any significant specific regulatory risk.

However, new regulations imposed on all foreign companies operating in Mahastan may come into force once the new government finds its feet. This could affect the ability of the company to operate effectively.

Fiscal risk

The uncertainty over the double tax position is an obvious risk for M Co. In addition, the country's tax legislation may not be well established and may be changed as the prime minister looks to encourage investment.

Risk mitigation

The recent political instability in Mahastan and the newness of the government, make this investment a very high-risk project.

Political risk

M Co already has a licence for the extraction of the minerals. It could attempt to negotiate further terms surrounding matters as diverse as levels of price increases, transfer of capital, transfer of remittances, transfer of products, access to local capital markets, transfer pricing, taxation and social and economic obligations.

However no matter what is negotiated the risk that the agreement will be not be honoured by this government (or subsequent ones should it fail) remains high.

The political risks can be best mitigated by gaining the goodwill of the community and ensuring that the wealth generated by the mineral extraction is not perceived to be entirely the preserve of M Co. Solutions may include:

- employing local workers where possible
- paying fair wages
- considering joint ventures with local companies over some parts of the construction or extraction processes
- investing some part of the profits in local opportunities.

It may be worth considering political risk insurance. However where the risk is so high the premiums may be prohibitive.

Economic risk

Since M Co has an international presence, the economic risk of the project will already be mitigated by diversification. However, if many of the areas in which it operates also trade in dollars then the benefits are reduced. Consideration should also be given to financing using dollar-based loans.

Regulatory risk

The risk that onerous regulations may be imposed on M Co cannot be easily avoided. The methods of mitigating political risk mentioned above, would also apply here, although they are unlikely to help with regulations aimed at all organisations.

M Co must ensure that it consistently monitors the changing regulatory environment and considers the impact on the firm. As the government is keen to encourage inward investment, it would be worth attempting to identify key ministers and open up lines of communication with them. Being viewed as an important stakeholder may mean that M Co is consulted on major regulatory changes before they are implemented.

Fiscal risk

Given the considerable uncertainty, fiscal risk may be best managed by assuming worst case tax treatment (based on current information) and only accepting the project if the NPV is still positive. Again constant monitoring of the situation and reforecasting as necessary will also be required.

Test your understanding 2

The project should be undertaken if there is a 90% probability of it having a positive NPV.

So start by calculating the value at risk for a 90% confidence level.

A 90% confidence level means that we need to find 0.40 (90% – 50%) in the normal distribution table – this corresponds to (approximately) 1.28 standard deviations.

Therefore the annual value at risk for a 90% confidence level is

1.28 × $0.3 million = $0.384 million.

Since this is a five year project though, the value at risk over five years will be needed:

i.e. $0.384 million × $\sqrt{5}$

= $0.859 million.

A five year value at risk of $0.859 million means that we can be 90% sure that the NPV won't fall by more than $0.859 million over the five year period.

The expected NPV is $1 million, so we can be 90% sure that the actual NPV will be at least (1m – 0.859m =) $0.141 million. This is still a positive NPV, so the project should be undertaken.

Hedging foreign exchange risk

Chapter learning objectives

Study guide section	Study guide outcome
E1: The role of the treasury function in multinationals	(b) Discuss the operations of the derivatives market (i) The relative advantages and disadvantages of exchange traded versus OTC agreements (iii) The source of basis risk and how it can be minimised.
E2: The use of financial derivatives to hedge against forex risk	(a) Assess the impact on an organisation to exposure in translation, transaction and economic risks and how these can be managed.
	(b) Evaluate, for a given hedging requirement, which of the following is the most appropriate strategy, given the nature of the underlying position and the risk exposure: (i) The use of the forward exchange market and the creation of a money market hedge (ii) Synthetic foreign exchange agreements (SAFEs) (iii) Exchange-traded currency futures contracts (iv) Currency swaps (v) FOREX swaps (vi) Currency options.

E2: The use of financial derivatives to hedge against forex risk (continued)

(c) Advise on the use of bilateral and multilateral netting and matching as tools for minimising FOREX transactions costs and the management of market barriers to the free movement of capital and other remittances.

Many aspects of forex risk management were introduced in Financial Management (FM). These are recapped briefly for completeness. In AFM the range of techniques considered is extended.

One of the PER performance objectives (PO11 – Identify and Manage Financial Risk) is to be able to identify, measure, and advise on the financial risks to the organisation.

PER

Working through this chapter should help you understand how to demonstrate that objective.

1 Introduction

Types of forex risk

Firms may be exposed to three types of foreign exchange risk:

Transaction risk

- The risk of an exchange rate changing between the transaction date and the subsequent settlement date on an individual transaction.

- i.e. it is the gain or loss arising on conversion.

- Associated with exports/imports.

- Hedge using a variety of financial products/methods – see below.

Economic risk

- Includes the longer-term effects of changes in exchange rates on the market value of a company (PV of future cash flows).

- Looks at how changes in exchange rates affect competitiveness, directly or indirectly.

- Reduce by geographic diversification.

Translation risk

- How changes in exchange rates affect the translated value of foreign assets and liabilities (e.g. foreign subsidiaries).

- Can hedge by borrowing in local currency to fund investment.

- Gains/losses usually unrealised so many firms do not hedge.

Types of foreign exchange risk

Transaction risk

Transaction risk the risk of an exchange rate changing between the transaction date and the subsequent settlement date, i.e. it is the gain or loss arising on conversion.

This type of risk is primarily associated with imports and exports. If a company exports goods on credit then it has a figure for debtors in its accounts. The amount it will finally receive depends on the foreign exchange movement from the transaction date to the settlement date.

As transaction risk has a potential impact on the cash flows of a company, most companies choose to hedge against such exposure. Measuring and monitoring transaction risk is normally an important component of treasury management.

The degree of exposure involved, which is dependent on:

(a) The size of the transaction, is it material?

(b) The hedge period, the time period before the expected cash flows occurs.

(c) The anticipated volatility of the exchange rates during the hedge period.

The corporate risk management policy should state what degree of exposure is acceptable. This will probably be dependent on whether the Treasury Department is been established as a cost or profit centre.

Economic risk

Transaction exposure focuses on relatively short-term cash flows effects; economic exposure encompasses these plus the longer-term effects of changes in exchange rates on the market value of a company. Basically this means a change in the present value of the future after tax cash flows due to changes in exchange rates.

There are two ways in which a company is exposed to economic risk.

Directly: If your firm's home currency strengthens then foreign competitors are able to gain sales at your expense because your products have become more expensive (or you have reduced your margins) in the eyes of customers both abroad and at home.

Indirectly: Even if your home currency does not move vis-à-vis your customer's currency you may lose competitive position. For example suppose a South African firm is selling into Hong Kong and its main competitor is a New Zealand firm. If the New Zealand dollar weakens against the Hong Kong dollar the South African firm has lost some competitive position.

Economic risk is difficult to quantify but a favoured strategy is to diversify internationally, in terms of sales, location of production facilities, raw materials and financing. Such diversification is likely to significantly reduce the impact of economic exposure relative to a purely domestic company, and provide much greater flexibility to react to real exchange rate changes.

> **Tutorial note: Borrowing in a foreign currency**
>
> In addition, when companies borrow in a foreign currency, committing themselves to regular interest payments and principal repayments they are exposing themselves to forex risk. This is a problem that beset a number of Far Eastern companies in the late 1990s. They had borrowed in US dollars or British pounds. This became a serious problem when their currency depreciated and the loan repayments became much more expensive. Of course if your firm takes out a loan in dollars and your home currency appreciates against the dollar the loan repayments become cheaper.

Translation risk

The financial statements of overseas subsidiaries are usually translated into the home currency in order that they can be consolidated into the group's financial statements. Note that this is purely a paper-based exercise – it is the translation not the conversion of real money from one currency to another.

The reported performance of an overseas subsidiary in home-based currency terms can be severely distorted if there has been a significant foreign exchange movement.

If initially the exchange rate is given by \$1 = £1 and an American subsidiary is worth \$500,000, then the UK parent company will anticipate a statement of financial position sheet value of £500,000 for the subsidiary. A depreciation of the US dollar to \$2 = £1 would result in only £250,000 being translated.

Unless managers believe that the company's share price will fall as a result of showing a translation exposure loss in the company's accounts, translation exposure will not normally be hedged. The company's share price, in an efficient market, should only react to exposure that is likely to have an impact on cash flows.

However, if the financial manager does want to hedge against the impact of translation risk, trying to make sure that foreign currency assets and liabilities are approximately equal in value is the simplest method. Then any gains or losses in asset values are offset by equivalent losses or gains in the values of the liabilities.

This can be achieved by funding foreign asset purchases by borrowing money in the same currency.

Hedging transaction risk – The internal techniques

Internal techniques to manage/reduce forex exposure should always be considered before external methods on cost grounds. Internal techniques include the following:

Invoice in home currency

- One easy way is to insist that all foreign customers pay in your home currency and that your company pays for all imports in your home currency.

- However the exchange-rate risk has not gone away, it has just been passed onto the customer. Your customer may not be too happy with your strategy and simply look for an alternative supplier.

- Achievable if you are in a monopoly position, however in a competitive environment this is an unrealistic approach.

Leading and lagging

- If an importer (payment) expects that the currency it is due to pay will depreciate, it may attempt to delay payment. This may be achieved by agreement or by exceeding credit terms.

- If an exporter (receipt) expects that the currency it is due to receive will depreciate over the next three months it may try to obtain payment immediately. This may be achieved by offering a discount for immediate payment.

- The problem lies in guessing which way the exchange rate will move.

Matching

- When a company has receipts and payments in the same foreign currency due at the same time, it can simply match them against each other.

- It is then only necessary to deal on the forex markets for the unmatched portion of the total transactions.

- An extension of the matching idea is setting up a foreign currency bank account.

- Bilateral and multilateral netting and matching tools are discussed in more detail later in the chapter.

Decide to do nothing?

- The company would 'win some, lose some'.

- Theory suggests that, in the long run, gains and losses net off to leave a similar result to that if hedged.

- In the short run, however, losses may be significant.

- One additional advantage of this policy is the savings in transaction costs.

2 Forward contracts

Characteristics

A forward contract allows a business to buy or sell a currency on a fixed future date at a predetermined rate, i.e. the forward rate of exchange.

Test your understanding 1
An Australian firm has just bought some machinery from a US supplier for US$250,000 with payment due in 3 months' time. Exchange rates are quoted as follows:

Spot rates: (US$... to A$1)	0.7785 – 0.7891
Three months forward rates:	0.7764 – 0.7873

Required:

Calculate the amount payable if a forward contract is used.

Availability and use

- Although other forms of hedging are available, forward cover represents the most frequently employed method of hedging.

- However, the existence and depth of forward markets depends on the level of demand for each particular currency.

- In the exam you need to consider; does the forward market exist and would it extend far enough into the future before you recommend it.

- For major trading currency like the $, £, Yen or Euro it can be up to 10 years forward. Normally forward markets extend six months into the future. Forward markets do not exist for the so-called exotic currencies.

Advantages and disadvantages

Advantages	Disadvantages
• OTC, so can be matched exactly to the future sums involved. • Simple and easy to understand.	• Availability – see above. • Binding contract for delivery, even if commercial circumstances change – e.g. a customer is late paying. • Eliminates exposure to upside as well as down-side movements.

Synthetic foreign exchange agreements (SAFEs)

- Some governments have banned forward FX trading – usually as a means to reduce exchange rate volatility.

- For example:

  - Brazilian Reals

  - Indian Rupee

  - Taiwan Dollars

  - South Korean Won

  - Chinese Renminbi (or Yuan).

- In such markets the use of non-deliverable forwards (NDFs) has developed.

- These are like forward contracts, except no currency is delivered. Instead the profit or loss (i.e. the difference between actual and NDF rates) on a notional amount of currency (the face value of the NDF) is settled between the two counter parties.

- Combined with an actual currency exchange at the prevailing spot rate, this effectively fixes the future rate in a similar manner to futures.

- One other feature is that the settlement is in US dollars.

SAFE illustration

Let the spot rate between the US$ and the Brazilian Real be 1.6983 Reals to $1 and suppose we agree a 3 month NDF to buy $1 million worth of Reals at 1.7000.

If the spot rate moves to 1.6800 in 3 months, then the counter-party will have to pay us 1 million × 0.02 = 20,000 Reals.

This will be settled in US$, so the actual receipt will be 20,000/1.6800 = $11,905.

3 Money market hedges

Characteristics

- The basic idea is to avoid future exchange rate uncertainty by making the exchange at today's spot rate instead.

- This is achieved by depositing/borrowing the foreign currency until the actual commercial transaction cash flows occur:

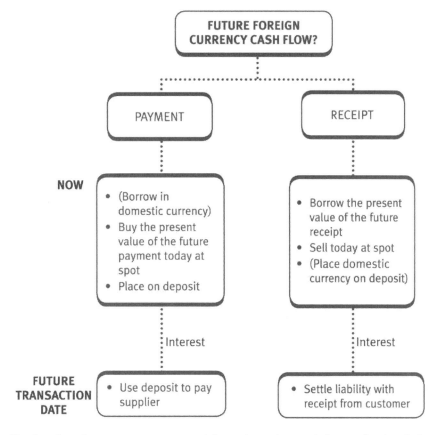

- In effect a foreign currency asset is set up to match against a future liability (and vice versa).

Test your understanding 2

Marcus Co is based in France has recently imported raw materials from the USA and has been invoiced for US$240,000, payable in three months' time.

In addition, it has also exported finished goods to Japan and Australia.

The Japanese customer has been invoiced for US$69,000, payable in three months' time, and the Australian customer has been invoiced for A$295,000, payable in four months' time.

Current spot and forward rates are as follows:

US$ ... /1 Euro

Spot:	0.9830 – 0.9850
3 months forward:	0.9520 – 0.9545

Euro... /1 A$

Spot:	1.8890 – 1.8920
4 months forward:	1.9510 – 1.9540

Current money market rates (per year) are as follows:

US$: 10.0% – 12.0%

A$: 14.0% – 16.0%

Euro: 11.5% – 13.0%

Required:

Show how the company can hedge its exposure to foreign exchange risk using:

(a) **forward contracts**

(b) **money market hedges**

and for each transaction, determine which is the best hedging technique.

Further comments

- Interest rate parity implies that a money market hedge should give the same result as a forward contract.

- Money market hedges may be feasible as a way of hedging for currencies where forward contracts are not available.

- This approach has obvious cash flow implications which may prevent a company from using this method, e.g. if a company has a considerable overdraft it may be impossible for it to borrow funds now.

Arbitrage profits

Although the theory of interest rate parity suggests that the financial position should be the same whether a forward contract or a money market hedge is used, in reality there may be differences caused by market imperfections. Then, differences can be exploited by investors aiming to make 'arbitrage profits'.

For example, an investor might be able to earn arbitrage profits by:

- borrowing currency X

- translating the amount to currency Y and putting the currency Y on deposit

- taking out a forward contract to convert Y back into X at some future date

- withdrawing the currency Y at the end of the period and translating it back to X under the forward contract

- repaying the borrowing in currency X (capital plus any interest accrued), and retaining the surplus.

Arbitrage profits will be made here if the forward rate of exchange doesn't exactly reflect the differential in interest rates between the two countries.

4 Futures contracts

Characteristics

- Futures contracts are standard sized, traded hedging instruments. The aim of a currency futures contract is to fix an exchange rate at some future date.

- A key issue with currency futures is to establish the 'currency of the contract' or CC. For example if the CC is € and your transaction involves buying €, you should buy futures now to set up the hedge. Note that the CC in an exam question is found by looking at the standard contract size. For example, if the contract size is quoted in $, the CC is $.

Contract sizes – Examples

Future	Contract size	Price quotation	Tick size	Value of one tick
£/US dollar	£62,500	US$ per £1	$0.0001	$6.25
€/US dollar	€200,000	US$ per €1	$0.0001	$20.00
Swiss franc/ US dollar	SFr 125,000	US$ per SFR1	$0.0001	$12.50
Yen/US dollar	12.5 million yen	US$ per 1 yen	$0.000001	$12.50
€/£	€100,000	£ per €1	£0.0001	£10

- The CC is the currency in which the contract size is quoted.

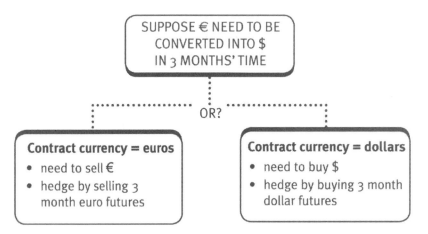

- We assume that the contracts mature or expire at the end of March, June, September and December. It is normal to choose the first contract to expiry after the conversion date.

- The range of available futures is limited and includes: $/£, $/Y, $/SFR, $/A$, $/C$ and $/€. Therefore if you are asked to give a hedge strategy for a 'minor' currency you should not recommend a futures contract.

Futures hedging calculations

Step 1: Set up the hedge by addressing 3 key questions:

- Do we initially buy or sell futures?

- How many contracts?

- Which expiry date should be chosen?

Step 2: Contact the exchange. Pay the initial margin. Then wait until the transaction/settlement date.

Step 3: Calculate profit or loss in the futures market by closing out the futures contracts, and calculate the value of the transaction using the spot rate on the transaction date.

Futures calculation

It is 15 October and a treasurer has identified the need to convert euros into dollars to pay a US supplier $12 million on 20 November. The treasurer has decided to use December Euro futures contracts to hedge with the following details:

- Contract size €200,000.

- Prices given in US$ per Euro (i.e. €1 = ...).

- Tick size $0.0001 or $20 per contract.

He opens a position on 15 October and closes it on 20 November. Spot and relevant futures prices are as follows:

Date	Spot	Futures price
15 October	1.3300	1.3350
20 November	1.3190	1.3240

Required:

Calculate the financial position using the hedge described.

Solution

Step 1	1	Buy or sell initially?	1	CC is €, and we need to sell € (to buy $), so sell futures now.
	2	How many contracts?		
	3	Which expiry date?	2	Cover $12m/1.3350 (Dec futures price – see below) = €8.99 million, using €200,000 contracts, hence €8.99m/€0.2m = 44.95 – round to 45 contracts.
			3	Transaction date is 20 November, so choose December futures (the first to expire after the transaction date).
Step 2	Contact the exchange – state the hedge		Sell 45 December futures (at a futures price of $1.3350/€1).	

| Step 3 | Calculate profit/loss in futures market by closing out the position. | Initially: Sell at 1.3350.

Close out: Buy at 1.3240.

Difference is $0.011 per €1 profit.

45 × €200,000 covered, so total profit is 0.011 × 45 × 200,000 = $99,000. |
| | Transaction at spot rate on 20 November:

Buy $11.901 m extra needed at spot rate of $1.3190/€1. | Cost in € is €9,022,745. |

Test your understanding 3

It is 4 May and the treasurer of a Swiss company has identified a net receipt of US$2 million on 10 June. These dollars will need to be converted into Swiss Francs (CHF). The treasurer has decided to use US dollar – Swiss Franc futures contracts to hedge with the following details:

- ICE Futures US (formerly NYBOT) options and futures exchange.
- Contract size $200,000.
- Prices given in Swiss francs per US dollar (i.e. $1 = ...).
- Tick size CHF 0.0001 or CHF20 per contract.

Expiry date	Futures price
June	1.2200
Sept	1.2510

The spot rate on 4 May is 1.2160 CHF/$1.

Required:

Calculate the financial position using the relevant futures hedge, assuming that the spot rate on 10 June is 1.2750 CHF/$1, and that the futures price is 1.2760 CHF/$1.

Forecasting futures prices

In the examples so far, the closing futures price has been given. This will not be available when the hedge is first set up, so we often try to estimate it to allow us to predict the likely result of the futures hedge.

An understanding of 'basis' enables us to estimate the closing futures price.

Basis

The basis within a futures hedge is defined as:

Spot rate – futures price

It is easy to calculate the basis when the hedge is first set up, since both the spot rate and the futures price will be known.

Also, the basis on the expiry date of the futures contract is always zero.

Therefore, the level of 'unexpired basis' can be estimated on the transaction date by assuming that the basis reduces from its opening value to zero in a linear manner.

Why does basis reduce to zero?

The futures price at any point in time represents the market's best estimate of the expected spot rate on the expiry date of the futures contract.

i.e. the futures price for a December futures contract is the market's estimate of the expected spot rate on 31 December.

As time goes by and new real world factors come to light, the estimate will change, so the futures price will change.

However, as the expiry date approaches, it is likely that the estimate will become more and more accurate until finally, when the expiry date arrives, the estimate will be completely accurate.

i.e. the futures price on 31 December, for a December futures contract, will be the same as the spot rate at that date.

Therefore, basis will always reduce to zero on the expiry date of a futures contract.

Illustration 1 – Basis calculation

Europe Co is expecting to receive $10m in 4 months' time, which it wants to translate into €.

The spot rate (quoted as €/$1) is 0.7343 – 0.7355.

Futures market information: ($500,000 contracts, prices quoted as €/$1)

2 month expiry 0.7335

5 month expiry 0.7300

Required:

Estimate the likely financial result of the hedge, assuming that the spot rate in 4 months is expected to be 0.7337 – 0.7366 €/$1, and that basis reduces to zero in a linear manner.

Solution: Hedge details

Set up the futures hedge by selling 20 contracts with a 5 month expiry date.

Likely result of the hedge:

	€
Transaction – sell $10m at spot in 4 months (0.7337€/$1)	7,337,000
Futures market: Sell at 0.7300, buy at 0.7328 (from basis workings below)	
Loss = 0.0028€/$1, multiplied by 20 × $500,000 covered	(28,000)
Net receipt	**7,309,000**

Basis workings

	Now	in 4 months		in 5 months
Spot	0.7343	0.7337		
Futures price	0.7300	0.7328	**(W3)**	
Basis (difference)	0.0043	0.0009	**(W2)**	0 **(W1)**

(W1) Basis will reduce to zero by the expiry date of the contract, because on that date, the futures price will equal the (known) spot rate.

(W2) Assuming basis reduces in a linear manner, the basis in 4 months should be 1/5 of the original 0.0043 i.e. the unexpired basis is 0.0009.

(W3) Basis is the difference between spot and the implied futures price, so implied futures price is 0.7337 − 0.0009 = 0.7328.

Exam shortcut – The 'lock-in rate'

The calculation of the likely financial result of the futures hedge was a lengthy calculation, and it also relied upon being able to estimate the spot rate on the transaction date.

There is a much simpler way of estimating the likely financial result of the futures hedge, by just calculating the overall 'lock-in rate' for the hedge, as follows:

Lock in rate = Opening futures price + unexpired basis on the transaction date

This will enable you to estimate the likely financial result of the hedge even if the spot rate on the transaction date is not known.

Illustration 2 – The lock-in rate

In the Europe Co illustration above, the lock-in rate would be:

Opening futures price + unexpired basis on the transaction date

= 0.7300 + 0.0009 (from the basis working) = 0.7309€/$1

Therefore the likely financial result of the futures hedge is $10m × 0.7309 = €7,309,000, exactly as before.

If ever you are asked in the exam to estimate the financial result of a futures hedge, try to use this lock-in rate shortcut if at all possible, because it significantly reduces the amount of workings you'll need to present in your answer.

Basis risk

We identified above that basis will fall to zero by the expiry date of the futures contract, but throughout our examples so far we have assumed that the reduction will occur in a linear manner. This might not be the case in reality.

Basis risk is the risk that the basis reduces in a non-linear manner, making our forecast of the unexpired basis on our transaction date inaccurate.

You will never have to present any more complex calculations in an exam, but make sure you refer to the existence of basis risk in your written answers, to highlight the potential for inaccuracy in your forecast of the unexpired basis and the lock-in rate.

Student Accountant article

Read the examiner's 'Basis Risk' article in the Technical Articles section of the ACCA website for more details.

5 Currency options

Introduction

- A currency option is a right, but not an obligation, to buy or sell a currency at an exercise price on a future date. If there is a favourable movement in rates the company will allow the option to lapse, to take advantage of the favourable movement. The right will only be exercised to protect against an adverse movement, i.e. the worst-case scenario.
    - A call option gives the holder the right to buy the underlying currency.
    - A put option gives the holder the right to sell the underlying currency.
- Options are more expensive than the forward contracts and futures.
- A European option can only be exercised on the expiry date whilst an American option can be exercised at any time up to the expiry date.

OTC options and exchange traded options

Currency options can be bought over the counter (OTC) or from major futures and options exchanges.

OTC options

- Like forward contracts, the OTC options are tailor made to fit a company's precise requirements. Branches of foreign banks in major financial centres are generally willing to write options against their home currency.

    - e.g. Australian banks in Chicago will write options on the Australian dollar.

- Option sizes are much larger on the OTC market, with most options being in excess of $1 million.

Exchange traded options

- Exchange traded options are also available but the OTC market is the larger.

    - e.g. the London International Financial Futures and Options exchange (now known as ICE Futures Europe) offers European style dollar: euro option contracts.

Traded options example

A typical pricing schedule for the US$/€ currency option on the Philadelphia exchange is as follows.

Strike price	CALLS			PUTS		
	Jun	Sept	Dec	Jun	Sept	Dec
115.00	1.99	2.25	2.47	0.64	1.32	2.12
116.00	1.39	2.03	2.28	1.00	1.56	–
117.00	0.87	1.55	1.81	1.43	2.22	–
118.00	0.54	1.08	1.30	–	–	–

- Here, the options are for a contract size of €125,000 and prices (both strike price and premia) are quoted in US$ (cents) per €1.

- So to buy a call option on €125,000 with an expiry date of September and at a strike price of €1 = $1.17 would cost 1.55 cents per euro, or $1,937.50.

- Similarly, the premium on a June put at a strike price of 115.00 (€1 = $1.15) would cost 0.64 cents per euro, or $800.

- The decision as to which exercise price to choose will depend on cost, risk exposure and expectations. If you have to choose in the exam then one approach is to consider the cost implications only for calculation purposes: The best exercise price is then the one which (incorporating the premium cost) is most financially advantageous.

Choosing an exercise price

Call option

Using the above schedule, determine which June call option would give the lowest net cost of **acquiring euros**.

Strike price	Premium	Total cost per €
115.00	1.99	116.99
116.00	1.39	117.39
117.00	0.87	117.87
118.00	0.54	118.54

The lowest cost would involve using call options with a strike price of 115.

Put option

Using the above schedule, determine which September put option would give the highest net receipt from **selling euros**.

Strike price	Premium	Net receipt from €1
115.00	1.32	113.68
116.00	1.56	114.44
117.00	2.22	114.78
118.00	–	–

The highest receipt would involve using put options with a strike price of 117.

Options hedging calculations

Step 1: Set up the hedge by addressing 4 key questions:

- Do we need call or put options?

- How many contracts?

- Which expiry date should be chosen?

- Which strike price/exercise price should be used?

Step 2: Contact the exchange. Pay the upfront premium. Then wait until the transaction/settlement date.

Step 3: On the transaction date, compare the option price with the prevailing spot rate to determine whether the option should be exercised or allowed to lapse.

Step 4: Calculate the net cash flows – beware that if the number of contracts needed rounding, there will be some exchange at the prevailing spot rate even if the option is exercised.

Test your understanding 4 – Pongo

Pongo plc is a UK-based import-export company. It has an invoice, which it is due to pay on 30 June, in respect of $350,000.

The company wishes to hedge its exposure to risk using traded options.

The current $/£ spot rate is 1.5190 – 1.5230.

On the ICE Futures Europe exchange, contract size is £25,000.

Exercise price ($/£)	June contracts	
	Calls	Puts
1.45	8.95	10.20
1.50	6.80	12.40

Option premia are given in cents per £.

Assume that it is now the 31 March.

Required:

Calculate the cash flows in respect of the payment if the spot rate is: $1.4810 – $1.4850 to £1 on the 30 June.

Test your understanding 5 – Pongo (continued)

Using the circumstances described in the previous example above, suppose Pongo plc is also due to receive $275,000 from a US customer on 30 September. ICE Futures Europe quotes for September option contracts are as follows:

Exercise price ($/£1)	September contracts	
	Calls	Puts
1.45	14.15	10.45
1.50	8.00	13.40

Required:

Calculate the cash flows in respect of the receipt if the spot rate is $1.5250 – $1.5285 to £1 on the 30 September.

Student Accountant article

The article 'Exchange traded foreign exchange derivatives' in the Technical Articles section of the ACCA website contains more details on currency futures and options.

6   Forex swaps

Characteristics

- In a forex swap, the parties agree to swap equivalent amounts of currency for a period and then re-swap them at the end of the period at an agreed swap rate. The swap rate and amount of currency is agreed between the parties in advance. Thus it is called a 'fixed rate/fixed rate' swap.

- The main objectives of a forex swap are:

    - To hedge against forex risk, possibly for a longer period than is possible on the forward market.

    - Access to capital markets, in which it may be impossible to borrow directly.

- Forex swaps are especially useful when dealing with countries that have exchange controls and/or volatile exchange rates.

Illustration 3

Suppose that A plc, a UK construction company, wins a contract to construct a bridge in Argentina. The bridge will require an initial investment now, and will be sold to the Argentinean Government in one year's time. The Government will pay in pesos.

The problem is the company's exposure to currency risk. They know how much will be received in one year's time in pesos but not in the home currency (British pounds, £) as the exchange rate changes daily.

Various possible hedging strategies:

1   **Decide to do nothing**, i.e. accept the risk – win some, lose some.

2   Lock into **a forward contract** for converting the amount receivable in one year's time into £, if a forward market exists.

3   Undertake **a money market hedge**: take out a loan in pesos to cover the initial cost, and repay the loan from the disposal proceeds in a year's time. We would then only be exposed on the profit we make (if we make any).

4   Enter into a **forex swap**. Instead of taking out a loan in pesos we

(a)   Swap £ today for the pesos required to cover the initial investment, at an agreed swap rate.

(b)   Take out a loan in £ today to buy the pesos.

(c)   In one year's time (in this example) arrange to swap back the pesos obtained in (a) for £ at the same swap rate.

(d)   Just like taking out a loan in pesos we are therefore only exposed on the profit that we make. We could of course use another hedging technique to hedge the profit element.

Calculations

Illustration 4

Say the bridge will require an initial investment of 100m pesos and is will be sold for 200m pesos in one year's time.

The currency spot rate is 20 pesos/£1, and the government has offered a forex swap at 20 pesos/£1. A plc cannot borrow pesos directly and there is no forward market available.

The estimated spot rate in one year is 40 pesos/£1. The current UK borrowing rate is 10%.

Required:

Determine whether A plc should do nothing or hedge its exposure using the forex swap.

Solution

£m	0	1
Without swap		
Buy 100m pesos @ 20	(5.0)	
Sell 200m pesos @ 40		5.0
Interest on £ loan (5 × 10%)		(0.5)
	(5.0)	4.5
With forex swap		
Buy 100m pesos @ 20	(5.0)	
Swap 100m pesos back @ 20		5.0
Sell 100m pesos @ 40		2.5
Interest on £ loan (5 × 10%)		(0.5)
Net receipt of (£2.0 million)	(5.0)	7.0

A plc should use a forex swap.

(**Key idea:** The forex swap is used to hedge foreign exchange risk. We can see that in this basic exercise that the swap amount of 100m pesos is protected from any deprecation, as it is swapped at both the start and end of the year at the swap rate of 20, whilst in the spot market pesos have depreciated from a rate of 20 to 40 pesos per £1.)

Test your understanding 6

Goldsmith Co, a mining company based in the fictitious country of Krownland, wishes to hedge 1 year foreign exchange risk, which will arise on an investment in Chile. The investment is for 800m escudos and is expected to yield an amount of 1,000m escudos in 1 years' time.

Goldsmith cannot borrow escudos directly and is therefore considering two possible hedging techniques:

(a) Entering into a forward contract for the full 1000m escudos receivable.

(b) Entering into a forex swap for the 800m escudos initial investment, and then a forward contract for the 200m escudos profit element.

The currency spot rate is 28 escudos to the krown, and the bank has offered a forex swap at 22 escudos/krown with Goldsmith making a net interest payment to the bank of 1% in krowns (assume at T_1).

Interest rates	Borrowing	Lending
Krownland	15%	12%
Chile	N/A	25%

A forward contract is available at a rate of 30 escudos per krown.

Required:

Determine whether Goldsmith should hedge its exposure using a forward contract or a forex swap.

7   Currency swaps

Characteristics

- A currency swap allows the two counterparties to swap interest rate commitments on borrowings in different currencies.

- In effect a currency swap has two elements:

  - An exchange of principals in different currencies, which are swapped back at the original spot rate – just like a forex swap.

  - An exchange of interest rates – the timing of these depends on the individual contract.

- The swap of interest rates could be 'fixed for fixed' or 'fixed for variable'.

Example of a currency swap

Warne Co is an Australian firm looking to expand in Germany and is thus looking to raise €24 million. It can borrow at the following fixed rates:

A$ 7.0%

€ 5.6%

Euroports Inc is a French company looking to acquire an Australian firm and is looking to borrow A$40 million. It can borrow at the following rates:

A$ 7.2%

€ 5.5%

The current spot rate is A$1 = €0.6.

Required:

Show how a 'fixed for fixed' currency swap would work in the circumstances described, assuming the swap is only for one year and that interest is paid at the end of the year concerned.

Solution

Timing		Warne Co	Euroports Inc
Now	Borrow from banks	A$40m at 7.0%	€24m at 5.5%
	Exchange principals	Pay A$40m to Euroports receive €24m	Pay €24m to Warne receive A$40m
End of year	Pay interest to banks	Pay A$2.8m interest	Pay €1.32m interest
	Exchange interest	Pay €1.32m to Euroports receive A$2.8m	Receive €1.32m Pay A$2.8m to Warne
	Swap back principals	Pay €24m to Warne receive A$40m	Pay A$40m to Euroports receive €24m

Net result:

Interest costs	Warne Co	Euroports Inc
Without swap (24 × 5.6%)		
(40 × 7.2%)	€1.344m	A$2.88m
With swap	€1.320m	A$2.80m
	———	———
Saving	€24,000	A$80,000
	———	———

Test your understanding 7

Wa Inc is a Japanese firm looking to expand in the USA and is looking to raise $20 million at a variable interest rate. It has been quoted the following rates:

$ SOFR + 60 points

¥ 1.2%

McGregor Inc is an American company looking to refinance a ¥2,400m loan at a fixed rate. It can borrow at the following rates:

$ SOFR + 50 points

¥ 1.5%

The current spot rate is $1 = ¥120.

Required:

Show how the 'fixed for variable' currency swap would work in the circumstances described, assuming the swap is only for one year and that interest is paid at the end of the year concerned.

Student Accountant article

The article 'Currency swaps' in the Technical Articles section of the ACCA website provides further details on this topic.

8 Bilateral and multilateral netting and matching agreements

Introduction

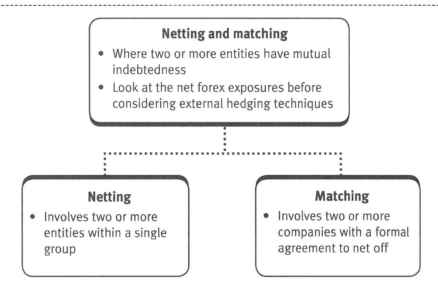

Netting and matching

Netting and matching are carried out to reduce the scale of external hedging required.

For example, Group X is expecting to receive $10 million in one subsidiary and pay $6 million at the same time in another subsidiary. Clearly the group only has a net exposure of a receipt of $4 million.

The terms 'netting' and 'matching' are often used interchangeably but strictly speaking they are different:

- Netting refers to netting off group receipts and payments, as in the example above.

- Matching extends this concept to include third parties such as external suppliers and customers.

When is multilateral netting used?

Multilateral netting involves minimising the number of transactions taking place through each country's banks. This limits the fees that these banks receive for undertaking the transactions and therefore some governments do not allow multilateral netting in order to maximise the fees their local banks receive.

On the other hand, some other governments allow multilateral netting in the belief that this will make companies more willing to operate from those countries and any banking fees lost will be more than compensated by the extra business these companies and their subsidiaries bring into the country.

Calculations

The calculations can be presented in one of two ways: the tabular method and the diagrammatical method.

Tabular method ('transactions matrix')

Step 1: Set up a table with the name of each company down the side and across the top.

Step 2: Input all the amounts owing from one company to another into the table and convert them into a common (base) currency (at spot rate).

Step 3: By adding across and down the table, identify the total amount payable and the total amount receivable by each company.

Step 4: Compute the net payable or receivable, and convert back into the original currency.

Diagrammatical method

Step 1: Convert all currency flows to a common ('base') currency using spot rates (NOT forward or future rates).

Step 2: Clear the overlap of any bi-lateral indebtedness.

E.g.

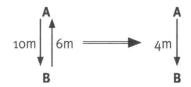

Step 3: Clear the smallest leg of any 3 way circuits.

E.g.

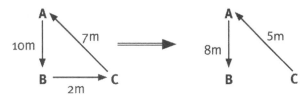

Step 4: Clear the smallest leg of any 4 way circuits (then 5, etc).

E.g.

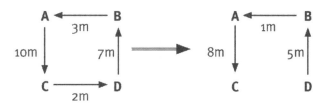

Step 5: Convert back into original currencies.

Step 6: Use the simplified figures for:

A   Settlement

B   Setting up appropriate hedging tools.

Multilateral netting – Worked example

P is the parent company of a group that contains 3 subsidiaries: Q (based in Europe), R (based in the USA) and S based in Canada. The following cash flows are due in 2 months' time between P and its subsidiaries:

Owed by	Owed to	Amount
P	S	CAN$ 3 million
P	R	US$ 5 million
Q	R	US$ 4 million
Q	S	CAN$ 7 million
R	S	CAN$ 2 million
R	P	US$ 6 million
S	Q	EUR 12 million
S	P	CAN$ 5 million

Mid-rate exchange rates in two months' time are expected to be:

£1 = US$ 1.60

£1 = EUR 1.20

£1 = CAN$ 1.50

Required:

Calculate, using a tabular format (transactions matrix), the impact of undertaking multilateral netting by P and its three subsidiary companies for the cash flows due in two months.

Solution

Note that all foreign currency amounts have been translated into £ using the given mid rates.

In £ million Paid to	P	Q	Paid R	by S	Total
P			3.750	3.333	7.083
Q				10.000	10.000
R	3.125	2.500			5.625
S	2.000	4.667	1.333		8.000
Total payment	(5.125)	(7.167)	(5.083)	(13.333)	
Total receipt	7.083	10.000	5.625	8.000	
Net receipt/(payment)	1.958	2.833	0.542	(5.333)	

So overall, S needs to pay amounts equivalent to the above figures to each of P, Q and R in two months' time.

Test your understanding 8 – Netting and matching

X, Y, and Z are three companies within the same UK based international group. W is a company outside of the group. The following liabilities have been identified for the forthcoming year:

Owed by	Owed to	Amount (millions)
X	Y	€39
Y	X	£10
Y	W	$20
Z	X	¥200
Z	Y	€15
W	X	$15
W	Z	¥100

Mid-market spot rates are:

£1 = $2.00

£1 = €1.50

£1 = ¥250

Required:

Establish the net indebtedness that would require external hedging.

9 Chapter summary

```
┌──────────────────────────┐
│   HEDGING FOREIGN         │
│   EXCHANGE RISK           │
└──────────────────────────┘
```

Techniques/instruments

- Forward contracts, including synthetic foreign exchange agreements (SAFEs)
- Money market hedges
- Futures
- Forex swaps
- Currency swaps
- Currency options
- Netting and matching agreements

Test your understanding answers

Test your understanding 1

Step 1: Get the appropriate spot rate from the spread – the lower of the two rates quoted (remember the bank always wins): 0.7785

Step 2: Now pick the correct forward rate – still the lower of the two rates quoted (0.7764).

Step 3: Use the rate: cost = 250,000/0.7764 = **A$ 322,000 CERTAIN SUM**.

Test your understanding 2

1 US$ exposure

As Marcus Co has a US$ receipt (US$69,000) and payment (US$240,000), maturing at the same time (3 months), they can match them against each other to leave a net liability of US$ 171,000 to be hedged.

Forward market hedge

Buy US$171,000 3 months forward at a cost of:

US$171,000/0.9520 = **(€179,622)** payable in 3 months' time.

Money market hedge

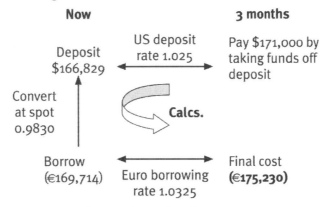

This is cheaper than the forward market hedge.

Note: Interest rates can simply be time-apportioned.

2 A$ exposure

Forward market hedge

Sell A$295,000 4 months forward to produce a receipt of:

A$295,000 × 1.9510 = **€575,545** receivable in 4 months' time.

Money market hedge

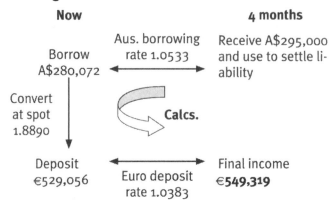

As this is smaller amount than received from the forward market hedge, we can conclude that the forward market hedge gives the better outcome.

Test your understanding 3		
Step 1	1 Buy or sell initially? 2 How many contracts? 3 Which expiry date?	1 CC is $, and we need to sell $ (to buy CHF), so sell futures now. 2 Cover $2m using $200,000 contracts, hence 10 contracts. 3 Transaction date is 10 June, so choose June futures (the first to expire after the transaction date).
Step 2	Contact the exchange – state the hedge.	Sell 10 June futures (at a futures price of CHF1.2200/ $1.

| Step 3 | Calculate profit/loss in futures market by closing out the position. | Initially: Sell at 1.2200.

Close out: Buy at 1.2760.

Difference is CHF0.056 per $1 loss.

10 × $200,000 covered, so total loss is 0.056 × 10 × 200,000 = CHF112,000. |
| | Transaction at spot rate on 10 June.

Sell $2m at spot rate of CHF 1.2750/$1. | CHF received is CHF2,550,000, hence net receipt is 2,550,000 – 112,000 = CHF2,438,000. |

Test your understanding 4 – Pongo

Step 1: 4 key questions:

Call or put options? – CC is £, we need to sell £ to get $ so buy put options on £.

Which expiry date? Only June quoted here, but that matches the transaction date exactly, so choose June contracts.

Which exercise price? The choice is between $1.50/£1 and $1.45/£1. Since we are selling £ to buy $, the $1.50 rate looks initially more attractive. However, the premium for the $1.50/£1 option is more expensive as a consequence. The final decision can only be made after looking at the net benefit of each alternative, as follows:

- the $1.45 option has a premium of $0.1020 so net receipt = $1.3480/£1.

- the $1.50 option has a premium of $0.1240 so net receipt is $1.3760/£1.

Hence, the better option is the $1.50/£1 exercise price.

How many contracts? Cover $350,000/1.50 = £233,333 using £25,000 contracts, so 233,333/25,000 = 9.33 – round to 9 contracts.

Step 2: Contact the exchange. We need to buy 9 June Put options at an exercise price of $1.50/£1.

Premium payable is 12.40c per £1 covered i.e. $0.1240 × (9 × £25,000) = $27,900, which has to be purchased at spot (1.5190) so costs $27,900/1.5190 = £18,367.

Step 3:	On the settlement date compare the option price ($1.50) with the prevailing spot ($1.4810) to determine whether the option would be exercised or allowed to lapse. Here, it is preferable to exercise ('sell the big number').
Step 4:	Determine net cash flows.
	£ payment under options = 9 × £25,000 = £225,000.
	Amount not hedged = $350,000 – (9 × £25,000 × 1.50) = $12,500.
	Assume these unhedged $ are bought at spot rate.
	Cost = $12,500 ÷1.4810 = £8,440
	Total payment under $1.50 options hedge (including premium).
	= £225,000 + £8,440 + £18,367 = **£251,807**.

Test your understanding 5 – Pongo (continued)

Step 1:	4 key questions:
	Call or put options? CC is £, we need to sell $ to get £ so buy call options on £.
	Which expiry date? Only September quoted.
	Which exercise price? The choice is between $1.50/£1 and $1.45/£1. Since we are selling $ to buy £, the $1.45 rate looks initially more attractive. However, the premium for the $1.45/ £1 option is more expensive as a consequence. The final decision can only be made after looking at the total cost of each alternative, as follows:
	• the $1.45 option has a premium of $0.1415 so total cost = $1.5915/£1.
	• the $1.50 option has a premium of $0.0800 so total cost is $1.5800/£1.
	Hence, the better option is in fact the $1.50/£1 exercise price.
	How many contracts? Cover $275,000/1.50 = £183,333 using £25,000 contracts, so 183,333/25,000 = 7.33 – round to 7 contracts.

Step 2:	Contact the exchange: We need to buy 7 September Call Options at an exercise price of $1.50.
	Determine option premium – usually payable upfront.
	Option premium = $0.08 × (£25,000 × 7) = $14,000.
	Assume the option premium is payable upfront $14,000/1.5190 = £9,217.
Step 3:	On the settlement date compare the option price ($1.50) with the prevailing spot ($1.5285) to determine whether the option would be exercised or allowed to lapse.
	Here it is best to exercise ('buy the low number').
Step 4:	Determine net cash flows.
	£ receipt under options = 7 × £25,000 = £175,000
	Amount not hedged = $275,000 – (7 × £25,000 × 1.50) = $12,500
	Assume these unhedged $ are sold at spot rate.
	Cost = $12,500 ÷ 1.5285 = £8,178
	Total receipt under $1.50 options hedge (net of premium)
	= £175,000 + £8,178 – £9,217 = **£173,961**

Test your understanding 6

Krowns (millions)	0	1
Forward hedge		
Buy 800m escudos @ 28	(28.57)	
Sell 1,000m escudos @ 30		33.33
Interest on krown loan (28.57 × 15%)		(4.29)
	(28.57)	29.04

Net receipt of **0.47** million krowns.

With forex swap and forward	0	1
Buy 800m escudos @ 22	(36.36)	
Swap 800m escudos back @ 22		36.36
Sell 200m escudos @ 30		6.67
Interest on krown loan (36.36 × 15%)		(5.45)
Swap fee (36.36 × 1%)		(0.36)
	(36.36)	37.22

Net receipt of **0.86** million krowns.

Goldsmith should use a forex swap.

Test your understanding 7

Timing		Wa Inc	McGregor Inc
Now	Borrow from banks	¥2,400m at 1.2%	$20m at S + 0.5%
	Exchange principals	Pay ¥2,400m to McGregor receive $20m	Pay $20m to Wa receive ¥2,400m
End of year	Pay interest to banks	Pay ¥28.8m interest	Pay $20 × (S + 0.5%) interest
	Exchange interest based on swap terms	Pay McGregor $20 × (S + 0.5%) receive ¥28.8m`	Receive $20 × (S + 0.5%) Pay ¥28.8m to Wa
	Swap back principals	Pay $20m to McGregor receive ¥2,400m	Pay ¥2,400m to Wa receive $20m

Net result:

Interest costs	Wa	McGregor
Without swap	$20m × (S + 0.6%)	2,400 × 1.5% = ¥36m
With swap	$20m × (S + 0.5%)	¥28.8m
Saving	$20m × 0.1% = $20,000	¥7.2m

Test your understanding 8 – Netting and matching

Tabular method

	X	Y	Z	W
X		€39m		
Y	£10m			$20m
Z	200m Yen	€15m		
W	$15m		100m Yen	

These amounts represent amounts owed BY the firm in the left hand column TO the firm listed across the top.

Now convert to £ at spot rate, and add across and down:

£m	X	Y	Z	W	Total (across)
X		26			26
Y	10			10	20
Z	0.8	10			10.8
W	7.5		0.4		7.9
Total (down)	18.3	36	0.4	10	
Total (across)	26	20	10.8	7.9	
Net total	(7.7)	16	(10.4)	2.1	

The easiest way to interpret this is for X and Z to pay £7.7m and £10.4m respectively to Y (which now receives £18.1 m in total). If Y then pays £2.1 m to W, all companies have the correct net payments or receipts.

Convert these back into the original currencies and the final transactions are:

X pays Y €11.55m

Z pays Y €15.6m

Y pays W $4.2m

Diagrammatical method:

The current position can be shown in a diagram as follows:

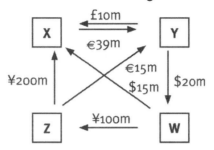

Step 1: Convert to base – here GB pounds.

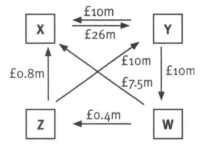

Step 2: Clear bilateral indebtedness.

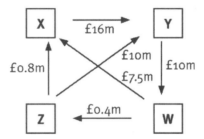

Step 3: Identify and clear 3 way circuits

(a)   XYW

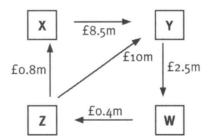

(b)   ZXY

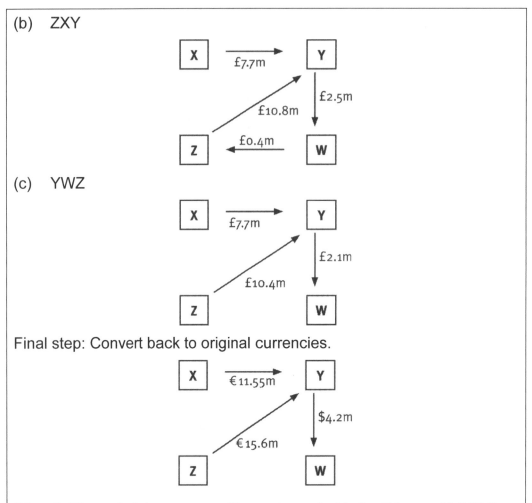

(c)   YWZ

Final step: Convert back to original currencies.

Step 6: The only intra-group settlement needed is for Z to pay Y €15.6m and X to pay Y €11.55m.

The final hedging tools needed for the group are for a payment of $4.2m to W.

Hedging interest rate risk

Chapter learning objectives

Study guide section		Study guide outcome
E1: The role of the treasury function in multinationals	(b)	Discuss the operations of the derivatives market (i) The relative advantages and disadvantages of exchange traded versus OTC agreements (iii) The source of basis risk and how it can be minimised.
E3: The use of financial derivatives to hedge against interest rate risk	(a)	Evaluate, for a given hedging requirement, which of the following is the most appropriate given the nature of the underlying position and the risk exposure: (i) Forward Rate Agreements (FRAs) (ii) Interest Rate Futures (iii) Interest rate swaps (iv) Interest rate options (including collars).

Many aspects of interest rate risk management were introduced in Financial Management (FM). These are recapped briefly for completeness. In AFM the range of techniques considered is extended.

One of the PER performance objectives (PO11 – Identify and Manage Financial Risk) is to be able to identify, measure, and advise on the financial risks to the organisation.

PER

Working through this chapter should help you understand how to demonstrate that objective.

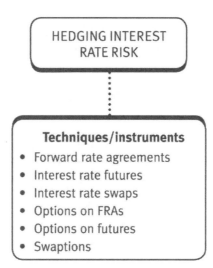

1 Introduction

Firms are exposed to interest rate movements in two ways:

- The cost of existing borrowings (or the yield on deposits) may be linked to interest rates in the economy. This risk exposure can be eliminated by using fixed rate products.

- Cash flow forecasts may indicate the need for future borrowings/deposits. Interest rates may change before these are needed and thus affect the ultimate cost/yield.

- The second type of risk is the focus of this chapter.

Student Accountant article

The article 'How to answer an interest rate risk management question' in the Technical Articles section of the ACCA website provides further details on the topics covered in this chapter.

 More explanation of interest rate risk

Interest rate risk exposure

Interest rate risk is the risk of incurring losses due to adverse movements in interest rates. An exposure to interest rate risk arises in the following situations.

- An organisation is expecting some income in the future, and the amount of income received will depend on the interest rate at that time.

- An organisation is expecting to make some payment in the future, and the amount of the payment will depend on the interest rate at the time.

- The organisation has an asset whose market value changes whenever market interest rates change.

The greatest exposures to interest rate risk are faced by banks and investment institutions. However, non-bank companies can also have substantial exposures to interest rate risk.

- Many companies borrow at a floating rate of interest (or variable rate of interest).

- For example, a company might borrow at a variable rate of interest, with interest payable every six months and the amount of the interest charged each time varying according to whether short-term interest rates have risen or fallen since the previous payment.

- Some companies also budget to receive large amounts of cash, and so budget large temporary cash surpluses that can be invested short-term. Income from those temporary investments will depend on what the interest rate happens to be when the money is available for depositing. Some investments earn interest at a variable rate of interest (for example money in bank deposit accounts) and some short-term investments go up or down in value with changes in interest rates (for example, Treasury bills and other bills).

- Some companies hold investments in marketable bonds, either government bonds or corporate bonds. These change in value with movements in long-term interest rates.

- Some companies borrow by issuing bonds. If a company foresees a future requirement to borrow by issuing bonds, it will have an exposure to interest rate risk until the bonds are eventually issued.

- Many companies borrow, and if they do they have to choose between borrowing at a fixed rate of interest (usually by issuing bonds) or borrow at a floating rate (possibly through bank loans). There is some risk in deciding the balance or mix between floating rate and fixed rate debt. Too much fixed rate debt creates an exposure to falling long-term interest rates and too much floating rate debt creates an exposure to a rise in short-term interest rates.

Interest rate risk can be significant. For example, suppose that a company wants to borrow $10 million for one year, but does not need the money for another three weeks. It would be expensive to borrow money before it is needed, because there will be an interest cost. On the other hand, a rise in interest rates in the time before the money is actually borrowed could also add to interest costs. For example, a rise of just 0.25% (25 basis points) in the interest rate on a one-year loan of $10 million would cost an extra $25,000 in interest.

2 Forward rate agreements (FRAs)

Introduction

- Using an FRA effectively fixes the rate of interest on a loan or deposit.

- In the terminology of the markets, an FRA for a three-month loan/deposit starting in five months' time is called a '5–8 FRA' (or '5v8 FRA').

- Two rates are usually quoted, the higher one for borrowing and the lower one for investing.

More detail on FRAs

Hedging using FRAs

Hedging is achieved by a combination of an FRA with the 'normal' loan or deposit.

When an FRA reaches its settlement date (usually the start of the notional loan or deposit period), the buyer and seller must settle the contract:

Borrowing (hence concerned about interest rate rises)

- The firm will borrow the required sum on the target date and will thus contract at the market interest rate on that date.

- Separately the firm will buy a matching FRA from a bank or other market maker and thus receive compensation if rates rise.

Depositing (hence concerned about a fall in interest rates)

- The firm will deposit the required sum on the target date and will thus contract at the market interest rate on that date.

- Separately the firm will sell a matching FRA to a bank or other market maker and thus receive compensation if rates fall.

In each case this combination effectively fixes the rate.

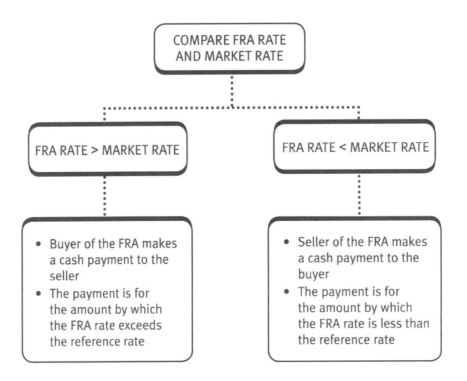

Illustration 1 – FRA

It is now the 1st November 20X6. Enfield Co's financial projections show an expected cash deficit in two months' time of $8 million, which will last for approximately three months. The treasurer is concerned that interest rates may rise before the 1st January 20X7, so she is considering using an FRA to fix the interest rate.

The bank offers a 2 – 5 FRA at 5.00% – 4.70%.

Required:

Calculate the interest payable if in two months' time the market rate is: (a) 7% or (b) 4%.

Solution

The rate for borrowing is 5% – the higher of the two rates quoted.

Loan payments		7%	4%
Interest payable on loan:	8m × 0.07 × 3/12 =	(140,000)	
	8m × 0.04 × 3/12 =		(80,000)

FRA payments

Compensation:

Receivable	8m × (0.07 – 0.05) × 3/12	=	40,000	
Payable	8m × (0.04 – 0.05) × 3/12	=		(20,000)
			————	————
Combination gives an effective interest rate of 5%.			**(100,000)**	**(100,000)**
			————	————

- In this case the company is protected from a rise in interest rates but is not able to benefit from a fall in interest rates – a FRA hedges the company against both an adverse movement and a favourable movement.

- The FRA is a totally separate contractual agreement from the loan itself and could be arranged with a completely different bank.

- FRAs are usually on amounts > $1m and enable you to hedge for a period of one month up to two years. However, as an 'over the counter' instrument, they can be tailor-made to the company's precise requirements.

Settlement payment on an FRA

Because the settlement payment is made at the start of the loan/deposit period, the actual payment made is the present value of the interest differential at that date, discounted using the market reference interest rate.

Illustration

Using the details for the Enfield Co example above with a 7% market rate:

- The difference in interest rates gave rise to a potential receipt of $40,000 from the bank.

- The actual amount received will be 40,000/(1 + 0.07 × 3/12) = $39,312.

- One approach is to use this to reduce the loan from $8 million to $7,960,688. If this sum is then borrowed at 7% for 3 months, then the final repayment will be:

  7,960,688 × (1 + 0.07 × 3/12) = 8,100,000

This gives an effective interest rate of $100,000 on $8m, or 5%.

How does the bank set the interest rate for an FRA?

FRA rates are set by the bank by analysing the individual company's spot yield curve (introduced in the earlier chapter on the weighted average cost of capital).

Illustration 2

Stone Co's yield curve has been calculated as:

Year	Individual yield curve (%)
1	3.96
2	4.25
3	4.56

This means that Stone Co will have to pay interest of 3.96% if it wants to borrow money for 1 year, 4.25% if it wants to borrow for 2 years etc.

An alternative to borrowing for 2 years at 4.25% throughout is to borrow for 1 year initially at 3.96% and then to borrow for another year in 1 years' time at an unknown rate. The company could fix the interest rate in one year's time by asking the bank to quote a rate for a 12 – 24 FRA.

The rate quoted by the bank would be the rate r, so that:

$$1.0396 \times (1 + r) = 1.0425^2$$

Rearranging this gives r = 4.54%.

Hence the 12 – 24 FRA rate for Stone Co would be 4.54%.

Test your understanding 1

Stone Co (the company in the previous Illustration) wants to borrow money in 2 years' time for a period of 1 year.

Required:

Using the company's spot yield information quoted above, calculate the rate of interest the bank would quote for a 24 – 36 FRA.

Student Accountant article

The examiner's article 'Determining interest rate forwards...' in the Technical Articles section of the ACCA website covers the calculation of FRA rates in more detail.

3 Options on FRAs

Interest rate guarantees (options on FRAs)

- An interest rate guarantee (IRG) is an option on an FRA and, like all options, protects the company from adverse movements and allows it take advantage of favourable movements.

- If borrowing money, a firm would buy an FRA (explained above), so a **call** option over FRAs would be used. Similarly a **put** option over FRAs would be used to cover a deposit.

- IRGs are usually written by banks and other financial houses (i.e. the same organisations that may offer FRAs).

Decision rules

If there is an adverse movement   If there is a favourable movement

Exercise the option to protect   Allow the option to lapse

- IRGs are more expensive than the FRAs as one has to pay for the flexibility to be able to take advantage of a favourable movement.

Illustration 3 – IRG

Harry Co wishes to borrow $8 million in two months' time for a period of three months.

An IRG is available at 5% for a premium of 0.1% of the size of the loan.

Required:

Calculate the interest payable if in two months' time the market rate is: (a) 7% or (b) 4%.

Solution

		7% – exercise	4% – allow to lapse
Interest	8m × 3/12 × 5%	(100,000)	
	8m × 3/12 × 4%		(80,000)
Premium =	Cost of option	(8,000)	(8,000)
Total payment		**(108,000)**	**(88,000)**

Note: There is no need to time apportion the premium percentage.

Test your understanding 2

RGI Co wishes to invest $12 million in 6 months' time for two months and considering the following hedging strategies.

1.   A 6 – 8 FRA quoted at 4%.

2.   An IRG at 4% for a premium of 0.1%.

Required:

Determine the costs if in six months' time the market rate is: (a) 5% (b) 3% and comment.

When to hedge using FRAs or IRGs

- If the company treasurer believes that interest rates will rise, will it be better use an FRA or an IRG? Use an FRA, as it is the cheaper way to hedge against the potential adverse movement.

- If the treasurer is unsure which way interest rates will move, it may be better to use the more expensive IRG to be able to benefit from a potential fall in interest rates.

4   Interest rate futures (IRFs)

Introduction

An interest rate futures contract fixes the interest rate on a future loan or deposit.

More details on interest rate futures

Types of IRFs

There are two broad types of interest rate futures:

- Short-term interest rate futures (STIRs). These are standardised exchange-traded forward contracts on a notional deposit (usually a three-month deposit) of a standard amount of principal, starting on the contract's final settlement date.

- Bond futures. These are contracts on a standard quantity of notional government bonds. If they reach final settlement date, and a buyer or seller does not close the position before then, the contracts must be settled by physical delivery.

Futures hedging calculations

Step 1: Set up the hedge by addressing 3 key questions:

- Do we initially buy or sell futures?

- How many contracts?

- Which expiry date should be chosen?

Step 2: Contact the exchange. Pay the initial margin. Then wait until the transaction/settlement date.

Step 3: Calculate profit or loss in the futures market by closing out the futures contracts, and calculate the value of the transaction using the market rate of interest rate on the transaction date.

Calculations – Particular characteristics of IRFs

Underlying assets

To understand whether you need to buy or sell contracts, interest rate futures are best understood as involving the sale or purchase of bonds.

- borrowing money equates to issuing (selling) bonds, so sell futures to set up the hedge.

- depositing funds equates to buying bonds, so buy futures to set up the hedge.

Futures prices

- Interest rate futures prices are stated as (100 – the expected market reference rate), so a price of 95.5 would imply an interest rate of 4.5%.

- Open and settlement prices – in an exam question, when setting up the hedge, you may be quoted 'Open' and 'Settlement' futures prices. When setting up the hedge, the 'Settlement' price should be used – the 'Open' price is not relevant in our calculations.

Calculating the number of contracts needed

$$\text{Number of contracts} = \frac{\text{Loan or deposit amount}}{\text{Contract size}} \times \frac{\text{Loan or deposit period in months}}{\text{Contract duration}}$$

More practical information on IRFs

Contract specifications

Short-term interest rate futures are traded on a number of futures exchanges. For example:

- STIRs for GB pounds (three-month SONIA) and the euro (three-month ESTER) are traded on ICE Futures Europe (formerly LIFFE), the London futures exchange.

- A STIR contract for the US dollar (eurodollar) is traded on the Chicago Mercantile Exchange (CME).

Here are just a few STIR contract specifications.

Short-term interest rate futures

Reference rate	Futures exchange	Notional deposit
3-month GB pounds	LIFFE	£500,000
3-month euro	LIFFE/Eurex	€1 million
3-month eurodollar	CME	$1 million
3-month euroyen	TFE/LIFFE	¥100 million

Ticks and tick values

- For STIRs, the minimum price movement is usually 0.01% or one basis point. The value of a tick is calculated as follows:

  - Tick value = unit of trading (i.e. amount of principal) × one basis point × fraction of year.

  - For three-month GB pounds sterling ('short sterling') futures, the underlying deposit for one contract is £500,000, so the value of one tick is £500,000 × 0.0001 × 3/12 = £12.50.

  - For three-month euro futures, the underlying deposit is €1,000,000, so the value of one tick is €1,000,000 × 3/12 × 0.0001 = €25.

  - For three-month eurodollar futures, the underlying deposit is $1,000,000, so the value of one tick is $1,000,000 × 3/12 × 0.0001 = $25.

Note: For three-month euroyen futures, the underlying deposit is ¥100 m but the tick size is 0.005%, so the value of one tick is ¥100 million × 3/12 × 0.00005 = ¥1250.

Illustration of an interest rate futures calculation

Global Co wishes to borrow €9 million for one month starting in 5 weeks' time. ESTER is currently 3% and the treasurer of Global decides to fix the rate by selling interest rate futures at 96.90. The market rate subsequently rises by 25 basis points to 3.25%. As soon as the loan is agreed, the treasurer closes out Global's position by buying a matching number of contracts at 96.65.

Required:

(a) **Calculate the number of contracts required (Note: One 3-month contract is for €1,000,000).**

(b) **Demonstrate that, in this case, the gain on the futures contracts exactly matches the extra interest on the loan.**

Solution

(a) Number of contracts = (9,000,000/1,000,000) × 1/3 = 3

(b) Extra interest cost on loan = 0.25% × 9,000,000 × 1/12 = €1,875

Gain on futures = 3 contracts × 25 ticks per contract × €25 per tick (W) = €1,875

(W: Value of tick = €1,000,000 × 3/12 × 0.0001 = €25)

Test your understanding 3

Assume that today is the 25th of January.

A company is going to borrow $2,000,000 in two months' time for a period of three months. It fears that the current interest rate will rise from its current level of 5%, so it wants to use $500,000 3-month interest rate futures to hedge the position.

Data from the futures market:

March futures price = 94.90

June futures price = 94.65

Required:

Calculate the result of the relevant futures hedge on the assumption that interest rates have risen to 7% and the futures price has moved to 92.90 in two months' time.

Basis in interest rate futures

In the previous chapter, we saw that basis for a currency futures contract was defined as:

Spot rate – futures price.

For an interest rate futures contract, because of the way the contract price is quoted as (100-expected interest rate) the calculation is slightly different. Basis in an interest rate futures contract is calculated as:

(100 – Spot rate of interest (e.g. the current SOFR rate)) – futures price.

Therefore, if the current SOFR rate is 5.00% and the futures price is 95.50, the basis is:

(100 – 5.00) – 95.50 = – 0.50%

The futures 'lock-in rate'

As with currency futures, we can use this basis value, together with the assumption that basis reduces steadily to zero over the period before the expiry date of the contract, to predict closing futures prices and the likely futures 'lock-in rate'.

With interest rate futures, the lock-in rate is calculated as:

100 – (current futures price + unexpired basis on the transaction date).

Test your understanding 4

Sopoph Co is using June interest rate futures to cover the interest rate risk on a 3 month $1 million borrowing starting on 31 May.

At the time the $500,000 futures contracts are set up on 1 January, the SOFR rate is 5.00% and the futures price is 95.48. Sopoph Co can borrow at the SOFR rate.

Assume that basis reduces in a linear manner.

Required:

(a) **Calculate the financial result of the futures hedge on the assumption that the SOFR rate on 31 May is 4.00%.**

(b) **Calculate the likely lock-in rate for this futures hedge, and hence the likely financial result of the hedge.**

(c) **Comment on your results to parts (a) and (b).**

5   Options on interest rate futures

Options on futures

*   Traded options are options to buy or sell futures.
*   A call option gives the holder the right to buy the futures contract.
*   A put option gives the holder the right to sell the futures contract.
*   You always buy the option – buy the right to buy or buy the right to sell.

Cash market	Deposits	Loan
	↓	↓
Futures market	Buy futures contracts	Self futures contracts
	↓	↓
Options market	Buy calls	Buy puts

Exercise prices and premium costs

- When you are setting up the hedge position for an option you have a number of prices (exercise prices) from which to choose (as opposed to the futures position where you buy or sell at the current price).

Option prices

ICE Futures Europe option price on three-month December futures.

Exercise price	Premium	
	Calls	Puts
93.50	2.20	1.25
94.00	1.74	1.84
94.50	1.32	2.90
95.00	0.87	3.46

- If a company had a deposit of £500,000 and the treasurer wanted to hedge the position using traded options, he would buy a call option. If he purchased it at an exercise price of 95.00 he would be buying the right to interest receipts at 5% this would cost him a premium 0.87% (i.e. 0.87% × 100) 87 ticks (i.e. 87 × £12.50) = £1,088 per contract.

- If he purchased it at 93.50 he would be buying the right to interest receipts at 6.50% this would cost him a premium 2.20% (i.e. 2.20% × 100) 220 ticks (i.e. 220 × £12.50) = £2,750 per contract.

- The premium cost of the option will obviously depend on the exercise price chosen. Buying a call option at 93.50 should be more expensive than buying at 95.00, as the company has a greater chance of a profit when it comes to closing out its futures position.

Choosing an exercise price

There are various ways of choosing an exercise price.

- **NB:** In a question, you may be told which exercise price to use, so check that first.

- One common way is to choose the exercise price closest to the current interest rate, so if the current interest rate were 6.00% then an exercise price of 94.00 would be chosen.

- Alternatively, choose the exercise price that will result in the highest net interest receipt or minimum total interest payment.

Choosing an exercise price

CALL OPTIONS – deposit – highest net receipt.

Exercise price	Deposit interest	Cost	Net receipt
	%	%	%
93.50	6.50	(2.20)	4.30
94.00	6.00	(1.74)	4.26
94.50	5.50	(1.32)	4.18
95.00	5.00	(0.87)	4.13

PUT OPTIONS – loan – lowest total payment.

Exercise price	Loan interest	Cost	Total payment
	%	%	%
93.50	6.50	1.25	7.75
94.00	6.00	1.84	7.84
94.50	5.50	2.90	8.40
95.00	5.00	3.46	8.46

Options hedging calculations

Step 1: Set up the hedge by addressing 4 key questions:

- Do we need call or put options?
- How many contracts?
- Which expiry date should be chosen?
- Which strike price/exercise price should be used?

Step 2: Contact the exchange. Pay the upfront premium. Then wait until the transaction/settlement date.

Step 3: On the transaction date, compare the option price with the prevailing market interest rate to determine whether the option should be exercised or allowed to lapse.

Step 4: Calculate the net cash flows – beware that if the number of contracts needed rounding, there will be some borrowing or deposit at the prevailing market interest rate even if the option is exercised.

Decision point – Exercise the option or allow it to lapse

General rule:

If there is an adverse movement	If there is a favourable movement
↓	↓
Exercise the option to protect	**Allow the option to lapse**

Double check:

- Would you ever exercise an option that results in a loss?

- Therefore you must always have a profit on the futures when exercising and a potential loss if you allow the option to lapse.

Test your understanding 5 – Interest rate options

It is now the 31st of July.

Tolhurst Co needs to borrow $10 million in 1 months' time, for a 6 month period. The current market interest rate is 5%.

The following information is available regarding $500,000 3-month September interest rate options:

Exercise price	Call	Put
94.50	1.39	–
94.75	1.02	0.18
95.00	0.65	0.65
95.25	0.21	1.12

Premia are quoted in %.

Required:

Calculate the result of the options hedge if the interest rate has risen to 7.5% and if the September futures price has moved to 93.00 in one month's time.

Comparison of options and futures

Note that interest rate options over futures contracts behave in exactly the same way as futures contracts if we decide to exercise. So, for example with a call option, if we exercise we buy futures at the option exercise price before selling at the 'normal' futures price on the transaction date.

If the closing futures price is not given, it might have to be calculated by estimating the amount of unexpired basis on the transaction date as detailed above in the examples on futures contracts.

Student Accountant article

The article 'How to answer an interest rate risk management question' in the Technical Articles section of the ACCA website provides a detailed example of how to answer an exam question on interest rate futures and options.

Test your understanding 6 – Futures and options

Chesterfield Co needs to borrow $5 million for 6 months, starting in 4 months' time on 1st August.

The current SOFR rate is 3.50% but there is a risk that interest rates will change over the next few months by up to 0.5% either way, so the company's treasurer is considering hedging the interest payments using futures contracts or options. Chesterfield Co can borrow at 25 basis points above the SOFR rate.

Current futures/options information:

Futures ($500,000 3 month contracts)

June	96.40
September	96.10
December	95.86

Options on futures (premia quoted as an annual percentage)

Exercise price	Calls			Puts		
	June	Sept	Dec	June	Sept	Dec
96.40	0.155	0.260	0.320	0.305	0.360	0.445

Required:

Estimate the likely financial position if Chesterfield Co hedges the interest rate risk using:

(a)   **futures contracts**

(b)   **options over futures contracts.**

and recommend which method the company should use in this case.

6 Caps, floors and collars

Options terminology – Caps and floors

Caps

We have seen above that a borrower will hedge against the risk of interest rate rises by buying a put option over interest rate futures.

A cap is another name for this put option over interest rate futures.

Floors

Similarly, a depositor will hedge against the risk of interest rate falls by buying a call option over interest rate futures.

Such an option can also be called a floor.

Options terminology – Collars

- A company buys an option to protect against an adverse movement whilst allowing it to take advantage of a favourable movement in interest rates. The option will be more expensive than a futures hedge. The company must pay for the flexibility to take advantage of a favourable movement.

- A collar is a way of achieving some flexibility at a lower cost than a straight option.

- Under a collar arrangement the company limits its ability to take advantage of a favourable movement.

- For example, for a borrower, it buys a cap (a put option) as normal but also sells a floor (a call option) on the same futures contract, but with a different exercise price.

- The floor sets a minimum cost for the company. The counterparty is willing to pay the company for this guarantee of a minimum income. Thus the company gets paid for limiting its ability to take advance of a favourable movement if the interest rate falls below the floor rate the company does not benefit therefore the counterparty does.

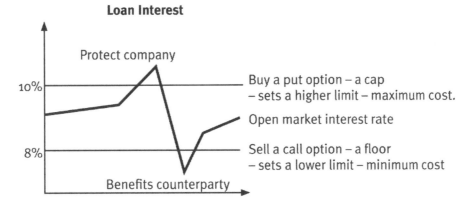

- It involves a company arranging both a minimum and a maximum limit on its interest rates payments or receipts. It enables a company to convert a floating rate of interest into a semi-fixed rate of interest.

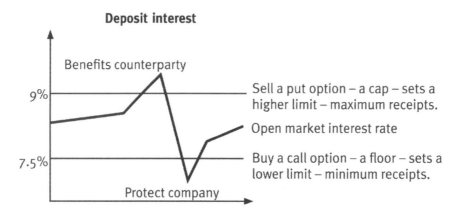

Test your understanding 7

A company wishes to borrow $10 million on the 1st of March for three months. The company can borrow at SOFR + a fixed margin of 2%. SOFR is currently 8%.

It is keen to hedge using options, to prevent an increase in SOFR rate causing the borrowing rate to rise above the existing level. However, having made initial enquiries, it has been discouraged by the cost of the option premium.

A member of its treasury team has suggested the use of a collar to reduce the premium cost of the purchased option.

Market data: Interest rate options

Exercise price	CALLS		PUTS	
	March	June	March	June
92.00	0.80	0.77	0.20	0.22
93.00	0.15	0.12	0.60	0.70

Required:

Calculate the effective interest rate the company will pay using a collar if:

(a) **SOFR rises to 9.5% and futures prices move to 90.20.**

(b) **SOFR falls to 4.5% and futures prices move to 96.10.**

7   Interest rate swaps

Introduction

An interest rate swap is an agreement whereby the parties agree to swap a floating stream of interest payments for a fixed stream of interest payments and via versa. There is no exchange of principal:

- The companies involved are termed 'counter-parties'.

- Swaps can run for up to 30 years.

- Swaps can be used to hedge against an adverse movement in interest rates. Say a company has a $200m floating loan and the treasurer believes that interest rates are likely to rise over the next five years. She could enter into a five-year swap with a counter party to swap into a fixed rate of interest for the next five years. From year six onwards, the company will once again pay a floating rate of interest.

- A swap can be used to obtain cheaper finance. A swap should result in a company being able to borrow what they want at a better rate under a swap arrangement, than borrowing it directly themselves.

Calculations based on splitting gains

- The precise details of the swap arrangement will depend on how the potential gains are split between the two counter-parties.

Illustration 4 – Interest rate swap

Company A wishes to raise $10 million and to pay interest at a floating rate, as it would like to be able to take advantage of any fall in interest rates. It can borrow for one year at a fixed rate of 10% or at a floating rate of 1% above SOFR.

Company B also wishes to raise $10 million. It would prefer to issue fixed rate debt because it wants certainty about future interest payments, but can only borrow for one year at 13% fixed or SOFR + 2% floating, as it has a lower credit rating than company A.

Required:

Calculate the effective swap rate for each company – assume savings are split equally.

Solution

Step 1: Identify the type of loan with the biggest difference in rates.

- *Answer:* Fixed

Step 2: Identify the party that can borrow this type of loan the cheapest.

- *Answer:* Company A

- Thus Company A should borrow fixed, company B variable, reflecting their comparative advantages.

Step 3:

- Company A has cheaper borrowing in both fixed and variable. Interest rate differentials are 3% for fixed and 1% for variable. The difference between these (2%) is the potential gain from the swap.

- Splitting this equally between the two counter parties, each should gain by 1%.

One way (there are many!) of achieving this is for A to pay B SOFR (variable) and for B to pay A 10%.

Summary

	A	B
Actual borrowing	(10%)	(SOFR + 2%)
A to B	(SOFR)	SOFR
B to A	10%	(10%)
Interest rates after swap	**(SOFR)**	**(12%)**
Open market cost – no swap	(SOFR + 1%)	(13%)
Saving	1%	1%

Test your understanding 8

Company X wishes to raise $50 million. It would prefer to issue fixed rate debt and can borrow for one year at 6% fixed or SOFR + 80 points.

Company Y also wishes to raise $50 million and to pay interest at a floating rate. It can borrow for one year at a fixed rate of 5% or at SOFR + 50 points.

Required:

Calculate the effective swap rate for each company – assume savings are split equally.

Calculations involving swap quotes from intermediaries

In practice a bank normally arranges the swap and will quote the following:

- The 'ask rate' at which the bank is willing to receive a fixed interest cash flow stream in exchange for paying a certain reference rate such as SOFR.

- The 'bid rate' that they are willing to pay in exchange for receiving SOFR.

- The difference between these gives the bank's profit margin and is usually at least 2 basis points.

Illustration 5 – Interest rate swap via an intermediary

Co A currently has a 12-month loan at a fixed rate of 5% but would like to swap to variable. It can currently borrow at a variable rate of SOFR + 12 basis points.

The bank is currently quoting 12-month swap rates of 4.90 (bid) and 4.95 (ask).

Required:

Show Co A's financial position if it enters the swap.

Solution

	Co A
Actual borrowing	(5.00%)
Payment to bank	(SOFR)
Receipt from bank (bid)	4.90%
	————————
Net interest rate after swap	**(SOFR + 0.10%)**
	————————
Open market cost – no swap	(SOFR + 0.12%)
Saving	2 basis points

Test your understanding 9

Co B has a 12-month loan at a variable rate of SOFR + 15 basis points but, due to fears over interest rate rises, would like to swap to a fixed rate. It can currently borrow at 5.12% fixed.

The bank is currently quoting 12-month swap rates of 4.90 (bid) and 4.95 (ask). Assume this is the same bank as in the previous illustration.

Required:

Show Co B's financial position if it enters the swap. Comment on the bank's position, bearing in mind the positions of Co A (in the previous Illustration) and Co B.

Further swap example

Company A has a 12 month loan at a variable rate of SOFR + 50 basis points but, due to fears over interest rate rises, would like to swap to a fixed rate. It can currently borrow at 5.40% fixed.

Company B currently has a 12 month loan at a fixed rate of 4.85% but would like to swap to variable. It can currently borrow at a variable rate of SOFR + 65 basis points.

The bank is currently quoting 12 month swap rates of 4.50 (bid) and 4.52 (ask).

Required:

Show how the swap via the intermediary would work.

Solution

- Co A already has a variable outflow so must receive SOFR from the bank to convert this to fixed. It will pay the bank the ask rate.

- Similarly Co B must pay the bank variable and receive fixed at the bid rate.

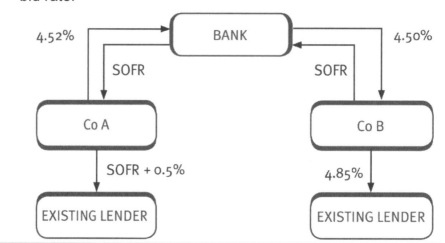

	A	B
Actual borrowing	(SOFR + 0.5%)	(4.85%)
Payment to bank	(4.52%)	(SOFR)
Receipt from bank	SOFR	4.50%
Net interest rates after swap	**(5.02%)**	**(SOFR + 0.35%)**
Open market cost – no swap	(5.40%)	(SOFR + 0.65%)
Saving	38 basis points	30 basis points

Note: In this case A can borrow variable cheaper but B can get the best fixed rates. In this case the total potential saving = D fixed + D variable = 55 + 15 = 70 basis points.

Of this, 2 basis points have gone to the bank via the spread in quoted prices, leaving 68 to be shared between the two companies.

Using the yield curve and FRA rates to set swap rates

In the examples of swap agreements above, the bank agreed to pay a fixed stream of payments to a company in exchange for a variable stream of payments made by the company to the bank (or vice versa).

The bank decides what the fixed payment should be by analysing the company's yield curve.

The key consideration is that at the inception of the swap:

PV of the variable rate payments = PV of the fixed rate payments

when both are discounted at the spot yield.

Notice how, in the Illustration below, the calculated swap rate payments are based on the forward interest rates/FRA rates (calculated earlier in this chapter). This is because the forward rates are our best estimate of what the actual interest rates might be in the future.

Numerical illustration

Stone Co has $10 million of debt finance, and it pays interest at a variable rate based on its current yield curve rates of:

Year	Individual yield curve (%)
1	3.96
2	4.25
3	4.56

There is a likelihood that interest rates will rise over the next few months, so the Stone Co financial manager has asked the bank to arrange a three year swap, where Stone Co will pay a fixed annual rate to the bank, in exchange for a variable rate based on the given yield curve rate less 30 basis points.

Required:

Assuming that Stone Co will receive a variable rate based on the given yield curve rate less 30 basis points from the bank, calculate the fixed rate of interest which Stone Co will have to pay to the bank in the swap.

Solution

The bank's variable payments under the swap agreement (based on the current yield curve rates) will be:

Year	%
1	3.96 – 0.30 = 3.66%, or $366k on $10m
2	4.54 **(W1)** – 0.30 = 4.24%, or $424k on $10m
3	5.18 **(W1)** – 0.30 = 4.88%, or $488k on $10m

(W1) The payments in year 2 and year 3 have to be estimated, using the forward interest rates calculated in TYU 1 earlier in this chapter. The 12 – 24 FRA rate for Stone Co was 4.54%, and the 24 – 36 FRA rate was 5.18%.

Hence, to make sure that the fixed payments (X per year) are equal in present value terms to these expected variable payments:

$(X/1.0396) + (X/1.0425^2) + (X/1.0456^3) = (366k/1.0396) + (424k/1.0425^2) + (488k/1.0456^3)$

Therefore $0.962X + 0.920X + 0.875X = 352k + 390k + 427k$

so $2.757X = 1,169k$

$X = 1,169k / 2.757$

$X = \$424k$

On the $10m debt, this is a rate of 4.24%.

Student Accountant article

The examiner's article 'Determining interest rate forwards and their application to swap valuation' in the Technical Articles section of the ACCA website covers the calculation of swap rates in more detail.

Options over swaps

- Swaptions are hybrid derivative products that integrate the benefits of swaps and options. They are options on swaps.

- The purchaser of an interest rate swaption has the right, but not the obligation, to enter into an interest rate swap at some future date on terms agreed today. An upfront premium is payable.

Swaption illustration

Shun Co has a $10 million loan, repayable in 5 years, at SOFR + 2%. SOFR is currently at 5.75%. The company is thus exposed to the risk of fluctuating interest rates.

The treasurer believes that SOFR will stay low for the next two years, after which period, however, the outlook is at best uncertain. She would like to hedge this risk but is not sure if the current swap rate is the best available. The treasurer wants to lock in the swap rate in two years' time for the following three years and have the flexibility to benefit from a lower swap rate should swap rates fall.

This is achieved by buying a 2-year option on a 3-year pay fixed 7% swap.

The decision that will have to be made in two years is illustrated below:

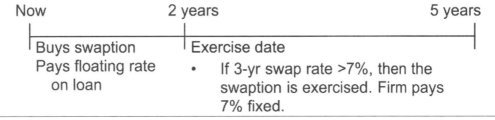

8 Chapter summary

Summary of terminology

	Borrowing	**Depositing**
FRA	Buy an FRA	Sell an FRA
IRG	Call option	Put option
Futures	Sell IR futures	Buy IR futures
Options	Buy put options	Buy call options

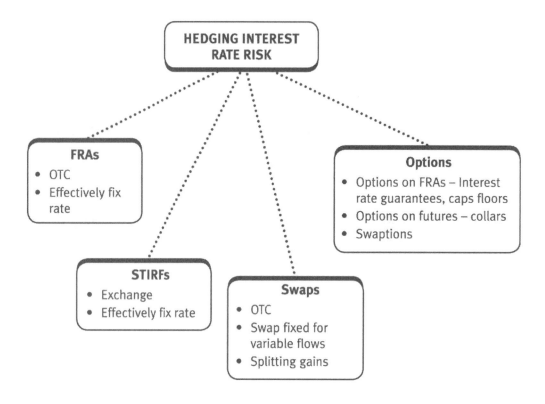

HEDGING INTEREST RATE RISK

FRAs
- OTC
- Effectively fix rate

STIRFs
- Exchange
- Effectively fix rate

Swaps
- OTC
- Swap fixed for variable flows
- Splitting gains

Options
- Options on FRAs – Interest rate guarantees, caps floors
- Options on futures – collars
- Swaptions

Test your understanding answers

Test your understanding 1

A 24 – 36 FRA will fix the rate of interest in 2 years for a 1 year loan.

The FRA rate will be r, such that:

$(1 + r) \times 1.0425^2 = 1.0456^3$

because Stone Co could borrow for 3 years at 4.56% or alternatively the first 2 years at 4.25% followed by the FRA rate for 1 year.

Therefore, r = 5.18%.

The interest rate for a 24 – 36 FRA would be 5.18%.

Test your understanding 2

	IRG at 4%		FRA at 4%	
Market rate	5% – lapse	3% – exercise	5%	3%
Interest	100,000	80,000	80,000	80,000
Premium	(12,000)	(12,000)	–	–
Net receipt	88,000	68,000	80,000	80,000

Comment: The choice between FRA and IRG will depend on expectations and the desired risk exposure of the firm.

Test your understanding 3

- Buy or sell futures? Sell, since we are borrowing

- Number of contracts = (2,000,000/500,000) × 3/3 = 4

- Which expiry date? March, since it expires soonest after the transaction date of 25 March.

Contact the exchange: We need to sell 4 March contracts at a price of 94.90.

Two months later:

Transaction: Interest will be $2m × 3/12 × 7% = $35,000

Futures market:

- Number of ticks movement per contract = (94.90 – 92.90) × 100 = 200

- Value of a tick = $500,000 × 3/12 × 0.0001 = $12.50

- Profit on futures = ticks per contract × tick value × no of contracts = 200 × 12.50 × 4 = $10,000

Hence, net cost = $35,000 – $10,000 = $25,000

Test your understanding 4

(a) The hedge is set up by selling 2 June futures at a futures price of 95.48.

Likely result of the hedge:

	$
Transaction – borrow $1 m for 3 months at SOFR on 31 May (4%)	(10,000)
Futures market: Sell at 95.48, buy at 96.08 (from basis workings below)	
Loss = 0.60%, multiplied by 2 × $500,000 covered for 3 months	(1,500)
Total payment	**(11,500)**

Basis workings:

	1 January	31 May		30 June
SOFR	5.00%	4.00%		
	i.e. 95.00			
Futures price	95.48	96.08	**(W3)**	
Basis	(0.48%)	(0.08%)	**(W2)**	0 **(W1)**

(W1) Basis will reduce to zero by the expiry date of the contract, because on that date, the futures price will equal 100 – the (known) SOFR rate.

(W2) Assuming basis reduces in a linear manner, the basis at 31 May should be 1/6 of the original –0.48% i.e. –0.08%.

(W3) Basis is the difference between (100 – SOFR) (i.e. 96.00 here) and the futures price, so futures price is 96.00 + 0.08% = 96.08.

(b) The lock-in rate is:

100 – (current futures price + unexpired basis on the transaction date).

= 100 – (95.48 – 0.08%) = **4.60%**

Therefore, the likely financial result of the hedge is a total payment of 4.60% × $1 m × 3/12 = **$11,500**

(c) The result is the same under both calculation methods. The lock-in rate method can be used as a shortcut, and it is particularly useful when the SOFR rate on the transaction date is not known.

Test your understanding 5 – Interest rate options

Set up hedge:

- Call or put options? Put here, to cover a borrowing.

- How many contracts? ($10m/$500k) × (6/3) = 40

- Expiry date? September – expires soonest after the transaction date of 31 August.

- Which exercise price?

Choice	Implied rate	Premium	Total cost
94.75	5.25%	0.18%	5.43%
95.00	5.00%	0.65%	5.65%
95.25	4.75%	1.12%	5.87%

So we can see that the 94.75 option is the cheapest total cost.

Contact exchange: We need to buy 40 September put options with an exercise price of 94.75.

Premium payable upfront = 0.18% × 40 × $500,000 × 3/12 = $9,000.

1 month later:

Transaction: Interest = 7.5% × $10m × 6/12 = $375,000

Futures/options market:

Exercise the put option i.e. sell at 94.75

Close out: Buy at futures price of 93.00

Gain is 1.75% (175 ticks) × 40 × $500,000 × 3/12 = $87,500

So, the net interest cost is $375,000 – $87,500 = $287,500 (plus the initial premium of $9,000).

Test your understanding 6 – Futures and options

Futures hedge

To set up the hedge, Chesterfield Co needs to sell 20 September futures contracts, at a price of 96.10.

Basis workings:

	1 April	1 August	30 Sept
SOFR	3.50%		
	(i.e. 96.50)		
Futures price	96.10		
Basis	0.40%	0.13% **(W2)**	0 **(W1)**

(W1) Basis will reduce to zero by the expiry date of the contract, because on that date, the futures price will equal 100 – the (known) SOFR rate.

(W2) Assuming basis reduces in a linear manner, the basis at 1 August should be 2/6 of the original 0.40% i.e. 0.13%.

From this information we can derive the lock-in rate as

100 – (current futures price + unexpired basis on the transaction date)

= 100 – (96.10 + 0.13%) = 3.77%

However, since Chesterfield Co can borrow at 25 basis points above SOFR, the rate applicable to Chesterfield Co is 3.77% + 0.25% = 4.02%.

Therefore, the likely financial result of this futures hedge is that 4.02% × $5m × 6/12 is payable, i.e. $100,500. This will be the case whatever the SOFR rate moves to on the transaction date.

Tutorial note: Although it wasn't necessary to calculate the closing futures price to find the financial result of the futures hedge, the workings below show how it would have been calculated in this case, using the example of a 0.50% increase and decrease in SOFR for reference – a possibility which was trailed by the question. The closing rates can then be used to prove the financial result figure shown above, but also to use in the options hedges below.

Basis workings (revisited)

	1 April	1 August	30 Sept
SOFR	3.50%	3.00% or 4.00%	
	(i.e. 96.50)	(i.e. 97.00 or 96.00)	
Futures price	96.10	96.87 or 95.87	
		(W3)	
Basis	0.40%	0.13%	0

(W3) Basis is the difference between (100 – SOFR) and the futures price, so (for the 3.00% SOFR rate) futures price is (100 – 3.00%) – 0.13% = 96.87.

Therefore, to confirm the financial result of the futures hedge calculated from the lock-in rate above:

$	4.00% SOFR	3.00% SOFR
Interest payable ($5m × 6/12 × (SOFR + 0.25%))	(106,250)	(81,250)
Futures market: Sell at 96.10		
– for 4% SOFR buy at 95.87, so gain = 0.23%	5,750	
– for 3% SOFR buy at 96.87, so loss = 0.77% (in both cases, apply the gain/loss % to the 20 × $500k × 3/12 contracts covered)		(19,250)
Net financial position	(100,500)	(100,500)
Effective interest rate (financial position/$5m) × (12/6) × 100	4.02%	4.02%

Exactly as calculated earlier, by the much quicker lock-in rate method.

Options hedge

To set up the hedge, Chesterfield Co needs to buy 20 September put options, at an exercise price of 96.40. The upfront premium payable will be 0.360% of the amount covered i.e. 0.360% × 20 contracts × $500,000 × (3/12) = $9,000.

The above forecasts of closing futures prices will now be useful to help calculate the financial position under the options hedge:

$	4.00% SOFR	3.00% SOFR
Exercise	Yes	No
Put options, so sell at (exercise price)	96.40	N/A
Buy at closing futures price	95.87	N/A
Therefore, gain on options	0.53%	N/A
Monetary gain on options (0.53% × 20 contracts × $500k × 3/12)	13,250	0
Interest payable ($5m × 6/12 × (SOFR + 0.25%))	(106,250)	(81,250)
Cost of option premium	(9,000)	(9,000)
Net financial position	(102,000)	(90,250)
Effective interest rate (financial position/$5m) × (12/6) × 100	4.08%	3.61%

Hedging using the interest rate futures market fixes the rate at 4.02%, whereas with options on futures, the net cost changes.

If interest rates fall in the future then a hedge using options gives the more favourable rate. However, if interest rates increase then a hedge using futures gives the lower interest payment cost.

Before deciding which method is preferred, the company needs to consider what the more likely future interest rate movement will be.

Test your understanding 7

When borrowing money, the standard option strategy is to buy PUT options. To prevent the interest cost rising above the current level, put options at 92.00 should be used.

Therefore, the collar will involve both buying PUT options and selling CALL options to reduce the overall premium cost.

March options will be used, since they expire sooner after the transaction date of 1st March.

Therefore, the company should buy March 92.00 put options for a cost of 0.20%, and sell March 93.00 call options for a cost of 0.15%.

(a)   Interest rates exceed the cap so the company will exercise its put option: (9.5%) + (2%) + (−0.20 + 0.15) + 92.00 − 90.20 = (9.75%).

(b)   Interest rates have fallen below the floor so the bank will exercise its call option: (4.5%) + (2%) + (−0.20 + 0.15) − 96.10 + 93.00 = (9.65%).

Test your understanding 8

Step 1: Identify the type of loan with the biggest difference in rates.

- Answer: Fixed.

Step 2: Identify the party that can borrow this type of loan the cheapest.

- Answer: Company Y should borrow fixed, company X variable.

Step 3: Split gains.

- Company Y has cheaper borrowing in both fixed and variable. Interest rate differentials are 1% for fixed and 0.3% for variable. The difference between these (70 basis points) is the potential gain from the swap.

- Splitting this equally between the two counter parties, each should gain by 35 basis points.

- One way of achieving this is for X to pay Y 4.85% and for Y to pay X SOFR (variable).

Summary

	X	Y
Actual borrowing	(SOFR + 0.8%)	(5%)
X to Y	(4.85%)	4.85%
Y to X	SOFR	(SOFR)
	————	————
Interest rates after swap	(5.65%)	(SOFR + 0.15%)
	————	————
Open market cost – no swap	(6%)	(SOFR + 0.5%)
Saving	35 points	35 points

Test your understanding 9

	B
Actual borrowing	(SOFR + 0.15%)
Payment to bank (ask)	(4.95%)
Receipt from bank	SOFR
Net interest rates after swap	**(5.10%)**
Open market cost – no swap	(5.12%)
Saving	2 basis points

Both Co A and Co B have saved 2 basis points by entering their swaps.

The bank has made a profit of 5 basis points – the difference between the bid and ask rates:

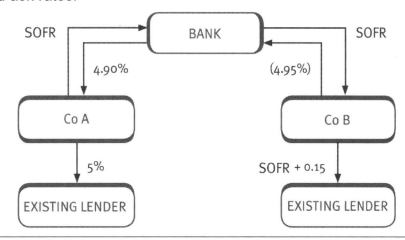

Strategic aspects of acquisitions

Chapter learning objectives

Study guide section	Study guide outcome	
C1: Acquisitions and mergers versus other growth strategies	(a)	Discuss the arguments for and against the use of acquisitions and mergers as a method of corporate expansion.
	(b)	Evaluate the corporate and competitive nature of a given acquisition proposal.
	(c)	Advise upon the criteria for choosing an appropriate target for acquisition.
	(d)	Compare the various explanations for the high failure rate of acquisitions in enhancing shareholder value.
	(e)	Evaluate, from a given context, the potential for synergy separately classified as: (i) Revenue synergy (ii) Cost synergy (iii) Financial synergy.
	(f)	Evaluate the use of the reverse takeover as a method of acquisition and as a way of obtaining a stock market listing.

C3: Regulatory framework and processes

(a) Demonstrate an understanding of the principal factors influencing the development of the regulatory framework for mergers and acquisitions globally and, in particular, be able to compare and contrast the shareholder versus the stakeholder models of regulation.

(b) Identify the main regulatory issues which are likely to arise in the context of a given offer and (i) assess whether the offer is likely to be in the shareholders' best interests (ii) advise the directors of a target entity on the most appropriate defence if a specific offer is to be treated as hostile.

C4: Financing acquisitions and mergers

(a) Compare the various sources of financing available for a proposed cash-based acquisition.

(b) Evaluate the advantages and disadvantages of a financial offer for a given acquisition proposal using pure or mixed mode financing and recommend the most appropriate offer to be made.

(c) Assess the impact of a given financial offer on the reported financial position and performance of the acquirer.

PER

One of the PER performance objectives (PO09 – Evaluate Investment and Financing Decisions) is to be able to select investment or merger and acquisition opportunities.

Working through this chapter should help you understand how to demonstrate that objective.

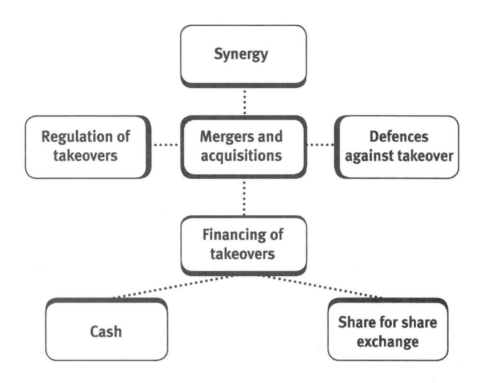

 1 Mergers and acquisitions – The terms explained

Terminology

The term 'merger' is usually used to describe the joining together of two or more entities.

Strictly, if one entity acquires a majority shareholding in another, the second is said to have been acquired (or 'taken over') by the first. If the two entities join together to submerge their separate identities into a new entity, the process is described as a merger.

In fact, the term 'merger' is often used even when an acquisition/takeover has actually occurred, because of the cultural impact on the acquired entity – the word merger makes the arrangement sound like a partnership between equals.

Types of merger/acquisition

Types of merger

The arguments put forward for a merger may depend on its type:

- Horizontal integration
- Vertical integration
- Conglomerate integration.

Horizontal integration

Two companies in the same industry, whose operations are very closely related, are combined, e.g. Volkswagen with Porsche, and the UK banks and building societies mergers, e.g. Lloyds TSB and HBOS.

Main motives: economies of scale, increased market power, improved product mix.

Disadvantage: can be referred to relevant competition authorities.

Vertical integration

Two companies in the same industry, but from different stages of the production chain merger.

e.g. major players in the oil industry tend to be highly vertically integrated.

Main motives: increased certainty of supply or demand and just-in-time inventory systems leading to major savings in inventory holding costs.

Conglomerate integration

A combination of unrelated businesses, there is no common thread and the main synergy lies with the management skills and brand name, e.g. General Electrical Company (GE) (management) or Virgin (brand).

Main motives: risk reduction through diversification and cost reduction (management) or improved revenues (brand).

2 The reasons for growth by acquisition or merger

Key reasons for acquisition

The potential for synergy is often given as the main reason for growth by acquisition. However, other more specific reasons are:

- Increased market share/power
- Economies of scale
- Combining complementary needs
- Improving efficiency
- A lack of profitable investment opportunities (surplus cash)

- Tax relief

- Reduced competition

- Asset-stripping

- Diversification – to reduce risk

- Shares of the target are undervalued.

More on the reasons for merger/acquisition

The following reasons have been suggested as to why entities merge or acquire.

- **Increased market share/power**. In a market with limited product differentiation, price may be the main competitive weapon. In such a case, large market share may enable an entity to drive prices – for example reducing prices in the short term to eliminate competition before increasing prices later.

- **Economies of scale**. These result when expansion of the scale of productive capacity of an entity (or industry) causes total production costs to increase less than proportionately with output. It is clear that a merger which resulted in horizontal or vertical integration could give such economies since, at the very least, duplication would be avoided. But how could a conglomerate merger give economies? Possibly through central facilities such as offices, accounting departments and computer departments being rationalised. (Indeed, both sets of management are unlikely to be needed in their entirety.)

- **Combining complementary needs**. Many small entities have a unique product but lack the engineering and sales organisations necessary to produce and market it on a large scale. A natural course of action would be to merge with a larger entity. Both entities gain something – the small entity gets 'instant' engineering and marketing departments, and the large entity gains the revenue and other benefits which a unique product can bring. Also if, as is likely, the resources which each entity requires are complementary, the merger may well produce further opportunities that neither would see in isolation.

- **Improving efficiency**. A classic takeover target would be an entity operating in a potentially lucrative market but which, owing to poor management or inefficient operations, does not fully exploit its opportunities. Of course, being taken over would not be the only way of improving such a poor performer, but such an entity's managers may be unwilling to give themselves the sack.

- **A lack of profitable investment opportunities – surplus cash.**
  An entity may be generating a substantial volume of cash, but sees
  few profitable investment opportunities. If it does not wish to simply
  pay out the surplus cash as dividends (because of its long-term
  dividend policy, perhaps), it could use it to acquire other entities.
  A reason for doing so is that entities with excess cash are usually
  regarded as ideal targets for acquisition – a case of buy or be
  bought.

- **Tax relief.** An entity may be unable to claim tax relief because it
  does not generate sufficient profits. It may therefore wish to merge
  with another entity which does generate such profits.

- **Reduced competition.** It is often one benefit of merger activity –
  provided that it does not fall foul of the competition authorities.

- **Asset-stripping.** A predator acquires a target and sells the easily
  separable assets, perhaps closing down or disposing of some of its
  operations.

The following reasons are of questionable validity:

- **Diversification, to reduce risk.** While acquiring an entity in a
  different line of activity may diversify away risk for the entities
  involved, this is surely irrelevant to the shareholders. They could
  have performed exactly the same diversification simply by holding
  shares in both entities. The only real diversification produced is in
  the risk attaching to the managers' and employees' jobs, and this is
  likely to make them more complacent than before – to the detriment
  of shareholders' future returns.

- **Shares of the target entity are undervalued.** This may well be the
  case, although it would conflict with the efficient markets theory.
  However, the shareholders of the entity planning the takeover would
  derive as much benefit (at a lower administrative cost) from buying
  such undervalued shares themselves. This also assumes that the
  acquirer entity's management are better at valuing shares than
  professional investors in the market place.

Advantages/disadvantages of organic growth and acquisition

Acquisition is often undertaken as an alternative to organic growth. It is important to understand the relative advantages and disadvantages of these two alternatives.

Advantages of organic growth (disadvantages of growth by acquisition)

- Organic growth allows planning of strategic growth in line with stated objectives.

- It is less risky than growth by acquisition – done over time.

- The cost is often much higher in an acquisition – significant acquisition premiums.

- Avoids problems integrating new acquired companies – the integration process is often a difficult process due to cultural differences between the two companies.

- An acquisition places an immediate pressure on current management resources to learn to manage the new business.

Advantages of growth by acquisition (disadvantages of organic growth)

- Quickest way is to enter a new product or geographical market.

- Reduces the risk of over-supply and excessive competition.

- Fewer competitors.

- Increase market power in order to be able to exercise some control over the price of the product, e.g. monopoly or by collusion with other producers.

- Acquiring the target company's staff highly trained staff – may give a competitive edge.

Corporate and competitive aspects of mergers

Methods of mergers and acquisitions

Though the terms are used loosely to describe a variety of activities, in every case the end result is that two companies become a single enterprise, in fact if not in name, the end result is achieved by:

- transfer of assets
- transfer of shares.

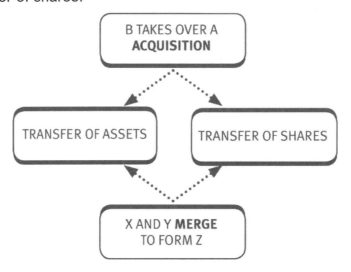

The two methods of undertaking acquisitions and mergers are summarised as follows:

	Transfer of assets	Transfer of shares
Acquisition (B takes over A)	B acquires trade and assets from A for cash. A is then liquidated, and the proceeds received by the old shareholders of A.	B acquires shares in A from A's shareholders in exchange for cash. A, as a subsidiary of B, may subsequently transfer its trade and assets to its new parent company (B).
Merger (X and Y merge to form Z)	Z acquires trade and assets from both X and Y in return for shares in Z. X and Y are then liquidated and the shares in Z distributed in specie to the shareholders of X and Y.	Z acquires shares in X and Y in return for its own shares. X and Y as subsidiaries of Z may subsequently transfer their trade and assets to their new parent company (Z).

Corporate issues arising on acquisition

Various corporate issues can arise on acquisition of one company by another:

- Impact on board structure – a power struggle among the directors will not help the post-acquisition integration of the two firms.

- Board hostility.

- Impact on corporate governance.

- Culture differences – this can be especially marked when the two companies are based in different countries.

- Loss of key personnel from target company.

- Integration difficulties – e.g. systems, operations.

- Adverse PR – especially if there is a threat of job losses as a consequence of the takeover.

Competitive issues

When considering acquisitions and mergers the competitive aspects need to be considered.

- One of the motives for acquiring a company is to remove competitive rivalry from the market.

For example, consolidation in the pharmaceuticals industry:

In 2014, Novartis AG and GlaxoSmithKline agreed a merger that reduced the number of competitors and as such the level of competition in this market.

They agreed to swap $20 billion in assets in what amounted to major restructurings for both firms.

Novartis bought GlaxoSmithKline's cancer drug business, GSK took Novartis's vaccine business, and the companies agreed to combine their respective over-the-counter and consumer drug businesses.

---

3 Identifying possible acquisition targets

When a company decides to expand by acquisition, its directors will produce criteria (size, location, finances, products, expertise, management) against which targets can be judged.

Directors and/or advisors then seek out prospective targets in the business sectors it is interested in.

The team then examines each prospect closely from both a commercial and financial viewpoint against the important criteria.

Steps in identifying acquisition targets

Steps to be taken

Assuming that external growth has been decided upon, the firm needs to consider the steps to be taken. A possible sequence of steps is as follows (given in the context of acquisitions, although much will apply to mergers as well):

- Strategic steps

    - **Step 1:** Appraise possible acquisitions.

    - **Step 2:** Select the best acquisition target.

    - **Step 3:** Decide on the financial strategy, i.e. the amount and the structure of the consideration.

- Tactical steps

    - **Step 1:** Launch a dawn raid subject to relevant regulation.

    - **Step 2:** Make a public offer for the shares not held.

    - **Step 3:** Success will be achieved if more than 50% of the target company's shares are acquired.

Information required for the appraisal of acquisitions

The following needs to be considered when appraising a target for acquisition:

- Organisation

- Sales and marketing

- Production, supply and distribution

- Technology

- Accounting information

- Treasury information

- Tax information.

When considering a target for acquisition a company need to assess carefully the following – this information would only be available pre-acquisition where an agreed bid was negotiated.

1 Organisation	2 Sales and marketing
Special requirements, e.g.	Special requirements, e.g.
• organisation chart, key management and quality • employee analysis, terms and conditions • unionisation and industrial relations • pension arrangements. Clearly, businesses are about people, and their quality and organisation requires examination. Further, comparison needs to be made with existing group remuneration levels and pensions, to determine the financial impact of their adoption, where appropriate, on the acquisition.	• historic and future sales volumes by product group and geographical location • market position, including customers and competition for major product groups • normal trading terms • historic sales and promotions expenditure by product group. This additional information should provide a detailed assessment of the market and customer base to be acquired.
3 Production, supply and distribution	4 Technology
Special requirements, e.g.	Special requirements, e.g.
• total capacity and current usage levels • need for future capital investment to replace existing assets, or meet expanded volume requirements. This would provide an assessment of the overhead burden due to under capacity production and of the potential future capital requirements to maintain the required productive capacity of the business.	• details of particular technical skills inherent in the acquisition • research and development organisation and historic expenditure. Thus, an analysis would be made of the technical assets acquired, and their past and potential future maintenance costs.

5 **Accounting information**	6 **Treasury information**
Special requirements, e.g.	Special requirements, e.g.
• company searches for all companies	• amounts, terms and security of bank facilities and all other external loans and leasing facilities (including capitalised value, if not capitalised)
• historic consolidated and individual company accounts	• details of restrictive covenants and trust deeds for such facilities
• detailed explanation of accounting policies	
• explanation of major fluctuations in sales, gross margins, overheads and capital employed.	• details of forward foreign exchange contracts, and exchange management policies.
These provide the background for basic financial analysis.	All this information will be useful in planning the financial absorption of the business into the acquiring group, and will in particular reveal any 'hidden assets' (e.g. low coupon loans) and 'hidden liabilities' (guarantees liable to be called, or hedged foreign exchange positions).

7 **Tax information**	8 **Other commercial/financial information**
Special requirements, e.g.	Special requirements, e.g.
• historic tax computations, agreed, submitted and unsubmitted by company • significant disputes with revenue • trading losses brought forward • potential tax liabilities, including deferred tax and sales tax • understanding of tax position of vendors, especially with respect to capital gains tax liability as a result of sale.	• details of ordinary and preference shareholders, with amounts held by each class, and voting restrictions if appropriate, together with share options held and partly paid shares • contingent liabilities, including litigation, forward purchase or sales contracts, including capital commitments and loss-making contracts not otherwise provided for • actuarial assessment of current pension funding, with assumptions.
This can identify any potential tax assets (e.g. utilisable losses) and liabilities (e.g. likely payments of tax not provided), and assist in pricing and structuring the transaction having regard to the vendor's tax position.	This relates primarily to a better understanding of the capital structure and shareholdings to be acquired, and any potential financial liabilities overhanging the acquired company, of which the most significant may well be underfunded pension schemes.

 4   Synergy

Definition

Synergy may be defined as two or more entities coming together to produce a result not independently obtainable.

For example, a merged entity will only need one marketing department, so there may be savings generated compared to two separate entities.

Importance of synergy in mergers and acquisitions

For a successful business combination we should be looking for a situation where:

MV of combined company (AB)   > MV of A + MV of B

Note: MV means Market Value here.

If this situation occurs we have experienced synergy, where the whole is worth more than the sum of the parts. This is often expressed as 2 + 2 = 5.

It is important to note that synergy is not automatic. In an efficient stock market A and B will be correctly valued before the combination, and we need to ask how synergy will be achieved, i.e. why any increase in value should occur.

Sources of synergy

There are several reasons why synergistic gains arise. These break down into the following:

- **revenue synergy**, such as market power and combining complementary resources

- **cost synergy**, such as economies of scale

- **financial synergy**, such as elimination of inefficiency.

Types of synergy

Revenue synergy

Sources of revenue synergy include:

Market power/eliminate competition

Firms may merge to increase market power in order to be able to exercise some control over the price of the product. Horizontal mergers may enable the firm to obtain a degree of monopoly power, which could increase its profitability by pushing up the price of goods because customers have few alternatives.

Economies of vertical integration

Some acquisitions involve buying out other companies in the same production chain, e.g. a manufacturer buying out a raw material supplier or a retailer. This can increase profits by 'cutting out the middle man', improved control of raw materials needed for production, or by avoiding disputes with what were previously suppliers or customers.

Complementary resources

It is sometimes argued that by combining the strengths of two companies a synergistic result can be obtained. For example, combining a company specialising in research and development with a company strong in the marketing area could lead to gains.

Cost synergy

Sources of cost synergy are:

Economies of scale

Horizontal combinations (of companies in a similar line of business) are often claimed to reduce costs and therefore increase profits due to economies of scale. These can occur in the production, marketing or finance areas. Economies of scale occur through such factors as:

- fixed operating and administrative costs being spread over a larger production volume

- consolidation of manufacturing capacity on fewer and larger sites

- use of space capacity

- increased buyer power, i.e. bulk discounts

- savings on duplicated central services and accounting staff costs.

These benefits are sometimes also claimed for conglomerate combinations (of companies in unrelated areas of business) in financial and marketing costs.

Economies of scope

May occur in marketing as a result of joint advertising and common distribution.

Financial synergy

Sources of financial synergy include:

Elimination of inefficiency

If the 'victim' company in a takeover is badly managed its performance and hence its value can be improved by the elimination of inefficiencies. Improvements could be obtained in the areas of production, marketing and finance.

Elimination of inefficiency – Bargain buying

If the 'victim' company in a merger is badly managed its performance and hence its value can be improved by the elimination of inefficiencies.

Tax shields/accumulated tax losses

Another possible financial synergy exists when one company in an acquisition or merger is able to use tax shields or accumulated tax losses, which would have been unavailable to the other company.

Surplus cash

Companies with large amounts of surplus cash may see the acquisition of other companies as the only possible application for these funds. Of course, increased dividends could cure the problem of surplus cash, but this may be rejected for reasons of tax or dividend stability.

Corporate risk diversification

One of the primary reasons put forward for all mergers but especially conglomerate mergers is that the income of the combined entity will be less volatile (less risky) as its cash flows come from a wide variety of products and markets. This is a reduction in total risk, but has little or no effect on the systematic risk.

Diversification and financing

If the future cash flow streams of the two companies are not perfectly positively correlated then by combining the two companies the variability of their operating cash flow may be reduced. A more stable cash flow is more attractive to creditors and this could lead to cheaper financing.

Others

Other sources of synergy are:

Surplus managerial talent

Companies with highly skilled managers can make use of this resource only if they have problems to solve. The acquisition of inefficient companies is sometimes the only way of fully utilising skilled managers.

Speed

Acquisitions may be far faster than organic growth in obtaining a presence in a new and growing market.

Test your understanding 1 – Williams and GSL

Williams Co is the manufacturer of cosmetics, soaps and shower gels. It also markets its products using its own highly successful sales and marketing department. It is seen as an employer of choice and as such has a talented and loyal work-force with a history of developing new and exciting products which have sold well. It is now considering extending its range, however it has currently a build-up of unfulfilled orders due to a lack of capacity.

GSL is a well-known herbal remedy for skin problems. GSL Co was founded by three brothers in the 1950s and until the death of the remaining brother in 2004 has performed well – however the new Chairman has limited experience and the company has not performed well over recent years. GSL has a dedicated team of herbalists who have developed products, which would find a ready market – however, there is insufficient funds and expertise to correctly market these products and market share is low.

Williams' products and GSL's products are made using similar production technologies and their financial and administrative systems are similar and it is hoped savings can be made here.

Required:

Identify any potential synergy gains that would emerge from a merger of Williams and GSL.

The impact of mergers and acquisitions on stakeholders

Impact on acquiring company's shareholders

The existence of synergy has been discussed above as a key benefit to shareholders of an acquisition. All companies have a primary objective to maximise shareholder wealth, so it is clear that if synergy can be achieved, an acquisition should benefit the acquiring company's shareholders.

Impact on the target company's shareholders

The acquiring company will often pay a premium to the shareholders of the target company, to encourage them to sell their shares. Therefore there is also a financial benefit to them when a takeover happens.

Impact on lenders/debt holders

Debt will often be repayable in the event of a change in control. It all depends on whether the bank borrowings and bonds contain a change in control clause. With bank borrowings they almost certainly will. The risk profile of the acquirer may be quite different from that of the original borrower and the bank will not wish to become exposed to a higher credit risk. Bonds may be the same.

The acquirer is therefore likely to need to arrange new financing, debt and/or equity financing as appropriate in advance of the takeover.

Impact on managers and staff

In many acquisitions, an easy way to generate synergy is to make some staff redundant to avoid there being duplication of roles. Therefore, the managers and employees, particularly of the target company, often view a takeover with dread. However, the managers of the acquiring company often see takeovers as an opportunity, to demand higher salaries and bonuses now that they manage a larger company.

The acquirer may wish to retain many managers whose knowledge and skills may be essential to the successful continuation of the business, at least in the short term. In such a case, the acquirer may seek assurance and contractual tie-ins to ensure that such people remain with the business for a certain period of time.

Impact on society as a whole

Governments monitor takeovers carefully, and if they feel that a takeover will not be in the best interests of society as a whole, the takeover can be investigated and sometimes stopped. Competition law in most countries prevents monopolies being created which might be able to exploit their power to take advantage of customers.

Problems with acquisitions

If an acquisition generates the expected synergy, shareholders in both the acquiring company and the target should see an increase in wealth.

However, not all mergers and acquisitions are successful.

Synergy will not automatically arise. Unless the management of the two entities can work together effectively, there is a chance that any forecast benefits of the new arrangement might not be realised.

In many cases, the forecast synergy is not achieved, or is not as large as expected. It may be that the premium paid on acquisition by the acquirer was too high, so the shareholder value of the acquirer actually reduced as a result of the acquisition.

Also, cultural clashes between the two companies can make the integration of the two businesses very difficult.

Another reason for failure is that the opportunity cost of the investment could be too high. This means that the acquirer realises that the funds tied up in the acquisition could have been better used, to generate higher returns elsewhere.

Detailed reasons why mergers/acquisitions fail

The fit/lack of fit syndrome

There may be a good fit of products or services, but a serious lack of fit in terms of management styles or corporate structure.

Lack of industrial or commercial fit

Failure can result from a horizontal or vertical takeover where the acquired entity turns out not to have the product range or industrial position that the acquirer anticipated. Usually in the case where a customer or supplier is acquired, the acquirer knows a lot about the acquired entity; even so, there may be aspects of the acquired entity's operations which may cause unexpected problems for the acquirer, such that, even in these cases, a prospective acquisition should be planned very carefully and not be based solely on experience gained from a direct relationship with the acquired entity.

Lack of goal congruence

This may apply not only to the acquired entity but, more dangerously, to the acquirer, whereby disputes over the treatment of the acquired entity might well take away the benefits of an otherwise excellent acquisition.

'Cheap' purchases

The 'turn around' costs of an acquisition purchased at what seems to be a bargain price may well turn out to be a high multiple of that price. In these situations, the amount of resources in terms of cash and management time could well also damage the acquirer's core business. In preparing a bid, a would-be acquirer should always take into account the likely total cost of an acquisition, including the input of its own resources, before deciding on making an offer or setting an offer price.

Paying too much

The fact that a high premium is paid for an acquisition does not necessarily mean that it will fail. Failure would result only if the price paid is beyond that which the acquirer considers acceptable to increase satisfactorily the long-term wealth of its shareholders.

Failure to integrate effectively

An acquirer needs to have a workable and clear plan of the extent to which the acquired company is to be integrated, and the amount of autonomy to be granted. At best, the plan should be negotiated with the acquired entity's management and staff, but its essential requirements should be fairly but firmly carried out. The plan must address such problems as differences in management styles, incompatibilities in data information systems, and continued opposition to the acquisition by some of the acquired entity's staff. Failure to plan can – and often does – lead to failure of an acquisition, as it leads to drift and demotivation, not only within the acquired entity but also within the acquirer itself.

Every aspect of a prospective acquisition, as it will affect the would-be acquirer, should be weighed up before embarking on a bid. Problems of integration have a much better chance of being resolved before bidding action is taken than they do after the event, when many more complications can ensue.

Even if a product fit is satisfactory, the would-be acquirer should be satisfied that the aspects of its own operation affected by the bid will be properly adaptable to the new activities. Running the rule carefully over one's own operations may yield vital information as to areas which may need adaptation before a bid can be contemplated, and provide vital clues to appropriate areas for search when a bid has actually been launched. One factor of special importance is a clear assessment of the flexibility of one's own information systems.

Inability to manage change

Several of the above points stress the need for an acquirer to plan effectively before and after an acquisition if failure is to be avoided. But this in itself calls for the ability to accept change – perhaps even radical change – from established routines and practices. Indeed, many acquisitions fail mainly because the acquirer is unable – or unwilling – reasonably to adjust its own activities to help ensure a smooth takeover. One such situation is where the acquired company has a demonstrably better data information system than the acquirer, which it might be greatly in the acquirer's interest to adopt.

5   Defences against hostile takeover bids

Any listed company needs to be aware that a bid might be received at any time.

The directors of a company subject to a hostile takeover bid should act in the best interests of their shareholders. However, in practice they will also consider the views of other stakeholders (such as employees, and themselves).

If the board of directors of a target company decides to fight a bid that appears to be financially attractive to their shareholders, then they should consider one of the following defences:

- Pre-bid defences

    – Communicate effectively with shareholders.

    – Revalue non-current assets.

    – Poison pill.

    – Change the Articles of Association (super majority).

- Post-bid defences

    – Appeal to their own shareholders.

    – Attack the bidder.

    – White Knight.

    – Counterbid ('Pacman').

    – Refer the bid to the Competition authorities.

 Details of takeover defences

Pre-bid defences

Communicate effectively with shareholders

This includes having a public relations officer specialising in financial matters liaising constantly with the entity's stockbrokers, keeping analysts fully informed, and speaking to journalists.

Revalue non-current assets

Non-current assets are revalued to current values to ensure that shareholders are aware of true asset value per share.

Poison pill strategy

Here a target company takes steps before a bid has been made to make itself less attractive to a potential bidder. The most common method is for existing shareholders to be given rights to buy future bonds or preference shares. If a bid is made before the date of exercise of the rights, then the rights will automatically be converted into full ordinary shares.

Super majority

The Articles of Association are altered to require that a higher percentage (say 80%) of shareholders have to vote for the takeover.

Post-bid defences

Appeal to their own shareholders

For example, by declaring that the value placed on the target company's shares is too low in relation to the real value and earning power of the company's assets, or alternatively that the market price of the bidder's shares is unjustifiably high and is not sustainable.

A well-managed defensive campaign would include:

(i)   Aggressive publicity on behalf of the company preferably before a bid is received. Investors may be told of any good research ideas within the company and of the management potential or merely be made more aware of the company's achievements.

(ii)   Direct communication with the shareholders in writing stressing the financial and strategic reasons for remaining independent.

Note: Under the City Code in the UK, any forecasts must be examined and reported on by the auditors or consultant accountants.

Attack the bidder

Typically concentrating on the bidder's management style, overall strategy, methods of increasing earnings per share, dubious accounting policies and lack of capital investment.

White Knight strategy

This is where the directors of the target company offer themselves to a more friendly outside interest. This tactic should only be adopted in the last resort as it means that the company will lose its independence. This tactic is acceptable provided that any information given to a preferred bidder is also given to a hostile bidder. The alternative company's management will be considered to be sympathetic to the target company's management.

Counterbid (Pacman defence)

Where the bidding company is itself the subject of a takeover bid by the target company.

Competition authorities

The target entity could seek government intervention by bringing in the Competition authorities. For this to be effective it would have to be proved that the takeover was against the public interest.

Test your understanding 2 – Development of bids

Follow the developments of bids in progress every day by reading a good financial newspaper and/or website. Can you see examples of where the above anti-takeover mechanisms have been used successfully?

Reverse takeovers

A reverse takeover is a type of acquisition/merger that is used by private companies that want to become public companies but want to avoid the high costs (time and money) that normally accompany stock market listings (initial public offerings, or IPOs).

How a reverse takeover works

First, the private company purchases a majority shareholding in a public company. Typically, the private company is larger than the public company.

Then, the private company's shareholders exchange their private company shares for shares in the public company. Effectively, this turns the private company into a public company - its shares can now be publicly traded.

Advantages and disadvantages of reverse takeovers

Reverse takeovers allow a private company to become public without raising capital, which considerably simplifies the process. While conventional IPOs can take months to organise, reverse takeovers can be completed much more quickly, saving management time and money.

After the reverse takeover, the company's shareholders should benefit from all the advantages of a stock market listing (e.g. shares are more marketable, the company's profile is increased).

However, it is sometimes the case that the company's managers are inexperienced in the additional regulatory and compliance requirements of being a public company. These burdens (and costs in terms of time and money) can prove significant.

Also, unless the company's performance makes it attractive to stock market investors, there is no guarantee that simply being a public company will make its shares any more marketable.

Student Accountant article

The article 'Reverse takeovers' in the Technical Articles section of the ACCA website provides further details on this topic.

---

 6   The form of consideration for a takeover

Introduction

When one firm acquires another, two questions must be addressed regarding the form of consideration for the takeover:

1   what form of consideration should be offered? Cash offer, or share exchange, or earnout are the three main choices.

2   if a cash offer is to be made, how should the cash be raised? The choice is generally debt finance or a rights issue to generate the cash (if the entity does not have enough cash already).

The key considerations regarding these two questions are outlined below:

Form of consideration

Cash

In a cash offer, the target company shareholders are offered a fixed cash sum per share.

This method is likely to be suitable only for relatively small acquisitions, unless the bidding entity has an accumulation of cash.

Advantages:

* When the bidder has sufficient cash the takeover can be achieved quickly and at low cost.

* Target company shareholders have certainty about the bid's value i.e. there is less risk compared to accepting shares in the bidding company.

* There is increased liquidity to target company shareholders, i.e. accepting cash in a takeover, is a good way of realising an investment.

* The acceptable consideration is likely to be less than with a share exchange, as there is less risk to target company shareholders. This reduces the overall cost of the bid to the bidding company.

Disadvantages:

* With larger acquisitions the bidder must often borrow in the capital markets or issue new shares in order to raise the cash. This may have an adverse effect on gearing, and also cost of capital due to the increased financial risk.

* For target company shareholders, in some jurisdictions a taxable chargeable gain will arise if shares are sold for cash, but the gain may not be immediately chargeable to tax under a share exchange.

* Target company shareholders may be unhappy with a cash offer, since they are 'bought out' and do not participate in the new group. Of course, this could be seen as an advantage of a cash offer by the bidding company shareholders if they want to keep full control of the bidding company.

Share exchange

In a share exchange, the bidding company issues some new shares and then exchanges them with the target company shareholders. The target company shareholders therefore end up with shares in the bidding company, and the target company's shares all end up in the possession of the bidding company.

Large acquisitions almost always involve an exchange of shares, in whole or in part.

Advantages:

* The bidding company does not have to raise cash to make the payment.

* The bidding company can 'boot strap' earnings per share if it has a higher P/E ratio than the acquired entity.

* Shareholder capital is increased – and gearing similarly improved – as the shareholders of the acquired company become shareholders in the post-acquisition company.

* A share exchange can be used to finance very large acquisitions.

Disadvantages:

- The bidding company's shareholders have to share future gains with the acquired entity, and the current shareholders will have a lower proportionate control and share in profits of the combined entity than before.

- Price risk – there is a risk that the market price of the bidding company's shares will fall during the bidding process, which may result in the bid failing. For example, if a 1 for 2 share exchange is offered based on the fact that the bidding company's shares are worth approximately double the value of the target company's shares, the bid might fail if the value of the bidding company's shares falls before the acceptance date.

Earn-out

Definition of an earn-out arrangement: A procedure whereby owners/managers selling an entity receive a portion of their consideration linked to the financial performance of the business during a specified period after the sale. The arrangement gives a measure of security to the new owners, who pass some of the financial risk associated with the purchase of a new entity to the sellers.

The purchase consideration is sometimes structured so that there is an initial amount paid at the time of acquisition, and the balance deferred.

Some of the deferred balance will usually only become payable if the target entity achieves specified performance targets.

Key issues relating to forms of consideration

Considerations of different stakeholders

In order to evaluate which form of consideration is appropriate in a particular case, it is important to assess the positions of both the target company's shareholders, and the bidding company and its shareholders.

Position of the target company's shareholders

The target company's shareholders may want to retain an interest in the business, in which case a cash offer would not be welcomed. However, there is a greater certainty of value with a cash offer (share prices fluctuate, so in a share exchange the target company's shareholders cannot be completely sure whether they are receiving an appropriate valuation for their shares).

> ### Position of the bidding company and its shareholders
>
> The bidding company will have to issue new shares if it is to undertake a share exchange. This may require the consent of shareholders in a general meeting. The shareholders may be concerned in a share exchange that their control of the bidding company will be diluted by the issue and exchange of shares.
>
> Another key consideration is the impact of the takeover on the bidding company's financial statements. An issue of new shares could reduce the level of earnings per share (a measure which is often used as a key performance measure by market analysts). However, if a cash offer is made, the raising of the necessary cash could have a significant impact on the gearing of the bidding company.

Methods of financing a cash offer

If the bidding company has a large cash surplus, it might be able to make a cash offer without raising any new finance.

However, in most cases, this will not be the case, so various financing options will have to be considered by the bidding company. The main two options are debt or a rights issue.

Debt

The bidding company could borrow the required cash from the bank, or issue bonds in the market.

The advantage of using debt in this situation is the low cost of servicing the debt. However, raising new debt finance will increase the bidding company's gearing. This will increase the risk to the bidding company's shareholders, so might not be acceptable to the shareholders.

Rights issue

If the bidding company shareholders do not want to suffer the increased risk which debt finance would bring, the alternative would be for the bidding company to offer a rights issue to its existing shareholders. In this case, the company's gearing (measured using market values) is not affected, although its earnings per share will fall as new shares are issued.

From the shareholders' point of view, the problem with this financing option is that it is the shareholders themselves who have to find the money to invest.

Evaluating a share for share exchange

One popular question is to comment on the likely acceptance of a share for share offer. The procedure is as follows:

- Value the predator company as an independent entity and hence calculate the value of a share in that company.

- Repeat the procedure for the victim company.

- Calculate the value of the combined company post-integration. This is calculated as:

Value of predator company as independent company	X
Value of victim company as independent company	X
Value of any synergy	X
	–––––
Total value of combined company	X
	–––––

- Calculate the number of shares post-integration:

Number of shares originally in the predator company	X
Number of shares issued to victim company	X
	–––––
Total shares post-integration	X
	–––––

- Calculate the value of a share in the combined company, and use this to assess the change in wealth of the shareholders after the takeover.

 Illustration 1

Company A has 200m shares with a current market value of $4 per share. Company B has 90m shares with a current market value of $2 per share.

A makes an offer of 3 new shares for every 5 currently held in B. A has worked out that the present value of synergies will be $40m.

Required:

Calculate the expected value of a share in the combined company (assuming that the given share prices have not yet moved to anticipate the takeover), and advise the shareholders in company B whether the offer should be accepted.

Solution

MV of A = $800m

MV of B = $180m

PV of synergies = $40m

TOTAL = $1,020m

No. of new shares = 200m + (3/5) × 90m = 254m

New share price = 1,020m/254m = $4.02

	Shares	MV	Old wealth	Change
A	200m	$804m	$800m	$4m
B	(3/5) × 90m = 54m	$216m	$180m	$36m

The wealth of the shareholders in company B will increase by $36m as a consequence of the takeover. This is a (36/180) 20% increase in wealth.

Company B's shareholders should be advised to accept the 3 for 5 share for share offer.

Further numerical illustration

Initial example – Cash offer

Summary of information regarding Entity A and Entity B, two UK companies (currency £):

	Entity A	Entity B
Market price per share (£)	75	15
Number of shares	100,000	60,000
Market value (£)	7,500,000	900,000

Required:

If A intends to pay £1.2m cash for B, what is the cost premium if:

(a) **the share price does not anticipate the takeover**

(b) **the share price of Entity B includes a 'speculation' element of £2 per share?**

Solution

(a) The share price accurately reflects the true value of the entity (in theory).

Therefore, the cost to the bidder is simply £1,200,000 – £900,000, that is, £300,000.

Entity A is paying £300,000 for the identified benefits of the takeover.

(b) The cost is £300,000 + (60,000 × £2), or £420,000.

The entity is therefore really worth only £13 × 60,000, or £780,000.

Follow up example – Share exchange

Suppose A offers 16,000 shares (£1.2m/£75) instead of £1.2m cash. The cost appears to be £300,000 as before, but because B's shareholders will own part of A, they will benefit from any future gains of the combined entity. Their share will be (16,000/(16,000 + 100,000)), or 13.8%.

Further, suppose that the benefits of the combination have been identified by A to have a present value of £400,000 (i.e. A thinks that B is really worth £900,000 + £400,000, or £1.3m). Therefore, the combined entity of A and B is worth £7.5m + £1.3m, or £8.8m.

Required:

Calculate the true cost of the takeover to the acquirer's shareholders.

Solution

Estimate of post-acquisition prices

	A	B
Proportion of ownership	86.2%	13.8%
Market value: £8.8m × proportion	£7.586m	£1.214m
Number of shares currently in issue	100,000	60,000
Price per share (£)	75.86	20.23

What we are attempting to do here is to value the shares in the entity before the takeover is completed, based on estimates of what the entity will be worth after the merger. The valuation of each entity also recognises the split of the expected benefits which will accrue to the combined form once the merger has taken place.

The true cost to A can now be calculated as follows:

	£
60,000 B shares at £20.23	1,213,800
Less: Current market value	(900,000)
Benefits being paid to B's shareholders	313,800

Test your understanding 3

Mavers Co and Power Co are listed on the Stock Exchange.

Relevant information is as follows:

	Mavers Co	Power Co
Share price today	$3.05	$6.80
Shares in issue	48 million	13 million

Mavers Co wants to acquire 100% of the shares of Power Co.

The directors are considering offering 2 new Mavers Co shares for every 1 Power Co share.

Required:

Evaluate whether the 2 for 1 share for share exchange will be likely to succeed.

If necessary, recommend revised terms for the offer which would be likely to succeed.

Test your understanding 4 – further share exchange example

Laguna Co and Venez Co are listed companies. Laguna is considering a takeover bid for Venez, using a share for share exchange.

Relevant information is as follows:

	Laguna Co	Venez Co
Share price today	$10	$8
Shares in issue	10 million	5 million

If the acquisition goes ahead, synergies with a total value of $20 million are expected to be achieved. The Venez Co shareholders have indicated that they would be happy to accept an offer that enabled them to achieve a 25% premium on acquisition.

Required:

Advise the directors of Laguna Co on a suitable share-for-share exchange offer which meets the criteria specified by Venez Co's shareholders.

7   The regulation of takeovers

Introduction to regulation

During a takeover, it is important that the companies comply with relevant legislation and regulations.

General principles of takeover regulation

The regulation of takeovers varies from country to country but focuses primarily on controlling the directors' behaviour and ensuring that the shareholders are treated fairly.

General principles include the following:

- At the most important time in the company's life – when it is subject to a takeover bid – its directors should act in the best interest of their shareholders, and should disregard their personal interests.

- All shareholders must be treated equally.

- Shareholders must be given all the relevant information to make an informed judgement.

- The board must not take action without the approval of shareholders, which could result in the offer being defeated.

- All information supplied to shareholders must be prepared to the highest with standards of care and accuracy.

- The assumptions on which profit forecasts are based and the accounting polices used should be examined and reported on by accountants.

- An independent valuer should support valuations of assets.

Examples of regulation

Although the exam questions will never test the details of any particular country's regulations, it might be useful to see how the general principles listed above are applied in the UK. Similar examples could be given for other countries.

The City Code

The acquisition of quoted companies in the UK is regulated by the City Code on Takeovers and Mergers ('the City Code'), which is the responsibility of the Panel on Takeovers and Mergers.

This code does not have the force of law. It is enforced by the various City regulatory authorities, including the Stock Exchange (which has the power to suspend a company which does not comply), and specifically by the Panel on Takeovers and Mergers (the 'Takeover Panel').

Its basic principle is that of equity between one shareholder and another and it sets out rules for the conduct of acquisitions.

Competition and Markets Authority

The Competition and Markets Authority (CMA) replaced both the Office of Fair Trading (OFT) and the Competition Commission on 1 April 2014.

Many bids, because of their size, will require review by the CMA, and a limited number will subsequently be investigated if the CMA thinks that a merger might be against the public interest (i.e. constraining of competition).

As a rule of thumb the CMA may investigate an acquisition if it will result in the combined entity acquiring 25% or more of market share.

The investigations may take several months to complete during which time the merger is put on hold, thus giving the target company valuable time to organise its defence. The acquirer may abandon its bid as it may not wish to become involved in a time consuming investigation.

The CMA may simply accept or reject the proposals or accept them subject to certain conditions.

In recent years, the Competition Commission (former name of the CMA) has investigated the several UK banking mergers and also mergers in the UK airport industry. BAA was told by the Commission in 2009 that it had to sell off three of its existing airports in order to open up the market.

In addition, if the offer gives rises to a concentration (i.e. a potential monopoly) within the EU, the European Commission may initiate proceedings. This can result in considerable delay, and constitutes grounds for abandoning a bid.

Shareholder/stakeholder models of regulation

In the UK and US the market-based 'shareholder model' of regulation is used:

- Shareholder model – to protect rights of shareholders.
- Wide shareholder base.

In contrast, the European model looks at regulation from a wider stakeholder perspective:

- Stakeholder perspective to protect all stakeholders in a company.
- Stakeholders include:
    - employees
    - creditors
    - government
    - suppliers
    - general public.

Which model is better?

There is a wide ranging debate as to whether the shareholder or stakeholder model is better from an economic and a more general public interest viewpoint.

- Stakeholder model appears to be more successful at dealing with the agency problem and managerial abuse of their power.

- Shareholder model appears to be more economically efficient.

- In practice the shareholder model is becoming more dominant:

    – Due to strength of UK/US economies.

    – Power of US/UK capital markets.

    – The move is reflected in legislation.

- Synergy is often gained through redundancies in an acquired firm. Many are concerned with what they see as an unethical practice. A stakeholder model is more likely to give emphasis to employee protection.

Specific examples of takeover regulation

The principle of equal treatment

This stipulates that all shareholder groups must be offered the same terms, and that no shareholder group's terms are more or less favourable than another group's terms.

The main purpose of this principle is to ensure that minority shareholders are offered the same level of benefits, as the previous shareholders from whom the controlling stake in the target company was obtained.

Squeeze-out rights

Squeeze-out rights allow the bidder to force minority shareholders to sell their stakes, at a fair price, once the bidder has acquired a specific percentage of the target company's equity. The percentage varies between countries but typically ranges between 80% and 95%.

The main purpose of this is to enable the acquirer to gain a 100% stake of the target company and prevent problems arising from minority shareholders at a later date.

The mandatory-bid condition through sell out rights

This allows remaining shareholders to exit the company at a fair price once the bidder has accumulated a certain number of shares. The amount of shares accumulated before the rule applies varies between countries. The bidder must offer the shares at the highest share price, as a minimum, which had been paid by the bidder previously.

The main purpose of this condition is to ensure that the acquirer does not exploit its position of power at the expense of minority shareholders.

Merger and acquisition accounting

- There are two different methods of consolidation designed to reflect the substance of two different types of business combination.

- Acquisition accounting is used for the purchase of one company by another with the purchaser controlling the net assets of the subsidiary.

  - Net assets acquired are included at their fair values.

  - Only post-acquisition profits of the subsidiary included in consolidated reserves.

- Merger accounting is when there is a pooling of interests of two or more roughly equal partners. Effectively adds the two sets of accounts together.

- The investment in a new subsidiary will be shown as a fixed asset investment in the parent company's own accounts.

- The amount at which this investment will be stated will depend upon whether merger accounting or acquisition accounting is used.

- Under acquisition accounting the investment will be recorded at cost (generally the fair value of the consideration given).

- If merger accounting is used the investment is recorded at the nominal value of the shares issued as purchase consideration plus the fair value of any additional consideration.

Comparison of merger and acquisition accounting – Illustration

Fred makes an offer to all the shareholders of Ginger to acquire their shares on the basis of one new $1 share (market value $3) plus 25 c for every two $1 shares (market value $1.10 each) in Ginger. The holders of 95,000 shares in Ginger (representing 95% of the total shares) accept this offer.

The investment in Ginger will be recorded in the books of Fred as follows:

If acquisition accounting is to be used on consolidation:

	$	$
Dr: Investment in Ginger plc	154,375	
Cr: $1 ordinary shares		47,500
Cr: Share premium		95,000
Cr: Cash		11,875
	154,375	154,375

If merger accounting is to be used on consolidation:

	$	$
Dr: Investment in Ginger plc	59,375	
Cr: $1 ordinary shares		47,500
Cr: Cash		11,875
	59,375	59,375

8 Chapter summary

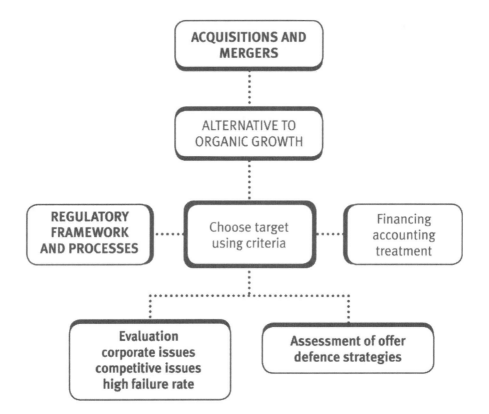

Test your understanding answers

Test your understanding 1 – Williams and GSL

- Operating efficiencies – the unused capacity at GSL can be used to produce William's products without adding to costs and capacity.

- Marketing synergies.

- If the cash flow streams of Williams and GSL are not perfectly positively correlated then by acquiring GSL – Williams may reduce the variability of their operating cash flow. This being more attractive to investors may lead to cheaper financing.

- The 'dedicated' herbalists of GSL and the R+D staff of Williams may be a complementary resource.

- Fixed operating and administrative costs savings.

- Consolidation of manufacturing capacity on fewer and larger sites.

- There may be bulk buying discounts.

- Possibility of joint advertising and distribution.

- GSL is badly managed – thus the elimination of inefficiency could allow for financial synergy.

Test your understanding 2 – Development of bids

There is no feedback to this activity.

Test your understanding 3

Calculations

Value of Mavers Co = $3.05 × 48m shares = $146.4m

Value of Power Co = $6.80 × 13m shares = $88.4m

Total value (assuming no synergistic gains) = 146.4 + 88.4 = $234.8m

Number of shares post-integration = 48 million + (2 × 13 million) = 74 million

So the post-integration share price will be:

$234.8m/74 million = $3.173

	Shares	MV	Old wealth	Change
Mavers	48m	$152.3m	$146.4m	+$5.9m
Power	2 × 13m = 26m	$82.5m	$88.4m	−$5.9m

Advice

The Power Co shareholders will not accept a 2 for 1 share for share exchange since it causes their wealth to reduce.

Recommendation

In order for the Power Co shareholders to be encouraged to accept the offer, it must offer them a gain in wealth.

To make sure that Mavers Co is valuing Power Co at its current market value, the value of the offer needs to be ($6.80 × 13m shares) $88.4m in total.

Given the current Mavers Co share price of $3.05, this amounts to $88.4m/$3.05 = 28.98m shares in Mavers Co.

An exchange of 28.98m Mavers Co shares for the 13m Power Co shares represents a ratio of 28.98m to 13m or 2.23 to 1.

However, if the terms of the offer were to be exactly 2.23 Mavers Co shares for every 1 share in Power Co, there would be no incentive for the Power Co shareholders to sell (financially, they'd be indifferent between keeping their existing shares and exchanging them for Mavers Co shares).

In order to encourage Power Co's shareholders to sell, a premium would have to be offered.

Hence, an offer of (say) 2.5 Mavers Co shares for every 1 share in Power Co would probably be needed to encourage the Power Co shareholders to sell.

Position of Mavers Co shareholders

In this situation, where no synergistic gains are included in the calculations, a gain to Power Co's shareholders will result in a corresponding loss to the Mavers Co shareholders. Clearly Mavers Co would not want to proceed with the takeover in these circumstances.

Unless some synergies can be generated, to improve the wealth of the overall company after the acquisition, there is no way of structuring the deal so that both sets of shareholders will be satisfied.

Test your understanding 4

Value of Laguna Co = $10 × 10m shares = $100m

Value of Venez Co = $8 × 5m shares = $40m

Total combined value before the acquisition = $140m

Total value after acquisition (assuming synergistic gains are achieved)

= 140m + 20m = $160m

Share for share exchange calculation:

	Laguna Co	Venez Co
Pre-acquisition value	$100m	$40m
Premium needed (25% × $40m)		$10m
Balance of value gain to Laguna	$10m	
($20m – (25% × $40m))		
Post-acquisition value	$110m	$50m
Relative valuation	2.2	1

Laguna Co has 10m shares in issue at the moment, so to make sure the valuation after the acquisition splits in a 2.2 to 1 ratio, it needs to issue (10m / 2.2 =) 4.55m new shares to give to the Venez Co shareholders.

Venez Co has 5m shares in issue at the moment, so the terms of the share for share exchange need to be 4.55m new shares in Laguna Co in exchange for the 5m existing shares in Venez Co.

This is approximately a 91 for 100 share exchange.

Business valuation

Chapter learning objectives

Study guide section		Study guide outcome
B4: Valuation and the use of free cash flows	(a)	Apply asset based, income based and cash flow based models to value equity. Apply appropriate models, including term structure of interest rates, the yield curve and credit spreads, to value corporate debt.
	(b)	Forecast an organisation's free cash flow and its free cash flow to equity (pre- and post-capital reinvestment).
	(c)	Advise on the value of an organisation using its free cash flow and free cash flow to equity under alternative horizon and growth assumptions.
C2: Valuation for acquisitions and mergers	(a)	Discuss the problem of overvaluation.
	(b)	Estimate the potential near-term and continuing growth levels of a corporation's earnings using both internal and external measures.

C2: Valuation for acquisitions and mergers (continued)

(c) Discuss, assess and advise on the value created from an acquisition or merger of both quoted and unquoted entities using models such as:

(i) 'Book value-plus' models

(ii) Market based models

(iii) Cash flow models, including free cash flows.

Taking into account the changes in the risk profile and risk exposure of the acquirer and the target entities.

(d) Apply appropriate methods, such as: risk-adjusted cost of capital, adjusted net present values and changing price-earnings multipliers resulting from the acquisition or merger, to the valuation process where appropriate.

(e) Demonstrate an understanding of the procedure for valuing high growth start-ups.

PER

One of the PER performance objectives (PO09 – Evaluate Investment and Financing Decisions) is to be able to select investment or merger and acquisition opportunities using appropriate appraisal techniques.

Working through this chapter should help you understand how to demonstrate that objective.

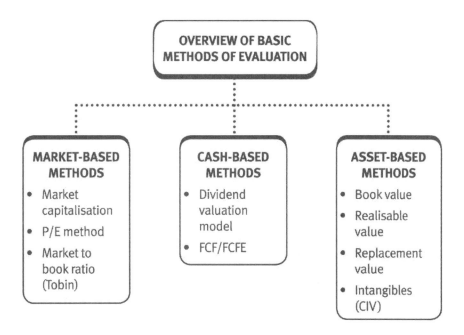

1 Introduction to business valuation

This chapter covers several different methods of business valuation. You should view the different methods as complementary which enable you to suggest a possible value region. It is essential that you are able to comment on the suitability of each approach in a particular scenario.

Do not put yourself under pressure in the exam to come up with a precise valuation, as business valuation is not an exact science. In reality the final price paid will depend on the bargaining skills and the economic pressures on the parties involved.

2 Overview of the different valuation methods

Three basic valuation methods

There are three basic ways of valuing a business:

- Cash based methods – the theoretical premise here is that the value of the company should be equal to the discounted value of future cash flows.

- Market based methods – where we assume that the market is efficient, so use market information (such as share prices and P/E ratios) for the target company and other companies. The assumption is that the market values businesses consistently so, if necessary, the value of one company can be used to find the value of another.

- Asset based methods – the firm's assets form the basis for the company's valuation. Asset based methods are difficult to apply to companies with high levels of intangible assets, but we shall look at methods of trying to value intangible as well as tangible assets.

We shall cover these methods in detail in the rest of this chapter.

3   Cash based methods

The free cash flow method

Free cash flows can used to find the value of a firm. This value can be used:

*   to determine the price in a merger or acquisition

*   to identify a share price for the sale of a block of shares

*   to calculate the 'shareholder value added' (SVA) by management from one period to another.

Calculating the value

Technically, in order for the value of the business to be accurately determined, free cash flow for all future years should be estimated. However rather than attempting to predict the free cash flows for every year, in practice a short cut method is applied. Future cash flows are divided into two time periods:

*   Those that occur during the 'planning horizon'.

*   Those that occur after the planning horizon.

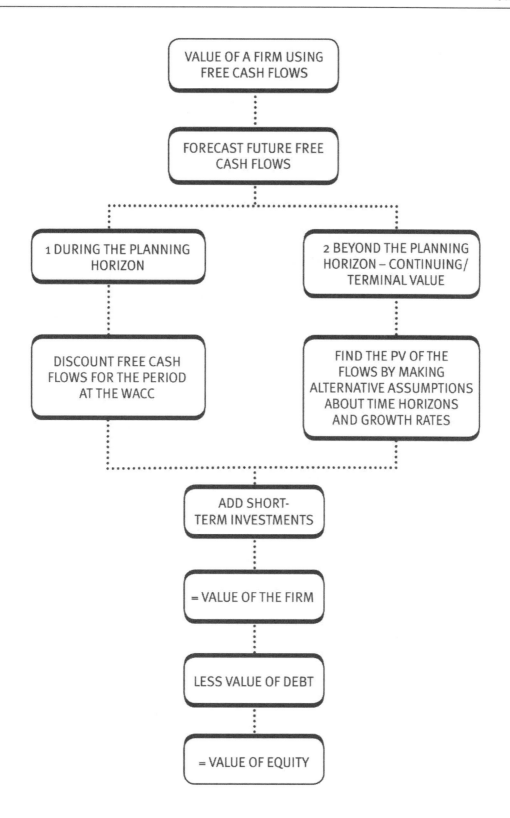

The planning horizon

The planning horizon is the period where:

- the firm can earn above average returns

- cash flows are assumed to grow over time.

Beyond the planning horizon, returns are expected to reach a steady state.

The planning horizon

In competitive industries, a business may have a period of 'competitive advantage' where it can earn excess returns on capital by maintaining a commercial advantage over the competition. However this period is unlikely to last indefinitely. Returns are likely to reach a steady state where the business earns on average its cost of capital but no more.

The planning horizon (which may last up to ten years or more) is the period during which the returns are expected to be higher than the cost of finance.

In period beyond the planning horizon it is usually assumed that the returns earned will continue at their current rate for the remainder of the investors' time horizon. This may be a given number of years or in perpetuity. Alternatively the value of the cash flows may be expressed as a lump sum using a P/E ratio.

Illustration 1

A company prepares a forecast of future free cash flow at the end of each year. A period of 15 years is used as this is thought to represent the typical time horizon of investors in this industry.

It is assumed that the planning horizon is three years – i.e. returns are likely to grow each year for the first three years after which they will reach a steady state.

The following data is available:

Free cash flows are expected to be $2.5 million in the first year, $4.5 million in the second year and $6.5 million in year 3. The stock market value of debt is $5m and the company's cost of capital is 10%.

Required:

Calculate the current value of the firm and the value of the equity.

Solution

	Year 1	Year 2	Year 3	Years 4–15
Free cash flow	2.5	4.5	6.5	6.5
PV factor @ 10%	0.909	0.826	0.751	6.814 × 0.751 *
PV	2.273	3.717	4.882	33.263
Total PV = value of the firm				44.135
Less value of debt				(5.000)
Value of equity				39.135

*12 year AF (gives T_3 value of CF years 4 – 15) × 3 year DF (to discount to T_0).

The valuation of debt

The value of debt was given in the previous illustration.

If you are not told the value in a question, the best way of estimating the value is by using the formula:

Value of debt = Present value of receipts to the lender (i.e. interest and redemption payment) discounted at the lender's required rate of return

The valuation of debt is covered in more detail later in this chapter.

Further illustration

The company in the previous illustration now believes that earnings after the planning horizon will:

(a)   continue at the year 3 level into perpetuity or

(b)   grow at 0.9% per year into perpetuity.

Required:

Recalculate the current value of the firm and the value of the equity.

Solution

(a)

	Year 1	Year 2	Year 3	Years 4 onwards
Free cash flow	2.5	4.5	6.5	6.5
PV factor @ 10%	0.909	0.826	0.751	$1/0.1 \times 0.751$*
PV	2.273	3.717	4.882	48.815
Total PV = value of the firm				59.687
Less value of debt				(5.000)
Value of equity				54.687

*$1/i$ (gives T_3 value of CF from year 4 onwards) × 3 year DF (to discount to T_0).

Note the higher value that results when the time horizon is altered.

(b)

	Year 1	Year 2	Year 3	Years 4–infinity
Free cash flow	2.5	4.5	6.5	6.5 (infl 0.9%)
PV factor @ 10%	0.909	0.826	0.751	See working
PV	2.273	3.717	4.882	54.126

Value of equity is 54.126 + 2.273 + 3.717 + 4.882 – (debt value) 5 = \$59.998m

Working:

The value of the growing perpetuity from Year 4 onwards can be calculated as:

$$[(6.5 \times 1.009)/(0.10 - 0.009)] \times 0.751 = 54.126$$

Calculating free cash flows from accounting information

When appraising an individual project in Chapter 2: Investment appraisal, the free cash flows could usually be estimated quite easily. However, identifying free cash flows for an entire company or business unit is much more complex, since there are potentially far more of them.

In these situations, the level of free cash flows is more usually determined from the already prepared accounting information and therefore is found by working back from profits as follows:

		Comment
Net operating profit (before interest and tax)	X	For future years, expected profits are predicted based on expected growth rates
Less taxation	(X)	A relevant cash flow and therefore deducted from profit
Add depreciation	X	Not a cash flow and therefore added back to profit
Operating cash flow	X	
Less investment:		
Replacement non-current asset investment (RAI)	(X)	Needed in order to continue operations at current levels. If no information available about amounts, it is assumed to be equal to current levels of depreciation
Incremental non-current asset investment (IAI)	(X)	Needed to sustain expected growth asset investment
Incremental working capital investment (IWCI)	(X)	Needed to sustain expected growth
Free cash flow	X	

This method gives the level of free cash flow to the firm as a whole.

Free cash flow to equity

The above approach calculates free cash flows before deducting either interest or dividend payments.

The **free cash flow to equity** only can be calculated by taking the free cash flow calculated above and:

- deducting debt interest paid
- deducting any debt repayments
- adding any cash raised from debt issues.

In practical terms, the free cash flow to equity determines the dividend capacity of a firm i.e. the amount the firm can afford to pay out as a dividend.

More details on free cash flow

Cash that is not retained and then reinvested in a business is called free cash flow. This in effect represents the cash flow available to all the providers of capital of a company, whether these be debt holders or shareholders. This could be used to pay dividends or finance additional capital projects, if the necessary organisational criteria were met. Free cash flow is a very good measure of performance and an indicator of value.

Some would suggest that it is a better indicator of performance than measures based on net income. Forecast free cash flow is the most theoretically sound way to place a fair value on a company. Apparently Warren Buffett, one of the world's richest investors, uses historic and forecast free cash flow to value the businesses that he buys.

Growing free cash flows are frequently a prelude to increased earnings and hence may be a positive sign for investors. Conversely a shrinking free cash flow may be an indicator of problems ahead, and a sign that companies are unable to sustain earnings growth. This may not always be the case, as many young companies put a lot of their cash into investments, which diminish their free cash flow. However, in this case questions might be raised about the sufficiency of short and long-term capital.

There can be variations in the definition. When calculating free cash flow over a number of years it is sensible to include the change in working capital and all investment spending. Over a long period of time the cash flow resulting from all investment is likely to be realised and so such a measure would be useful to those undertaking business valuations and using data forecast into the future.

However, when calculating free cash flow for a single year it would be sensible to omit the change in working capital and discretionary non-maintenance capital spending, because the ultimate payoff from those investments is not yet included in the operating cash flow. However, this in turn may give rise to debate about what represents the level of sustaining capital expenditure that should be deducted. When analysing figures for free cash flow it is also important to be aware of any unusual events in a particular year, which may impact on the cash flow.

Figures calculated for free cash flow can be used in determining a company's cash flow ratios.

For example:

Dividend cover in cash terms = Free cash flow to equity/Dividends paid.

It is argued that this measure of dividend cover is better than the conventional ratio of earnings divided by dividends paid, since dividends are paid in cash, and with no cash there can't be any dividends.

Also, since the free cash flow to equity determines the company's dividend capacity (explained in detail in Chapter 5: The dividend decision) we can see from the breakdown of free cash flow to equity that there is a strong link between new investments and dividend capacity i.e. if a new investment project increases the cash inflows of a business, its free cash flow to equity and hence its dividend capacity will increase.

Illustration of calculations of free cash flow

Calculate the free cash flow based on the following figures:

(a) **using the standard approach**

(b) **to show the free cash flow to equity.**

	$000
Operating profit	300
Depreciation	120
Increase in working capital	50
Capital expenditure to replace existing assets	10
Capital expenditure on new investments	15
Interest paid	5
Loans repaid	20
Tax paid	140

Solution

(a) Standard approach

	$000
Net operating profit (before interest and tax)	300
Plus depreciation	120
Less taxation	(140)
Operating cash flow	280

	Less investment:	
	Replacement non-current asset investment	(10)
	Incremental non-current asset investment	(15)
	Incremental working capital investment	(50)
		———
	Free cash flow	205
		———
(b)	Free cash flow to equity	
		$000
	Free cash flow to the firm	205
	Less debt interest paid	(5)
	Less loans repaid	(20)
		———
	Free cash flows to equity	180
		———

Forecasting growth in free cash flows

The methods above have identified a figure for the free cash flow of the business based on its current financial statements. In order to value the business, the future free cash flows need to be forecast and then discounted.

To forecast the likely growth rate for the free cash flows, the following three methods can be used:

Historical estimates

For example, if the business has achieved growth of 5% per year each year for the last five years, 5% may be a sensible growth rate to apply to future free cash flows.

Analyst forecasts

Particularly for listed companies, market analysts regularly produce forecasts of growth. These independent estimates could be a useful indicator of the likely future growth rate.

Fundamental analysis

The formula for Gordon's growth approximation ($g = r \times b$) can be used to calculate the likely future growth rate, where r is the company's return on equity (cost of equity) and b is the earnings retention rate. The formula is based on the assumption that growth will be driven by the reinvestment of earnings.

Alternatively, in an exam question, you may simply be told which growth rate to apply. When applying any growth rate in an exam question, the rate's use should be questioned, particularly if the figure seems high.

Test your understanding 1

A company is preparing a free cash flow forecast in order to calculate the value of equity.

The following information is available:

Sales: Current sales are $500 million. Growth is expected to be 8% in year 1, falling by 2% per year (e.g. to 6% in year 2) until sales level out in year 5 where they are expected to remain constant in perpetuity.

The operating profit margin will be 10% for the first two years and 12% thereafter.

Depreciation in year 1 will be $7 million increasing by $1 million per year over the planning horizon before levelling off and replacement asset investment is assumed to equal depreciation. Incremental investment in assets is expected to be 8% of the increase in sales in year 1, 6% of the increase in sales in each of the following two years, and 4% of the increase in year 4.

Tax will be charged at 30%. The WACC is 15%.

The market value of short-term investments is $4 million and the market value of debt is $48 million.

Required:

Calculate the value of equity.

Use of free cash flow to equity (FCFE) in valuation

The previous calculations have found equity value by:

- discounting free cash flow to present value using the WACC, and then deducting debt value. This is known as the free cash flow to firm methodology.

Alternatively, the value of equity can be found directly by:

- discounting free cash flow TO EQUITY at the cost of equity.

In the simplest case (if FCFE is assumed to be growing at a constant rate into perpetuity), the following formula can be applied:

$FCFE_0(1 + g)/(k_e - g)$

The formula is based on the dividend valuation model theory (see below for more details on using DVM in business valuation).

Test your understanding 2

Chassagne Co is considering making a bid for Butler Co, a rival company.

The following information should be used to value Butler Co.

Statement of profit or loss for the most recent accounting period

	$m
Revenue	285.1
Cost of sales	(120.9)
	———
Gross profit	164.2
Operating expenses (inc depreciation $12.3m)	(66.9)
	———
Profit from operations	97.3
Finance costs	(10.0)
	———
Profit before tax	87.3
Taxation	(21.6)
	———
Profit after tax	65.7

Other information

- Selling prices are expected to rise at 3% per year for the next 3 years and then stay constant thereafter.

- Sales volumes are expected to rise at 5% per year for the next 3 years and then stay constant thereafter.

- Assume that cost of sales is a completely variable cost, and that other operating expenses (including depreciation) are expected to stay constant.

- Butler Co invested $15m in non-current assets and $2m in working capital last year. These annual amounts are expected to stay constant in future.

- Butler Co's financing costs are expected to stay constant each year in the future.

- The marginal rate of tax is 28%, payable in the year in which the liability arises.

- Assume that book depreciation equals tax depreciation.

- Butler Co has 500 million shares in issue.

- The WACC of Butler Co is 9% and its cost of equity is 12%.

Required:

Calculate the value of the equity in Butler Co (in total and per share) by forecasting future free cash flow to equity and discounting to present value using the cost of equity.

The dividend valuation model (DVM)

Theory: The value of the share is the present value of the expected future dividends discounted at the shareholders' required rate of return.

Assuming a constant growth rate in dividends, g:

$P_0 = D_0(1 + g)/(k_e - g)$

Note that:

If D_0 = Total dividends P_0 = Total value of the company's equity.

If D_0 = Dividends per share P_0 = Value per share.

If the growth pattern of dividends is not expected to be stable, but will vary over time, the formula can be adapted.

Explanation of terms in DVM formula

k_e = cost of equity.

g = constant rate of growth in dividends, expressed as a decimal.

$D_0(1 + g)$ = dividend just paid adjusted for one year's growth.

DVM calculations

Basic application of DVM formula

A company has just paid a dividend of 20 cents. The company expects dividends to grow at 7% in the future. The company's current cost of equity is 12%.

Required:

Calculate the market value of the share.

Solution

$P_0 = 20(1 + 0.07)/(0.12 - 0.07) = 428c = \$4.28$

More advanced application of the DVM formula

C Co has just paid a dividend of 25 cents per share. The return on equities in this risk class is 20%.

Required:

Calculate the value of the shares assuming:

(i)   **no growth in dividends**

(ii) **constant growth of 5% per year**

(iii) **constant dividends for 5 years and then growth of 5% per year to perpetuity.**

Solution

(i) $P_0 = 0.25/0.2 = \$1.25$

(ii) $P_0 = 0.25(1.05)/(0.2 - 0.05) = \$1.75$

(iii) Present value of first
      5 years' dividends   = 0.25×5 yr 20% AF   0.748
                           = 0.25×2.991

Present value of growing
dividend   =   Value at T5 × 5 yr DF
                           =   [0.25(1.05)/
                               (0.2 − 0.05)] × 0.402   0.704
                                                              _____

Share value $1.452
                                                              _____

Test your understanding 3

C Co has just paid a dividend of 32 cents per share. The return on equities in this risk class is 16%.

Required:

Calculate the value of each share, assuming constant dividends for 3 years and then growth of 4% per year to perpetuity.

The model is highly sensitive to changes in assumptions:

- Where growth is high relative to the shareholders' required return, the share price is very volatile.

- Even a minor change in investors' expectations of growth rates can cause a major change in share price contributing to the share price crashes seen in recent years.

Illustration of sensitivity of DVM

Consider the impact of a change in growth predictions of 0.5% in two cases – the first where growth is low compared to the firm's required return, the other where it is high.

A firm's k_e is 7% and D_0 is 10 cents.

The change in share price as a result of changing growth predictions is shown.

Assuming:

(i)   a growth rate of 2% dropping to 1.5%

(ii)   a growth rate of 5% dropping to 4.5%.

Assumption (i)

Share price at g = 2% $10 \times 1.02/(0.07 - 0.02) = 204$

Share price at g = 1.5% $10 \times 1.015/(0.07 - 0.015) = 184.55$

Fall in share price is $(204 - 184.55)/204 = 9.5\%$

Assumption (ii)

Share price at g = 5% $10 \times 1.05/(0.07 - 0.05) = 525$

Share price at g = 4.5% $10 \times 1.045/(0.07 - 0.045) = 418$

Fall in share price is $(525 - 418)/525 = 20.4\%$

The share price shows far greater volatility where growth is high relative to required return.

DVM is more suitable for valuing minority stakes, since it only considers dividends. In practice the model does tend to accurately match actual stock market share prices.

4   Market based methods

Stock market value (market capitalisation)

For a listed company, the stock market value of the shares (or 'market capitalisation') is the starting point for the valuation process.

In a perfectly efficient market, the market price of the shares would be fair at all times, and would accurately reflect all information about a company. In reality, share prices tend to reflect publicly available information.

The market share price is suitable when purchasing a minority stake. However, a premium usually has to be paid above the current market price in order to acquire a controlling interest.

The price-earnings ratio (P/E) method

The P/E method is a very simple method of valuation. It is the most commonly used method in practice.

P/E valuation method formula

Value per share = EPS × P/E ratio

Total equity value of the company = Total post-tax earnings × P/E ratio

Using the P/E valuation formula

The P/E ratio method is the simplest valuation method. It relies on just two figures (the post-tax earnings and the P/E ratio).

Post-tax earnings

The current post-tax earnings, or EPS, for a company can easily be found by looking at the most recent published accounts. However, these published figures will be historic, whereas the earnings figure needed for valuation purposes should be an expected, future earnings figure.

It is perfectly acceptable to use the published earnings figure as a starting point, but before performing the valuation, the historic earnings figure should be adjusted for factors such as:

- one-off items which will not recur in the coming year (e.g. debt write offs in the previous year)

- directors' salaries which might be adjusted after a takeover has been completed

- any savings ('synergies') which might be made as part of a takeover.

P/E ratio

The P/E ratio for a listed company is a simple measure of the company's share price divided by its earnings per share.

The P/E indicates the market's perception of the company's current position and its future prospects. For example, if the P/E ratio is high, this indicates that the company has a relatively high share price compared to its current level of earnings, suggesting that the share price reflects good growth prospects of the company.

An unlisted company has no market share price, so has no readily available P/E ratio. Therefore, when valuing an unlisted company, a proxy P/E ratio from a similar listed company is often used.

Proxy P/E ratios

As explained above, an unlisted company will not have a market-driven P/E ratio, so an industry average P/E, or one for a similar company, will be used as a proxy.

However, proxy P/E ratios are also sometimes used when valuing a listed company – of course if a listed entity's own P/E ratio is applied to its own earnings figure, the calculation will just give the existing share price.

Test your understanding 4

Molier is an unquoted entity with a recently reported after-tax earnings of $3,840,000. It has issued 1 million ordinary shares. A similar listed entity has a P/E ratio of 9.

Required:

Calculate the value of one ordinary share in Molier using the P/E basis of valuation.

The strengths and weaknesses of P/E valuations

The main strengths of P/E valuations are:

- they are commonly used and are well understood
- they are relevant for valuing a controlling interest in an entity.

The main weaknesses of P/E valuations are:

- they are based on accounting profits rather than cash flows
- it is difficult to identify a suitable P/E ratio, particularly when valuing the shares of an unlisted entity
- it is difficult to establish the relevant level of sustainable earnings.

ABC Co is considering making a bid for the entire equity capital of XYZ Co, a firm which has a P/E ratio of 9 and annual earnings of $390 million.

ABC Co has a P/E of 13 and annual earnings of $693 million, and it is thought that $125 million of annual synergistic savings will be made as a consequence of the takeover. The P/E of the combined company is expected to be 12.

Required:

Calculate the minimum value acceptable to XYZ's shareholders, and the maximum amount which ABC should consider paying.

Earnings yield method

In some questions, you may not be given the P/E ratio, but you may be given the Earnings Yield instead.

The earnings yield is the reciprocal of the P/E ratio

i.e. Earnings Yield = 1 /(P/E ratio).

Hence

Value of company = Total earnings/Earnings Yield

Value per share = EPS/Earnings Yield

Understanding and interpretation of earnings yield

Some deeper analysis is desirable, for example examining the trend of share price over a number of quarters in the light of any events such as profits warnings and acquisitions (or rumours thereof), and the likely effect that they have had on earnings.

The stability of Earnings Yield is often as important as its growth, bearing in mind that in a general way the market is absorbing new information to try to assess a sustainable level of EPS on which to base growth for the future. Clearly, effective growth is dependent on a stable base, and the trend of Earnings Yield over time is to an extent a reflection of this factor.

A prospective acquirer would, of course, be concerned to assess the worth of a prospective target on the basis of its becoming part of the acquiring entity, and the valuation will especially need to take into account the expectations of the target's shareholders.

Tobin's market to book ratio

Market to book ratio (based on Tobin's Q)

Market value of target company = Market to book ratio × book value of target company's assets

where market to book ratio = (Market capitalisation/Book value of assets) for a comparator company (or take industry average)

This method assumes a constant relationship between market value of the equity and the book value of the firm.

Problems with the model:

- Choosing an appropriate comparator – should we use industry average, or an average of similar firms only?

- The ratio the market applies is not constant throughout its business cycle, so strictly the comparator should be taken only from other companies at the same stage.

 Illustration of Tobin's Q

The industry sector average Market to Book ratio for the industry of X Co is 4.024.

The book value of X Co is $3,706 million and it has 1,500 million shares in issue.

Required:

Calculate the predicted share price.

Solution

Predicted value of X Co = $3,706m × 4.024 = $14,912.94m.

Predicted share price = $14,912.94m/1,500m = $9.94

5 Asset based methods

The basic model

The traditional asset based valuation method is to take as a starting point the value of all the firm's statement of financial position assets less any liabilities. Asset values used can be:

- book value – the book value of assets can easily be found from the financial statements. However, it is unlikely that book values (which are based on historic cost accounting principles) will be a reliable indicator of current market values.

- replacement cost – the buyer of a business will be interested in the replacement cost, since this represents the alternative cost of setting up a similar business from scratch (organic growth versus acquisition).

- net realisable value – the seller of a business will usually see the realisable value of assets as the minimum acceptable price in negotiations.

However:

- replacement cost is not easy to identify in practice, and

- the business is more than just the sum of its constituent parts. In fact the value of the tangible assets in many businesses is minimal since much of the value comes from the intangible assets and goodwill (e.g. compare a firm of accountants with a mining company).

Test your understanding 6

The summarised balance sheet (statement of financial position) of Owen at 31 December 20X7 is as follows:

Assets	$000
Non-current assets	23,600
Current assets	8,400
	———
	32,000
	———

Equity and liabilities	
Capital and reserves	
$1 Ordinary shares	8,000
Retained earnings	11,200
	———
	19,200
Non-current liabilities:	
6% Unsecured bond	8,000
Current liabilities	4,800
	———
	32,000
	———

Required:

Calculate the value of one ordinary share in Owen, using an asset based valuation method.

Test your understanding 7

Fowler is planning to make a bid for Owen (see details for Owen in the previous example).

It has estimated that the replacement cost of Owen's non-current assets is $40 million.

Required:

Calculate the value of a share in Owen from Fowler's perspective.

6 Intangible asset valuation methods

Definition of intangible assets

Intangible assets are those assets that cannot be touched, weighed or physically measured. They include:

- assets such as patents with legal rights attached
- intangibles such as goodwill, purchased and valued as part of a previous acquisition
- relationships, networks and skills built up by the business over time.

A major flaw with the basic asset valuation model is that it does not take account of the true value of intangibles.

Basic intangible valuation method

The simplest way of incorporating intangible value into the process is by the following basic formula:

Firm value = [book or replacement cost of the real assets] + [multiplier × annual profit or revenue]

The multiplier is negotiated between the parties to compensate for goodwill.

Effectively, some attempt is being made to estimate the extra value generated by the intangible assets, above the value of the firm's tangible assets.

This simple formula provides the basis for the two main intangible valuation methods: CIV (Calculated Intangible Value) and Lev's method.

More detail on intangible assets

Often intangible assets, making up a significant part of the real worth of the company, are formed by the staff of a company – their skills, knowledge and creativity. Such assets are created by spending on areas such as R&D, advertising and marketing, training and staff development. This type of expenditure serves to enhance the underlying value of the firm rather than assisting directly in earning this year's profits.

A significant problem with the basic asset valuation model is that the assets to be valued are taken to be those identified on the statement of financial position. Where a firm has significant levels of intangible assets, accounting conventions mean they will be either not be included at all, or included at amounts well below their real commercial value.

If the asset based model is to be of use, a way of valuing these intangibles must be found.

Calculated intangible value (CIV)

This method is based on comparing (benchmarking) the return on assets earned by the company with:

- a similar company in the same industry or

- the industry average.

The method is similar to the residual income technique you may remember from your earlier studies. It calculates the company's **value spread** – the profit it earns over the return on assets that would be expected for a firm in that business.

Method

1   A suitable competitor (similar in size, structure etc.) is identified and their return on assets calculated:

Operating profit/Assets employed

2   If no suitable similar competitor can be identified, the industry average return may be used.

3   The company's value spread is then calculated.

	$
Company operating profit	X
Less:	
Appropriate ROA × Company asset base	(X)
	——
Value spread	X
	——

4   Assuming that the value spread would be earned in perpetuity, the Calculated Intangible Value (CIV) is found as follows:

–   Find the post-tax value spread.

–   Divide the post-tax value spread by the cost of capital to find the present value of the post-tax value spread as a perpetuity (the CIV).

5   The CIV is added to the net asset value to give an overall value of the firm.

CIV calculation

CXM operates in the advertising industry. The directors are keen to value the company for the purposes of negotiating with a potential purchaser and plan to use the CIV method to value the intangible element.

In the past year CXM made an operating profit of $137.4 million on an asset base of $307 million. The company WACC is 6.5%.

A suitable competitor for benchmarking has been identified as R. R made an operating profit of $315 million on assets employed in the business of $1,583 million.

Corporation tax is 30%.

Required:

Calculate the value of CXM, including the CIV.

Solution

1   R is currently earning a return of 315/1,583 = 19.9%

2   The value spread for CXM is:

	$m
Company operating profit	137.40
Less	
Appropriate ROA × Company asset base (19.9% × 307)	61.09
Value spread	76.31

3   Calculate the CIV:

  –   Find the post-tax value spread

    $76.31 × (1 – 0.3) = 53.42$

  –   Find the CIV by calculating the PV of the post-tax value spread (assuming it will continue into perpetuity)

    CIV = 53.42/0.065 = $822m

4   The overall value of the firm = CIV + asset base

    Firm value = $822m + $307m = $1,129m.

Test your understanding 8

DCH operates in a specialised sector of the telecommunications industry. A company value is needed as part of merger talks and the CIV method has been chosen to value the intangible element of the business.

In the past year DCH made an operating profit of $256.8 million on an asset base of $522 million. The company WACC is 9%.

The average return on assets for the industry sector in which DCH operates is 16%.

Corporation tax is 30%.

Required:

Calculate the value of DCH, including the CIV.

Problems with the CIV model:

- Finding a similar company in terms of industry, similar asset portfolio, similar cost gearing etc.

- Since the competitor firm presumably also has intangibles, CIV actually measures the surplus intangible value our company has over that of the competitor rather than over its own asset value.

Lev's knowledge earnings method

An alternative method of valuing intangible assets involves isolating the earnings deemed to be related to intangible assets, and capitalising them. However it is more complex than the CIV model in how it determines the return to intangibles and the future growth assumptions made.

In practice, this model does produce results that are close to the actual traded share price, suggesting that is a good valuation technique.

However, it is often criticised as over complex given that valuations are in the end dependent on negotiation between the parties.

Risk in acquisitions and mergers

An acquisition may expose an acquiring company to risk. It is important to distinguish between:

- business risk
- financial risk.

Business risk

This is the variability in the earnings of the company, which results from the uncertainties in the business environment. If the merger or acquisition is with another company operating in the same business area, the underlying business risk (measured by the asset beta) of the acquirer will be unaffected.

Financial risk

Financial risk is the additional volatility caused by the firm's gearing structure. If an acquisition is significant in size relative to the acquirer or requires an alteration to the firm's capital structure, it will change the acquirer's exposure to finance risk.

Valuation and risk

It is a key principle that the most an acquirer should ever pay for a target company is the increase in the value of the acquiring firm arising from the acquisition.

However, it is rarely a simple matter of valuing the target and assuming that will be the level of increase experienced. This ignores the impact of:

- potential synergy gains – although there is an argument that they are so rarely achieved in practice that they should be very conservatively estimated, and only then if they are arising because of the target itself (that is they wouldn't arise from any merger)
- the change in potential risk profile of the combined entity as discussed above.

The valuation techniques used must therefore depend on the type of acquisition being considered.

For example, if an NPV based approach is being used for valuation, a risk adjusted cost of capital (appropriate to the risk of the cash flows being considered) may need to be calculated and used for discounting.

In fact, the methods introduced in the earlier Chapter 7: Risk adjusted WACC and adjusted present value are equally relevant in business valuation. So the risk adjusted WACC can be used as a discount rate when dealing with a change in business risk and/or a small change in financial risk, whereas the APV method can be used when there is a significant change in capital structure. Some examples of these approaches are shown below.

Similarly, if a price-earnings (P/E) valuation method is being used, the proxy P/E ratio used in the calculation must reflect the risk profile and growth prospects of the company's earnings being valued.

Worked example using risk adjusted WACC in valuation

A risk adjusted WACC approach is often used when discounting the expected cash flows of the combined company after an acquisition or merger.

Overview of method

Step 1: Calculate the asset beta of both companies before the acquisition.

Step 2: Calculate the average asset beta for the new combined company after the acquisition.

Step 3: Regear this beta to reflect the post-acquisition gearing of the new combined company.

Step 4: Calculate the combined company's WACC.

Step 5: Discount the post-acquisition free cash flows using this WACC.

Step 6: Calculate the NPV and deduct the value of debt to give the combined company's value of equity.

A worked example using this method follows.

Worked example

Anderson Co is planning to take over Webb Co, a company in a different business sector, with a different level of risk. Anderson Co's free cash flows are forecast to be $50m per year in perpetuity, Webb Co's free cash flows are forecast to be $10m per year into perpetuity and there are expected to be annual post-tax cash synergies of $5m if the acquisition goes ahead.

The combined company will pay tax at 30% and will have a pre-tax cost of debt of 5%. The risk free rate is 3% and the equity risk premium is 5.8%.

Currently, Anderson Co has an asset beta of 1.25 and Webb Co has an asset beta of 1.60. Assume that the beta of debt is zero.

The current financing of the two companies is:

$million	Debt	Equity
Anderson Co	50	450
Webb Co	20	80

Anderson Co is planning to make a cash offer of $80m to buy 100% of the shares of Webb Co. The cash offer will be funded by additional borrowing.

Required:

Calculate the gain in wealth for Anderson Co's shareholders if the acquisition goes ahead.

Solution

The **asset beta** of the combined company is $(1.25 \times (500/600)) + (1.60 \times (100/600)) = 1.31$

Therefore, the **equity beta** of the combined company is (using the asset beta formula from the formula sheet and assuming the new gearing is 150 debt to 450 equity):

$1.31 \times (1 + [0.7 \times (150/450)]) = 1.62$

Hence, using **CAPM**, the cost of equity is: $3\% + (1.62 \times 5.8\%) = 12.4\%$

and so the **WACC** $= (12.4\% \times (450/600)) + (5\% \times (1 - 0.30\%) \times (150/600)) = 10.2\%$

Therefore, the **discounted free cash flows** of the combined company are (as a perpetuity):

($50m + $10m + $5m)/0.102 = $637m.

The **value of equity** is then this NPV – the value of debt, i.e.

$637m – $150m = $487m

Hence the **shareholder wealth** of the Anderson Co shareholders has increased from $450m to $487m as a consequence of the acquisition.

Worked example using APV in valuation

In the earlier Chapter 7: Risk adjusted WACC and adjusted present value (APV), we saw that the APV method can be used to appraise a project when there is a significant change in financial risk (capital structure).

The application of the APV method to valuation

In the context of project appraisal, the APV was found by discounting the project cash flows at the ungeared cost of equity, and then adjusting for the costs and benefits associated with the actual financing used.

The approach used in valuation is very similar. In fact, to value a target company using APV, the method is:

1   calculate the present value of the target's free cash flows, using the ungeared cost of equity as a discount rate

2   add the present value of the tax saved as a result of the debt finance used in the acquisition (using either the risk free rate or the pre-tax cost of debt as a discount rate)

3   find the value of the target's equity (by deducting the value of the target's debt from the value calculated in step 2 above).

Then this value of the target's equity can be compared with the proposed acquisition cost to assess whether the acquisition should proceed.

Worked example

Derman Co is considering the acquisition of Weaver Co, an unquoted company. The shareholders of Weaver Co are hoping to receive $75 million for the sale of their shares.

The ungeared (asset) beta factor for Weaver Co is 1.20, the risk free rate of interest is 3% and the market risk premium is 5.8%.

Forecast free cash flows for Weaver Co are as follows:

$ million	Year 1	Year 2	Year 3	Year 4
Free Cash Flow	10.3	11.5	13.8	14.9

Annual cash flows after year 4 are expected to stay constant into perpetuity.

Weaver Co has $50 million of 6% debt, repayable in 4 years. The tax rate is 30%.

Required:

Using the APV method of valuation, calculate whether Derman Co should be prepared to pay the $75 million required by the shareholders of Weaver Co.

Solution

$ million	Year 1	Year 2	Year 3	Year 4 etc
Free cash flow	10.3	11.5	13.8	14.9
DF at 10% (see **W1**)	0.909	0.826	0.751	(1/0.10) × 0.751
PV	9.36	9.50	10.36	111.90

NPV = $141.12 million

(W1) CAPM: Ungeared cost of equity = 3% + (1.20 × 5.8%) = 9.96%, say 10%.

PV of tax relief on debt interest:

The interest paid will be 6% × $50 million = $3 million from year 1 to year 4.

Therefore, tax relief is 30% × $3 million = $0.9 million per year

Discounted at 6% (the pre-tax cost of debt) this has a present value of:

$0.9m × Annuity factor for 4 years at 6%

= $0.9m × 3.465 = $3.12 million

APV

So the total APV is $141.12m + $3.12m = $144.24 million

Thus, the equity value of Weaver Co is $144.24m – $50m = $94.24 million.

This is significantly more than the $75 million that the shareholders are hoping for, so Derman Co should pay the $75 million and take over Weaver Co.

Student Accountant article

The article 'Business valuations' in the Technical Articles section of the ACCA website provides further details on the various valuation methods shown in this chapter.

7   The valuation of debt

Introduction

Throughout this chapter so far, we have been calculating a value for the equity of a business, on the basis that on an acquisition, the acquirer has to purchase the equity (or certainly a controlling share of it). Therefore, equity valuation is a critical issue in every acquisition.

The value of the debt in a company is often quite easy to determine, and not as subjective as the value of equity. For example, a bank loan is not traded so its value doesn't fluctuate. However, traded debt (such as bonds) will have a fluctuating value so it is important that we can calculate a theoretical value for such debt.

Basic debt valuation model

The basic model for valuing a bond (or indeed any other type of debt) is similar to the cash based valuation methods discussed earlier i.e. the value of the bond will be the present value of the expected future receipts from the bond, discounted at the lender's required rate of return.

In this case, the receipts to the investor are the interest payments and the redemption amount from the bond.

Illustration 2 – Basic debt valuation

Frank Co has some $100 nominal value, 6% coupon bonds in issue. The bonds are redeemable at par in 5 years and investors require a return of 4% from investments of this level of risk.

Required:

Calculate the value of each Frank Co bond.

Solution

PV of receipts = ($6 × annuity factor for 5 years at 4%) + ($100 × discount factor for 5 years at 4%)

= (6 × 4.452) + (100 × 0.822) = $108.91

Estimating the required return to the debt holder

In the example above, the calculations were simple because we knew what the required return of the debt holder was. However, we saw in the earlier chapter on the weighted average cost of capital that the required return of the debt holder (sometimes called the 'yield' on the debt) is not always easy to estimate. In this earlier chapter, we saw how to derive the yield by either:

- adding a given credit spread onto the risk free rate, or

- deriving a yield curve for bonds with different redemption dates.

Therefore, exam questions might well link these two parts of the syllabus together i.e. you might first have to derive the yield on a bond, as seen in the earlier chapter on the weighted average cost of capital, and then use the yield as a discount rate to calculate the bond's value.

Illustration 3 – Use of credit spreads

Paper Co has some 5 year bonds in issue. It is an A rated company according to the main credit rating agencies.

The risk free rate of interest is 2.5%.

The current table of credit spreads (in basis points) published by one of the main agencies gives the following information:

Rating	1 yr	3 yr	5 yr	10 yr	20 yr
AAA	12	25	60	100	150
AA	19	40	80	150	211
A	28	56	99	221	276

Therefore, the yield on Paper Co's five year bonds can be found by adding the relevant credit spread to the risk free rate.

i.e. 2.5% + 99 basis points = 3.49%

The value of Paper Co's bonds can now be calculated by discounting future interest and redemption payments at this 3.49%.

Illustration 4 – Use of the yield curve

Stone Co is about to issue some 3 year, $100 par value, 5% coupon bonds.

The issue price (bond value) should be calculated by discounting each year's forecast cash flow from the bond at the relevant rate from the yield curve.

For Stone Co, assume the yield curve is:

Year	Individual yield curve (%)
1	3.96
2	4.25
3	4.56

Therefore, these 3 year, 5% coupon bonds should be issued at:

$(\$5/1.0396) + (\$5/1.0425^2) + (\$105/1.0456^3)$

= $101.26 (per $100 par value).

Student Accountant article

The examiner's article 'Bond valuation and bond yields' in the Technical Articles section of the ACCA website covers the calculation of bond yield curves and values in more detail.

8 High growth start-ups

A start-up business that wishes to attract equity investment will need to put a value on the business.

Valuing start-up businesses presents a different challenge from valuing an existing business, because unlike well-established firms many start-ups have:

- little or no track record
- ongoing losses
- few concrete revenues
- unknown or untested products
- little market presence.

In addition, they are often staffed by inexperienced managers with unrealistic expectations of future profitability and the lack of past data makes prediction of future cash flows extremely difficult.

Any mathematical valuation will inevitably be only an early starting point in the negotiations.

More detail on valuation of start-up businesses

Estimating growth

Growth for a start-up can be estimated based on:

- industry projections from securities analysts
- qualitative evaluation of the company's management, marketing strengths and level of investment.

However, both of these are essentially subjective and are unlikely to be reliable.

Since high-growth start-ups usually cannot fund operating expenses and investment needs out of revenues, long-term financial projections will be essential.

High growth is one thing, profitable high growth is another.

Growth in operating income is a function of:

- management's investment decisions:
    - How much a company reinvests.
    - The effectiveness of the investment in achieving results.
- the markets acceptance of the product and the action of competitors
- management's skills
- the riskiness of the industry.

Valuation methods

Since the estimate of growth is so unpredictable and initial high growth can so easily stagnate or decline, valuation methods that rely on growth estimates are of little value:

- Cash is key indicator of start-up success and asset models are therefore an important starting point.

However, they cannot provide an accurate value, since value rests more on potential than on the assets in place:

- DCF models are problematic because of the non-linear and unpredictable performance often exhibited in the early years, rendering the estimates highly speculative.

- Market based models are difficult to apply because of the problem of finding similar companies to provide a basis for comparison.

---

9 Problems of overvaluation

A share is overvalued if it is trading at a price that is higher than its underlying value.

In an efficient market this can still occur if:

- the market doesn't properly understand the business (as with internet businesses in the late 1990s) and overestimates the expected returns

- the managers running the company do not convey full company information honestly and accurately.

Management responses to overvaluation

Managers may be reluctant to correct the markets' mistaken perceptions. This can lead to:

- the use of creative accounting to produce the results the city is expecting

- poor business decisions aimed at giving the impression of success

- 'poor' acquisitions made using inflated equity to finance the purchase.

The impact of overvaluation on reported earnings

Since managers may manipulate reported earnings to produce more favourable results, the financial data they supply should be treated with caution. When valuing a company the financial statements should first be analysed and adjusted as necessary.

Why firms may be overvalued

Empirical evidence suggests that stock markets are semi-strong efficient – i.e. equity prices reflect all publicly available information. However, this does not necessarily mean that the shares will be fairly valued:

- If the market doesn't fully understand the information available – as was the case in the late 1990s and early 2000s with some high-tech, telecommunications, and internet ventures – it tends to overestimate the potential returns and so overvalue the equity.

- The price of overvalued equity may not be corrected by the market if:

  - the data provided by managers is deliberately misleading; a particular problem where the agency relationships within companies breaks down

  - there is collusion by gatekeepers including investment and commercial banks, and audit and law firms (many of whom have been accused of knowingly contributing to the misinformation and manipulation that fed the overvaluation of stocks such as Enron and Worldcom amongst others).

The response of management

When a firm produces earnings that beat analysts' forecasts, the share price rises by 5.5% on average. For unexpected negative earnings, the share price falls on average by 5.05%. Even where shares are fairly priced shares, managers may hide the inherent uncertainty in the business by smoothing earnings figures – delaying expenses and bringing forward revenue recognition, for example to ensure they consistently meet investor expectations.

If equity remains overpriced, the company will not be able to deliver – except by pure luck – the performance to justify its value. Where the management of an overvalued company is unwilling to accept the pain of a stock market correction, earnings smoothing can escalate into false accounting and outright lying. In addition, projects that give the appearance of potential earnings may be adopted even where the true likely outcome is a negative NPV, in order to forestall city concerns.

Research has also shown that companies are more likely to make acquisitions when their shares are overvalued. This is because they can use the shares to buy assets (which have true worth). However, these mergers often do not make good business sense and can destroy the core value of the firm.

Case study

At the time of Enron's peak market value of $60 billion, the company was worth about 70 times its earnings and 6 times its book value of assets. The company was a major innovator, and the business had a viable future. However, senior managers were unwilling to see the excess valuation diminished. Rather than communicate honestly with the market to reduce its expectations, they tried to hide the overvaluation by manipulating the financial statements and exaggerating the value of new ventures. By the time the market had realised the extent of the problem, the core value of the company had been destroyed.

Implications for valuations

In valuing a company, reported results form an essential core of data. Since reported earnings may be manipulated to produce more favourable results (aggressive accounting) the financial statements should be scrutinised and restated as necessary before being used as the basis for any valuation.

The detailed techniques are outside the syllabus but would include:

- Calculating the Cash to Operating Profit (COP) ratio. This involves comparing EBITDA (Earnings before Interest, Tax, Depreciation and Amortisation) with operating cash flow – they should be about equal. A figure above one is an indicator of aggressive accounting.

- Adjusting for changes in:

    - depreciation/amortisation policy

    - bad debt provisions.

- Considering whether the amortisation of intangibles and R&D is appropriate and adjusting if necessary.

- Making changes if necessary to the way leases and hire purchase agreements have been accounted for:

    - Removing any exceptional items.

    - Removing any exceptional payments such as directors' severance payments.

10 Chapter summary

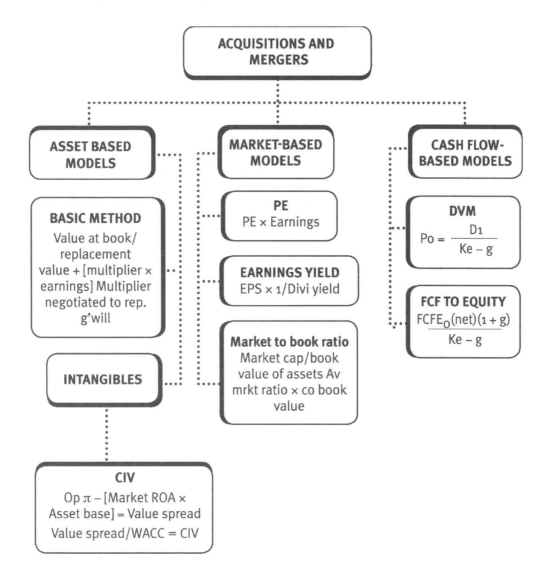

Test your understanding answers

Test your understanding 1

Free cash flows ($m)	Planning horizon				Beyond
Year	**1**	**2**	**3**	**4**	**5 onwards**
Sales	540	572.4	595.3	607.2	607.2
Operating profit	54	57	71.4	72.9	72.9
Tax	(16.2)	(17.1)	(21.4)	(21.9)	(21.9)
Depreciation	7.0	8.0	9.0	10.0	10.0
Operating cash flow	44.8	47.9	59	61	61
Replacement assets	(7.0)	(8.0)	(9.0)	(10.0)	(10.0)
Incremental assets (W1)	(3.2)	(1.9)	(1.4)	(0.5)	(0.0)
Free cash flows	34.6	38	48.6	50.5	51
PV factor	0.870	0.756	0.658	0.572	1/0.15 × 0.572
PV	30.1	28.7	32.0	28.9	194.5
Total PV			314.2		
Short-term investments			4.0		
Value of firm			318.2		
Market value of debt			(48.0)		
Value of equity			270.2		

(W1)

$8\% \times (540 - 500) = 40 \times 0.08$

$6\% \times (572.4 - 540) = 32.4 \times 0.06$

$6\% \times (595.3 - 572.4) = 22.9 \times 0.06$

$4\% \times (607.2 - 595.3) = 11.9 \times 0.04$

Test your understanding 2

$m	Year 1	Year 2	Year 3 etc
Sales (× 1.03 × 1.05)	308.3	333.5	360.6
Cost of sales (× 1.05)	(126.9)	(133.3)	(140.0)
	—	—	—
Gross profit	181.4	200.2	220.6
Operating expenses	(66.9)	(66.9)	(66.9)
Financing costs	(10.0)	(10.0)	(10.0)
	—	—	—
Forecast profit before tax	104.5	123.3	143.7
Less Taxation (28%)	(29.3)	(34.5)	(40.2)
Add back depreciation	12.3	12.3	12.3
Less Capital expenditure	(15.0)	(15.0)	(15.0)
Less Working capital investment	(2.0)	(2.0)	(2.0)
	—	—	—
Forecast free cash flows to equity	70.5	84.1	98.8
	—	—	—
DF 12%	0.893	0.797	0.797/0.12
	—	—	—
Present value	63.0	67.0	656.2

So the net present value = $786.2m

This is the total value of the equity in Butler Co.

With 500 million shares in issue, this corresponds to a value of 786.2/500 = $1.57 per share.

Test your understanding 3

Present value of first 3 years' dividends	0.719
= 0.32 × 3 yr 16% AF = 0.32 × 2.246	
Present value of growing dividend	1.778
= Value at T_3 × 3 yr DF = [0.32(1.04)/(0.16 – 0.04)] × 0.641	
	———
Share value	$2.497
	———

Test your understanding 4

EPS = 3,840,000/1,000,000 = $3.84

Value = P/E × EPS = 9 × 3.84 = $34.56

Test your understanding 5

The minimum acceptable value to XYZ's shareholders will be the current value of the equity, i.e.

9 × $390m = **$3,510m**

However, from ABC's perspective, it is important to estimate the value created by the likely synergies as well as the basic value of XYZ. Hence:

Value of XYZ to ABC = Value of the combination – Value of ABC at the moment

This measures the likely increase in value to ABC if XYZ is acquired, so will indicate the maximum amount payable.

Therefore,

Value of XYZ to ABC =

(New P/E × Total forecast earnings) – (13 × $693m)

$$= (12 × (\$693m + \$390m + \$125m)) - \$9,009m$$

$$= \$14,496m - \$9,009m = \mathbf{\$5,487m}$$

In reality, following negotiations between ABC and XYZ, the final value is likely to be somewhere between these two figures.

Test your understanding 6

Assuming the statement of financial position values are realistic, the valuation is:

	$000
Non-current assets	23,600
Current assets	8,400
Less: 6% Unsecured bond	(8,000)
Less: Current liabilities	(4,800)
	19,200

So the value per share is $19,200,000/8,000,000 = $2.40

(Note that the asset value of $19,200,000 is equal to the value of the ordinary share capital plus reserves.)

Test your understanding 7

Value per share =

($19,200,000 + $40,000,000 − $23,600,000)/8,000,000

= $4.45

Test your understanding 8

1   The value spread for DCH is:

	$m
Company operating profit	256.80
Less	
Appropriate ROA × Company asset base	
(16% × 522)	83.52
Value spread	173.28

2   Calculate the CIV

–   Find the post-tax value spread

$173.28 × (1 − 0.3) = $121.30

–   Find the CIV by calculating the PV of the post-tax value spread (assuming it will continue into perpetuity)

CIV = 121.30/0.09 = $1,348 million

3   The overall value of the firm = CIV + asset base

Firm value = $1,348m + $522m = $1,870m

Corporate failure and reconstruction

Chapter learning objectives

Study guide section	Study guide outcome	
D1: Financial reconstruction	(a)	Assess an organisational situation and determine whether a financial reconstruction is the appropriate strategy for a given business situation.
	(b)	Assess the likely response of the capital market and/or individual suppliers of capital to any reconstruction scheme and the impact their response is likely to have upon the value of the organisation.
D2: Business reorganisation	(a)	Recommend, with reasons, strategies for unbundling parts of a quoted organisation.
	(b)	Evaluate the likely financial and other benefits of unbundling.
	(c)	Advise on the financial issues relating to a management buy-out and buy-in.
A2: Financial strategy formulation	(a)	Assess organisational performance using methods such as ratios and trends.

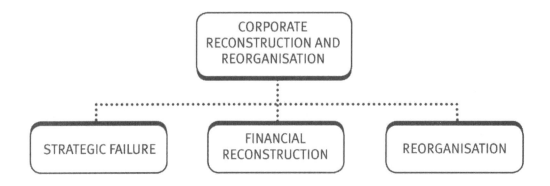

1 Financial distress and corporate failure

What is corporate failure?

Corporate failure occurs when a company cannot achieve a satisfactory return on capital over the longer term. If unchecked, the situation is likely to lead to an inability of the company to pay its obligations as they become due.

If a company is in financial distress, corporate failure will follow unless the company's problems can be identified and corrected.

Therefore, it is important that we can recognise the main causes of financial distress.

2 The five core causes of financial distress

The five core causes of financial distress in a business are:

- **Revenue failure**, caused by either internal or external factors. Revenue failure may be through a loss of orders (market failure) or through the acceptance of business which does not contribute to the growth of shareholder value.

- **Cost failure**, caused by weak cost control, changes in technology, inappropriate accounting policies, inadvertent or exceptional cost burdens, poor financial management or failure of effective governance.

- **Failure in asset management**, through failure to invest in appropriate technology, poor working capital management, inappropriate write off and reinvestment or poor organisation of the available assets.

- **Failure in liability management**, through failure to manage the company's relationship with the money markets, weak control of interest rate risk and currency risk or unsustainable credit policies.

- **Failure of capital management**, through either over or under-capitalisation or poor management of the company's relationship with the capital markets and in particular the company's debt portfolio and the optimisation of its cost of capital.

In practice problems rarely occur in isolation. A business is an internal and external network of relationships of assets and individuals, so problems in one area invariably have consequences elsewhere.

Research into the causes of corporate failure

A major study (Grinyer, Mayes et al., 1988) examined reasons why firms experience decline. Chief among the reasons found (in order of frequency) in the study were:

- adverse changes in total market demand
- intensification of competition
- high cost structure
- poor financial controls
- weak management
- failure of a large project
- poor marketing effort
- poor acquisitions
- poor quality.

Clearly, some of these are not, in themselves, strategic issues. Much can be done, by strong management accounting, to reduce costs, improve financial information and controls, improve project management and quality control systems, without changing strategy. It is always worth repeating the adage that strategic management builds on good operations management. No strategy can compensate for operational inefficiency in the long run.

However, many of the items listed involve changes in the market place, and the way that competition is carried out. Strategy is chiefly about adapting the firm to such changes, and strategic failure results when the organisation does not change as quickly as the market.

An illustration of financial distress

Norman English was a mechanical engineer, who founded his own company in the early 1980s, producing automotive parts. His early successes enabled him to diversify into a wide range of component manufacturing, and eventually into assembly of unbranded products. Many households are entirely unaware that the product they identify by an expensive, foreign brand was actually made locally.

In the mid-1990s, the company was floated and attracted favourable City opinion. New investment was used to launch into several new projects, and exporting. The latter was particularly well received and, with his forthright views, made Norman English a minor spokesperson for industry. Public speaking and committee work took a great part of his time. During the 2000s, company size increased by more than five times.

By 2018, Norman was ageing, unwell, and thinking about retirement. For several years, his involvement as CEO had been somewhat peripheral, and he was aware that his middle managers spent some time fighting each other. In the past, he had seen off such problems with his forceful personality and understanding of the business. The geographical spread of the company, and the proliferation of information made it extremely hard for him to keep the issues clear in his mind.

Further, the company's financial performance was not good and dividends were low. Manufacturing plant was old, and needed replacement. Product design was also looking dated; the firm had been slow to incorporate microchip technology into its products and was increasingly forced into producing budget models with little margin.

A widely-circulated report suggested that the export initiative had never been profitable, but had consumed a great deal of capital. Nonetheless, investors and lenders wanted to feel that Norman English was still in control.

Is this corporate failure? Give reasons for your answer. How has this arisen?

Solution

Although the company has not yet failed, it would seem to be only a question of time. When we look back at the purpose of a strategy, we see that the company is under-performing in most respects. The firm has failed to adapt to the environment – it is no longer producing goods that top firms wish to be associated with. It has failed to develop its resource base, both in terms of plant and learning about the capabilities of recent technologies. It no longer has a sense of purpose about the future, rather it seems that middle and senior managers cannot even agree on how to manage the business in its present state. Finally, it has confused a strategy – exporting – with the purpose of the strategy, to produce a return on investment.

The problem may have arisen in several ways, but it is likely that a formerly dramatic leader has lost his touch, leaving an absence of strategic thinking and energy. There is the added problem that the obvious solution, succession planning, leading to replacement of the CEO, would not be well received by the City. Consequently, this situation has been allowed to continue for longer than usual.

Identifying financial distress

It is possible to identify a business in financial distress by analysing its financial statements.

- Trends in ratios (such as return on capital employed and receivables collection period) can be used to identify the first signs of distress.

- Free cash flow analysis can also give an indication of likely problems.

3   Ratio analysis

A comprehensive analysis of performance will cover the following four areas: profitability, liquidity, gearing and stock market ratios.

Key ratios are listed under each of these headings below:

Profitability

Return on capital employed (ROCE), which can be measured as either net operating profit before tax or net operating profit after tax (NOPAT) as a percentage of capital employed.

Asset turnover is the ratio of revenue to capital employed.

Operating profit margin is operating profit expressed as a percentage of revenue.

Liquidity

The most basic measure of liquidity is the **current ratio** (current assets/current liabilities). However, this ratio is so simplistic that it is difficult to use it for any meaningful analysis. Instead, it is better to focus on the individual elements of working capital separately.

Debtor days (receivables collection period) = (Receivables/Credit sales revenue) × 365

Creditor days (payables payment period) = (Payables/Purchases) × 365

Inventory holding period = (Inventory/Cost of sales) × 365

The firm's **cash operating cycle** is calculated as Debtor days + Inventory holding period – Creditor days

Generally, a reduction in the overall length of the cycle indicates an improvement in the entity's liquidity position.

Gearing

If gearing is too high, the entity might be unable to service its debts. There are two ways of looking at gearing:

Balance sheet (statement of financial position) gearing

Debt value/Equity value, or

Debt value/(Value of equity + debt)

Note that equity value in the accounts is the share capital AND the reserves.

Statement of profit or loss gearing

The key measure is **interest cover** = Profit before interest and tax/Interest (Finance charges).

It is usually easier to identify potential problems from the statement of profit or loss figure, since a low figure close to unity gives an immediate and obvious cause for concern. Statement of financial position gearing ratios need to be compared (to industry averages and/or prior years) before they can be properly interpreted.

Stock market ratios

Note that if the entity being analysed is not listed, no calculations will be possible in this area.

However, if the entity is listed, this is arguably the most important area, since the ratios in this area will show whether the rest of the market perceives the entity positively or not.

Price-earnings (P/E) ratio = Share price/Earnings per share

Dividend cover = Earnings per share/Dividend per share

Dividend yield = Dividend per share/Share price

Test your understanding 1 – Performance analysis

The following shows the balance sheet (statement of financial position) and statement of profit or loss for Zed Manufacturing for the years ended 31 December 20X7 and 31 December 20X8:

Summarised statement of profit or loss ($m)

	20X7	20X8
Sales revenue	840	830
Cost of sales	554	591
Gross profit	286	239
Selling, distribution and administration expenses	186	182
Profit before interest	100	57
Interest	6	8
Profit before tax	94	49
Tax (standard rate 50%)	45	23
Profit for the year	49	26

Summarised statement of financial position (balance sheet) ($m)

	20X7		20X8
Non-current assets:			
Intangible assets	36		32
Tangible assets at net book value	176		222
	——		——
	212		254
Current assets:			
Inventory	237	265	
Receivables	105	132	
Bank	52	13	
	——	——	
	394		410
	——		——
Total assets	606		664
	——		——
Equity			
Share capital(ordinary 50c shares)	100		100
Retained earnings	299		348
	——		——
	399		448
Non-current liabilities:			
Long-term loans	74		94
	——		——
	473		542
Current liabilities:			
Payables	133		122
	——		——
Total equity and liabilities	606		664
	——		——

The current share price is $0.80 (it was $1.60 at the end of 20X7).

Required:

Summarise the performance of Zed Manufacturing in 20X8 compared with 20X7.

4 Assessing the risk of corporate failure – Other considerations

Limitations of corporate failure prediction models

There are a number of limitations of ratio analysis as a predictor of corporate failure:

- Ratios are a snapshot – they give an indication of the situation at a given point in time but do not determine whether the situation is improving or deteriorating.

- Further analysis is needed to fully understand the situation, for example a comparison with industry average ratio figures.

- Ratios are only good indicators of performance in the short term.

Practical indicators of financial distress

You should not think that ratio analysis of published accounts and free cash flow analysis are the only ways of spotting that a company might be running into financial distress. There are other possible indicators too. Some of this information might be given to you in an exam case study.

- Information in the published accounts, for example:

  - a worsening cash and cash equivalents position shown by the cash flow statement

  - very large contingent liabilities

  - important post-balance sheet events.

- Information in the chairman's report and the directors' report (including warnings, evasions, changes in the composition of the board since last year).

- Information in the press (about the industry and the company or its competitors).

- Information about environmental or external matter. You should have a good idea as to the type of environmental or competitive factors that affect firms.

More practical indicators

Going concern evaluation

A useful source of guidance on the troubled company is the International Standard on Auditing (ISA) 570, which identifies possible symptoms of going concern problems. Examples are outlined below. Again, if you come across any of these features in a case study the warning bells should start to sound.

Financial issues

- Net liability or net current liability position.

- Necessary borrowing facilities have not been agreed.

- Fixed-term borrowings approaching maturity without realistic prospects of renewal or repayment; or excessive reliance on short-term borrowings to finance long-term assets.

- Major debt repayment falling due where refinancing is necessary to the entity's continued existence.

- Major restructuring of debt.

- Indications of withdrawal of financial support by debtors and other creditors.

- Negative operating cash flows indicated by historical or prospective financial statements.

- Adverse key financial ratios.

- Substantial operating losses or significant deterioration in the value of assets used to generate cash flows.

- Arrears or discontinuance of dividends.

- Inability to pay creditors on due dates.

- Inability to comply with the terms of loan agreements.

- Change from credit to cash-on-delivery transactions with suppliers.

- Inability to obtain financing for essential new product development or other essential investments.

Operating issues

- Loss of key management without replacement.

- Loss of key staff without replacement.

- Loss of a major market, franchise, licence, or principal supplier.

- Labour difficulties or shortages of important supplies.

- Fundamental changes in the market or technology to which the entity is unable to adapt adequately.

- Excessive dependence on a few product lines where the market is depressed.

- Technical developments which render a key product obsolete.

Other issues

- Non-compliance with capital or other statutory requirements.

- Pending legal or regulatory proceedings against the entity that may, if successful, result in claims that are unlikely to be satisfied.

- Changes in legislation or government policy expected to adversely affect the entity.

Test your understanding 2

You have been asked to determine whether a company is failing. What areas would your analysis cover?

5   Corporate reconstruction

Corporate reconstruction of a failing company

Companies in financial distress often undergo corporate reconstructions to enable them to remain in business rather than go into liquidation. Corporate reconstruction in a failing company often involves raising some new capital and persuading creditors/lenders to accept some alternative to the repayment of their debts. This will ensure that the business continues in the short term.

Longer term, the management need to consider whether the reconstruction will help the company develop a sustainable competitive advantage, and provide opportunities for raising further finance.

Options open to failing companies

Options open to failing companies not wishing to go into liquidation, and which allow space for the development of recovery plans, usually include:

- a Company Voluntary Arrangement (CVA)
- an administration order.

Reconstruction of failing companies

1   **A Company Voluntary Arrangement (CVA)**

This is a legally binding arrangement between a company and its creditors. It may involve writing off debt balances on the profit and loss account against shareholders' capital and creditors' capital and therefore affects creditors' rights. However it is designed to ensure that the return to creditors is maximised. It is useful in companies under pressure from cash flow problems.

The procedure is as follows:

- An application is made to the court, asking it to call a meeting between the company and its creditors or a class of creditor, e.g. debenture holders.

- The scheme of reconstruction is put to the meeting and a vote taken.

- If there is 75% in value and including proxies vote in favour the court will be asked to sanction it.

- If the court sanctions it, the scheme is then binding on all the creditors.

2 Administration orders

Administration orders were introduced to allow space for a recovery plan to be put in place. The company, its Directors or one of the creditors can apply for an order. The company continues to trade whilst plans are put in place to rescue the company or achieve a better return for the creditors than if the company were liquidated immediately.

The use of an administration order

Consider the case of a manufacturing company which has become insolvent. There are also indications of poor credit control, and production problems including long lead times, high defect rates and high levels of stock. However there is a growing market for the company's products which are well-designed.

The company was put into administration to allow for a recovery plan to be developed. Its debts were written down and creditors and the bank given equity in the business. New management was brought in which improved the production and financial management and turned round the company which is now profitable.

Test your understanding 3

Why might the decision be made to liquidate a failing company rather than attempt to carry out a reconstruction?

Corporate reconstruction of a solvent company

Corporate reconstructions can also be undertaken by successful companies. The specific objectives of the reorganisation/reconstruction maybe one or more of the following:

- To reduce net of tax cost of borrowing.

- To repay borrowing sooner or later.

- To improve security of finance.

- To make security in the company more attractive.

- To improve the image of the company to third parties.

- To tidy up the statement of financial position.

Options for solvent companies

There are four main types of reorganisation used by solvent companies, depending on the individual situation. These are:

- conversion of debt to equity

- conversion of equity to debt

- conversion of equity from one form to another

- conversion of debt from one form to another.

Reconstruction of solvent companies

1 **Conversion of debt to equity**

   The most likely reasons for converting debt to equity are:

   – Automatically by holders of convertible debentures exercising their rights.

   – In order to improve the equity base of a company. This situation is particularly likely to arise when a company has financed expansion by short-term borrowings. Sooner or later, it will run into working capital problems, and if long-term loan funds are not available (because, for example, they would make the gearing excessively high) the only solution is to issue new shares, possibly by way of a rights issue.

2 **Conversion of equity to debt**

   Conversion of equity to debt usually involves the conversion of preference shares to some form of debenture. Although through the eyes of both companies and investors there is little to choose between debentures or preference shares bearing a fixed rate of return, in the eyes of both tax and company law they are very different:

   – From the tax point of view, payments to preference shareholders are dividends, and are not, therefore, an allowable charge in computing taxable profits.

   – From the legal point of view, conversion of preference shares into debentures constitutes a reduction of capital. Company law provisions relating to redemption of shares must therefore be followed. In accounting terms the broad effect of these provisions is to reduce distributable profits by the nominal value of the preference shares redeemed (by transferring amounts from distributable profit to capital redemption reserve).

3 Conversion of equity from one form to another

This includes:

–   Simplifying the capital structure. It was once common to have a variety of types of share capital, designed to appeal to a variety of investors. This has now become less favoured, and the tendency is to have only one, or at most two, classes of share capital. Conversion of shares from one type to another can only be carried out in accordance with the procedures in the articles, normally approved by a prescribed majority of the class affected, subject to rights of appeal to the court.

–   Making shares more attractive to investors, for example by subdivision into smaller units, or conversion into stock.

–   Eliminating reserves by issuing fully paid bonus shares. This is very much a tidying up operation, and may be especially useful to remove share premium accounts and capital redemption reserves. Additionally, in a period of inflation, it may be recognising the fact that a substantial part of the revenue reserves could never be paid out as dividends.

4 Conversion of debt from one form to another

This procedure might be undertaken to improve security, flexibility or cost of borrowing. For example:

–   Security – Consider the example of a company financing itself out of creditors and overdraft facilities, neither of which give any security. Rather than a rights issue, converting the creditors to long-term loans, e.g. debentures, would be equally satisfactory in that it would give security as to the source of funds.

–   Flexibility – Again, a company financing itself out of short-term borrowings has little room to manoeuvre. Flexibility could be improved by arranging more permanent financing. Alternatively, a company already borrowing to the limits of its ability could reduce its borrowings and improve flexibility by using other sources of finance – leasing for example.

–   Cost – Some loan finance is cheaper than others for example secured loans compared with unsecured loans. An opportunity may arise to shift from a relatively high cost to a relatively low cost source of funds.

The legal aspects of corporate reconstruction

Reconstruction schemes may be undertaken in companies which are healthy or those in financial difficulties.

The boundary line between these two types of scheme is not clear cut. Some provisions of company law can be used by both types of company.

For example the capital reduction provisions of S641 in the UK Companies Act 2006 can be used by a company to tidy up its statement of financial position reserves or to write off debt balances arising from trading losses so that further finance can be obtained.

6 Devising a corporate reconstruction scheme

General principles in devising a scheme

In most cases the company is ailing:

- Losses have been incurred with the result that capital and long-term liabilities are out of line with the current value of the company's assets and their earning potential.

- New capital is normally desperately required to regenerate the business, but this will not be forthcoming without a restructuring of the existing capital and liabilities.

The general procedure to follow would be:

1 Write off fictitious assets and the debit balance on profit and loss account. Revalue assets to determine their current value to the business.

2 Determine whether the company can continue to trade without further finance or, if further finance is required, determine the amount required, in what form (shares, loan stock) and from which persons it is obtainable (typically existing shareholders and financial institutions).

3 Given the size of the write-off required and the amount of further finance required, determine a reasonable manner in spreading the write off (the capital loss) between the various parties that have financed the company (shareholders and creditors).

4 Agree the scheme with the various parties involved.

The impact on stakeholders

The interests of a number of different stakeholder groups must be taken into account in a reconstruction. A reconstruction will only be successful if it manages to balance the different objectives (risk and potential return) of:

- ordinary shareholders

- preference shareholders

- creditors, including trade payables, bankers and debenture holders.

In a failing company, the reconstruction should be organised so that the main burden of any loss falls on the ordinary shareholders.

Test your understanding 4

Why is it important to consider the interests of shareholders in developing a reconstruction scheme?

Different stakeholder requirements

- Solvent companies often enter reconstruction schemes to improve their ability to raise finance in the future by making security in the company more attractive or to improve the image of the company to third parties. The view taken of the scheme by banks and investors is therefore vital in ensuring that this aim is achieved.

- Banks have been criticised in the past for being too quick to close down failing companies in order to protect their investment at the expense of others – it is important that they are initially supportive and allow time for decisions about the company's future to be made with the full co-operation of all stakeholders.

- The design of a reconstruction scheme for a failing company needs to take into account the interests of:
  - ordinary shareholders
  - preference shareholders
  - creditors.

- In a failing company the main burden of the losses should be borne primarily by the ordinary shareholders, as they are last in line in repayment of capital on a winding up. In many cases, the capital loss is so great that they would receive nothing upon a liquidation of the company. They must, however, be left with some remaining stake in the company if further finance is required from them.

- Preference shares normally give holders a preferential right to repayment of capital on a winding up. Their loss should be less than that borne by ordinary shareholders. They may agree to forgo arrears of dividends in anticipation that the scheme will lead to a resumption of their dividends.

- If preference shareholders are expected to suffer some reduction in the nominal value of their capital, they may require an increase in the rate of their dividend or a share in the equity, which will give them a stake in any future profits.

- Creditors, including debenture and loan stock-holders may agree to a reduction in their claims against the company if they anticipate that full repayment would not be received on liquidation. Like preference shareholders, an incentive may be given in the form of an equity stake.

- In addition trade creditors may also agree to a reduction if they wish to protect a company which will continue to be a customer to them.

Test your understanding 5 – Wire Construction Case Study Part 1

Case study – Wire Construction

Wire Construction has suffered from losses in the last three years. Its statement of financial position (balance sheet) as at 31 December 20X1 shows:

		$
Non-current assets		
Land and buildings		193,246
Equipment		60,754
Investment		27,000
		281,000
Current assets		
Inventory	120,247	
Receivables	70,692	
		190,939
Total assets		471,939
Equity and liabilities		
Ordinary shares – $1		200,000
5% Cumulative preference shares – $1		70,000
Profit and loss		(39,821)
		230,179
Non-current liabilities		
8% Debenture 20X4		80,000
Current liabilities		
Trade payables	112,247	
Interest payable	12,800	
Overdraft	36,713	
		161,760
		471,939

Sales have been particularly difficult to achieve in the current year and inventory levels are very high. Interest has not been paid for two years. The debenture holders have demanded a scheme of reconstruction or the liquidation of the company.

Required:

Show the likely position of the key stakeholders (ordinary shareholders, preference shareholders and debenture holders) if the firm goes into liquidation.

Assume that

1   The investment is to be sold at the current market price of $60,000.

2   10% of the receivables are to be written off.

3   The remaining assets were professionally valued as follows:

	$
Land	80,000
Building	80,000
Equipment	30,000
Inventory and work-in-progress	50,000

Illustration 1 – Wire Construction Part 2

Continuing with the information on Wire Construction from the previous TYU.

During a meeting of shareholders and directors, it was decided to carry out a scheme of internal reconstruction. The following scheme has been proposed:

1   Each ordinary share is to be re-designated as a share of 25c.

2   The existing 70,000 preference shares are to be exchanged for a new issue of 35,000 8% cumulative preference shares of $1 each and 140,000 ordinary shares of 25c each.

3   The ordinary shareholders are to accept a reduction in the nominal value of their shares from $1 to 25c, and subscribe for a new issue on the basis of 1 for 1 at a price of 30c per share.

4   The debenture holders are to accept 20,000 ordinary shares of 25c each in lieu of the interest payable. It is agreed that the value of the interest liability is equivalent to the nominal value of the shares issued. The interest rate is to be increased to 9.5% and the repayment date deferred for three years. A further $9,000 of this 9.5% debenture is to be issued and taken up by the existing holders.

5   The profit and loss account balance is to be written off.

6   The bank overdraft is to be repaid.

7   It is expected that, due to the refinancing, operating profits will be earned at the rate of $50,000 per year after depreciation but before interest and tax.

8   Corporation tax is 21%.

Required:

Prepare the statement of financial position (balance sheet) of the company, assuming that the proposed reconstruction has just been undertaken.

Solution

Tutorial note: In a question like this, do not waste time producing a statement of financial position unless it is specifically asked for by the examiner.

Statement of financial position at 1 January 20X2 (after reconstruction)

	$	$
Non-current assets		
Land at valuation		80,000
Building at valuation		80,000
Equipment at valuation		30,000
		190,000
Current assets		
Inventory	50,000	
Receivables (70,692 × 90%)	63,623	
Cash (W1)	92,287	
		205,910
		395,910
Called up share capital	$	$
Issued ordinary shares of 25c each (W2)		140,000
Issued 8% cumulative preference shares of $1 each (W2)		35,000
Share premium account (W2)		17,800
Capital reconstruction account (balancing figure)		1,863
		194,663
Non-current liabilities: 9.5% Debenture 20X7		89,000
Current liabilities: Trade payables		112,247
Total equity and liabilities		395,910

Workings

(W1) Cash

	$
New share issue – Ords	
200,000 × 30c	60,000
New debentures	9,000
Sale of investment	60,000
	129,000
Less: Overdraft	36,713
	92,287

(W2) Shareholdings

	Ords No.	Ords $	Prefs No.	Prefs $	Share premium $
Per SOFP	200,000	200,000	70,000	70,000	
Redesignation		50,000			
Exchange	140,000	35,000	(35,000)	(35,000)	
New issue	200,000	50,000			10,000
Debenture interest	20,000	5,000			7,800
(12,800 – 5,000)					
	560,000	140,000	35,000	35,000	17,800

Tutorial note: As $12,800 of debenture interest is to be cancelled for $5,000 nominal of ordinary shares the excess is share premium (i.e. the consideration for the shares is deemed to be the liability removed).

Test your understanding 6 – Wire Construction Part 3

Advise the shareholders and debenture-holders as to whether they should support the Wire Construction reconstruction.

More detail on the Wire Construction Case Study

Reconstruction account, relating to the second part of the case study

Note: The capital reconstruction account can be proved as follows:

Book value:		Revised values:	
Non-current assets	281,000	Land and buildings	160,000
Inventory	120,247	Equipment	30,000
Receivables written off		Investment	60,000
10% × 70,692	7,069	Inventory	50,000
Profit and loss balance	39,821	Share capital reduced	
		200,000 × 75c	150,000
Balance – Capital reserve	1,863		
	450,000		450,000

Detailed advice to shareholders and debenture holders, relating to the third part of the case study

It follows that the scheme must be favourable to the debenture-holders if it is to have success. The holders are being offered an increased rate of interest but an extended repayment date.

The expected interest cover is reasonable:

	$
Expected profits	50,000
Interest	
9.5% × 89,000	8,455
Interest cover = 5.9	

In financial terms it is a matter of comparing the prospective rate of interest with interest rates currently available elsewhere.

The preference shareholders are having half of their investment turned into equity. They will have 140,000/560,000 × 100 = 25% of the ordinary share capital. In addition they will have an increased dividend rate and are not required to contribute any further capital.

The ordinary shareholders retain part of their stake in the company if they participate 200,000/560,000 = 36% without any further cash investment. The further cash investment required of $50,000 leaves them with the majority holding.

The expected available earnings will be:

	$
Profit	50,000
Interest	(8,455)
	———
	41,545
Tax at 21%	(8,724)
	———
	32,821
Preference dividend 35,000 × 8%	(2,800)
	———
Available to equity	30,021
	———
EPS 30,021/560,000 × 100 =	5.4c
	———

However, as the shareholders would receive nothing on a liquidation, the additional expected return to them is twice 5.4c per share i.e.:

On old shareholding

200,000 × 5.4c

On new shareholding

200,000 × 5.4c

This therefore seems a reasonable proposition to the ordinary shareholders.

Test your understanding 7 – Another reconstruction example

BDJR Computers Global is a company that manufactures a range of personal computers that are sold to retailers, and also directly to individuals and businesses through online sales.

Due to a number of technical problems the company's sales have fallen significantly over the last year resulting in an operating loss of $160,000. The company has, as a result, built up losses on its retained earnings and there is a significant risk of insolvency.

To avoid this, the company's financial advisers have proposed a scheme of reconstruction.

Balance Sheet at 31/12/20X9 (statement of financial position)

Assets	$000	$000
Non-current assets		1,100
Current assets		
Inventory	410	
Receivables	220	
Cash	25	
	―――	
Net Current Assets		655
		―――
Total Assets		1,755
		―――
Equity and Liabilities		
Share Capital ($1 shares)		200
Retained Earnings		(50)
		―――
Total Equity		150
Non-current liabilities – Bank loan		1,200
Current liabilities		
Payables	205	
Overdraft	200	
	―――	
		405
		―――
Total Equity and Liabilities		1,755
		―――

Notes:

1   If the company was liquidated all of the assets could be sold for their book values except for inventory. Following a review it was discovered that $220k of the inventory is obsolete but the remainder could be sold for book value. In addition $90k of the receivables is irrecoverable.

2   To be successful a scheme of reconstruction would need to raise $195k of cash to invest in new manufacturing processes.

3   Given the risk attached to the company any providers of new equity capital will require a return of at least 18%.

4   The current interest rates are 8% on the bank loan and 6% on the overdraft. The bank loan is secured.

The following scheme of reconstruction is proposed:

1   The nominal value of each existing share will be reduced to 50c.

2   Goodwin Bank (who provide both the overdraft and loan) will convert half of the overdraft and 1/3 of the loan into a total of 200,000 new shares.

3   New finance of $400k will be raised from a venture capital company, PC ventures, who will buy new shares for $1.25 per share. In addition to investing in the new manufacturing process the finance will also be used to repay the payables.

4   Following the reconstruction it is expected that the company will generate $320K of profit before interest and tax per year. Tax is payable at 28%. Assume no tax losses.

Required:

(a) Determine how much each of the original investors in likely to get in the event of a liquidation.

(b) Following the reconstruction calculate the expected EPS, and the return on equity to the venture capital company, and advise as the whether the venture capital company is likely to invest in BDJR computers.

(c) From the post-reconstruction EPS calculation above calculate the effective return that the bank is likely to receive on the capital converted into equity.

(d) Determine whether the existing ordinary shareholders, and the bank, are likely to accept the scheme.

Assessing the impact of the reconstruction scheme

The examples above have shown that the key to assessing the impact of a reconstruction scheme is to look at the likely impact on major stakeholders. In order to do this effectively, it is often useful to assess the likely impact of the scheme on the company's forecast:

- statement of financial position (SOFP)

- earnings (in total and/or per share).

Several recent past exam questions have first asked students to calculate the impact of a reconstruction scheme on the SOFP and earnings, and then to comment on the implications.

A tabular approach can help to present the answer in an efficient and easily understandable way.

Tabular method

Step 1: Set up a table with the current forecast earnings and SOFP in the first column. Set up columns to the right for each of the suggested reconstruction options.

Step 2: Deal with each of the suggested reconstruction options separately – start with the one that sounds most straightforward.

Step 3: Deal with the simple parts of the reconstruction first. Usually these will be the SOFP figures e.g. if the plan is to increase debt finance by $5 million, simply add $5 million to the non-current liabilities and write the updated figure in the correct column.

Step 4: Now move on to the more tricky parts. Usually these will be the adjustments to earnings caused by (one or more of) paying more interest on the higher amount of debt finance identified in Step 3, generating more income from assets purchased and identified in Step 3, generating less income because assets have been disposed of and identified in Step 3.

Step 5: Having calculated the revised forecast earnings figure in Step 4, adjust the forecast retained earnings (reserves) in the SOFP to reflect this.

Step 6: Balance off the SOFP by entering anything that is still unknown as a balancing figure.

Step 7: Repeat steps 3 to 6 for each of the reconstruction options.

Test your understanding 8

Ray Co is a company with a diversified range of business units. One of its business units, a training business, is underperforming. The Finance Director estimates that this business unit could be disposed of by selling its non-current assets for their book value of $25 million.

At the recent Board meeting, the directors discussed the possible disposal, and two proposals for the use of the $25 million proceeds:

Proposal 1: Use half the proceeds to pay off some debt finance, and the other half to invest in some new non-current assets for an existing publishing business unit.

Proposal 2: Use the full amount to purchase some new non-current assets and set up a new business unit in the advertising industry.

At the end of the Board meeting, the Finance Director was asked to prepare some calculations to show the likely impact of these two proposals on Ray Co's forecast statement of financial position and forecast earnings for the coming year.

Ray Co, financial information

Extract from the forecast statement of financial position for next year

	$000
Non-current assets	92,650
Current assets	16,620
	————
Total assets	109,270
	————
Equity and liabilities	
Share capital – $1 par value	50,000
Reserves	20,550
	————
Total equity	70,550
Non-current liabilities	30,000
Current liabilities	8,720
	————
	109,270
	————

Ray Co's forecast after-tax profit for next year is $15.6 million.

Other information:

- The training business contributes 10% of Ray Co's overall after-tax profit.

- Ray Co pays tax at a rate of 20% per year and its after-tax return on the publishing business unit is estimated at 8%. The after-tax return on the advertising investment is expected to be 13%.

- The non-current liabilities are bank loans with a fixed interest rate of 6%.

Required:

(a) Estimate the impact of the two proposals on next year's forecast earnings and forecast financial position.

(b) Evaluate the decision to sell the training business unit, and advise the Board of Directors which (if either) proposal should be accepted.

7 Business reorganisation methods

Unbundling companies

Unbundling is the process of selling off incidental non-core businesses to release funds, reduce gearing and allow management to concentrate on their chosen core businesses. The main aim is to improve shareholder wealth. Unbundling can take a number of forms:

- Spin-offs, or demergers, in which the ownership of the business does not change, but a new company is formed with shares in the new company owned by the shareholders of the original business. This results in two or more companies instead of the original one.

- Sell-offs, which involves the sale of part of the original company to a third party, usually in return for cash.

- Management buyouts, in which the management of the business acquires a substantial stake in and control of the business which they managed.

- Liquidation, when the entire business is closed down, the assets sold and the proceeds distributed to shareholders. This is done when the owners of the business no longer want it or the business is not seen as viable.

The rest of this chapter explains these unbundling options in detail.

Test your understanding 9

Explain why shareholders might support the unbundling of a diversified organisation.

Spin-offs or demergers

Demergers

The aim of a demerger is to create separate businesses which together have a higher value than the original company. Following a demerger:

- shareholders own the same proportion of shares in the new business or businesses as they did in the previous one

- each company owns a share of the assets of the original company

- the new company or companies generally have new management who can take the individual companies in diverging directions; and each company could eventually be sold separately

- the original company may no longer exist, with all its assets distributed to the new business.

Sell-offs

A company may sell-off parts of the business for a number of reasons, such as:

- to raise cash

- to prevent a loss-making part of the business from lowering the overall performance business

- to concentrate on the core areas of the business

- to dispose of a desirable part of the business to protect the rest from the threat of a takeover.

Management buy-outs

What is a management buy-out?

Overall the distinguishing feature of an MBO is that a group of managers acquires effective control and substantial ownership and forms an independent business. Several variants of an MBO may be identified and are explained below:

- **Management buy-out** – where the executive managers of a business join with financing institutions to buy the business from the entity which currently owns it. The managers may put up the bulk of the finance required for the purchase.

- **Leveraged buyout** – where the purchase price is beyond the financial resources of the managers and the bulk of the acquisition is financed by loan capital provided by other investors.

- **Employee buyout** – which is similar to the above categories but all employees are offered a stake in the new business.

- **Management buy-in** – where a group of managers from outside the business make the acquisition.

- **Spin-out** – this is similar to a buyout but the parent company maintains a stake in the business.

The difference between a management buy-out and a management buy-in

A management buy-out (MBO) involves the purchase of a business by the management team running that business.

However, a management buy-in (MBI) is the purchase a business by a management team brought in from outside the business.

The benefits of a MBO relative to a MBI (to the company being acquired) are that the existing management is likely to have detailed knowledge of the business and its operations. Therefore they will not need to learn about the business and its operations in a way which a new external management team may need to. It is also possible that a MBO will cause less disruption and resistance from the employees when compared to a MBI. If the former parent company wants to continue doing business with the new company after it has been disposed of, it may find it easier to work with the management team which it is more familiar with. The internal management team may be more focused and have better knowledge of where costs can be reduced and sales revenue increased, in order to increase the overall value of the company.

The drawbacks of a MBO relative to a MBI (to the company being acquired) may be that the existing management may lack new ideas to rejuvenate the business. A new management team, through their skills and experience acquired elsewhere, may bring fresh ideas into the business. It may be that the external management team already has the requisite level of finance in place to move quickly and more decisively, whereas the existing management team may not have the financial arrangements in place yet. It is also possible that the management of the parent company and the company being sold off have had disagreements in the past and the two teams may not be able to work together in the future if they need to.

Example of a MBO (Springfield ReManufacturing Corporation)

One of the most well-known examples of a management buy-out is the Springfield ReManufacturing Corporation (SRC).

Prior to the buyout the company was the Springfield, Missouri unit of International Harvester, a manufacturer of agricultural and construction equipment in the USA. The unit remanufactured components for the company's construction division.

Although the business unit was profitable, International Harvester was in significant difficulties and decided it no longer needed the Springfield unit.

However a group of managers led by Jack Stack, who became CEO of SRC Holdings Corporation, kept the plant running and eventually bought the unit.

SRC Holdings now owns many other successful companies.

Reasons for a management buy-out

Opportunities for MBOs may arise for several reasons:

- The existing parent company of the 'victim' firm may be in financial difficulties and therefore require cash.

- The subsidiary might not 'fit' with the parent's overall strategy, or might be too small to warrant the current management time being devoted to it.

- In the case of a loss-making part of the business, selling the subsidiary to its managers may be a cheaper alternative than putting it into liquidation, particularly when redundancy and other wind-up costs are considered.

- The victim company could be an independent firm whose private shareholders wish to sell out. This could be due to liquidity and tax factors or the lack of a family successor to fill the owner-manager role.

Advantages of buy-outs to the disposing company

There are a number of advantages to the parent company:

- If the subsidiary is loss-making, sale to the management will often be better financially than liquidation and closure costs.

- There is a known buyer.

- Better publicity can be earned by preserving employee's jobs rather than closing the business down.

- It is better for the existing management to acquire the company rather than it possibly falling into the hands of competitors.

Advantages to the acquiring management

The advantages to the acquiring management are that:

- it preserves their jobs

- it offers them the prospect of significant equity participation in their company

- it is quicker than starting a similar business from scratch

- they can carry out their own strategies, no longer having to seek approval from head office.

Issues to be addressed when preparing a buy-out proposal

MBOs are not dissimilar to other acquisitions and many of the factors to be considered will be the same:

- Do the current owners wish to sell? The whole process will be much easier (and cheaper) if the current owners wish to sell. However, some buy-outs have been concluded despite initial resistance from the current owners, or in situations of bids for the victim from other would-be purchasers.

- Will the new business be profitable? Research shows that MBOs are less likely to fail than other types of new ventures, but several have collapsed. As the new owners the management team must ensure that the business will be a long-run profit generator. This will involve analysing the performance of the business and drawing up a business plan for future operations.

- If loss-making, can the new managers return it to profitability? Many loss-making firms have been returned to profitability via management buyouts. Managers of a subsidiary are in a unique position to appreciate the potential of a business and to know where cost savings can be made by cutting out 'slack'.

- What will be the impact of loss of head office support? On becoming an independent firm many of the support services may be lost. Provision will have to be made for support in areas such as finance, computing, and research and development. Although head office fees might be saved after the buyout these support services can involve considerable expense when purchased in the outside market.

- What is the quality of the management team? The success of any MBO will be greatly influenced by the quality of the management team. It is important to ensure that all functional areas are represented and that all managers are prepared to take the required risks. A united approach is important in all negotiations and a clear responsibility structure should be established within the team.

- What is the price? The price paid will be crucial in determining the long-term success of the acquisition. Care must be taken to ensure that all relevant aspects of the business are included in the package. For example, trademarks and patents may be as important as the physical assets of the firm. In a similar way responsibilities for costs such as redundancy costs must be clearly defined.

- Is the deal in the best interests of shareholders? Managers known to the existing owners may be able to secure the buyout at a favourable price, and the final price paid will be a matter for negotiation. However, the current directors of the firm have a responsibility to shareholders to obtain the best deal possible, which may mean a full 'commercial' price being paid for the victim company.

Sources of finance for buy-outs

For small buy-outs the MBO, the price may be within the capabilities of the management team, but the acquiring group usually lack the financial resources to fund the acquisition. Several institutions specialise in providing funds for MBOs. These include:

- the clearing banks
- pension funds and insurance companies
- merchant banks
- specialist institutions such as the 3i group and Equity Capital for Industry
- government agencies and local authorities, for example regional development agencies.

Different types of finance

The types of finance and the conditions attached vary between the institutions. Points to be considered include:

- The form of finance – Some institutions will provide equity funds. However, more commonly loan finance will be advanced. Equity funds will dilute the management team's ownership but on the other hand high gearing could put substantial strain on the firm's cash flow. Leveraged buyouts, with gearing levels up to 20:1, have been known.

- Duration of finance – Some investors will require early redemption of loans and will provide funds in the form of redeemable loan stock or preference shares. Others may accept longer-term involvement and look to an eventual public flotation as an exit from the business.

- The involvement of the institution – Some institutions may require board representation as a condition of providing funds.

- Ongoing support – The management team should also consider the institution's willingness to provide funds for later expansion plans. Some investors also offer other services such as management consultancy to their clients.

- Syndication – In large buyouts it is possible that a syndicate of institutions may be required to provide the necessary funds.

- The need for financial input from the management team – All institutions will look for a 'significant' input of finance from the management team relative to their personal wealth as a demonstration of their commitment. Managers can expect to have to plough in their redundancy payments, take second mortgages on their homes and often provide personal guarantees on loans.

- The need for a business plan – Institutional investors will also expect to see a well-prepared business plan and usually an investigating accountant and a technical advisor will be employed to investigate the proposal.

- Other sources of finance – The management team can also look for other sources of finance to assist in the MBO. Hire purchase or leasing of specific assets may ease initial cash flow problems. Government grants might be available for certain firms, and the managers' and employees' pension scheme may be available to provide some of the required finance.

MBO terminology

The management buy-out industry has developed a range of colourful jargon terms over its period of existence, such as:

- **BIMBO** – A deal involving both a buy-in by outside managers and a buy-out by current managers was coined a bimbo by Investors in Industry (the 3i group) and unfortunately the name has stuck. Around 50% of recent deals take this form.

- **Caps, floors and collars** are limits to which the interest rate charged in a leveraged buy-out can respectively rise, fall and range between.

- **Junk bonds** are tradeable high yielding unsecured debt certificates issued by companies in US leveraged buy-outs. Their equivalent in the UK is mezzanine finance, though this is less easily traded than junk bonds since it is not usually issued in certificate form.

- **Lemons** are deals that go wrong.

- **Plums** are successful deals.

- **The living dead** are companies which just earn enough cash to pay the interest on their borrowings, but no more. They can continue indefinitely, but are never expected to flourish.

- **A ratchet arrangement** permits managers to be allocated a larger share of the company's equity if the venture performs well. It is intended as an incentive arrangement to encourage managers to be committed to the success of the company.

Assessing the viability of buy-outs

Both the management buy-out team and the financial backers will wish to be convinced that their proposed MBO will succeed. It is important to ask the following questions:

- Why do the current owners wish to sell? If the owners are trying to rid themselves of a loss-making subsidiary, are the new management being over-confident in believing that they can turn it round into profitability?

- Does the proposed management team cover all key functions? If not, new appointments should be made as soon as possible.

- Has a reliable business plan been drawn up, including cash flow projections, and examined by an investigating accountant?

- Is the proposed purchase price too high?

- Is the financing method viable? The trend is now away from highly geared buy-outs.

Test your understanding 10

Identify some advantages and disadvantages of management buy-outs.

Numerical example of a management buy-out

Example question – Management buy-out

(a) The following information relates to the proposed financing scheme for a management buy-out of a manufacturing company.

	%	€000
Share capital held by		
Management	40	100
Institutions	60	150
		250
10% redeemable preference shares (redeemable in ten years' time)		1,200
		1,450
Loans		700
Overdraft facilities		700
		2,850

Loans are repayable over the next five years in equal instalments. They are secured on various specific assets, including properties. Interest is 12% per year.

The manufacturing company to be acquired is at present part of a much larger organisation, which considers this segment to be no longer compatible with its main line of business. This is despite the fact that the company in question has been experiencing revenue growth in excess of 10% per year.

The assets to be acquired have a book value of €2,250,000, but the agreed price was €2,500,000.

You are required to write a report to the buy-out team, appraising the financing scheme.

(b) What problems are likely to be encountered in assembling a financing package in a management buy-out of a service company as opposed to a manufacturing company?

Solution

(a) **Report**

To: Buy-out team

From: Consulting accountant

Date: X-X-20XX

Subject: MBO Financing Scheme Overview

The financing scheme involves the purchase of assets with a net book value of €2,250,000 for an agreed price of €2,500,000. The finance that will be raised will provide funds of €2,850,000 in the form of:

	€000
Equity	250
Preference shares	1,200
Loan	700
Overdraft	700
	———
	2,850
	———

Of the funds raised only €350,000 will be available to the business after the purchase price has been paid. This will be in the form of unused overdraft facilities.

Gearing

As is common to MBOs the gearing level will be very high. There is only €250,000 of equity compared to €2,250,000 of debt finance (including the preference shares and excluding the unused element of the overdraft). The gearing level will mean that the returns to equity will be risky, but the buyout team own 40% of a €2.5 million company for an investment of only €100,000. The rewards are potentially very high.

One consequence of the level of gearing is that it will be difficult to raise any additional finance. There are unlikely to be any assets that are not secured, and in any case the level of interest and loan repayments would probably prohibit further borrowing.

Cash commitments

The annual cash commitments from the financing structure are summarised below:

(i) **Loan repayments**

Annual payments will have to be made in the repayment of capital and interest on the €700,000 loan. The annual amount will be:

€700,000/3.605* = €194,175

* The cumulative discount factor for 5 years at 12%.

(ii) **Redeemable preference shares**

The redeemable preference shares will be either cumulative or non-cumulative. Assuming that they are cumulative €120,000 will, on average, have to be paid every year. There is a little flexibility in that if the dividend cannot be met it can be postponed (but not avoided).

The redeemable preference shares will have to be repaid after 10 years. This can either be provided for over the 10 years, or an alternative source of finance found to replace the funds. Assuming that they will be required to be provided for according to the terms of the financing package this will require a commitment of €120,000 per year.

(iii) **Overdraft**

The element of the overdraft used to finance the purchase price is effectively a source of long term finance. The rate of interest is not known but if we make the (unrealistic) assumption that it is also at 12%, then the €350,000 drawn down will cost €42,000 per year.

Overall summary

In total there will be a commitment to pay approximately €476,000 per year. This will be the first priority of the new company. The management team will need to generate sufficient funds from the only available source, operations, in order to meet this commitment.

Other cash requirements

Apart from the need to generate cash to satisfy the requirements of the financing scheme the company will also need to generate funds to invest in working capital and fixed assets as required. At the moment these capital requirements are unknown. In the context of 10% annual growth in revenue, however, they might exceed the unused element of the overdraft facility.

Institutional involvement

By virtue of their stake in the company of 60% of the equity the financial institutions hold the controlling stake. This will be enhanced by their position as the providers of the remainder of the finance. Consequently the institutions will able to determine many aspects of the company's management, including the appointment of directors. The institutions are likely to have two overriding objectives:

(i) The security of loan and interest repayments. Any breach of the loan arrangements might trigger the appointment of administrators or receivers, and the institutions' investment would almost certainly be lost.

(ii) Realising their equity investment. The institutional investors will probably expect to realise their investment in a relatively short time frame. This is commonly set at between 5 and 7 years.

Profit growth

Apart from the requirement to generate cash as noted above the company must also generate steady profit growth. The institutional investors will require a history of profit growth in order to enable the sale of their stake through either flotation or a trade sale.

Conclusion

The financing scheme will place a heavy cash burden on the company, particularly in the early years. The involvement of the institutions will perhaps prove unwelcome, but the MBO would be impossible without accepting it.

(b) There are three main problems particular to arranging a finance package for a service company.

(i) **The lack of tangible assets**

Because MBOs normally have to be highly geared there is a requirement to provide security for the loans in a package. Service companies commonly have a very low level of tangible assets. It will therefore be difficult to attract much debt finance.

(ii) **'People' businesses**

The success of service companies depends on their staff. Institutions tend to view such success with suspicion because people, unlike plant and machinery, can resign. Unless the people in question are tied into the company within the MBO financing package by, for example, insisting on their investing in equity there is little guarantee that they will stay with the company.

(iii) Working capital

The nature of most service businesses is that they have unusually high working capital requirements. The main expense for a service company is staff costs. It is almost impossible to take extended credit from staff without losing their services. The supplies of service companies often involve a long period of work before customers can be billed. Consequently, a finance package would have to provide for the working capital, and working capital finance is particularly risky because it is difficult to secure and so may be equally difficult to raise.

Evaluating the benefits of reorganisations

Concentration of growth and maximisation of shareholder value

Following the unbundling of a company the resulting value of the new businesses can exceed that of the original business. This suggests that the shares in the original business were selling for less than their potential value and can be for a number of reasons:

- The splitting-off of non-core activities from the rest of the business may increase the visibility of an under-valued asset which is then valued more highly by the market.

- Businesses may be valued more highly in the hands of the new managers than under the previous management.

- The sale of less profitable parts of the business may be viewed favourably by the market, result in an increased valuation for the remainder.

- The performance of the individual businesses may improve, also resulting in a higher valuation.

Reduction in complexity and improved managerial efficiency

In recent years, increasing numbers of demergers and sell-offs have taken place in order to reduce the complexity of the organisation:

- Diversified businesses are complex to manage. As the pace of change and uncertainty facing organisations has increased, the complexity of large businesses becomes more difficult to cope with and absorbs management time and energy which is diverted from the business itself.

- Smaller companies tend to be more flexible and respond more easily to change.

- Following a demerger, the new companies have a clearer, more focused management structure.

- Improved managerial effectiveness also results from the splitting off of non-core businesses as managers are free to concentrate on what they do best.

- Changes in the market can also mean that benefits of synergy no longer exist, and there is no longer any business reason for the organisation to retain unrelated businesses.

The release of financial resources for new investment

Unbundling parts of the company can also release financial resources:

- selling a loss-making part of the business which is absorbing funds can release cash to invest in the core businesses or new activities

- a reduction in the size and complexity of the organisation can reduce the central management costs, freeing up resources

- unbundling generates a lump sum in proceeds which can be invested in a specific project.

Illustration

In October 2006 GUS plc, a major UK retail and business services conglomerate, completed the process of demerger into three separate businesses. Burberry, a luxury brand, was demerged first, and the remaining company was demerged in October 2006 into Experian, a provider of analysis and information services, and Home Retail Group, a major home and general retailer.

This demerger was the culmination of a strategy to maximise shareholder wealth by focusing on a small number of high-growth businesses. Other parts of the business were sold off to raise funds for reinvestment. Among the reasons given for the demerger were:

- the lack of synergy between the businesses

- separate opportunities for investment for shareholders

- allowing the independent businesses to pursue individual strategies and benefit from a better management focus.

8 Chapter summary

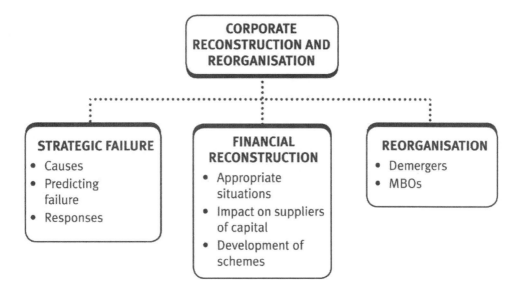

Test your understanding answers

Test your understanding 1 – Performance analysis

Profitability ratios

Return on Capital Employed (based on pre-tax operating profit)

20X7: 100/473 = 21.1%

20X8: 57/542 = 10.5%

Return on Capital Employed (based on post-tax operating profit)

20X7: 100 (1 – 0.50)/473 = 10.6%

20X8: 57 (1 – 0.50)/542 = 5.3%

In 20X7, Zed had a much higher level of ROCE, indicating that the firm was generating far more profit from its capital invested. However, as profitability fell in 20X8, the ROCE fell too. It may be that the percentage return being generated is not sufficient to meet the required returns of the investors.

Liquidity ratios

Debtor days

= (Receivables/Credit sales revenue) × 365

20X7: (105/840) × 365 = 46 days

20X8: (132/830) × 365 = 58 days

Creditor days

= (Payables/Cost of sales) × 365

(Cost of sales used since purchases is not given)

20X7: (133/554) × 365 = 88 days

20X8: (122/591) × 365 = 75 days

Inventory holding period

= (Inventories/Cost of sales) × 365

20X7: (237/554) × 365 = 156 days

20X8: (265/591) × 365 = 164 days

Cash operating cycle

= Debtor days + Inventory holding period – Creditor days

20X7: 46 + 156 – 88 = 114 days

20X8: 58 + 164 – 75 = 147 days

The liquidity position of Zed has worsened between 20X7 and 20X8.

Both inventory holding period and debtor days have increased, indicating perhaps a lack of control over working capital levels. At the same time, the creditor days figure has fallen, indicating that Zed is being pushed by its creditors to pay sooner. This may indicate that creditors are becoming worried about the ability of Zed to meet its obligations.

Gearing ratios

SOFP: Debt/Equity

20X7:   74/399 = 19%

20X8:   94/448 = 21%

Statement of profit or loss: Interest cover = Profit before interest/Interest

20X7: 100/6 = 16.7 times

20X8: 57/8 = 7.1 times

Gearing is not a problem at the moment for Zed.

The gearing ratio is low and relatively stable, while the interest cover is high. Even with the drop in profitability in 20X8, Zed's profit is still large enough to cover the low level of debt interest payable.

Market ratios

Share price

20X7: $1.60

20X8: $0.80

P/E ratio

= Share price/Earnings per share

NB: Zed has 100m/0.50 = 200m shares

20X7:   1.60/(49/200m) = 6.5

20X8:   0.80/(26/200m) = 6.2

The share price has halved between 20X7 and 20X8, and the P/E ratio has also fallen. This is a worrying trend. The market seems to be losing confidence in Zed.

Test your understanding 2

The analysis is likely to include:

- An analysis of key ratios, including trends.

- Changes in the cash flow of the business.

- An analysis of the company report to identify any significant changes over the year.

- An assessment of the environment facing the company and any opportunities and threats.

- An assessment of the strengths and weaknesses of the company.

Test your understanding 3

Possible reasons include:

- The main reason for the company's failure is that there is no longer a market for its products.

- The level of assets is so low that there is no chance of covering any of the company's debts.

- The management of the company and the creditors are not prepared to co-operate with one another, making it impossible to agree a way forward.

Test your understanding 4

The shareholders are important for the future financing of the business. If they are not happy with the scheme or don't retain a stake in the business they will not invest in the company in the future.

However, the ordinary shareholders have the most to gain if the company performs well, so it is only fair that if the company is failing, they should bear the greatest loss.

Balancing these two factors is key to the success of the reconstruction.

Test your understanding 5 – Wire Construction Case Study Part 1

Position of interested parties in a liquidation (assuming assets can be sold at going concern value)

	$	$
Value of non-current assets		190,000
Inventory		50,000
Receivables		63,623
Investment		60,000
		———
Assets available		363,623
Secured debts		
Debentures		(80,000)
		———
		283,623
Other payables		
Overdraft	36,713	
Interest	12,800	
Trade payables	112,247	
	———	
		161,760
		———
Available to shareholders		121,863
		———

The above statement of assets reflects the position of the three interested parties with no reconstruction scheme. The debenture holders would be sure of their capital repayment on a liquidation and most probably the arrears of interest. The preference shareholders would also receive their repayment of $70,000. $51,863 would then be left for the ordinary shareholders (unless there is a difference between going concern and break up values of the assets).

Test your understanding 6 – Wire Construction Part 3

Ordinary shareholders

Before the reconstruction, the ordinary shareholders own 100% of the control and voting rights in the company. After the reconstruction, their control will be diluted to 71.4% (400,000 shares out of a total of 560,000) assuming they take up their rights.

These shareholders may be unwilling to take up their rights given that the company is failing, but clearly if the company cannot raise any new finance it will slide into liquidation and the shareholders will receive little return (shown in the first part of this case).

This should be the key consideration of the ordinary shareholders: if they don't accept the reconstruction, they may well end up with nothing. Accepting the reconstruction will mean that they keep control of the company and will benefit in the future if the company's performance improves.

On balance it appears that the scheme is acceptable to the shareholders.

Preference shareholders

Before the reconstruction, the preference shareholders are guaranteed a return of $3,500 per year (5% × 70,000 $1 shares). Initially they may well be unhappy about exchanging this income stream for a new proposal of 8% on 35,000 $1 shares (i.e. $2,800), but there are two other factors which make the scheme more appealing on further examination:

- the preference shareholders will also own some ordinary shares, so that if the company's performance improves, they will receive more dividends (and capital growth) from these shares in the future.

- as mentioned above with the ordinary shareholders, the risk is that if the company goes into liquidation, the shareholders may receive a lower than hoped for return. (Admittedly the preference shareholders' position is less risky than the ordinary shareholders' position, but some risk remains).

Again, on balance, it seems that the scheme is acceptable to the preference shareholders.

Debenture holders

The debenture holders' patience is wearing thin: no interest has been paid for two years, so the debenture holders could apply to the courts to liquidate the company, in which case (according to part one of this case study) they would receive a full settlement of all that is owed to them. However, in a liquidation there is no guarantee that the debenture holders would get back all that is owed to them (assets may not be worth as much as was first thought), so a reconstruction may well be more appealing.

The terms of this reconstruction seem quite favourable to the debenture holders. Despite having to forgo interest in the short term, the debenture holders are being offered:

- ordinary shares – i.e. the chance of capital growth and dividends in the longer term if the company's performance improves.

- higher longer term interest rates (9.5% per year will be paid until 20X7 rather than 8% until 20X4 as at present).

Providing the debenture holders are not struggling for cash in the short term, the scheme should be appealing to them in the long term. If the debenture holders do have a preference for short term income, a liquidation may be a better option, since we have forecast that they will receive all their money back.

Test your understanding 7 – Another reconstruction example

(a) **Liquidation**

Assuming that there are no liquidator's fees, in the event of liquidation the distribution will be as follows:

Assets to distribute		$000
Per SOFP		1,755
Less inventory write off		(220)
Less receivables write off		(90)
		———
Net		1,445
Distribution:		
Secured Bank Loan		(1,200)
		———
		245
Unsecured		
Payables	205	
Overdraft	200	
	———	
		(405)
		———
		(160)
		———

Notes:

1 Unsecured creditors will only receive 245/405 = 60% of the amount owing.

2 Ordinary shareholders will receive nothing.

(b) **Post-reconstruction EPS**

Earnings post-reconstruction	$000
PBIT	320
Bank loan interest (2/3 × 1,200 × 8%)	(64)
Overdraft interest (1/2 × 200 × 6%)	(6)
PBT	250
Tax at 28%	(70)
PAT	180

Number of shares post-reconstruction

= 200,000 (existing s/h) + 200,000 (bank) + 320,000 (venture capitalist)

= 720,000

Post-reconstruction forecast EPS

= 180/720 = 25c per share.

Return on equity to venture capital company = 25c/125c = 20%

This is above the target required return of 18% and is therefore acceptable to the venture capital company.

(c) **Effective return to bank on converted capital**

Capital foregone = (1/2 × 200,000) + (1/3 × 1,200,000) = $500,000

Number of shares in exchange = 200,000

Earnings generated = 200,000 × 25c = $50,000

Therefore return = $50,000/$500,000 = 10%

(d) **Acceptability of the scheme**

Existing ordinary shareholders.

If the company is liquidated then the existing ordinary shareholders will get nothing.

In a reconstruction the existing ordinary shareholders will lose control of the company (they will only own 200/720 = 28% of the equity) but they are likely to earn 25c per new ordinary share. Based on the original nominal value of each share this represents a return of 25c/$1 = 25%.

Given the return that the providers of new capital are likely to receive the scheme seems very generous to the existing shareholders. It is likely that the bank and the venture capital providers would want the scheme to be amended so as to make it less generous to the existing shareholders.

Bank

If the company is liquidated the bank is likely to recover the full amount of the secured loan but will only recover 60% of the overdraft. Following the reconstruction the bank will only get a return of 10% on the capital converted into equity but will continue to receive interest on the remaining loan and overdraft at the existing rate.

Given that 1/3 of the secured loan is converted into equity and the forecast return on this is only 2% more than the current loan interest, this is unlikely to be acceptable to the bank.

Test your understanding 8

(a) **Impact on SOFP and earnings**

Earnings	Current $000	Proposal 1 $000	Proposal 2 $000
Forecast after-tax profit	15,600	15,600	15,600
Profits foregone by selling training business (10%)		(1,560)	(1,560)
Interest saved by paying off debt ($12.5m × 6% × (1–0.20))		600	
Extra returns generated:			
– 8% on publishing investment (8% × $12.5m)		1,000	
– 13% on advertising investment			3,250
Adjusted profit after tax	15,600	15,640	17,290
Change		+40	+1,690

SOFP	Current	Proposal 1	Proposal 2
	$000	$000	$000
Non-current assets	92,650	80,150	92,650
Current assets	16,620	16,660	18,310
Total assets	109,270	96,810	110,960
Equity and liabilities			
Share capital	50,000	50,000	50,000
Reserves	20,550	20,590	22,240
Total equity	70,550	70,590	72,240
Non-current liabilities	30,000	17,500	30,000
Current liabilities	8,720	8,720	8,720
	109,270	96,810	110,960

Workings and notes:

Proposal 2 (looks like the easier option, so start with that)

Easy figures: Reduce NCA by $25m to show sale of training, but then increase it by $25m to show investment in advertising. No net impact.

No change to financing, so share capital and NCL stay the same.

No information to the contrary so assume CL stay the same.

Adjust reserves figure to reflect likely increase in earnings of $1.690m.

Balance off SOFP, entering CA as a balancing figure.

Proposal 1

Easy figures: Reduce NCA by $25m to show sale of training, but then increase it by $12.5m to show investment in publishing.

Reduce NCL by $12.5m (no change in share capital).

No information to the contrary so assume CL stay the same.

Adjust reserves figure to reflect likely increase in earnings of $0.040m.

Balance off SOFP, entering CA as a balancing figure.

(b) Evaluation of the proposals

The training business unit is underperforming, so it does seem sensible to consider disposing of it. However, it is not clear whether the under-performance is a long-term problem, or whether it is just a short-term blip. Before making a final decision, it would be sensible to assess the possibility of the training business performance improving in the near future.

The training business has non-current assets worth $25 million, and is expected to generate after-tax profits of $1.56 million – a return of 6.24%. This is lower than the return on investment in both the publishing and the advertising sectors, so the proposals to sell the training business and re-invest the proceeds elsewhere make good financial sense.

Proposal 2 in particular looks very attractive. Earnings are expected to increase significantly because of the high level of return expected in the advertising sector. The only concern is whether the directors have the necessary expertise to invest in this new sector. If not, it might be very difficult for Ray Co to achieve this high level of return.

Proposal 1 is not as financially attractive – the after-tax profit figure is likely to stay almost the same. Also, it is not clear why the directors are considering paying off some of the debt here. Interest rates are fairly low, the company's gearing is not excessive, and the interest cover is high. An excessive amount of debt finance can cause problems for a company, but a moderate amount of debt (like Ray Co has) is actually a positive thing, given that it enables a company to benefit from tax relief on its interest payments.

Recommendation

As long as it can be shown that the training business under-performance is a long-term problem, it makes sense to dispose of this business unit.

On balance, Proposal 2 looks a more attractive option, given that it involves investment in a highly profitable industry, and avoids the unnecessary repayment of debt under Proposal 1.

Test your understanding 9

- There is potential for improved performance leading to increased shareholder value.

- There may be an increase in the total value of the investment.

- Selling off unrelated or loss-making businesses may improve financial performance.

- There is an opportunity to choose how much to invest in particular parts of the business.

Test your understanding 10

Advantages:

- Although the risks are high so are the potential rewards. In the situation of leveraged buyouts, where the bulk of the equity is in the hands of the management team, the returns to shareholders once the loans have been covered can be very large.

- They are usually considered to be less risky than starting a new business from scratch.

- Firms that have been subject to MBOs tend to operate at a higher level of efficiency. The traditional divorce between ownership and control is effectively ended and managers (and shareholding employees) have great incentive to improve the efficiency of the firm.

Disadvantages:

- They are risky (approximately one in ten fail) and can involve managers losing their personal wealth as well as their jobs.

- Problems will be encountered when the new company becomes independent. For example, head office support services will be lost, and existing customers may go elsewhere if they see the new firm being too risky.

Employability and technology skills

Chapter learning objectives

This chapter contains an overview of the employability and technology skills syllabus area. This is relevant for all ACCA Applied Skills (except LW) and Strategic Professional exams.

1 Purpose of chapter

This chapter explains the content included within the employability and technology skills syllabus area. A similar syllabus area is included in all Applied Skills (except LW) and Strategic Professional level syllabi.

ACCA exams utilise software and technology similar to those used in the modern workplace. By studying ACCA exams, candidates will be equipped with both technical syllabus knowledge and practical, applied software skills. The employability and technology skills syllabus area is included within the syllabus to acknowledge this acquired skillset.

2 Content of the employability and technology skills syllabus area

The employability and technology skills syllabus area is outlined in the syllabus and study guide. It consists of the following:

1   Use computer technology to efficiently access and manipulate relevant information.

2   Work on relevant response options, using available functions and technology, as would be required in the workplace.

3   Navigate windows and computer screens to create and amend responses to exam requirements, using the appropriate tools.

4   Present data and information effectively, using the appropriate tools.

By using a computer-based examination (CBE), the ACCA has enabled the use of word processing, spreadsheet, screen navigation and data processing functionalities to become part of their assessment range. This replicates the skills used in the modern workplace, whether in accounting practice, in industry or outside of accountancy altogether.

Whilst sitting an exam, candidates will be using the functionality of the CBE software in a variety of ways e.g. to prioritise information within the question data provided, to organise and present their answers in a manageable fashion, to use shortcuts and software functionality to increase efficiency. Skills garnered in the workplace can be used in the examination and vice versa.

This reflects that exams offered at Applied Skills and Strategic Professional are designed to be relevant and accessible to all students. The delivery mode and assessment types require students to demonstrate similar skills to those required in the modern workplace. Offering computer-based exams (CBE) at all levels gives students the opportunity to focus on the application of knowledge to scenarios, using a range of tools – spreadsheets, word processing and presentations. This not only allows students to demonstrate their technical and professional skills, but also their use of the technology relevant to the modern workplace. CBEs, therefore, offers the candidate an examination delivery method that allows them to demonstrate their knowledge and skills with the technology they are most familiar with, in the classroom or at work.

3   CBE support and the ACCA Exam Practice Platform

ACCA candidates can access the ACCA's Exam Practice Platform to practice attempting questions using the CBE software. It is imperative that candidates are familiar with the software before attempting the exam.

The link to the AFM Exam Practice Platform access gateway can be found here:

https://bit.ly/2VJJYxw

This requires a MyACCA login to access the platform.

Support, access to other papers, tutorial videos and CBE advice can be found here:

https://bit.ly/2IIBV6Y

4   Contents of the CBE and Exam Practice Platform

On entering the Exam Practice Platform, candidates will access their dashboard, as follows:

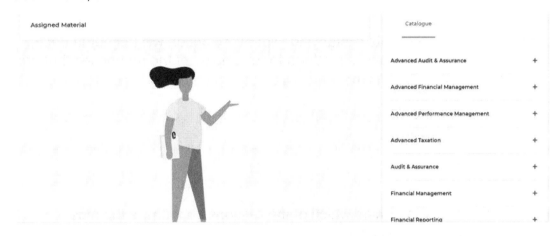

Candidates should click their appropriate paper in the right hand side menu. There they will be able to 'assign' content to their workspace. Candidates can assign a blank workspace or ACCA official resources (which include past papers presented using the CBE software for the candidates to attempt) to their workspace.

This will be added to the candidate's 'Self-Assigned Material' listing as below:

When working within the assignment the candidate will use response options to provide their answer.

The **Response Options** are where the candidate will attempt their answers.

There are up to three types of response option provided, dependent upon the specific syllabus a candidate is studying. Not every option will appear in each exam. Check the exam practice platform for examples of the responses that are commonplace within your exam.

The response options are:

- the word processor,

- the spreadsheet, and

- the slides.

The candidate must determine which of the response options is the most suitable for their specific answer.

These replicate the functionality of widely used software packages. The ACCA has developed this software, for use during home question practice and under exam conditions, to replicate the practical skill sets and work-based behaviours adopted by various industries throughout the world. By studying the ACCA qualification, candidates will improve, not only on their technical knowledge and understanding, but also on skills applied on a daily basis within their work environments. Candidates should practise questions using the CBE platform to ensure they are familiar with the various functions available within their specific examination.

Word Processor

The word processor response option, when relevant, will appear as follows:

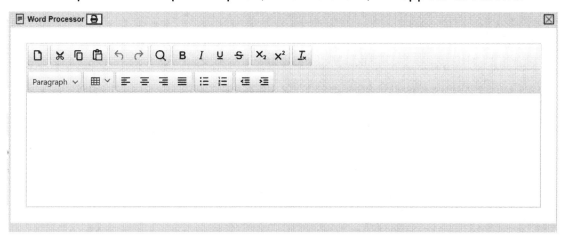

This resource has the following advantages and disadvantages:

Advantages	Disadvantages
It is easier to continue typing without entering new cells or becoming concerned about cell width	It cannot automatically perform calculations
Answers can be more easily split into paragraphs to make them more visually appealing and easier to mark	Numerical tables can be difficult to label and align
Bullet points can be used to present lists	
Text can be easily aligned and justified	
Superscript and subscript can be easily added to express terms such as 4^2, for example	

It is, therefore, best suited to discursive answers where candidates are asked, for example, to discuss, analyse or evaluate issues from a scenario or calculation.

The word processing software application could be used in the workplace within the writing of meeting agendas, meeting minutes, external letters, marketing output, briefings, audit reports, textbooks and instructional documentation.

Spreadsheet

The spreadsheet response option, when relevant, will appear as follows:

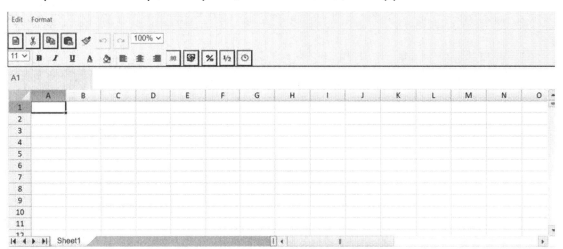

The spreadsheet software uses the same functionality as other commonly used spreadsheet software. Basic formulae functionality, such as SUM, power functions (e.g. SQRT) and the use of brackets are all reproduced within the ACCA software. Candidates are advised to practise questions using the software so that they are familiar with the functions available and how they can be utilised to the candidate's advantage through improved efficiency.

This resource has the following advantages and disadvantages:

Advantages	Disadvantages
This can quickly and easily perform calculations (e.g. using sums for totals or formulae for calculations)	Text will carry over beyond one cell and may go across and beyond the page width making answers difficult to follow (and mark)
Data within tables can be easily aligned	Bullet points are difficult to use
Shortcut icons can be used to quickly round figures, change numbers to percentages etc	
Tables can easily and quickly be copied when calculations need to be reperformed (e.g. for sensitivity analysis, tax calculations for more than one person, financial statements for more than one company etc)	
Column width can be adjusted to label length	

It is, therefore, best suited for performing calculations within the examination e.g. NPVs, tax computations, goodwill calculations.

Spreadsheet software is ubiquitous in the modern workplace. It has the capacity to record, store and organise huge swathes of data and information relating to all aspects of a business. Examples of only a few of its possible practical applications include the preparation of management and financial accounts, operational controls and record-keeping e.g. expense claims, data analytics, project appraisals, sample size selection and tax computations.

Slides

The slides response option, when relevant, will appear as follows:

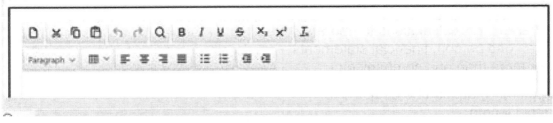

This resource has the following advantages and disadvantages:

Advantages	Disadvantages
Key messages are easier to see	There is limited space and ability to contain detail outside of the speaker notes
Tables can be easily added	It cannot automatically perform calculations
Speaker notes can be added for the detail	
Bullet points can be used to provide lists	
Titles can be given more prominence	

This is best suited for requirements that ask for presentations. This is not a common response option and is not applicable to most papers. Expect to see it within SBL.

The simple, aesthetically pleasing visual information provided by slide software is effectively used in the workplace when material is required to be shared with a wider audience. Slide software will be used during sales pitches, job interviews, presentations, key note speeches and product launches.

5   Chapter summary

The CBE software will replicate the work that is performed by accountants in a typical workplace. It will be used across the syllabus to support a candidate's answer by providing suitable response options for different types of answers.

These response options will be most suitable in the following instances (when available):

- For discursive answers: it is best to use the word processing option
- For calculations: it is best to use the spreadsheet option
- For presentations: it is best to use the slides option.

Questions and Answers

1   The role and responsibility of the financial manager

Influence on objectives

Discuss, and provide examples of, the types of non-financial, ethical and environmental issues that might influence the objectives of companies. Consider the impact of these non-financial, ethical and environmental issues on the achievement of primary financial objectives such as the maximisation of shareholder wealth.

(15 marks)

2   Investment appraisal

Breckhall

Assume that you have been appointed finance director of Breckhall Co. The company is considering investing in the production of an electronic security device, with an expected market life of five years.

The previous finance director has undertaken an analysis of the proposed project; the main features of his analysis are shown below.

Proposed electronic security device project:

	Year 0 $000	Year 1 $000	Year 2 $000	Year 3 $000	Year 5 $000	Year 5 $000
Investment in depreciable non-current assets	4,500					
Cumulative investment in working capital	300	400	500	600	700	700
Sales		3,500	4,900	5,320	5,740	5,320
Materials		535	750	900	1,050	900
Labour		1,070	1,500	1,800	2,100	1,800
Overhead		50	100	100	100	100
Interest		576	576	576	576	576
Depreciation		900	900	900	900	900
		3,131	3,826	4,276	4,726	4,276
Taxable profit		369	1,074	1,044	1,014	1,044
Taxation		129	376	365	355	365
Profit after tax		240	698	679	659	679

All of the above cash flow and profit estimates have been prepared in terms of present day costs and prices as the previous finance director assumed that the sales price could be increased to compensate for any increase in costs.

You have available the following additional information:

1   Selling prices, working capital requirements and overhead expenses are expected to increase by 5% per year.

2   Material costs and labour costs are expected to increase by 10% per year.

3   Tax allowable depreciation (tax deduction) is allowable for taxation purposes against profits at 25% per year on a reducing balance basis.

4   Taxation of profits is at a rate of 35% payable one year in arrears.

5   The non-current assets have no expected salvage value at the end of five years.

6   The company's real after-tax discount rate (or weighted average cost of capital) is estimated to be 8% per year and nominal after-tax discount rate 15% per year.

7   Assume that all receipts and payments arose at the end of the year to which they relate except those in year 0 which occur immediately.

Required:

(a)   Estimate the net present value of the proposed project. State clearly any assumptions that you make.

(16 marks)

(b)   Calculate by how much the discount rate would have to change to result in a net present value of approximately zero.

(4 marks)

(Total: 20 marks)

3   International operations and international investment appraisal

Growth of multinationals

The global revenue of the largest multinational companies is greater than the gross national product of many countries.

Required:

Discuss factors that might explain the successful growth of large multinational companies.

(10 marks)

Axmine

The managers of Axmine Co, a major copper processor based in the UK are considering a joint venture with Traces, a company owning significant copper reserves in a South American country. The proposed joint venture with Traces would be for an initial period of four years.

Copper would be mined using a new technique developed by Axmine. Axmine would supply machinery at an immediate cost of 800 million pesos and 10 supervisors at an annual salary of £40,000 each at current prices. Additionally Axmine would pay half of the 1,000 million pesos per year (at current prices) local labour costs and other expenses in the South American country.

The supervisors' salaries, local labour, and other expenses will be increased in line with inflation in the United Kingdom and the South American country respectively.

Inflation in the South American country is currently 100% per year and in the UK, it is expected to remain stable at around 8% per year. The government of the South American country is attempting to control inflation and hopes to reduce it each year by 20% of the previous year's rate.

The joint venture would give Axmine a 50% share of Traces' copper production, with current market prices at £1,500 per 1,000 kilograms. Traces' production is expected to be 10 million kilograms per year, and copper prices are expected to rise by 10% per year (in British pounds, £) for the foreseeable future. At the end of four years, Axmine would be given the choice to pull out of the venture or to negotiate another four-year joint venture, on different terms.

The current exchange rate is 140 pesos/£1. Future exchange rates may be estimated using the purchasing power parity theory.

Axmine has no foreign operations. The cost of capital of the company's UK mining operations is 16% per year. As this joint venture involves diversifying into foreign operations, the company considers that a 2% reduction in the cost of capital would be appropriate for this project.

Corporate tax is at the rate of 20% per year in the South American country and 35% per year in the UK. A tax treaty exists between the two countries and foreign tax paid is allowable against any UK tax liability. Taxation is payable one year in arrears and 25% straight-line tax allowable depreciation is available on the machinery in both countries.

Cash flows may be assumed to occur at the year-end, except for the immediate cost of machinery. The machinery is expected to have negligible terminal value at the end of four years.

Required:

(a) **Prepare a report discussing whether Axmine Co should agree to the proposed joint venture. Relevant calculations must form part of your report or an appendix to it.**

State clearly any assumptions that you make.

(20 marks)

(b) **Explain whether you consider Axmine's proposed discount rate for the project to be appropriate.**

(5 marks)

(c) **If, once the investment has taken place, the government of the South American country imposed a block on the remittance of dividends to the UK, discuss how Axmine might try to avoid such a block on remittances.**

(5 marks)

(Total: 30 marks)

4   The financing decision

There are no additional questions on this chapter.

5   The dividend decision

HGT Co

HGT Co is a UK based multinational company with two overseas subsidiaries. The company wishes to minimise its global tax bill, and part of its tax strategy is to try to take advantage of opportunities provided by transfer pricing.

HGT has subsidiaries in Glinland and Rytora.

Taxation	UK	Glinland	Rytora
Corporation tax on profits	30%	40%	25%
Withholding tax on dividends	–	10%	–
Import tariffs on all goods (not tax allowable)	–	–	10%

The subsidiary in Glinland produces 150,000 graphite golf club shafts per year which are then sent to Rytora for the metal heads to be added and the clubs finished off. The shafts have a variable cost in Glinland of $6 each, and annual fixed costs are $140,000. The shafts are sold to the Rytoran subsidiary at variable cost plus 75%.

The Rytoran subsidiary incurs additional unit variable costs of $9, annual fixed costs of $166,000, and sells the finished clubs at $30 each in Rytora.

Bi-lateral tax agreements exist which allow foreign tax paid to be credited against the domestic (UK) tax liability.

All transactions between the companies are in $. The Rytoran subsidiary remits all profit after tax to the parent company each year, and the Glinland subsidiary remits 50% of its profit after tax.

Required:

The parent company is considering instructing the Glinland subsidiary to sell the shafts to the Rytoran subsidiary at full cost. Evaluate the possible effect of this on tax and tariff payments, and discuss briefly any possible problems with this strategy.

(10 marks)

6   The weighted average cost of capital (WACC)

There are no additional questions on this chapter.

7 Risk adjusted WACC and adjusted present value

Goddard Co

Goddard Co, a company in the educational sector, is evaluating two new projects. One is in the leisure industry and the other is in the publishing industry. Goddard's summarised statements of financial position, and those of Cottons Co and Blackwell Co, quoted companies in the leisure and publication industry respectively, are shown below:

	Goddard Co $m	Cottons Co $m	Blackwell Co $m
Non-current assets	96	42	102
Current assets	95	82	65
Total assets	191	124	167
Ordinary shares[1]	15	10	30
Reserves	50	27	20
Medium and long-term loans[2]	56	15	69
Current liabilities	70	72	48
Total equity and liabilities	191	124	167
Ordinary share price (cents)	380	180	230
Debenture price ($)	104	112	–
Equity beta	1.1	1.3	1.2

1 Goddard and Blackwell 50 cents par value, Cottons 25 cents par value.

2 Goddard 12% debentures 20X8-20Y0, Cotton 14% debentures 20Y2, Blackwell medium-term bank loan.

Goddard's capital structure will remain unchanged if both or either of the projects are undertaken. Goddard's investors currently require a return on debt of 11%. The risk free rate of interest is estimated to be 6% per year and the market return 14% per year. Corporate tax is at a rate of 30% per year.

Required:

(a) Calculate the appropriate discount rate to use for each of these projects. Explain your answer and state clearly any assumptions that you make.

(10 marks)

(b) Goddard's marketing director suggests that it is incorrect to use the same discount rate each year for the leisure project, as the early stages of the investment are more risky and should be discounted at a higher rate. Another board member disagrees saying that more distant cash flows are riskier and should be discounted at a higher rate. Discuss the validity of the views of each of the directors.

(5 marks)

(Total: 15 marks)

8 Option pricing

Option valuation

An investor holds 200,000 shares in D Co and is considering buying some put options to hedge her investment. D's current share price is $6. The risk free interest rate is currently 12% per year and the recent volatility of D Co shares has been 30% per year. She requires European put options with an exercise price of $5 for exercise in two years' time.

Required:

(a) Calculate the value that the bank is likely to charge for 200,000 put options of the investor's required specification.

(8 marks)

(b) Calculate the investor's change in wealth if she buys 200,000 put options to hedge her portfolio and the share price in two years' time is a) $3 per share or b) $10 per share.

(4 marks)

(c) A friend informs the investor that she could achieve a safer position by selling call options to construct a delta hedge. Calculate the number of call options to be sold to construct a delta hedge.

(3 marks)

(Total: 15 marks)

9   An introduction to risk management

Political risk

The finance department of Beela Electronics has been criticised by the company's board of directors for not undertaking an assessment of the political risk of the company's potential direct investments in Africa. The board has received an interim report from a consultant that provides assessment of the factors affecting political risk in three African countries. The report assess key variables on a scale of –10 to +10, with –10 the worst possible score and +10 the best.

	Country 1	Country 2	Country 3
Economic growth	5	8	4
Political stability	3	–4	5
Risk of nationalism	3	0	4
Cultural compatibility	6	2	4
Inflation	7	–6	6
Currency convertibility	–2	5	–4
Investment incentives	–3	7	3
Labour supply	2	8	–3

The consultant suggests that economic growth and political stability are twice as important as the other factors.

The consultant states in the report that previous clients have not invested in countries with total weighted score of less than 30 out of a maximum possible 100 (with economic growth and political stability double weighted). The consultant therefore recommends that no investment in Africa should be undertaken.

Required:

(a)   **Discuss whether or not Beela electronics should use the technique suggested by the consultant in order to decide whether or not to invest in Africa.**

(8 marks)

(b)   **Discuss briefly how Beela might manage political risk if it decides to invest in Africa.**

(7 marks)

(Total: 15 marks)

10   Hedging foreign exchange risk

There are no additional questions on this chapter.

11 Hedging interest rate risk

Murwald (Interest rate hedging)

The corporate treasury team of Murwald Co (a UK company) are debating what strategy to adopt towards interest rate risk management. The company's financial projections show an expected cash deficit in three months' time of £12 million, which will last for a period of approximately six months. Base rate is currently 6% per year, and Murwald can borrow at 1.5% over base, or invest at 1% below base. The treasury team believe that economic pressures in the euro zone will soon force the European Central Bank (ECB) to raise interest rates on the euro by 2% per year, which could lead to a similar rise in UK interest rates. The ECB move is not certain, as there has recently been significant economic pressure on the bank from the governments of euro zone countries not to raise interest rates.

In the UK, the economy is still recovering from a recession and representatives of industry are calling for interest rates to be cut by 1%. Opposing representations are being made by pensioners, who do not wish their investment income to fall further due to an interest rate cut.

The corporate treasury team believes that interest rates are more likely to rise than to fall, and does not want interest payments during the six month period to increase by more than £10,000 from the amounts that would be paid at current interest rates. It is now 1 March.

LIFFE prices (1 March)

Futures

£500,000 three month sterling interest rate (points of 100%)

March	93.45
June	93.10

Options

£500,000 short sterling options (points of 100%)

	CALLS	PUTS
Exercise price	June	June
9200	3.33	–
9250	2.93	–
9300	2.55	0.92
9350	2.20	1.25
9400	1.74	1.84
9450	1.32	2.90
9500	0.87	3.46

Required:

(a) **Illustrate results of futures and options hedges if, by 1 June:**

   (i) **Interest rates rise by 2%. Futures prices move by 1.8%.**

   (ii) **Interest rates fall by 1%. Futures prices move by 0.9%.**

   Recommend with reasons, how Murwald Co should hedge its interest rate exposure. All relevant calculations must be shown. Taxation, transactions costs and margin requirements may be ignored. State clearly any assumptions that you make.

(b) **Discuss the advantages and disadvantages of other derivative products that Murwald might have used to hedge the risk.**

12 Strategic aspects of acquisitions

Rayswood Co

In a recent meeting of the board of directors of Rayswood Co the chairman proposed the acquisition of Pondhill Co. During his presentation the chairman stated that: 'As a result of this takeover we will diversify our operations and our earnings per share will rise by 13%, bringing great benefits to our shareholders.'

No bid has yet been made, and Rayswood currently owns only 2% of Pondhill.

A bid would be based on a share for share exchange, which would be one Rayswood share for every six Pondhill shares.

Financial data for the two companies include:

	Rayswood	Pondhill
	$m	$m
Revenue	56.0	42.0
Profit before tax	12.0	10.0
Profit available to ordinary shareholders	7.8	6.5
Dividends	3.2	3.4
Retained earnings	4.6	3.1
Issued ordinary shares	40m	150m
Market price per share	320 cents	45 cents

Rayswood 50 cents par value, Pondhill 10 cents par value.

A non-executive director has recently stated that she believes 'the share price of Rayswood will rapidly increase to $3.61 following the announcement of the bid.'

> **Required:**
>
> Explain whether you agree with the chairman's and the non-executive director's assessment of the benefits of the proposed takeover.
>
> Support your explanation with relevant calculations, including your assessment of the likely post-acquisition share price of Rayswood if the bid is successful.
>
> State clearly any assumptions that you make.
>
> **(15 marks)**

13 Business valuation

Predator

The board of directors of Predator Co is considering making an offer to purchase Target Co, a private limited company in the same industry. If Target is purchased it is proposed to continue operating the company as a going concern in the same line of business.

Summarised details from the most recent set of financial statements for Predator and Target are shown below:

	Predator SOFP as at 31 March		Target SOFP as at 31 March	
	$m	$m	$000	$000
Freehold property		33		460
Plant & equipment		58		1,310
Inventory	29		330	
Receivables	24		290	
Cash	3		20	
	——	56	——	640
Total assets		**147**		**2,410**
Equity and liabilities				
Ordinary shares		35		160
Reserves		43		964
		——		——
Shareholders' funds		78		1,124
Medium term bank loans		38		768
Current liabilities		31		518
		——		——
		147		**2,410**

Predator, 50 cents ordinary shares, Target, 25 cents ordinary shares.

Year	Predator PAT $m	Predator Dividend $m	Target PAT $000	Target Dividend $000
T5	14.30	9.01	143	85.0
T4	15.56	9.80	162	93.5
T3	16.93	10.67	151	93.5
T2	18.42	11.60	175	102.8
T1	20.04	12.62	183	113.1

T5 is five years ago and T1 is the most recent year.

Target's shares are owned by a small number of private individuals. Its managing director who receives an annual salary of $120,000 dominates the company. This is $40,000 more than the average salary received by managing directors of similar companies. The managing director would be replaced, if Predator purchases Target.

The freehold property has not been revalued for several years and is believed to have a market value of $800,000.

The statement of financial position (SOFP) value of plant and equipment is thought to reflect its replacement cost fairly, but its value if sold is not likely to exceed $800,000. Approximately $55,000 of inventory is obsolete and could only be sold as scrap for $5,000.

The ordinary shares of Predator are currently trading at 430 cents ex-div. A suitable cost of equity for Target has been estimated at 15%.

Both companies are subject to corporation tax at 33%.

Required:

Estimate the value of Target Co using the different methods of valuation and advise the board of Predator as to how much it should offer for Target's shares.

Note: There has been no increase in the share capital of Target over the last five years. Explain why this is relevant.

14 Corporate failure and reconstruction

Last Chance Saloon Co

Last Chance Saloon Co has experienced considerable losses in the last few years, leading to a debit balance on its revenue reserves and thus a deterioration of its cash position. The company has developed a wonder product to revive its fortunes. The wonder product will require a total investment of $7 million. The finance director has drafted a scheme of reconstruction:

1   Existing shareholders are to be offered a cash payment 25 cents per share to redeem their shares which would then be cancelled.

2   10 million new shares 50 cents (par value) are to be issued at $1.20 each.

3   An increase of $500,000 in inventory (working capital) is required.

4   The 10% debentures would be repaid immediately.

5   The bank is willing to provide a $1 million overdraft facility at an increased cost of 9% to replace the existing overdraft. The bank would purchase a $3 million 12% debenture. Both loans will be secured.

If the new wonder product is not launched the company earnings before interest and tax will be a ridiculously low figure from which you should immediately realise that it is over for the company unless it goes ahead will the new product.

If the scheme is organised the earnings before interest and tax is estimated to be $1 million in the first year of trading.

Summarised balance sheet (statement of financial position) as at 31 December 20X4

	$000	$000
Land and buildings		2,200
Plant and machinery		6,300
		8,500
Inventory	2,000	
Receivables	1,500	
Cash	500	
		4,000
Total assets		12,500

Ordinary share capital (50c shares)		3,000
Share premium		2,000
Revenue reserves		(1,000)
		─────
Shareholders' funds		4,000
10% Debentures 20X5		5,000
Current liabilities		
Payables	2,300	
Bank overdraft	1,200	
	─────	
		3,500
		─────
Total equity and liabilities		**12,500**
		─────

The realisable values of assets upon liquidation are estimated to be:

	$000
Land and buildings	1,500
Plant and machinery	3,450
Inventory	1,000
Receivables	1,000

The current market price of ordinary shares is 22 cents per share. The corporate tax rate is 30%.

Required:

Prepare a report analysing whether the proposed scheme of reconstruction will be successful. State clearly any assumptions that you make.

Test your understanding answers

Influence on objectives

Non-financial issues, ethical and environmental issues in many cases overlap, and have become of increasing significance to the achievement of primary financial objectives such as the maximisation of shareholder wealth. Most companies have a series of secondary objectives that encompass many of these issues.

Traditional **non-financial issues** affecting companies include:

(i) **Measures that increase the welfare of employees** such as the provision of housing, good and safe working conditions, social and recreational facilities. These might also relate to managers and encompass generous perquisites.

(ii) **Welfare of the local community and society as a whole**. This has become of increasing significance, with companies accepting that they have some responsibility beyond their normal stakeholders in that their actions may impact on the environment and the quality of life of third parties.

(iii) **Provision of, or fulfilment of, a service**. Many organisations, both in the public sector and private sector provide a service, for example to remote communities, which would not be provided on purely economic grounds.

(iv) Growth of an organisation, which might bring more power, prestige, and a larger market share, but might adversely affect shareholder wealth.

(v) **Quality**. Many engineering companies have been accused of focusing upon quality rather than cost effective solutions.

(vi) **Survival**. Although to some extent linked to financial objectives, managers might place corporate survival (and hence retaining their jobs) ahead of wealth maximisation. An obvious effect might be to avoid undertaking risky investments.

Ethical issues of companies were brought into sharp focus by the actions of Enron and others.

There is a trade-off between applying a high standard of ethics and increasing cash flow or maximisation of shareholder wealth. A company might face ethical dilemmas with respect to the amount and accuracy of information it provides to its stakeholders. An ethical issue attracting much attention is the possible payment of excessive remuneration to senior directors, including very large bonuses and 'golden parachutes'.

Key answer tips: Should bribes be paid in order to facilitate the company's long-term aims? Are wages being paid in some countries below subsistence levels? Should they be? Are working conditions of an acceptable standard? Do the company's activities involve experiments on animals, genetic modifications etc? Should the company deal with or operate in countries that have a poor record of human rights? What is the impact of the company's actions on pollution or other aspects of the local environment?

Environmental issues might have very direct effects on companies. If natural resources become depleted the company may not be able to sustain its activities, weather and climatic factors can influence the achievement of corporate objectives through their impact on crops, the availability of water etc. Extreme environmental disasters such as typhoons, floods, earthquakes, and volcanic eruptions will also impact on companies' cash flow, as will obvious environmental considerations such as the location of mountains, deserts, or communications facilities. Should companies develop new technologies that will improve the environment, such as cleaner petrol or alternative fuels? Such developments might not be the cheapest alternative.

Environmental legislation is a major influence in many countries. This includes limitations on where operations may be located and in what form, and regulations regarding waste products, noise and physical pollutants.

All of these issues have received considerable publicity and attention in recent years. *Environmental pressure groups* are prominent in many countries; companies are now producing social and environmental accounting reports, and/or corporate social responsibility reports. Companies increasingly have multiple objectives that address some or all of these three issues. In the short-term non-financial, ethical and environmental issues might result in a reduction in shareholder wealth; in the longer term it is argued that only companies that address these issues will succeed.

Breckhall

(a) As there is more than one inflation rate, we must calculate the money cash flows and hence discount them by the money (nominal) rate.

Net present value calculation for Breckhall Co

Year	0	1	2	3	4	5	6
	$000	$000	$000	$000	$000	$000	$000
Receipts							
Sales							
(5% increase)		3,675	5,402	6,159	6,977	6,790	
Payments:							
Materials							
(10% increase)		(589)	(908)	(1,198)	(1,537)	(1,449)	
Labour							
(10% increase)		(1,177)	(1,815)	(2,396)	(3,075)	(2,899)	
Overheads							
(5% increase)		(53)	(110)	(116)	(122)	(128)	
TAD		(1,125)	(844)	(633)	(475)	(1,423)	
(W1)							
Taxable Profits		731	1,725	1,816	1,768	891	
Tax:							
Corporation tax			(256)	(604)	(636)	(619)	(312)
Add Capital allowances		1,125	844	633	475	1,423	
Non-current assets	(4,500)						
Working capital	(300)	(120)	(131)	(144)	(156)	(42)	893
(W2)							
Net cash flow	(4,800)	1,736	2,182	1,701	1,451	1,653	581
Discount rate (15%)	1	0.870	0.756	0.658	0.572	0.497	0.432
Present values	(4,800)	1,510	1,650	1,119	830	822	251
Net present value	**$1,382**						

A positive NPV is when the expected return on a project more than compensates the investor for the perceived level of (systematic) risk.

(W1) Tax allowable depreciation calculation

		W.D.A.	Year
Cost	4,500		
TAD year 1	(1,125)	1,125	1
	‾‾‾‾		
TAD year 2		X0.75	
TAD year 3		844	2
TAD year 4		633	3
Scrap value		475	4
Balancing allowance	Balancing figure	1,423	5
		‾‾‾‾	
Check Line	**0**	**4,500**	
		Cost – Scrap = 4,500	

(W2) Working capital requirements

Year	0	1	2	3	4	5	6
Total in real terms	300	400	500	600	700	700	
Inflation	1	1.05	1.05^2	1.05^3	1.05^4	1.05^5	
Total in money terms	300	420	551	695	851	893	
Movement	(300)	(120)	(131)	(144)	(156)	(42)	893

(W3) Sales – $3,500,000*1.05 = $3,675,000

$4,900,000*1.052 = $5,402,000 etc.

(b) Calculation of IRR

15% gave a positive NPV, therefore I will choose a higher discount rate to try and achieve a negative NPV, to enable the calculation of the IRR by linear interpolation. Under exam conditions I would simply pick the highest discount rate from the tables i.e. 20%.

Year	Cash flow	20% Discount Rate	Present Value
0	(4,800)	1	(4,800)
1	1,736	0.833	1,446
2	2,182	0.694	1,514
3	1,701	0.579	985
4	1,451	0.482	699
5	1,653	0.402	665
6	581	0.335	195
			‾‾‾‾
			704
			‾‾‾‾

The estimate of the IRR by extrapolation:

15 + ((1382/1382 – 704) × (20 – 15)) = 25.20%

Growth of multinationals

Multinational companies are normally able to take more advantage of imperfections in product markets, factor markets or financial markets than companies that only operate in a domestic market. Taking advantage of market imperfections gives a competitive advantage and facilitates the organic growth of multinationals. By virtue of their size they are also well placed to grow through acquisition, often in the form of vertical or horizontal integration.

Many market imperfections result from government actions, for example through tariffs, quotas, exchange controls, and investment incentives. Multinationals often avoid government imposed barriers through foreign direct investment, and may take advantage of favourable tax and other incentives.

Multinationals may benefit from locating production in different countries in order to take full advantage of economies of scale and scope, low labour costs, and control of raw material supplies. Economies of scale and scope may be in production (operating at an optimum unit size, and specialising production in those countries where comparative advantages are greatest), purchasing (quantity discounts and use of market power), marketing (utilising an internationally known brand image, and an efficient international marketing structure), research and development (superior technology and/or differentiated products) or financing (access to international financial markets with the potential to raise finance at relatively low cost, and to earn higher yields on financial investments). Multinationals also often have the ability to reduce their global tax payments by locating activities in tax efficient countries, reducing taxable income or shifting tax liability from one country to another through devices such as transfer pricing, royalty fees and management fees, and eliminating or deferring taxation through the use of tax havens.

In many countries multinationals may be in an oligopolistic or even monopolistic situation, which may be exploited to generate abnormally good profitability and growth.

Internalisation of comparative advantages

Competitive advantage can be maintained by possession of unique information and skills which employees can use to create further advantage through research and development, marketing and other commercial skills. The multinational company is motivated to create an internal market for this information and to keep possession of their unique advantage specific to the firm.

Taking advantage of market imperfections is important, but a prerequisite for a successful multinational is high quality management, and the ability to survive against other multinationals in a competitive world.

Axmine

(a) **REPORT**

To: The management, Axmine Co

From: The chief accountant

Date: X-X-20XX

Subject: Proposed joint venture with Traces

Introduction

Axmine Co is considering entering into a joint venture with Traces in order to import copper from XX country in South America.

Financial analysis

The discounting exercise reveals that the projected cash flows have a positive net present value of £4.71 m.

Once this decision has been made public the share price will increase if the market is at least semi strong efficient. Therefore as directors can you can achieve your primary duty, which is to maximise shareholders wealth.

Accuracy and completeness of cash flows

Be question specific

The price of copper grows by 10% per year in British pounds terms. Metals prices are notoriously volatile and the implications of this assumption should be investigated.

The justification of the discount rate is unreliable, i.e. the 16% minus 2%, as this does not appear to reflect the systematic risk of this project.

General comments

Purchasing Power Parity Theory can be used as our best predictor of future spot rates, however it is not accurate because of the following:

– The future inflation rates are only estimates.

– The market is dominated by speculative transactions (98%) as opposed to trade transactions; therefore purchasing power theory breaks down.

Are the various revenues and costs likely to be subject to the same level of inflation?

Corporate tax rates and tax allowances may change over the project life.

Risk analysis

General risk comment

When accepting a project we also accept the risk associated with that project. Thus I would suggest we analysis the project risk in more detail before accepting the project. The level of analysis will depend on the complexity and materiality of the project. The risk can be analysed in a number of ways, i.e. sensitive analysis, scenario analysis, and simulation analysis.

International risk comment

Axmine should undertake a political risk assessment, it may adopt both macro and micro techniques to help reach its evaluation. Joint ventures have historically been more at risk of expropriation by host governments than wholly owned subsidiaries.

A review of economic exposure should also be undertaken.

Qualitative factors

The relationship with Traces

Will Traces honour its obligations under the joint venture? What will happen at the end of the four years? Will Traces have acquired all the technical knowledge to be able to go it alone? Why is the initial period only for four years? Would it benefit Axmine to have this period extended?

Communication to sophisticated shareholders

Will our shareholders believe it is a worthwhile project to be undertaken? Does the project fit into our previously communicated strategy? Our shareholders' confidence is crucial to maintaining or increasing our share price.

Future opportunities

Axmine should undertake a review of all real options.

Effect on other stakeholders

Employees, creditors, debentures holders and the local community.

Managerial resources

Have we the in house managerial resources to deliver this project. What will the impact be, on our current operational capabilities?

Conclusions and recommendations

It is therefore concluded that the joint venture should be proceeded within the absence of any more lucrative proposals, subject to clarification of the above reservations.

Workings:

(W1) Estimated future exchange rates: based on PPPT

Year	Forecast South American inflation %	Forecast UK inflation %	Forecast exchange/rate (pesos/£1)
1	80	8	140 × 1.80/1.08 = 233.3
2	64	8	233.3 × 1.64/1.08 = 354.3
3	51.2	8	354.3 × 1.512/1.08 = 496.0
4	41	8	496.0 × 1.41/1.08 = 647.6
5	32.8	8	647.6 × 1.328/1.08 = 796.3

(W2) Sales

Year	Volume	Unit price	Inflation	Exchange	Total m pesos
1	5m	£1.5	1.1	233.3	1,925
2	5m	£1.5	1.1^2	354.3	3,215
3	5m	£1.5	1.1^3	496.0	4,951
4	5m	£1.5	1.1^4	647.6	7,111

(W3) Labour and other expenses

Year	Total	Inflation	Exchange rate	Total m pesos
1	500m pesos	1.8		900
2	500m pesos	1.8 × 1.64	–	1,476
3	500m pesos	1.8 × 1.64 × 1.512	–	2,232
4	500m pesos	1.8 × 1.64 × 1.512 × 1.41	–	3,147

(W4) Supervisors' costs

Year	Total	Inflation	Exchange rate	Total m pesos
1	£0.4m	1.08	233.3	101
2	£0.4m	1.08^2	354.3	165
3	£0.4m	1.08^3	496.0	250
4	£0.4m	1.08^4	647.6	353

(W5) UK tax on foreign taxable profits

Tax has been paid in South America at only 20%. A further 15% is therefore payable in the UK.

Year 2 $\dfrac{724m}{233.3} \times 15\% = £0.47m$

Year 3 $\dfrac{1{,}374m}{353.3} \times 15\% = £0.58m$

Year 4 $\dfrac{2{,}269m}{496.0} \times 15\% = £0.69m$

Year 5 $\dfrac{3{,}412m}{647.6} \times 15\% = £0.79m$

Axmine Co

The net cash flow projections of the proposed joint venture with Traces

Year	0	1	2	3	4	5
	Pesos m	Pesos m	Pesos m	Pesos m	Pesos m	Pesos m
Sales – (W2)		1,925	3,215	4,951	7,111	
Payments:						
Labour and other expenses – **(W3)**		(900)	(1,476)	(2,232)	(3,147)	
Supervisors salaries – **(W4)**		(101)	(165)	(250)	(352)	
TAD		(200)	(200)	(200)	(200)	
Taxable profits		724	1,374	2,269	3,412	
Foreign tax @ 20%			(145)	(275)	(454)	(682)
TAD		200	200	200	200	
Machinery	(800)					
Net foreign cash flow	**(800)**	**924**	**1,429**	**2,194**	**3,158**	**(682)**
Exchange rate – **(W1)**	140	233.3	354.3	496.0	647.6	796.3
£ Cash flow (£m)	(5.71)	3.96	4.03	4.42	4.88	(.86)
UK tax on foreign profits @15% – **(W5)**			(.47)	(.58)	(.69)	(.79)
Net £ cash flows	(5.71)	3.96	3.56	3.84	4.19	(1.65)
Discount rate – 14%	1	.877	.769	.675	.592	.519
Present value	(5.71)	3.47	2.74	2.59	2.48	(.86)
Net present value	**4.71 m**					

(b) **Is the proposed discount rate of 14% appropriate?**

The first point is the each discount rate must be bespoke, i.e. calculated specifically for each project and based on the perceived systematic risk of the inherent cash flows of that project. To base the discount rate of the foreign project on the rate for UK mining operations is not satisfactory as the systematic risk of the project may be significantly different.

The logic of the 2% reduction is also questionable:

One argument put forward for overseas expansion is that of risk diversification, i.e. that the income of the combined company will be less volatile as its cash flows come from a variety of markets. However, this is a reduction in total risk, but has little or no effect on the systematic risk.

Will this benefit the shareholders? Basic answer: No

Shareholders should diversify for themselves, because a shareholder can more easily and cheaply eliminate unsystematic risk by purchasing an international unit trust.

If the diversification is into foreign markets where the individuals cannot directly invest themselves this may lead to a reduction in their systematic risk.

This could be possible for a South American country, where exchange controls and other market imperfections often exist. However, as it gets easier for individuals to gain access to foreign markets the value of this argument has diminished.

(c) **Blocked remittances might be avoided by means of:**

1   Increasing transfer prices paid by the foreign subsidiary to the parent company.

2   Lending the equivalent of the dividend to the parent company.

3   Making payments to the parent company in the form of royalties, payment for patents, or management fees.

4   Charging the subsidiary additional head office overhead.

5   Parallel loans, whereby the subsidiary in the South American country lends cash to the subsidiary of another a company requiring funds in the South American country. In return the parent company would receive the loan of an equivalent amount of cash in the UK from the other subsidiary's parent company.

The government of the South American country might try to prevent many of these measures being used.

HGT Co

Key answer tips: What appears to be an amazingly complex question for 10 marks is nothing much more than a relevant cost exercise. That said, the numbers take time and it would be sensible, if short of time, to cover the discussion points with assumed numbers if necessary.

Under the current scheme:

		Glinland	Rytora
		$000	$000
Sales	(150,000 units)	1,575	4,500
		———	———
Variable costs		900	1,350
Costs from Glinland		–	1,575
Fixed costs		140	166
		———	———
Profit before tax		535	1,409
Local corporate tax	(40% Glinland, 25% Rytora)	214	352
		———	———
Profit after corporate tax		321	1,057
Withholding tax	(Glinland: 10% of 50% of 321)	16	–
Import tariff	(10% of 1,575)	–	157
Retained	(Glinland: 50% of 321)	161	–
Remitted	(Glinland: 321 – 161 – 16)	144	900
UK taxation:			
Taxable profit		535	1,409
		———	———
Tax at UK tax rate	(30%)	160	423
Tax credit	(Rytora: Limited to Rytora tax)	160	352
		———	———
Tax paid in the UK		0	71
		———	———

Total tax paid	$000	$000
In Glinland		
Corporate tax	214	
Withholding tax	16	
	———	
		230
In Rytora		
Corporate tax	352	
Import taxes	157	
	———	
		509
In the UK		71
		———
Total		810
		———

If goods are sold at cost by the Glinland subsidiary

(i.e. at variable cost of 900 + fixed costs of 140 = 1,040):

		Glinland $000	Rytora $000
Sales		1,040	4,500
		———	———
Variable costs		900	1,350
Costs from Glinland		–	1,040
Fixed costs		140	166
		———	———
Profit before tax		0	1,944
Local corporate tax	(25% Rytora)	–	486
Profit after corporate tax		–	1,458
Withholding tax		–	–
Import tariff	(10% of 1,040)	–	104
Retained		–	–
Remitted	(1,458 – 104)	–	1,354
UK taxation:			
Taxable profit		–	1,944
		———	———
Tax at UK tax rate	(30%)	–	583
Tax credit	(Limited to Rytora tax)	–	486
		———	———
Tax paid in the UK		0	97
			———

Total tax paid	$000	$000
In Glinland		0
In Rytora		
Corporate tax	486	
Import taxes	104	
	———	
		590
In the UK		97
		———
Total		687
		———

The proposed change would result in an overall saving of $123,000 per year.

The proposal might not be acceptable to:

(i)   The tax authorities in Glinland, where $230,000 in taxation would be lost. The tax authorities might insist on an arm's length price for transfers between Glinland and Rytora.

(ii)   The subsidiary in Glinland, which would no longer make a profit, or have retentions available for future investment in Glinland. Depending upon how performance in Glinland was evaluated, this might adversely affect rewards and motivation in Glinland.

Goddard Co

(a)   The overview – What method should I use to calculate the discount rate for a project in a different industry (different business risk), when the capital structure of our company remains unchanged (same financial risk) post-project implementation.

The Leisure Project

I have assumed the business risk (the beta asset) of the leisure industry can be estimated by de-gearing the equity beta of Cottons Co.

Goddard's existing gearing ratio/capital structure based on market values is:

		$m	%
Equity	15/0.5 × 3.80	114.00	**66**
Debt	56 × 1.04	58.24	**34**
		———	
Total		172.24	100

Cotton's gearing ratio/capital structure based on market values is:

		$m	%
Equity	10/0.25 × 1.80	72.00	**81**
Debt	15 × 1.12	16.80	**19**
Total		88.8	100

1 Find the business risk asset beta $ß_a$ of the new project/industry.

$$ß_a = ß_e × V_e/[V_e + V_d(1 - T)]$$
$$= 1.3 × 81/[81 + 19 (0.70)]$$
$$= 1.12$$

2 Calculate the equity beta of the **new project**.

$$ß_a = ß_e × V_e/[V_e + V_d(1 - T)]$$
$$1.12 = ß_e × 66/[66 + 34(0.70)]$$
$$1.12 = 0.73 ß_e$$

$ß_e = 1.12/0.73 = 1.53$ – **Reflects the systematic risk of the project**

3 k_{eg}

$R_f + (R_M - R_f) ß_e.$

$6\% + (14 - 6) 1.53 = 18.24\%.$

4 k_{dat}

The investors' required return = k_d = 11%. Therefore to find the current cost of debt adjust for the tax relief on interest.

$k_d(1 - t) = 11(0.70) = 7.70.$

$k_d(1 - t) = 7.70\%.$

5 **WACC**

$= 18.24\% × 0.66 + 7.70\% × 0.34 = 14.66\%.$

The Publication Project

I have assumed the business risk (the beta asset) of the publication industry can be estimated by de-gearing the equity beta of Blackwell Co.

Blackwell's gearing ratio/capital structure based on market values is:

		$m	%
Equity	30/0.50 × 2.30	138.00	**67**
Debt		69.00	**33**
Total		207.00	100

As the gearing ratio/financial risk of Blackwell is almost identical to that of Goddard, there is no need to take out the financial risk (degear) and then put back in the same level of financial risk (re gear).

3　k_{eg}

　$R_f + (R_M - R_f) ß_e.$

　$6\% + (14 - 6)\ 1.2 = 15.60\%.$

4　k_{dat}

　$= 7.7\%.$

5　**WACC**

　$= 15.60 \times 0.66 + 7.7 \times 0.34 = 12.91.$

(b)　The marketing director might be correct. If there is initially a high level of systematic risk in the packaging investment before it is certain whether the investment will succeed or fail, it is logical to discount cash flows for this high risk period at a rate reflecting this risk. Once it has been determined whether the project will be successful, risk may return to a 'more normal' level and the discount rate reduced commensurate with the lower risk. If the project fails there is no risk (the company has a certain failure!).

The other board member is incorrect. If the same discount rate is used throughout a project's life the discount factor becomes smaller and effectively allows a greater deduction for risk for more discount cash flows. The total risk adjustment is greater the further into the future cash flows are considered. It is not necessary to discount more distant cash flows at a higher rate.

Option valuation

(a) **Option valuation**

First use Black-Scholes to value the equivalent call.

Step 1: Calculate d_1 and d_2

$d_1 = [\ln (P_a/P_e) + (r+0.5s^2)t]/s\sqrt{t}$

$d_1 = [\ln (6/5) + (0.12 + 0.5 \times 0.3^2)2]/(0.3 \times \sqrt{2})$

$d_1 = \mathbf{1.21}$

$d_2 = d_1 - s\sqrt{t} = 1.21 - 0.3\sqrt{2}$

$d_2 = \mathbf{0.79}$

Step 2: $N(d_1) = 0.5 + 0.3869 = 0.8869.$

$N(d_2) = 0.5 + 0.2852 = 0.7852.$

Step 3: **Plug these numbers into the Black-Scholes formula**

Value of a call option $= P_a N(d_1) - P_e N(d_2)e^{-rt}$

$= 6.00 \times 0.8869 - 5.00 \times 0.7852 \times e^{-(0.12*2)}$

$= 5.32 - 3.08$

$= \mathbf{2.24}$

(**Reasonableness check:** This exceeds the intrinsic value of $1.00 so it looks ok.)

Step 4: Then use the put call parity rule to value a put option.

$2.24	**$6.00**
Call price	**Share price**
+	+
PV of the exercise price	**Put price**
$5.00e^{-(0.12*2)}$	(Balancing Figure)

(middle column has "=")

$= \$2.24 + \$3.93 - \$6.00 =$ value of a put

$= \mathbf{\$0.17}$

200,000 puts would therefore cost $= 200,000* 0.17$

$= \mathbf{\$34,000}$

(**Reasonableness check:** This option is out of the money so we would expect a low value.)

(b)

Shares only:	Share prices	
	$3	$10
Share price movement	–$600,000	$800,000

Shares with Put options

	Adverse Exercise*	Favourable Abandon
Share price movement	–$600,000	$800,000
Profit on options*	$400,000	
Less premium	–$34,000	–$34,000
Net	**–$234,000**	**$766,000**

The hedge would save $366,000 ($600,000 – $234,000) if the share price fell, and would lose $34,000 if the share price increased i.e. the cost of the options that were not exercised.

(c) The investor purchased 200,000 shares and wishes to hedge the position, how many call options would she have to sell to construct a risk free investment?

= 200,000/0.8869 = Sell 225,505 call options

Political risk

(a) The consultant's report should not be used as the only basis for the African investment decision, for the following reasons.

(i) The decision should be taken after evaluating the risk/return trade-off; financial factors (e.g. the expected NPV from the investments); strategic factors; and other issues including political risk. Political risk is only one part of the decision process (although in extremely risky countries it might be the most important one).

(ii) The scores for the three countries are, giving double weighting to economic growth and political stability:

Country 1   29

Country 2   24

Country 3   28

Just because previous clients have not invested in countries with scores of less than 30 does not mean that Beela should not. The previous countries may not have been comparable with these in Africa. This decision rule also ignores return. If return is expected to be very high, a relatively low score might be acceptable to Beela.

(iii) The factors considered by the consultant might not be the only relevant factors when assessing political risk. Others could include the extent of capital flight from the country, the legal infrastructure, availability of local finance and the existence of special taxes and regulations for multinational companies.

(iv) The weightings of the factors might not be relevant to Beela.

(v) Scores such as these only focus on the macro risk of the country. The micro risk, the risk for the actual company investing in a country, is the vital factor. This differs between companies and between industries. A relatively hi-tech electronics company might be less susceptible to political actions than, for example, companies in extractive industries where the diminishing bargain concept may apply.

(vi) There is no evidence of how the scores have been devised and how valid they are.

(b) Prior to investing Beela might negotiate an agreement with the local government covering areas of possible contention such as dividend remittance, transfer pricing, taxation, the use of local labour and capital, and exchange controls. The problem with such negotiations is that governments might change, and a new government might not honour the agreement.

The logistics of the investment may also influence political risk:

(i) If a key element of the process is left outside the country it may not be viable for the government to take actions against a company as it could not produce a complete product. This particularly applies when intellectual property or know-how is kept back.

(ii) Financing locally might deter political action, as effectively the action will hurt the local providers of finance.

(iii) Local sourcing of components and raw materials might reduce risk.

(iv) It is sometimes argued that participating in joint ventures with a local partner reduces political risk, although evidence of this is not conclusive.

(v) Control of patents and processes by the multinational might reduce risk, although patents are not recognised in all countries.

Governments or commercial agencies in multinationals' home countries often offer insurance against political risk.

Murwald (Interest rate hedging)

(a) The treasury team believe that interest rates are more likely to increase than to decrease, and any hedging strategy will be based upon this assumption. There is also a requirement that interest payments do not increase by more than £10,000 from current interest rates.

Current expectations

The current expectation is a £12m deficit in three months' time for a six-month period. At current rates, the company could borrow at 6% + 1.5% = 7.5%. Interest costs at current borrowing rates would therefore be: £12m × 7.5% × 6/12 = £450,000.

Alternative 1: Futures hedges

Use June contracts to hedge a deficit of £12 million. To hedge against the risk of a rise in interest rates, the company should sell futures.

Tutorial note: We sell futures because if interest rates do rise, the market price of the futures will fall. The company can then close its position by buying futures, and making a gain on the futures trading to offset the 'loss' from higher interest rates in the loans market.

(i) If interest rates rise by 2% and the futures price moves by 1.80%.

As a six months hedge is required and each future is for a three-month interest period, the number of contracts will be £12m/£500k × 6/3 = 48 contracts.

The tick value is £500,000 × 0.0001 × 3/12 = £12.50.

		£
Cost of borrowing at current rate		450,000
Cost if rates rise 2%		
(£12m × 9.5% × 6/12)		570,000
		————
'Loss' from extra borrowing cost		(120,000)
Futures		
Sell 48 contracts at	93.10	
Buy 48 contracts at (93.10 – 1.80)	91.30	
	———	
Gain per contract	1.80	
	———	
Value of gain 180 × 48 × £12.50		108,000
		————
Net additional cost with hedging		(12,000)
		————

(ii)   If interest rates fall by 1% and the futures price moves by 0.9%

		£
Cost of borrowing at current rate		450,000
Cost if rates fall 1% (£12m × 6.5% × 6/12)		390,000
'Gain' from fall in borrowing cost		60,000
Futures		
Sell 48 contracts at	93.10	
Buy 48 contracts at (93.10 + 0.90)	94.00	
	————	
Loss per contract	0.90	
	————	
Value of loss 90 × 48 × £12.50		(54,000)
Net gain with hedging		6,000

Based on these futures prices, hedging in the futures market does not allow the company to guarantee that interest costs in the case of a deficit do not increase by more than £10,000.

Alternative 2: Options hedges

The expectation is for interest rates to rise, therefore put options on futures will be purchased. This will allow the company to sell futures contracts at the exercise price for the options. The company should buy 48 options, since this is the number of futures contracts that might be required. (If interest rates rise the value of the put options will also increase.)

For example using the 9400 exercise price:

(i)   If interest rates rise by 2% and the futures price moves by 1.8%.

		£
Cost of borrowing at current rate		450,000
Cost if rates rise 2% (£12m × 9.5% × 6/12)		570,000
		————
'Loss' from extra borrowing cost		(120,000)
Options		
Buy 48 puts at	(1.84)	
Exercise – sell futures at (exercise price)	94.00	
Buy 48 futures contracts at (93.10 – 1.80)	(91.30)	
	————	
Gain per contract	0.86	
	————	
Value of gain 86 × 48 × £12.50		51,600
		————
Net additional cost with hedging		(68,400)
		————

In reality the options are likely to be sold rather than exercised. This is because they are June contracts, so they will still have time value that will be reflected in the option price. The gain from the options sale is therefore likely to be higher than the gain from exercising the options and selling futures. However, no data is provided on option prices on 1 June.

(ii)   If interest rates fall by 1% and the futures price moves by 0.9%

	£
Cost of borrowing at current rate	450,000
Cost if rates fall 1% (£12m × 6.5% × 6/12)	390,000
	————
'Gain' from fall in borrowing cost	60,000
Options	
Buy 48 puts at 1.84.	
Cost = 184 × 48 × £12.50	(110,400)
	————
Net additional cost with hedging	(50,400)
	————

Different outcomes will exist for using options if different put option exercise prices are selected. The best exercise price to select if the put options are exercised will be the 9350 option.

If interest rates rise by 2% and the futures price falls by 180 to 91.30, this will give a gain from the options of:

93.50 – 91.30 – 1.25 = 0.95 or 95 ticks

95 × 48 × £12.50 = £57,000

If interest rates fall by 1% and the futures price rises to the futures price moves to 94.00, the option will not be exercised. The loss from hedging with options will be the premium paid off:

125 × 48 × £12.5 = £75,000

Outcomes with options at 9350

2% increase: £(120,000) + £57,000 = £(63,000) 1% decrease: £60,000 – £75,000 = £(15,000).

Neither futures nor options hedges can satisfy, with certainty, the requirement that the interest payment should not increase by more than £10,000.

Collar

However, one way to achieve this would be to use a collar option, whereby downside risk is protected, but potential gains are also limited. A collar effectively fixes a maximum and minimum interest rate.

If a company expects to be borrowing and is worried about interest rate increases, a suitable collar can be achieved by buying put options and selling call options, to reduce the cost of protection.

For example a collar could be achieved by buying forty eight 9400 put options at 1.84 and selling 9400 call options at 1.74, a net premium cost of 0.10 (other alternatives are possible).

Murwald doesn't want interest to move adversely by more than £10,000 for a six month period on a £12 million loan.

In annual terms this is £10k/£12m × 2 = 0.167%.

A put option at the current interest rate (6%) and a total premium cost of less than 0.167% will satisfy the company's requirement. In the above example the total premium cost is 0.10%, and no matter what happens to interest rates Murwald can fix its borrowing cost at 7.6% (= 100 − 94.00 + 0.10 net option premium, plus the 1.5% premium over base rate for borrowing).

This satisfies the requirement. (Interest payments would be £12m × 7.6% × 0.5 = £456,000 which is £6,000 worse than current interest rates.)

The use of a collar is the recommended hedging strategy, but the company should consider the implications of the collar if a cash surplus was to occur rather than a cash deficit.

(b) Alternative interest rate hedges include:

(i) Forward rate agreements (FRAs).

(ii) OTC interest rate options – including interest rate guarantees.

(iii) Interest rate swaps.

(i) A forward rate agreement (FRA) is a contract to agree to pay a fixed interest rate that is effective at a future date. As such Murwald could fix now a rate of interest of 6.1% (for example) to be effective in three months' time for a period of six months. If interest rates were to rise above 6.1% the counter-party, usually a bank, would compensate Murwald for the difference between the actual rates and 6.1%. If interest rates were to fall below 6.1% Murwald would compensate the counter-party for the difference between 6.1% and the actual rate.

(ii) OTC options. Instead of market traded interest rate options such as those that are available on LIFFE, Murwald might use OTC options through a major bank. This would allow options to be tailored to the company's exact size and maturity requirements. An OTC collar would be possible, and the cost of this should be compared with the cost of using LIFFE options. Interest rate options for periods of less than one year are sometimes known as interest rate guarantees.

(iii) Interest rate swaps. Murwald expects to borrow at a floating rate of interest. It might be possible for Murwald to swap its floating rate interest stream for a fixed rate stream, pegging interest rates to approximately current levels (the terms of the swap would have to be negotiated). Interest rate swaps are normally for longer periods than six months.

Rayswood Co

Assumptions:

1. Share price is the present value of future cash flows i.e. the economic model.

2. The stock market is weak and semi strong efficient most of the time, therefore once new information is communicated to the market it is rapidly reflected in the share price.

3. In an efficient market shares are fairly priced i.e. a zero NPV transaction. They give investors the exact return to compensate them for the perceived level of systematic risk of the shares.

4. If shares are zero NPV transactions, takeovers/mergers could only be successful due to value created as a result of the merger i.e. the synergies.

5. Therefore it is absolutely essential that one undertakes an exhaustive review to identify all the synergies. In this question no synergies have been identified, therefore before any final advice would be given to the client one would request an immediate review of all synergies.

6. The question will therefore have to be answered on the basis of the unrealistic assumption that there are no synergies.

Post-acquisition share price:

The Add Company Approach:

Market values:	$m
Rayswood – 40 × 3.2 =	128.0
Pondhill – 150 × 0.45 =	67.5
Value of combined company	195.5
No of shares:	65m
Share price of the combined company	3.01

Rayswood buys Pondhill in a 1 for 6 shares for share exchange. Rayswood already has 40m shares and buys Pondhill for (150 × 1/6) = 25m shares, thus 65m shares in total.

Tutorial note:

In fact the takeover has been a wealth decreasing decision in relation to the shareholders of Rayswood. The new share price of $3.01 is lower than current market price of $3.20. Which reflects the fact that premium payment to Pondhill's shareholders has reduced the wealth of Rayswood's shareholders.

Calculation of the acquisition premium – Value per one share of Pondhill:

Pondhill shareholders get 1 share in Rayswood ($3.01) for every 6 shares of Pondhill.

$(1 \times 3.01)/6 = \$0.50$

$(0.50 - 0.45)/0.45 = 11.11\%$

Therefore before an acquisition premium is paid consideration should be given to ensure that it does not exceed the synergistic effects of the acquisition.

Director's comments:

'As a result of this takeover we will diversify our operations and our earnings per share will rise by 13%, bringing great benefits to our shareholders.'

Risk diversification:

One of the primary reasons put forward for all mergers is that the income of the combined entity will be less volatile (less risky) as its cash flows come from a wide variety of products and markets. However this is a reduction in total risk, but has little or no effect on the systematic risk.

Will this benefit the shareholders?

Basic answer: No. Shareholders should diversify for themselves, because a shareholder can more easily and cheaply eliminate unsystematic risk by purchasing an international unit trust. As the majority of investors in quoted companies have well diversified portfolios they are only exposed to systematic risk. Thus the reduction of total risk by the more expensive company diversification option is generally not recommended. The Director's comment is incorrect.

Earnings per share will rise by 13%:

Calculation of EPS:

	Rayswood	Pondhill	Enlarged Rayswood
Profit available to			
Ordinary shareholders	7.8m	6.5m	14.3
EPS	19.5c	4.33c	22c

% increase in the Earnings per share: $(22 - 19.5)/19.5 \times 100 = 13\%$

An increasing EPS does not automatically result in an increase share price, as the P/E ratio may fall to reflect the lower growth potential of the enlarged company.

The P/E ratios:

	Rayswood	Pondhill	Enlarged Rayswood
Share price	320	45	301
EPS	19.5	4.33	22
	16.41	10.39	13.68

In the absence of synergy from the acquisition, purchasing Pondhill, with relatively low growth expectations, will depress the growth of the enlarged Rayswood's post-acquisition and thus the post-acquisition P/E ratio falls.

The Director's comment is incorrect, the increasing earnings per shares does not bring great benefits to the shareholders, in fact it masks a potential decrease in the share price.

Non-executive comments:

"The share price of Rayswood will rapidly increase to $3.61 following the announcement of the bid."

Bootstrapping:

A company is able to increase its EPS by merging with a company on a lower P/E ratio than its own. The bootstrapping argument states that the

Share price of the enlarged Rayswood = Post-acq EPS × Pre-acq P/E ratio of Rayswood.

$3.61 = 22c × 16.41 times

It contends that the market may believe that when that merger is completed that the management team of Rayswood can increase growth potential of Pondhill earnings to the same level as Rayswood earnings. It may then assign the Rayswood's higher P/E ratio to the combined earnings of both companies (i.e. the post-acquisition EPS).

There have been some well documented cases of bootstrapping occurring in the 50s and 60s in America however as the stock markets have become more and more efficient it much less likely to occur today. The investors would request a detail analysis of the synergies so they could calculate the present value of future cash flows.

If there are no synergies identified the higher post-acquisition EPS simply results in a lower post-acquisition P/E multiple as we have seen. Therefore the non-executive is also incorrect in her views.

Predator

Predator Co

The approaches to use for valuation are:

1   Net asset valuation.

2   Dividend valuation model.

3   P/E ratio valuation.

   1   **Net asset valuation**

   Target is being purchased as a going concern, so realisable values are irrelevant.

	$000
Net assets per accounts (1,892 – 768)	1,124
Adjustment to freehold property (800 – 460)	340
Adjustment to inventory	(50)
Valuation	**1,414**

   Say $1.4m

   2   **Dividend Valuation Model**

   The average rate of growth in Target's dividends over the last 4 years is 7.4% on a compound basis.

   The estimated value of Target using the dividend valuation model is therefore:

   Valuation $113,100 × 1.074/(0.15 – 0.074) = $1,598,281

   Say $1.6m

3 P/E ratio Valuation

A suitable P/E ratio for Target will be based on the P/E ratio of Predator as both companies are in the same industry.

P/E of Predator (70m × $4.30)/$20.04m or 430/28.63 = **15.02**

The adjustments: – Downwards by 20% or 0.20 i.e. multiply by 0.80.

1   Target is a private company and its shares may be less liquid.

2   Target is a private company and it may have a less detailed compliance environment and therefore maybe more risky.

A suitable P/E ratio is therefore 15.02 × 0.80 = 12.02 (Multiplying by 0.80 results in the 20% reduction).

Target's PAT + Synergy after tax:

$183,000 + ($40,000 × 67%) = $209,800.

After adjusting for the savings in the director's remuneration.

The estimated value is therefore $209,800 × 12.02 = $2,521,796

Say $2.5m

Advice to the board

On the basis of its tangible assets the value of Target is $1.4m, which excludes any value for intangibles.

The dividend valuation gives a value of around $1.6m.

The earnings based valuation indicates a value of around $2.5m, which is based on the assumption, that not only will the current earnings be maintained, but that they will increase by the savings in the director's remuneration.

On the basis of these valuations an offer of around $2m would appear to be most suitable, however **a review of all potential synergies is recommended**. The directors should, however, be prepared to increase the offer to maximum price.

Maximum price comment

It is worth noting that the maximum price Predator should be prepared to offer is:

The maximum price Predator should pay for target is:

$PV_{\text{Target Company}} + PV_{\text{Synergy}}$

The comment on the maximum price is particularly appropriate in this question, as this an example of horizontal acquisition where considerable synergies normally exist.

Last Chance Saloon Co

Report on the proposed reconstruction scheme of The Last Chance Saloon

The scheme of reconstruction is likely to be successful if:

A   It raises adequate finance.

B   If the issue price of the new shares is fair.

C   It treats all parties fairly.

D   No group is worst off under the scheme.

The reason why the scheme is required

As a result of the recent considerable losses there are inadequate funds available to finance the redemption of the $5m debentures in 20X5.

Does the scheme raise adequate finance?

Cash in:	$m	Cash out:	$m
Equity (new shares to be issued)	12.0	Scheme funding	7.0
12% Debenture issued	3.0	Equity (old shares cancelled) 6m × 0.25	1.5
		Stock	0.5
		10% Debentures repaid	5.0
Total raised	15.0	**Total Out**	**14.0**
Total Out	(14.0)		
Scheme Surplus	1.0		
Current cash balance	0.5		
New cash balance	1.5		

The Capital Repayment position

	Immediate Liquidation	Cash	Post Scheme Capital Risk
Land and Buildings	1,500		1,500
Plant and machinery	3,450		3,450
Inventory	1,000	500	1,500
Receivables	1,000		1,000
Cash	500	1,000	1,500
New Assets – (realisable value may be considerably lower)		7,000	7,000
	7,450		15,950
Less: Secured creditors			
10% Debentures	(5,000)	5,000	–
12% Debenture		(3,000)	(3,000)
Bank overdraft			(1,000)
	(5,000)		(4,000)
Funds available to pay unsecured creditors	2,450		11,950
Less: Unsecured creditors:			
Bank overdraft	(1,200)		
Other creditors	(2,300)		(2,300)
	(3,500)		(2,300)
Funds available to pay shareholders		nil	9,650
Calculation of payment	2,450	70c	
in the $ to unsecured creditors	3,500		

An estimate of the liquidation expenses to be incurred would be necessary in practice.

Is the issue price of the new shares fair?

	$000	$000
Profit before interest and tax		
Interest:		
12% Debentures – 3,000 × 0.12 =	360	
9% Overdraft – 1,000 × 0.09 =	90	
		(450)
Earnings before tax		550
Tax		(165)
PAT		385
Interest cover (EBIT/Interest) =		2.2

The interest cover is below the minimum acceptable level of 2.5 times and is therefore cause for concern.

E.P.S = PAT/No. of Shares = 385/10,000 = 3.85c P/E ratio: Issue price/E.P.S

> 120c/3.85 = 31.17 times

Assume that the industry average P/E is 16 times. Therefore would investors also be willing to pay 31.17 times the estimated earnings of Last Chance for a share?

The answer is no, they would want to be able to buy the shares at a discount given the fact that earnings would be perceived to be less reliable as a result of its recent poor performance. Therefore the current issue price may be unacceptable to investors.

A discount of 25% would seem reasonable i.e. 16 times × 0.75 = 12 times. Then a more reasonable issue price would appear to be 3.85c × 12 times = 46.2c.

Conclusion: The shares could not be sold for $1.20. Thus the financial viability of the scheme is called into question. (As the 12m cash in from the issue of new shares will not occur.)

Is the scheme acceptable to all parties?

Unsecured creditors:

In the event of liquidation they would receive 70c in the pound (ignoring liquidation expenses). However under the scheme they should receive a full repayment. The scheme is clearly beneficial to them.

The Bank:

	Current position (sunk)	**Liquidation**	**Scheme**
	$000s	$000s	$000s
Bank overdraft	1,200	840	1,000

The reality of the situation is that the scheme will be organised (and the overdraft will be $1 m) or the company will be liquidated and the bank will only receive $840,000. The current position of an overdraft of $1.2m as denoted in the statement of financial position is a sunk position.

Thus the bank has a simple choice have $840,000 on liquidation or agree to a reduced overdraft of $1,000,000 under the scheme, which will be secured. If the bank agrees to the scheme the capital loss on the overdraft is reduced from $360,000 to $160,000 – a saving of $200,000.

Thus the bank will probably agree to the reduced overdraft (thus the reduced overdraft does not give rise to a cash flow).

However the low interest cover would be of concern to the Bank, and raises doubts about the company's ability to repay the interest. Therefore the bank may which to scrutinise the company profit forecasts in some details to ensure that they are based on realistic assumptions.

Existing shareholders:

Per share	Current position	Liquidation	Scheme – cash repayment
Capital	22c	Nil	25c

The current share of 22c does not represent a realistic exit strategy of all the existing shareholders, because if a sizeable proportion of shareholders try to sell, this would drive down the share price.

Thus existing shareholders will probably agree to the scheme.

The company may consider offering the existing shareholders a share for share exchange as opposed to offering them a cash repayment as this would reduce the need for financing and allow those existing shareholders who wish to remain the opportunity to do so.

Conclusion (have the reconstruction principles been adhered to?):

1 The shares appear to be overpriced at $1.20. This need to be reviewed immediately and possibly reduced to a more realistic level.

2 As the shares are overpriced – the $12m cash inflow from their issue is therefore unrealistic. Thus the scheme in its current form will not raise adequate finance.

3 The planning horizon needs to be extended beyond one year.

4 I recommend that the company valuation be taken using the present value of the free cash flows approach, if the information is available. Together with some evaluation of the risk inherent in the scheme. Risk analysis methods, which may be considered, are scenario planning, sensitivity analysis and simulation.

Index